All
That
Jesus
Asks

"Stan Guthrie is one of the most incisive writers I read. I'm always informed and challenged by his thinking."

—Jerry B. Jenkins, novelist; owner, Christian Writers Guild

"Atheists attempt to put Christians on the defensive by questioning the authority and goodness of God—the God whose existence they call into question. This book turns the tables by allowing Jesus to ask the questions. *All That Jesus Asks* will touch your head and your heart. I highly recommend it."

—Dinesh D'Souza, author, *What's So Great about Christianity*

"People's sentiments about Jesus can run strong. . . . We prefer a sentimental picture because it requires nothing from us, neither conviction nor commitment. And because it lacks truth, it lacks power. In this new book, Stan Guthrie is out to change that picture. Using the questions that Jesus actually asked of those around him, Stan leads us into a deeper look at Christ's humanity, authority, and mission. In *All That Jesus Asks*, you will discover the rugged truth about Christ and what that truth asks of *you*."

—Joni Eareckson Tada, Joni and Friends
International Disability Center

"Rigorously presenting the Jesus of the Gospels as our interrogator and digging deep into the realities of discipleship as he taught it, Guthrie's book is a landmark. I urge you to buy it and read it again and again."

—J. I. Packer, Board of Governors' Professor of Theology,
Regent College

"We all have our questions for Jesus and about Jesus—as if his job is to stand at our beck and call and answer our questions. Stan Guthrie encourages us to start in a completely different place: thinking about the questions Jesus asks us! That approach, along with Guthrie's gracious and thoughtful writing, will no doubt help many readers meet Jesus afresh."

—Mark Galli, senior managing editor, *Christianity Today*;
author, *Jesus Mean and Wild*

"Stan Guthrie's *All That Jesus Asks* is one-of-a-kind because it is the only book to date to deal with *all* the questions that Jesus asked—all three hundred of them! . . . The carefully crafted discussion questions at the end of each chapter are sure to enliven study and group discussion. And the question index, which lists the entirety of Jesus's questions according to their themes, will prove to be a unique resource to teachers and preachers alike. Thanks be to God for Stan Guthrie's great idea and his life-giving work."

—R. Kent Hughes, senior pastor emeritus, College Church in Wheaton

"Through the eyes of a seasoned journalist, you may meet a Jesus you have never experienced. This unique telling of the old story is refreshingly framed by the almost three hundred questions the master Teacher asked. Here you will find solid scholarship engagingly presented and lavishly illustrated."

—**J. Robertson McQuilkin**, president emeritus,
Columbia International University

"Stan's book is amazing. It's rich with wisdom and insights. . . . This book will be extremely helpful to others seeking an authentic relationship with Jesus."

—**Mary Schaller**, president, Q Place

"Stan Guthrie's *All That Jesus Asks* slices through the fog of culture and history to place us in an uncomfortable but privileged seat at the feet of Jesus as he teaches and confronts those who would follow him—or challenge him. Whether you worship in the congregation or stand behind the pulpit, you will find Jesus's questions to be both spiritually inspiring and unsettling as you truly realize *All That Jesus Asks*."

—**Chuck Colson**, founder, Prison Fellowship and
the Colson Center for Christian Worldview

All That Jesus Asks

HOW HIS QUESTIONS CAN TEACH AND TRANSFORM US

Stan Guthrie

BakerBooks

a division of Baker Publishing Group
Grand Rapids, Michigan

© 2010 by Stan Guthrie

Published by Baker Books
a division of Baker Publishing Group
P.O. Box 6287, Grand Rapids, MI 49516-6287
www.bakerbooks.com

Printed in the United States of America

Library of Congress Cataloging-in-Publication Data

Guthrie, Stan.
    All that Jesus asks : how his questions can teach and transform us / Stan Guthrie.
       p.   cm.
    Includes bibliographical references (p.   ) and index.
    ISBN 978-0-8010-7154-6 (pbk.)
    1. Jesus Christ—Words. 2. Christianity. 3. Christian life. 4. Bible. N.T. Gospels—Criticism, interpretation, etc. 5. Bible. N.T. Acts—Criticism, interpretation, etc. I. Title.
BT306.G88 2010
232—dc22
                                                             2010017089

10   11   12   13   14   15   16   7 6 5 4 3 2 1

For Laura, Peter, and Evan:

May you find in him the answers to all your questions

Contents

Section 4: Why Is Character So Vital?

Section 5: What Are Some Critical Doctrines?

Acknowledgments

No one benefits more from a book than the one who writes it, and I am no exception. Walking with Jesus as he asks his questions is the most exhilarating spiritual journey I have ever undertaken, but I have not trod it alone.

My "indescribably beautiful" wife, Christine, to whom I dedicated my first book, has been beside me through the entire expedition, offering her usual encouragement, advice, and flexibility while running home and hearth as I attempted to stick to a disciplined writing schedule amid the usual (and some not so usual) challenges of life.

My children—Laura, Peter, and Evan—have stood by me while I put together a very long book. As a writer, I scrounge for stories wherever I can find them, and you will see some of theirs in these pages. Christine and I have been warmed and enlightened by these three incandescent beings more than we ever imagined possible—and much more than I deserve.

My sincere thanks also go to Bob Hosack of Baker, who saw the potential in this project and offered advice and encouragement along the way. I am grateful also to J. I. Packer, who sat down with me over breakfast one morning and helped me to better understand Jesus in his first-century setting and encouraged me to press on.

Though they probably didn't know it, Robertson McQuilkin and Kent Hughes have served as role models. I remain in the debt of my parents, Morris and Irene Guthrie, for the wonderful example they have set through the decades. Thanks also to Gary Chase, who read drafts of the early chapters and provided valuable feedback.

Attentive readers may wonder about the Bible translation used in the lion's share of this work. Because of its beauty, clarity, and accuracy, I have chosen the English Standard Version. My grateful thanks go to the people at Crossway for their generosity. The other translation I turned to frequently is the New International Version, a fine one, published by Zondervan.

There are undeniable dangers in this endeavor, such as giving the questions Jesus asked more weight than they deserve or taking them out of context. As a non-scholar, I have carefully tried to avoid these hermeneutical minefields. But in a work of this size and complexity (and perhaps even in smaller, simpler ones), errors are unavoidable, and I accept all responsibility for mine.

I unknowingly wrote my first book, *Missions in the Third Millennium*, as my time with one employer was coming to a close and a new period was about to begin. Such is also the case with this volume, which marks another career transition for me. While my allotted periods and boundaries in this stage of life are not entirely clear, I trust that the God who has kept me from stumbling spiritually even as I stumble from time to time physically will continue to lead me in his path, answering my questions along the way.

Introduction

*"Why are you afraid,
O you of little faith?"*

At 7:51 a.m. on January 12, 2007, the musician picked up his violin outside the Metro in Washington, DC. During the next three-quarters of an hour, the man, wearing jeans and a long-sleeved T-shirt, began to play six classical pieces, to no one in particular. As he performed, more than a thousand people went on their way, oblivious to the music. Most probably assumed he was just another street musician seeking the largesse of commuters. A few stopped, but most hurried on to their jobs in the federal bureaucracy, absorbed in their own concerns. Forty-three minutes later, the man had earned a few coins over thirty-two dollars.

But this musician was no ordinary fiddler, and his instrument no common violin. He was the world-renowned Joshua Bell, recognized as one of the great musical artists of his generation. A middling ticket to a sold-out Bell concert at Boston's Symphony Hall three days earlier had cost one hundred dollars, yet this morning he was offering his artistry for free, playing a priceless instrument hand-crafted by Antonio Stradivari in 1713.

J. T. Tillman, a computer specialist for the Department of Housing and Urban Development, had planned to give Bell a dollar or two, but had spent all his cash on the lottery. When told he had "stiffed" a world-renowned musician, Tillman said, "I didn't think nothing of it—just a guy trying to make a couple of bucks." Then Tillman asked, "Is he ever going to play around here again?"

"Yeah," came the reply, "but you're going to have to pay a lot to hear him."[1]

Passion about the Christ

People are fascinated with Jesus. The huge numbers who saw *The Passion of the Christ* and *The Da Vinci Code* testify to this enduring interest, and have sparked a boom in family- and faith-friendly films—everything from *Evan Almighty* to *The Lion, the Witch and the Wardrobe*. The Library of Congress says more than seventeen thousand books exist about Jesus, and more such volumes (including the one you hold in your hands) are churned out every week.

And yet like a thousand passersby at the DC Metro on an ordinary winter morning, we risk missing his awesome beauty amid our busy daily pursuits. Despite the countless words written about the man from Galilee, we sometimes seem no nearer to figuring out who Jesus was than his disciples, who experienced shock and awe on a suddenly calm lake two millennia ago.

> And when [Jesus] got into the boat, his disciples followed him. And behold, there arose a great storm on the sea, so that the boat was being swamped by the waves; but he was asleep. And they went and woke him, saying, "Save us, Lord; we are perishing." And he said to them, "*Why are you afraid, O you of little faith?*" Then he arose and rebuked the winds and the sea, and there was a great calm. And the men marveled, saying, "What sort of man is this, that even winds and sea obey him?"[2]

This teacher from the ancient Middle East remains a revered and yet enigmatic figure in Western culture. Nearly everyone has a theory about who he is. No matter the level of our faith or skepticism, we all find ourselves asking, "Who *is* this man?"

- Modern Jews, who mostly reject him as Messiah, nonetheless often see him as a Torah-observant Jewish reformer who stirred up trouble and was the unfortunate victim of a political witch-hunt.
- Doubters of the orthodox Christian message, such as Bart Ehrman and Marcus Borg, allow that Jesus was a great (albeit misunderstood) human teacher who never intended to be worshiped.
- Political or religious revolutionaries see Jesus as a kindred spirit who was seeking to liberate the poor from injustice.
- According to scholar Stephen Prothero, "Buddhists revere him as a bodhisattva, Hindus as an avatar of God."[3]
- The unknown author of the Gnostic Gospel of Judas presents Jesus as an essentially spiritual being who longed to escape this corrupt earth.

- Novelist Dan Brown presents Jesus as a misunderstood feminist who was husband of Mary Magdalene.
- Muslims see Jesus as a great prophet who will come again (but not as the Son of God).
- Christians see Jesus as Immanuel, God with us. In this vein, the Nicene Creed of the fourth century calls him "the only begotten Son of God, begotten of the Father before all worlds, God of God, light of light, Very God of Very God."

However sincerely (or vehemently) these theories are held, they can't all be right. Like Joshua Bell, the identity of Jesus, though available to the crowds, is often hidden from our downcast eyes. How do we decide who Jesus was and what was most important to him? And what difference does it make in our lives today? How can we know?

Knowing and Doing

Pastor John Piper, author of *What Jesus Demands from the World*, says we can know the answers to these questions because Jesus has told us both who he is and what matters to him. But knowing and doing are two separate things. We know, for example, how he wants us to live as his followers—and yet we fail so consistently to turn the other cheek, to give to the one who asks, to go the second mile.

In *Jesus Mean and Wild*, Mark Galli says the problem is that we have a "Jesus-lite" image, hearing only what we want to hear, having "become deaf to the richer parts of the symphony of love." Galli says we have averted our gaze from the uncontrollable Christ of the Gospels, in favor of Sunday school flannel graphs depicting a cartoonish, lamb-cuddling softy: "We hear the melody played by the strings but ignore the brass and wind and especially the percussion sections. We don't notice the strong harmonies, the counterpoint, and the dissonant chords."[4]

Getting Closer

These perspectives are surely right and helpful. And yet we must get closer, or else we might commit the error of the crowds who may have heard his symphony but never bothered to stop and listen.

Imagine you are walking a dusty path with Jesus and the disciples, or climbing into a nerve-wrackingly small fishing boat with this motley crew. Yes, you will have ample opportunities to ask Jesus your questions (though, surprisingly perhaps, the documents handed down from those days record instances when bystanders "asked him no more questions" or "were afraid to ask him" about a matter).

Further, you can listen to his beautiful ethical teaching, the highest the world has known. Sit with him on the mountain as he calls on you to rejoice when you are persecuted, to lay up treasures in heaven, to love your enemies.

And yet, at the end of the day, we are still left with this question: who *is* this man? To get closer to an answer, we have to grasp a fundamental but little-noted fact about the life and ministry of Jesus of Nazareth. He engaged his listeners, both friend and foe, in conversation. Jesus didn't just teach; he didn't just command; he also asked questions—and lots of them. The four Gospels—Matthew, Mark, Luke, and John—plus Acts, reproduce nearly three hundred questions from the lips of Jesus, such as the one he asked the cowering disciples in the boat.[5]

While many have analyzed Jesus's commands and acts as recorded in the New Testament, few have delved deeply into the questions he asked during his brief time of earthly ministry. Jesus scholars break down his teaching ministry in many different ways. Marcus Borg, for example, separates out parables and aphorisms as primary (doubting the historicity of some of the longer discourses), and blends in Jesus's questions with the rest of his teachings.[6] And yet many of these questions have vital application for our lives today and deserve our close attention.

Mary Schaller of Q Place (formerly Neighborhood Bible Studies) notes that Jesus's questions possess contemporary application for a church increasingly swamped by a Western secularism that craves relationship. She contrasts his dialogical approach with our penchant for monologue. "Questions make us think," Schaller says. "As a church culture, we want to *tell* people, and it's really not effective. Good questions, such as Jesus asked, create dialogue."[7]

The Lord's commands invite obedience and fear. His actions, such as his death and resurrection, provoke awe and thankfulness. But his questions prompt our participation, inspection, and reflection. His questions draw us into the mind of God and invite us to grow as we walk with him. As we grapple with Jesus's questions, we learn what we truly believe—and what we don't.

Though obedience is always the right response to his commands, Jesus does not expect us to mindlessly absorb and implement them. He respects us as valuable creatures made in the image of God who can and must participate in our salvation. That's what this book is about.

Jesus, the master teacher of history, asked probing questions of all who came to him: friend and foe, skeptic and follower, seeker and betrayer. And he still asks today. Jesus didn't just present abstract theological truths. He was intensely personal and "in your face." He frequently turned the tables on those around him, forcing them through his questions to confront issues of life and death, love and hate, heaven and hell.

These questions force all professing Christians and spiritual seekers to face ultimate issues about Christ's identity and mission, and our faith and priorities. They also provide key insights into Christ's view of human nature and intellectual capacity, the priority of the Scriptures, and other topics. Further, we gain understanding of the discipling implications of Christ's brilliant teaching methods.

The Plan of This Book

In analyzing Jesus's questions, we will focus mainly on what he actually said in the Gospels and in the book of Acts, for this is where we find the questions and where we truly encounter Jesus. While scholars can bring great learning and insights to bear on the life of Christ—and we will look to them at times for guidance—there is no substitute for wrestling with the source documents themselves.[8] As John Piper notes, "no reliable or lasting portrait of Jesus has ever been reconstructed from going behind what the four Gospels portray. There is no reason to think this will change."[9]

But before we get into the questions, let's look at where this book is going.

In section 1, we seek an answer to the vital question, "Who Is Jesus?" Jesus was intensely interested in knowing what people thought of him, because our relationship to him determines our eternal destiny. The Gospels record questions reflecting this interest scores of times. We cannot understand his questions without understanding who he was . . . and is.

In section 2, "How Do You Follow Him?" his questions force us to count the cost of casting our lot with him. Buddhism has the Eightfold Path; Islam, the Five Pillars; Hinduism, karma; Judaism, the law. All religions want us to follow a way. Only Christianity invites us to follow a person.

Section 3, "Where Is Your Thinking?" puts the lie to the old canard that Christians are "poor, uneducated, and easy to command."[10] Three sets of questions focus on our loving the Lord with all of our minds—and the difference that should make. Section 4, "Why Is Character So Vital?" deals with the qualities Jesus expects us to exhibit in our hearts and lives. Section 5, "What Are Some Critical Doctrines?" allows us to explore life-changing areas of faith suggested by Jesus's queries.

While space will not allow us to examine every question in detail (even in a book this big), we will take a comprehensive look at them. Each chapter will deal with a different subject suggested by his questions, such as his humanity, authority, or mission. Using the questions as our primary guides, we will listen to what Jesus asked, consider what the question means, and discern how it applies in our lives today.

For individuals and groups seeking to dig deeper, I have provided voluminous notes and discussion questions at the end of every chapter, suggestions for further reading, and an appendix listing all of the recorded questions, complete with Scripture references. When the Gospels present the same question more than once, I will occasionally examine it more than once, depending on the topic. According to the English Standard Version, which is the main translation I use for this book, Matthew records Jesus asking questions eighty-five times; Mark, sixty-four; Luke, ninety-one; John, fifty-two; and Acts, three.

As a professional journalist for over two decades, I know that asking the right question is vital if you want to elicit the right information. Without sharp questions, public figures can be very skilled at avoiding the key issues, or in steering conversations onto an unthreatening rabbit trail. Interviews then become an unenlightening transmission of mere talking points.

Some tricks of the journalistic trade include asking the same question in different ways, building a relationship with the interviewee before asking the toughest questions, and allowing the silence after a question to work for you. At *Christianity Today*, editors often solicit questions from one another before key interviews, to make sure they have the best opportunity to learn the truth from a source.

As an ink-stained wretch, I appreciate the almost journalistic approach of Jesus Christ. Like a master journalist, he knew how to ask questions in order to learn the truth, and to gently force those around him to face that truth. Jesus rarely let people pass by, like busy commuters at the DC Metro, without engaging their hearts and minds. Questions were one of his primary tools to get people to stop, think, and change their lives. May this book do the same for you.

Who Is Jesus?

1

His Forerunner

*"What did you go out into
the wilderness to see?"*

A common gambit of interviewers to gain insights into someone's likes, dislikes, and character is to ask, "What person from history would you most like to invite over for dinner?" The answers usually range from the classic (Alexander the Great, Julius Caesar, Cleopatra, FDR) to the contemporary (Tom Hanks, Beyoncé, Jon Stewart). More often than not, these choices reflect how we want others to see us, not necessarily the people with whom we would like to actually break bread.

Of course, religious figures are often named as desirable dinner companions, too. Jesus, the Dalai Lama, or a favorite guru (perhaps the Maharishi Mahesh Yogi or author Deepak Chopra) might get the invitation. After all, despite all the talk from skeptics such as Nietzsche that "God is dead" or, in the words of atheist pundit Christopher Hitchens, "God is not great," the fact is, spirituality is in. From *feng shui* to yoga to gospel music, people wear their faiths on their sleeves and invite friends, neighbors, and other strangers to share in their spiritual discoveries. While it may no longer be fashionable in the current pluralistic climate to claim one's belief system is the only way, it is perfectly acceptable to celebrate your understanding of metaphysics—even if it makes no logical sense.

But I have never heard anyone name a certain mysterious man from the New Testament as a wanted guest for dinner. He is not mentioned in the book *Religious Literacy*. This is odd, for if ancient Israel had had rock stars, he would have been one. The documents handed down from that time two millennia ago name him as a counter-cultural iconoclast who drew gaping crowds of common folk and the intelligentsia.

"Then Jerusalem and *all* Judea and *all* the region about the Jordan were going out to him."[1] Seeing this towering figure was like traveling on pilgrimage to the United Center to see Michael Jordan in his prime.

A Voice in the Wilderness

This mighty man, of course, was John, commonly known as "the Baptist." As Matthew's eyewitness-derived testimony points out:

> In those days John the Baptist came preaching in the wilderness of Judea, "Repent, for the kingdom of heaven is at hand." For this is he who was spoken of by the prophet Isaiah when he said,
>
> > "The voice of one crying in the wilderness:
> > 'Prepare the way of the Lord;
> > make his paths straight.'"
>
> Now John wore a garment of camel's hair and a leather belt around his waist, and his food was locusts and wild honey.[2]

If we invited John to dinner, what would we feed him? Then, as now, most people allow their superstars to be different, whether that difference be in speech, sartorial predilections, or lifestyle. That's usually part of the act. The late Michael Jackson is a case in point. In John's case, it was all three (but it was no act). John was so big, in fact, that at one point, people thought Jesus was John come back from the dead.[3]

Of course, the lives of Jesus and John were linked well before then. Luke the physician, regarded by scholars such as the late F. F. Bruce as a precise ancient historian, tells how a godly couple, Zechariah and Elizabeth, who were too old to have children, nevertheless conceived John after an announcement by an angelic visitor, Gabriel. The birth of Jesus is much better known, but similar: some months later Gabriel tells Mary, a virgin, that she will miraculously have a son, Jesus.

Luke includes an important detail of foreshadowing, which occurred when a pregnant Mary visited a slightly further along Elizabeth, who was a relative: "And when Elizabeth heard the greeting of Mary, the baby [John] leaped in her womb. And Elizabeth was filled with the Holy Spirit. . . . [Elizabeth said,]

'And why is this granted to me that the mother of my Lord should come to me? For behold, when the sound of your greeting came to my ears, the baby in my womb leaped for joy.'"[4]

The Gospel narratives tell us nothing of John as he grew to manhood, but we can guess he spent much of that time as an orphan, given the advanced ages of Zechariah and Elizabeth at the time of his birth. John's seemingly crude attire and way of life as an adult about thirty years later recall the vows of an ancient Nazirite,[5] a member of a Jewish religious order that emphasized both a rejection of the corrupt outer world plus utter devotion to Israel's God. Such devotion, similar to that of the ancient Essene community at Qumran, expressed itself by vows to drink no wine, nor to eat anything considered unclean. John's single-minded commitment—uncharitable observers today might call it fanaticism—soon drew a following.

But John was no cult leader constructing a personal Jonestown. Yes, he had disciples, those who walked with him and helped in the growing ministry. But most he simply instructed to return to their old lives with new hearts, waiting expectantly for Israel's deliverer.

"Whoever has two tunics is to share with him who has none, and whoever has food is to do likewise," John told the anxious crowds. To the corrupt tax collectors, who made their comfortable livings by fleecing the flock, John said, "Collect no more than you are authorized to do." To the hated Roman soldiers, who "supplemented" their salaries the way many police officers do today in poor parts of the world—by bribe-taking and extortion—John said, "Do not extort money from anyone by threats or by false accusation, and be content with your wages."[6]

Radical stuff, yes. (If you doubt this, try to remember the last time you heard a similar sermon about contentment, workplace honesty, and generously sharing with the needy.) But it was hardly comparable to a call to mass suicide.

Ruffled Feathers

But not all Israel was taken with the mysterious celebrity. To the Pharisees (who constructed elaborate rules in addition to and on par with Scripture) and Sadducees (who did not believe in the life to come) John was sterner, even mocking: "You brood of vipers!" he thundered (and Scripture records no response from his stunned hearers). "Who warned you to flee from the wrath to come? Bear fruit in keeping with repentance."[7]

He evidently ruffled enough feathers to provoke the religious establishment in Jerusalem to send priests and Levites to find out more about this possible usurper. "Who are you?" they demanded to know, and you can almost hear their nervousness tinged with exasperation. John certainly could have said, "I am John, the leader of a new, purified Israel. Join me, or face annihilation!" Instead, he answered by saying who he was *not*: "I am not the Christ." Now the Christ (or, to use the

Hebrew word, *messiah*) was the long promised figure in the Old Testament who would establish his kingly rule, destroy Israel's enemies, and bring the people back to God. John was saying that the current religious leaders, who ruled under the watchful eye of Rome, had nothing to fear from him on that score.

The interrogation continued:

> "What then? Are you Elijah?"
> "I am not."
> "Are you the Prophet?"
> "No."
> "Who are you? We need to give an answer to those who sent us. What do you say about yourself?"
> "I am the voice of one crying out in the wilderness, 'Make straight the way of the Lord,' as the prophet Isaiah said."[8]

Though he was too humble to directly say so, John (in the later words of Jesus) had come in the spirit and power of the Old Testament prophet Elijah, attempting to bring the nation back from the moral precipice and prepare the people for One who was to come. He confidently prophesied to the shocked crowds,

> I baptize you with water for repentance, but he who is coming after me is mightier than I, whose sandals I am not worthy to carry. He will baptize you with the Holy Spirit and fire. His winnowing fork is in his hand, and he will clear his threshing floor and gather his wheat into the barn, but the chaff he will burn with unquenchable fire.[9]

Even for those of us unused to the ancient farming imagery, the meaning of John's words is clear enough. And terrifying.

And yet for all his certainty, John was soon taken aback by a Jesus he never expected—and not for the last time. Matthew (a former tax collector) reports, "Then Jesus came from Galilee to the Jordan to John, to be baptized by him. John would have prevented him, saying, 'I need to be baptized by you, and do you come to me?'"[10] This Jesus did not fit his expectations. John knew, from personal experience or a touch of spiritual insight, that Jesus was the greater, the mightier, the holier. John knew that his own ministry was to prepare not only others for Messiah's coming, but himself. As he was to tell his disciples elsewhere, "He must increase, but I must decrease."[11]

A Man with Doubts

Such maturity and humility—and yet we see that John struggled with Jesus and his even greater humility, at least at first. Evidently John expected not only the Lamb of God who takes away the sin of the world, but an avenging judge. What kind of judge would stoop to the water? But Jesus, as was his habit, met questioning faith with gentleness. "Let it be so now," he told John by the river, "for thus it is fitting for us to fulfill all righteousness."[12]

And decrease John did, losing followers to Jesus and eventually ending up in Herod's prison cell. As Israel's checkered history taught, being a prophet usually ended badly. John had publicly condemned the corrupt ruler for taking his brother's wife, and Herod made an executive decision to shut the prophet up—behind bars. Using his few remaining disciples now as his eyes and ears, John, the seemingly all-but-forgotten star, tried to follow the progress of Jesus's growing ministry from afar.

But Jesus, as before, did not match John's portrait of a conquering messiah. The Romans remained firmly in control, and Jesus's ministry to that point consisted mainly of teaching and healing. Where was the promised kingdom of God? When was Jesus going to get *on* with it?

Matthew recounts John's doubts with refreshing honesty: "Now when John heard in prison about the deeds of the Christ, he sent word by his disciples and said to him, 'Are you the one who is to come, or shall we look for another?'"[13]

Again, Jesus meets John's questioning faith with gentleness, referring to a messianic prophecy from the book of Isaiah that John knew well: "Go and tell John what you hear and see: the blind receive their sight and the lame walk, lepers are cleansed and the deaf hear, and the dead are raised up, and the poor have good news preached to them." Then Jesus adds the mildest rebuke possible; you can almost imagine him winking as he says it: "And blessed is the one who is not offended by me."[14]

More Than a Prophet

Then as John's disciples head back to their teacher, Jesus launches into a series of questions about John for the crowds, who presumably had heard the entire exchange. This cluster actually consists of six questions about the forerunner, stacked one on top of the other, followed by a detailed answer that his audience could only find shocking. Let's look at the questions in detail.

> *What did you go out into the wilderness to see? A reed shaken by the wind? What then did you go out to see? A man dressed in soft clothing?* Behold, those who wear soft clothing are in kings' houses. *What then did you go out to see? A prophet?*[15]

Jesus knew who he was and didn't feel the time was right to explain his messiahship further to the crowds. After all, if John had stumbled over his identity, surely they would, too. The issue these people could grasp was not Jesus, but

John. Jesus would use that firsthand knowledge to his advantage, reminding his listeners through these questions why they went out to see the Baptist.

Appealing to their highest motives, Jesus said they had not sought a spiritual weakling, a person tossed by every wind and wave of doctrine, a soft man who was too isolated and pampered to understand them and their needs. No, John had stood tall, putting even the official religious leaders, who cared little for the people, in their places. At the same time, he had given the crowds what they most needed, permission to repent, and instructions to begin rebuilding their lives. A true prophet, he had stood with them in the river, pouring the refreshing water with his own rough-hewn hands.

Then, having thus engaged his listeners, Jesus answers his own questions.

> Yes, I tell you, and more than a prophet. This is he of whom it is
> written,
>   "Behold, I send my messenger before your face,
>   who will prepare your way before you."[16]

Luke, a Gentile physician who would later travel with another great itinerant preacher to many Roman outposts, records the reaction of the crowds: "When all the people heard this, and the tax collectors too, they declared God just, having been baptized with the baptism of John, but the Pharisees and the lawyers rejected the purpose of God for themselves, not having been baptized by him."[17]

In other words, Jesus confirmed the common man's conviction that John was indeed a prophet—and more. Surely Jesus was also disabusing anyone present of the notion that John was less of a prophet because he had struggled with Jesus and his mission. Matthew Henry, a great Puritan pastor, notes, "Some of Christ's disciples might take occasion from the question John sent, to reflect upon him as weak and wavering, and inconsistent with himself."[18] No, doubt shadows the walk of every true follower of Christ, who gently leads each one back on the true path.

But as we also see here, John the Baptist forces us to choose, and not all will stoop in repentance, not all will accept God's gracious call. Later, when Jesus was reaching the climax of his ministry in Jerusalem, the leading priests and elders confronted him, much as they had John, with angry questions: "By what authority are you doing these things, and who gave you this authority?" Jesus answered their questions with his own:

> I will also ask you one question, and if you tell me the answer, then I also will
> tell you by what authority I do these things. *The baptism of John, where did it
> come from? From heaven or from man?*[19]

The lives and ministries of Jesus and John were linked. It was a package deal, and still is. Many see Jesus as a grand liberator, or a kindly figure whose goal is to comfort them, a magician, a teacher, a myth. But Jesus cannot be poured into any mold whatsoever. John, before anyone else, interprets Jesus.

John also tests our sincerity. When the elders and chief priests refused to say from where John had received his authority, Jesus refused to answer their questions. Religion is no game. Seek honestly, or not at all. Those who approach with sincerity will find the doors open. Those who don't will hear only the echo of their own voices.

So before we can embrace Jesus, we must wrestle with John. Instead of standing off to the side and interrogating this man wearing odd clothing and eating strange food, we must go down to the river and listen to this messenger who was announced by an angel.

And the message is simple enough for anyone to understand. John tells us, "You are a sinner. You have broken God's holy law. Repent—turn back to God and do what he says. Hurry, because the Judge is coming soon." Jesus asked his hearers, as he asks us today, "Do you believe John?"

I love watching the diminutive Kiwi evangelist Ray Comfort and his sidekick, Kirk Cameron. Like Batman and Robin, they regularly head out to Gotham City—usually, sunny Southern California—to confront the everyday sinners they meet on the streets. Ray and Kirk usually don't mince words. They can't. The encounters are brief, people are in a hurry, and they need to get to the point.

Ray takes the listeners quickly through the Ten Commandments—and, if need be, their elucidation by Jesus in the Sermon on the Mount—to inform them that they have broken God's law and stand under God's judgment. While some of the people they meet laugh in derision or even spit on Ray and Kirk, others are surprisingly honest about their sins, which run the gamut from lust to theft to worshiping false gods. And some of these people are ready to take the next step and hear about God's solution.

Before we can effectively tell people about Christ, we must introduce them to John. The bad news in most cases must precede the good news. Without facing the bad, the good will not make sense. Like John, we must draw the stark contrast for people. We must tell them the problem before we can offer the solution. Even Jesus's first words of ministry were, "Repent, for the kingdom of heaven is at hand."[20] Logically, we cannot repent from our sin if we do not know we are sinners.[21]

The church doesn't do enough of this kind of preaching today. We think if we are perceived as too radical, we will drive people away. But John tells us the opposite. People know, deep down, that they are sick. Radical surgery, unpleasant as it is, is required to save the patient. Perhaps this reluctance to speak out is why we find so few non-Christians actually entering our sanctuaries. They see little difference between us and the world.

And perhaps there is not a clear enough picture of our sinfulness even inside our doors. Sociologists have discovered that many Christian teens unconsciously think of their faith as "moralistic therapeutic deism," as a way to feel good about themselves while following a list of rules that supposedly will give them a successful and fulfilling life.[22]

But there is no power here. As the book *Forbidden Fruit* points out, most teens classified as evangelicals live sexual lives that are no different than their peers—in some cases, they are even *more* likely to engage in sexual activity: "evangelical teenagers don't display just average sexual activity patterns, but rather above average ones."[23] And this should hardly shock us, since their parents who profess evangelical faith seemingly do little better than outright pagans in keeping their marital vows. According to author and activist Ron Sider, approximately one in three evangelicals approves of premarital sex, and one in six condones adultery.[24]

Having It Both Ways

Pressing the matter, Jesus, with another question, confronts those in his audience who were looking for any excuse not to believe.

> *But to what shall I compare this generation?* It is like children sitting in the marketplaces and calling to their playmates,
>
> > "We played the flute for you, and you did not dance;
> > we sang a dirge, and you did not mourn."
>
> For John came neither eating nor drinking, and they say, "He has a demon." The Son of Man [Jesus] came eating and drinking, and they say, "Look at him! A glutton and a drunkard, a friend of tax collectors and sinners!" Yet wisdom is justified by her deeds.[25]

In other words, Jesus is calling the majority of his generation those who want to have it both ways. They reject John because he is supposedly too ascetic; they eschew Jesus because he is supposedly too worldly. The real problem is not John or Jesus; it is the people.

Now, of course, Christians have been known to go off the proverbial deep end upon their conversions and alienate those people they seek to convince. Sudden changes in eating habits, in dress, in friendships, and in treatment of nonbelieving family members sometimes can become unhealthy, even cultish, causing loved ones understandably to worry. A new follower of Jesus who has made radical changes and pompously lectures confused friends and family has fractured many a relationship. While these excesses are usually curbed as one matures in the faith, the initial damage done can be long lasting indeed. Missiologists and church-growth experts often counsel that it is best for new Christian believers to resist the urge to withdraw from their social circles and instead to spread the faith in a gentle and winsome way for as long as possible.

However, it is often true that unbelieving friends and acquaintances will not like the change in a new believer's allegiance to Christ, no matter what packaging it comes in. Jesus recognized this reality, and so must we.

More Than One Way

But we also see another point implicit in Jesus's question—that there is no one best way to serve him. Some may well be called to a life of renunciation in order to grab the rest of us by our spiritual throats, as John was. Others will be called to rub shoulders with the world in an effort to save the world. In both cases, the aim is not withdrawal, but engagement.

Many Christians, perhaps most, will be called to lay aside their camelhair tunics and locusts and wild honey to engage the culture in a different way. They will be recognizable not by their dress or their diet, but by their deeds. William Wilberforce was one.

Wilberforce, an eighteenth-century child of privilege and wealth, became a Member of Parliament who later was drawn to Christ. In secret he went to see John Newton, a former captain of a slave ship who was now a Christian pastor. As the two conversed, Wilberforce confided that he was thinking of leaving Parliament to become a minister. Newton, however, told Wilberforce to stay at his post "for such a time as this" and use his considerable gifts to help end the nefarious slave trade. That happened after over two decades of work.

Another follower of Christ whom Newton counseled was author Hannah More. "Wilberforce and the playwright and poet Hannah More were both prominent public figures when they experienced crisis conversions," says Charles Colson, who had a similar experience after Watergate. "After their conversions, both considered retiring from public life in order to engage fully in the spiritual life. . . . As they faced potential scorn, withdrawal into quietism was tempting."[26]

They didn't, and instead joined the battle against slavery. British society and the victims of the slave trade were better off for their effort to stay engaged as full participants. The slave trade was abolished in 1807.

Another kind of Christian, more in the mold of John the Baptist, was J. Hudson Taylor, who renounced his comforts in England to win Chinese people to Christ, who himself put on our rags so we could put on his riches.

By today's standards, J. Hudson Taylor was an extremist. To prepare himself for expected missionary hardships in China, this nineteenth-century Englishman subsisted on a loaf of bread and a pound of apples each day, seriously undermining his own frail health. Once in China, he was drawn to the interior, where hardships were many and Christians were few. In an attempt to remove Western cultural impediments, Taylor donned Chinese dress and dyed his sandy hair black and pulled it together in a Chinese pigtail, prompting rebukes and derision from other missionaries. Yet at its zenith, the organization Taylor founded, the China Inland Mission, had more than thirteen hundred missionaries at one time in China, six thousand in all, laying the foundation for the explosive growth of the church there today.[27]

We can find such John the Baptists even closer to home than the sepia-tinted nineteenth century, of course. A new evangelical movement seeks to serve the poor by radical identification with the poor. Like the best of the ancient Catholic monastic orders, these "new monastics" live in poor, inner-city areas and seek creative approaches to social pathologics such as crime and homelessness. Scott Bessenecker of InterVarsity Christian Fellowship calls them the "new friars." According to *Christianity Today*'s Rob Moll, "these communities are the latest wave of evangelicals who see in community life an answer to society's materialism and the church's complacency toward it. Rather than enjoy the benefits of middle-class life, these suburban evangelicals choose to move in with the poor."[28]

Another John the Baptist figure is the late Mother Teresa of Calcutta. Born in 1910 in the Albanian town of Skopje, Agnes Gonxha made her vows of poverty, chastity, and obedience with the Sisters of Loretto in India, where she served. There, in 1931, she changed her name to Teresa, in honor of Saint Therese of Lisieux, proclaimed by Pius XI as patroness of missions. In 1946, Teresa renounced still more: "On my way to Darjeeling, . . . I received an invitation to leave everything behind, to follow Jesus in the slums, and to serve him among the poorest of the poor. I knew it was his will and I had to follow him. The message was very clear."[29]

Mother Teresa is best known for her work among the sick and dying of Calcutta, work that draws few critics even among those who disagree with her theology, particularly her statements that she was "married" to Christ. In a critical biography, Gezim Alpion acknowledges, "Mother Teresa's attachment to Christ may have been indeed 'bizarre' or 'controversial,' as some of her statements seem to indicate. As far as she was concerned, however, there was nothing bizarre or controversial in how she felt about Jesus. She was so immersed in him that she was prepared to face any challenge to serve him fully."[30]

But her outspoken opposition to abortion has ruffled more than a few feathers. At the National Prayer Breakfast in 1994, Mother Teresa abandoned the polite niceties that invited speakers usually observe. Like John the Baptist and in the presence of a pro-choice president and vice president, her message was a shocking call to repentance:

> I feel that the greatest destroyer of peace today is abortion, because it is a war against the child—a direct killing of the innocent child—murder by the mother

herself. And if we accept that a mother can kill her own child, how can we tell other people not to kill one another? . . . Any country that accepts abortion is not teaching the people to love, but to use any violence to get what they want.[31]

Like the stunned elites whom John the Baptist stared down in his day, President Bill Clinton and his entourage refused to join the standing ovation.

Of course, sometimes the penalty for speaking the unvarnished truth is much more severe, as John the Baptist discovered. Imprisoned for speaking out against Herod—who took his brother's wife, Herodias, for his own—John was beheaded at the infuriated order of Herodias.[32]

No, being a John won't get you many dinner invitations. It won't protect you against doubt, discouragement, even death. In fact, it may make troubles even more likely. But it will also bring you the everlasting commendation of Jesus, who said of his forerunner, "Truly I say to you, among those born of women there has arisen no one greater than John the Baptist."[33]

Suggested Reading

Elwell, Walter A., ed. "John the Baptist." In *Baker Encyclopedia of the Bible.* 2 vols. Grand Rapids: Baker, 1988.

Mother Teresa. *My Life for the Poor.* San Francisco: HarperSanFrancisco, 2005.

Discussion Questions

1. How important is it to you to fit in with the crowd?
2. Does John the Baptist strike you as an iconoclast, or as an oddball—or both? Why?
3. What were John's greatest strengths and weaknesses?
4. Name some occasions when you put the career or reputation of someone else ahead of your own.
5. Why is this so hard to do?
6. When you see the word "repent," what images does it evoke?
7. Do you see yourself as a sinner in need of repentance?
8. Which do you think God might be calling you to—a life of renunciation or a life of immersion in the world? Why?

2

His Teaching in Context

"Can a blind man lead a blind man?"

During the 1980s, communism's hold on Poland seemed brutally secure. Yes, Lech Walesa and the Solidarity labor movement were irritants. Yes, Ronald Reagan and John Paul II continued to speak out for freedom, religious liberty, and human dignity. Yes, even Mikhail Gorbachev, the new Kremlin leader, was tentatively implementing *perestroika* ("economic and governmental restructuring"). But communist domination of this proud land at the crossroads of Europe appeared drearily inevitable, like the black smog that coated the ancient city of Krakow.

In 1988, my wife and I traveled to Poland as part of a church group, not sure what to expect. The country, with a thousand years of history, was heavily Catholic. Russian propagandists, however, asserted that the Polish people celebrated their place in the expanding Soviet—and atheistic—empire. A statue erected by Poland's communist masters depicts a burly man, symbolizing the Soviet Union, with his arm around a smaller man—Poland. On the Polish coat of arms, the crown over the eagle's head had been quietly removed.

Our flight aboard the Polish airline, Lot, was in some ways quaint. We were offered fresh bread and butter (Poland has a long history of farming). The flight attendants were kind, and there was no hint that the jet was under the control of a dictatorship that had slaughtered or exiled untold millions (except for the clunky ads appearing in the in-flight magazine).

But when we stepped off the jet, all doubt was removed. We were immediately taken to the terminal aboard a special bus. This bus carried more than international travelers. It had a contingent of grim-faced guards wearing military fatigues and bearing submachine guns. Needless to say, we knew we weren't in Kansas anymore.

Under Dictatorship

Separated by twenty centuries, the Poland of the 1980s nonetheless shared much in common with the world of Jesus's day. Like Poland before the implosion of the Soviet Union, Israel was under the thumb of a brutal military dictatorship—imperial Rome. Israel, once ruled by King David, now had to answer to Caesar. Like the Soviets, the Romans allowed their subjugated peoples a fig leaf of simulated self-rule, within limits. For the Jews who lived in Israel, that meant the Sanhedrin (a ruling council of rabbis, Pharisees, and scribes) could decide all matters religious.

Cruel King Herod, described without irony by historians as "the Great," ruled under the watchful eye of Rome, even building the magnificent second Jewish temple. It was Herod who, upon hearing reports of a new king in Israel, unsuccessfully attempted to murder the baby Jesus in Bethlehem—only to slaughter other innocents instead.[1]

Local synagogues could meet, as long as members did not foment revolution. Occasionally, however, rebels would rise, only to be crushed either by the Roman troops stationed in Jerusalem or other cohorts elsewhere in the countryside. While comparatively few Israelites took up arms against the legions—such acts were suicidal—all Jews hated the pagan Romans.

When Herod died, three of his sons—Archelaus, Philip, and Herod Antipas—divided the faux-kingdom between them. Tiberias was emperor in this dangerous time. Scholar N. T. Wright notes,

First-century Judaism, with all its pluriformity, had certain dynamics running through it, not least an undercurrent of potential or actual revolution. This was not confined to the lowest social classes, but enjoyed the support of at least some Pharisees, and, eventually, even some aristocrats. . . . There is plenty of evidence for revolutionary movements smouldering away throughout the period, coming into explicit confrontation with the authorities from time to time. . . . Sometimes violent intent was there from the start. Sometimes those who followed a new leader seemed to assume that their god would intervene on their behalf, as had happened when the walls of Jericho fell before Joshua and his company. But at least we can be sure of this: anyone who was heard talking about the reign of Israel's god would be assumed to be referring to the fulfillment of Israel's long-held hope. The covenant god would act to reconstitute his people, to end their exile, to forgive their sins. When that happened, Israel would no longer be dominated by the pagans. She would be free. The means of liberation were no doubt open to debate. The goal was not.[2]

The tensions evident in Jesus's day would eventually tear Israel apart. To put down a Jewish rebellion, in AD 70 the Romans destroyed the temple, ended the ancient sacrificial system, and laid waste to Jerusalem. In such a context, predictions of divine judgment made perfect sense. No wonder John the Baptist expressed doubt and confusion in the face of Jesus's enigmatic ministry! Thus, as easy as it might appear, we cannot examine Jesus's teaching—or, for that matter, his questions—in isolation from his historical context. That's what this chapter is about.

Jesus a Jew

Jaroslav Pelikan, the late New Testament scholar from Yale, noted, "It is obvious—and yet, to judge by the tragedies of later history, not at all obvious—that Jesus was a Jew."[3] For centuries large segments of the Christian church downplayed the obvious fact that Jesus was a Jew. And Jewish people, because of the centuries of painful interaction between the two faiths, were none too eager to emphasize it.

No more. In fact, many modern Jews have decided they may safely embrace Jesus, not as their messiah, perhaps, but nonetheless as a Jew *par excellence*. "There is every reason for Judaism to lose its reluctance toward Jesus," wrote Norman Cousins, former editor of the *Saturday Review*. Cousins added,

> His own towering spiritual presence is a projection of Judaism, not a repudiation of it. Jesus is not to be taxed for the un-Christian ideas and acts of those who have spoken in his name. Jesus never repudiated Judaism. He was proud to be a Jew, yet he did not confine himself to Judaism. . . . No other figure—spiritual, philosophical, political or intellectual—has had a greater impact on human history. To belong to a people that produced Jesus is to share in a distinction of vast dimension and meaning.[4]

While Christians disagree with contemporary observers who see "the historical Jesus" as merely "embedded" in first-century Judaism, we cannot go to the other extreme and simply hold that Jesus dropped out of the sky to teach timeless moral truths. As Wright says, "Jesus cannot be separated from his Jewish context, but neither can he be collapsed into it so that he is left without a sharp critique of his contemporaries."[5]

The Context

His context touched Jesus in specific ways and is key to helping us observe what he said, interpret what he meant, and apply that meaning to our lives in the twenty-first century. That will be the method of this book. For indeed

Jesus meant his questions not just for his contemporaries, but also for us. As he said, "Heaven and earth will pass away, but my words will not pass away."[6]

Jesus invested much of his ministry in Galilee. He grew up in this region, on the northern outskirts of Israel, a place of peasants and ill repute. Galilee, to borrow a phrase from Jim Croce, was "the south side of Chicago . . . the baddest part of town."[7] When the new disciple Philip told Nathanael that Jesus was from the Galilean town of Nazareth, you can almost see Nathanael's lip curl as he answers, "Can anything good come out of *Nazareth*?"[8] After Jesus was arrested at the end of his public ministry, the disciple Peter very nearly was arrested, too, with the accusation, "Certainly this man also was with him, for he too is a Galilean."[9]

And Jesus generally hung out in the least important towns of this little-noticed region. Adrian Curtis, senior lecturer in Hebrew Bible at the University of Manchester, notes, "With the exception of Jerusalem, the places associated with Jesus in the Gospel accounts were not particularly important in the wider context of the times. On the other hand, cities which were important, such as Sepphoris, the most important town in Galilee and not far from Nazareth, are not mentioned in the Gospels."[10]

Religious Groups

Also key to that context were the various religious groups in Israel, some of which cooperated with one another, and some of which fought one another, as is often the case among minorities struggling to survive under dictatorships. Let's briefly examine the key groups with which Jesus interacted, and not always gently. Well does Wright speak of the period's "pluriformity"!

- *Rabbis*: Jesus himself was called "Rabbi" or "Rabboni" many times. The term means "teacher," or even "great one." The position was not specifically mentioned in the ancient Hebrew Scriptures and did not begin to take shape until half a millennium before Christ. The position is evidence of a growing, merit-based democratization of Judaism. Rabbi Arthur Blecher calls the rabbinate "the triumph of intellect over lineage."[11] Rabbis were highly regarded for their ability to interpret the law of Moses for a Judaism that no longer found itself in the wilderness. Blecher notes that while the monarchy and the priesthood were based on heredity, the rabbinate was based on study. The monarchy, which was for all intents and purposes crushed once Jerusalem fell to the Babylonian invaders in 586 BC, and the priesthood, those authorized to run the sacrificial system until Herod's temple was destroyed by the Romans in AD 70, were ended; the rabbinate continues to this day. And rabbis were not simply wandering sages or gurus, but men who were expected to raise up disciples who would become rabbis in their own right. Of course, there were many rabbis within first-century Judaism, when the term was first used, including Gamaliel the Elder, who had a seat on the Sanhedrin.

- *Pharisees*: The Pharisees, mentioned by Wright above, were rabbis who had started a purity movement within Judaism. They were held in high esteem for their genuine commitment to both the written law and the oral laws that they had constructed to help people obey the written law. Most of the literature about the Pharisees is positive. But Jesus, who frequently called the Pharisees he interacted with "blind guides" for setting their traditions above the law of Moses, blasted them for their foolish priorities: "*And why do you break the commandment of God for the sake of your tradition? For God commanded, 'Honor your father and your mother,' and, 'Whoever reviles father or mother must surely die.' But you say, 'If anyone tells his father or his mother, "What you may have gained from me is given to God," he need not honor his father.' So for the sake of your tradition you have made void the word of God. You hypocrites!*"[12]

- *Scribes*: The scribes, another target of Jesus's ire, taught, copied, and interpreted the law so that the people could understand it. Their word was considered authoritative both in the synagogues and in the temple. In the Gospels, however, the scribes detested Jesus for disregarding (1) their interpretations of proper Sabbath observance, (2) the need for ceremonial washings, and (3) their regimen for fasting.[13]

- *Sadducees*: This final group, addressed by John the Baptist as a "brood of vipers," opposed the detailed teachings of the Pharisees, probably accepted only the five books of Moses as authoritative (and not the rest of the Hebrew Scriptures), and disbelieved in the general Jewish understanding of physical resurrection (held by the Pharisees) and the overruling providence of God (in which the Pharisees and the Essenes of Qumran believed). "Souls die with the bodies," these early Jewish skeptics said. The Sadducees also "had a greater tendency to compromise with the ways of the Gentiles than other Jewish parties."[14] This last point is no surprise. Communist rulers from Poland to Russia to China have ever kept their eyes on committed believers, knowing that those who have hope beyond this life are least afraid of earthly tyrants. As Jesus said, "And do not fear those who kill the body but cannot kill the soul. Rather fear him who can destroy both soul and body in hell."[15] Such fear is freeing in this world. The Sadducees, however, had no such fear, and so were pliable tools in the hands of those who cared little for Israel's God.

Busting the Paradigms

So how are we to regard Jesus of Nazareth? His life and ministry resembled the priorities of several of these groups—but with paradigm-busting extras:[16]

- In his concern to help people obey God's law, Jesus was like a *Pharisee*. But he was concerned with the goal of the law, righteousness, and changed hearts more than outward performance. He did not consider the Pharisees' oral traditions to be nearly as important as the written law, given by God. As Jesus warned the people, "For I tell you, unless your righteousness exceeds that of the scribes and Pharisees, you will never enter the kingdom of heaven."[17]
- In his reverence for God's Word, Jesus was like a *scribe*, saying, "But it is easier for heaven and earth to pass away than for one dot of the law to become void."[18] But he proclaimed his own words as equally authoritative. At the end of the Sermon on the Mount, the people got the message: "And when Jesus finished these sayings, the crowds were astonished at his teaching, for he was teaching them as one who had authority, and not as their scribes."[19]
- In his concern to interpret the law and raise up disciples to carry on his work, Jesus was like a *rabbi*. However, he was a rabbi with a difference, in that he was not seeking to train new rabbis to eventually build their own followings,[20] but students to faithfully pass on his teachings to the world.[21] Jesus, in this sense, remains the *final* rabbi.

The Disciples

We cannot fully appreciate Jesus's teaching without pondering the men he taught. Socrates had Plato, but Jesus seemingly had no one so promising. Jesus's disciples were mostly simple fishermen from Galilee, little regarded by the world's movers and shakers. They were what today is humorously called "slow on the uptake." The Gospels consistently, if not uniformly, present Jesus's inner circle as doubting and prone to pride and outbursts of temper, jealousy, and cowardice. They expected Jesus to inaugurate the messianic kingdom next week, if not sooner, and crush the hated Romans.

"At the time of their call they were exceedingly ignorant, narrow-minded, superstitious, full of Jewish prejudices, misconceptions, and animosities," observes A. B. Bruce, a great nineteenth-century pastor.[22] In a sense, Jesus had few options, Bruce notes:

> The truth is, that Jesus was obliged to be content with fishermen, and publicans, and . . . zealots, for apostles. They were the best that could be had. Those who

deemed themselves better were too proud to become disciples, and thereby they excluded themselves from what all the world sees to be the high honor of being chosen princes of the kingdom.[23]

And yet they were eager to learn, men with whom Jesus could work, who could grow under his influence. And work he did, not simply to drum his teaching into their heads, but to mold them into apostles who could carry on his work to reach the masses. Jesus told his new disciples, in a metaphor they could not miss, "from now on you will be catching men."[24]

As good disciples, one of their main tasks was simply to be with him and to learn via observation and participation. As the Gospel of Mark notes, "And [Jesus] went up on the mountain and called to him those whom he desired, and they came to him. And he appointed twelve (whom he also named apostles) so that they might be with him and he might send them out to preach and have authority to cast out demons."[25] Being a disciple—and further, an apostle—meant more than simply learning his teaching or a set of career skills. A key task in the disciple's life was simply to "be with" the master. One might even say that it is the *first* task.[26]

Robert Coleman points out that while Jesus did not neglect the masses that flocked to him, his main focus was on the apostles. He was training these simple men to carry on the work after he was gone. "The multitudes of discordant and bewildered souls were potentially ready to follow Him, but Jesus individually could not possibly give them the personal care they needed," Coleman observes. "His only hope was to get men imbued with His life who would do it for Him. Hence, He concentrated Himself on those who were to be the beginning of this leadership."[27]

Almost everything Jesus did presented a "teachable moment" to his sometimes slow-witted disciples and the crowds. Coleman identifies the following guiding principles Jesus used in training the disciples, only a few of which actually involved teaching as we might recognize it in a contemporary school setting: selection, association, consecration, impartation, demonstration, delegation, supervision, and reproduction.

Coleman points out that none of Jesus's investment in the lives of his followers was done haphazardly: "His life was ordered by his objective. Everything that he did and said was a part of the whole pattern. It had significance because it contributed to the ultimate purpose of His life in redeeming the world for God."[28]

Questions and Context

Questions, though the focus of this book, were but one arrow in the pedagogical quiver of Jesus. There were also long sermons, or discourses (such as the Sermon on the Mount);[29] parables, which, like the parable of the Prodigal Son,[30] imparted a spiritual lesson using figures from everyday life; and pithy sayings (such as "The last will be first and the first will be last"[31]), to help people remember his points. Jesus scholar Marcus Borg notes that Jesus's parables (like his questions) "invite the audience to make a judgment" and are "an interactive form of teaching. . . . They tease the mind into active thought and engage the listener in the question, 'What do you think?' . . . [They] provoked interaction among the hearers and between the hearers and Jesus."[32] And unlike many other teachers of the time, Jesus did not start a lesson with the words, "You shall" or "You shall not," nor with the prophetic utterance, "Thus says the Lord."[33] Instead, as in the Sermon on the Mount, Jesus said, "I say to you. . . ."[34]

Jesus also performed miracles, demonstrating his power over nature and the supernatural, and fed the hungry. Borg notes, "Indeed, it was his reputation as a healer and exorcist that generated an audience for him as a teacher."[35]

In sum, we cannot look at Jesus's questions in isolation from all he said and did. They are part of the whole, at the same time interpreting, and being interpreted, by the rest. There is a guiding principle that helps us understand parts of the Bible: in J. Robertson McQuilkin's words, "Context is king." While we might like to lift a question directly from a passage and act as if Jesus is speaking directly to us, there are dangers in immediately spiritualizing the text without doing our exegetical homework.[36]

To use a silly example, let's say a mother doesn't know what to fix her family for dinner, so she opens her Bible to John chapter six, verse five, where Jesus asks, "*Where are we to buy bread, so that these people may eat?*" The woman might decide to use this question as a sort of magical incantation telling her to give her husband and kids a loaf of bread for supper.

However, if she knew anything about biblical interpretation, she would instead first read the surrounding verses for the literary and historical context of Jesus's question. In this case, it makes a huge difference. In fact, this question comes amid a scene where a large crowd is following Jesus because they have seen him healing the sick. The question is directed at Philip the disciple; and the narrator—who is John, another of the disciples—gives us inside information about the motive of Jesus in asking it: "He said this to test him, for he himself knew what he would do."[37] Jesus, who was planning to feed the crowd miraculously, here is testing Philip's faith in his ability to provide. Scholars have noted that Jesus's feeding of the five thousand—emulating Moses with the Israelites in the wilderness—demonstrated that he was the ultimate "bread of life."[38] The question has absolutely nothing to do with planning a dinner menu in the twenty-first century, and it is an abuse of Scripture—as well as common sense—to think otherwise.

To get the full picture, we must study *all* that Jesus said and did. This book examines one facet in the diamond that is the ministry of Jesus. As beautiful as that facet is, don't become so focused on it that you miss the even greater splendor of the whole. We will return to this important theme in chapter 20.

Wright notes that Jesus's words and deeds were two sides of the same coin. He captures something of the energy and urgency of Jesus as he preached a message of repentance and radical commitment to himself:

> Modern western culture does not have too many obvious models for the kind of thing he was doing, and that may be just as well; if we did, we might be tempted to make them fit despite residual anachronisms. But we may catch something of the required flavour if we say that Jesus was more like a composer/conductor than a violin teacher; more like a subversive playwright than an actor. He was a herald, the bringer of an urgent message that could not wait, could not become the stuff of academic debate. He was issuing a public announcement, like someone driving through town with a loudhailer. He was issuing a public warning, like a man with a red flag heading off an imminent railway disaster.[39]

Living Words

Jesus's questions were not simply timeless moral truths launched like a space shuttle into the vacuum. They were spoken to specific people in concrete situations. They were also part of unique Gospel narratives, each with its own author and pedagogical objectives. As scholarly critics such as Bart Ehrman have pointed out, there are undeniable differences in the wording of some accounts treated by more than one Gospel, and there are not always easy ways to harmonize them.

Several explanations exist. Sometimes the differences exist because the writers are reporting similar but separate events. Other times, they are emphasizing differing, but complementary, aspects of the same event. Still other times, they are melding separate historical events into one to make a larger teaching point related to the life of Jesus. This does not mean they are inaccurate, but it does mean we need to study the Gospel genre to understand what kind of claims it is making about history and what it isn't.

We do well to remember that the first century did not have journalism and biography as they are understood today. But this does not make the Gospels untrue. The writers' aim was not to produce an "objective" piece of work, as by simply turning on a tape recorder and letting it run. They were seeking to persuade and teach about this Jesus who had so captured their lives. But there is nothing wrong with persuasion, as long as we tell the truth.

Of course the New Testament is firmly rooted in history, too. Jesus was born during the reigns of Augustus and Herod the Great in the insignificant town of Bethlehem. Characters such as Pilate and Gamaliel glide across the ancient narratives. We can cross-check other ancient sources to see that these were real people. But the Gospels, no matter how detailed in their descriptions, were written not as history texts, but as calls to faith.[40]

And yet, the questions don't remain trapped in these narratives as historical curiosities or disembodied utterances. They still probe us. As living words, they speak to us every bit as much as they did to first-century Pharisees, Sadducees, and disciples. Yes, they were given in a historical moment, in a specific literature, to a particular people, but they have enduring application today.

My wife and I have tried to instill in our children a love for great literature. But even classic works that are no more than a few centuries old, such as *Gulliver's Travels* and *Around the World in Eighty Days*, sound stilted and archaic today. Even bright children—and I count mine (in the words of Garrison Keillor) in the "above average" category—can struggle with the unfamiliar sentence patterns and references.

Not so the words of Jesus. They still possess the penetrating power they had two millennia ago to impel us to drop our nets, leave everything, and follow him. So while Jesus was at home in first-century Judaism, he was not imprisoned there. He is as comfortable in the twenty-first century as he was in the first. His words still speak with the freshness of early morning. His questions cut through our pretensions and evasions like a double-edged sword.

Of all people, Napoleon had it right when he reportedly said, "Superficial minds see a resemblance between Christ and the founders of empires, and the gods of other religions. That resemblance does not exist. There is between Christianity and whatever other religions the distance of infinity."[41]

Spinning the Tumblers

Jesus, of course, was not the first great teacher to employ questions. The Greek philosopher Socrates (469–399 BC) used them to force people to "recognize on their own what is true, real, and good . . . a new, and thus suspect, approach to education. He was known for confusing, stinging, and stunning his conversation partners into the unpleasant experience of realizing their own ignorance, a state sometimes superseded by genuine intellectual curiosity."[42]

In the 1973 movie *The Paper Chase*, Harvard Law Professor Kingsfield uses the Socratic method—a question, followed by an answer, then another question, and so on—to force students not just to learn facts, but to teach themselves. "My little questions spin the tumblers of your mind," Kingsfield intones to his class in contract law. "You teach yourselves the law, and I train your mind. You come in here with a skull full of mush. You leave thinking like a lawyer."[43]

Jesus, while not using the Socratic method, by his questions forces people to think through issues vital not to their schooling, but to their souls. By my count, the Gospels and Acts record nearly three hundred of his questions.

(Often the questions come in clusters, one right after the other, building on each other, probing, looking at a subject from multiple angles.) Many times the questions gauge listeners' comprehension of a lesson just taught. Other times they grab listeners' attention at the outset. Jesus's questions may not always get an audible response, but they always seek to spark an inner one.

For example, in Luke 14, after telling the "great crowds" following him of the serious costs involved in being his disciple, Jesus warns them that only those who "renounce all" can truly follow him (truly Jesus had more in mind than the acclaim of the crowds). Then he asks, "*Salt is good, but if salt has lost its taste, how shall its saltiness be restored?*"[44] In this context, his listeners could not fail to get the message that following him will cost them everything, and to wonder whether they have indeed given up everything. Then Jesus makes his meaning crystal clear: "[Such tasteless salt] is of no use either for the soil or for the manure pile. It is thrown away. He who has ears to hear, let him hear."[45] The question, coming at the end of Jesus's lesson about discipleship, helps his listeners participate in and personalize the message. As Professor Kingsfield said, it spins the tumblers of their minds. And ours.

Engaging the Listener

Before we move on to the meat of this book—the questions arranged by topic—let's look at how Jesus employs his questions to engage listeners. In his discourses, parables, and actions, Jesus takes nothing for granted, not even his hearers' interest. At key times, the master teacher uses queries simply to jump-start his lesson. With his intimate knowledge of first-century Palestinian culture, his biting sense of humor, and his understanding of the human heart, Jesus could do a monologue better than David Letterman or Jay Leno. But often he was after a dialogue.

In Luke 13, Jesus asks the crowds a question in two ways, "*What is the kingdom of God like? And to what shall I compare it?*" You can almost hear the excited people shouting out answers that emphasize a return to the nation's ancient power and glory, each answer being topped by the next one. Then Jesus answers his own question: "It is like a grain of mustard seed that a man took and sowed in his garden, and it grew and became a tree, and the birds of the air made nests in its branches."[46] The promised kingdom was indeed among them, but its key attribute was not power, but weakness. More on that later.

Sometimes Jesus uses questions that make a humorous point. "*Can a blind man lead a blind man?*" he asks. "*Will they not both fall into a pit?*"[47] Having earned his hearers' attention, and perhaps a chuckle, Jesus is ready to make his point. Jesus also engages his disciples by (as we have seen) asking them where the bread is or by having them ask an anonymous homeowner in Jerusalem a question in his stead: "*Where is my guest room, where I may eat the Passover with my disciples?*"[48]

Near Herod's great temple in Jerusalem, the disciples point out the impressive architecture. Then Jesus says of the buildings, "*You see all these, do you not?*" Yes, of course. What point could he possibly be making? Then, when his men are fully engaged, probably intently peering at the temple itself, Jesus delivers the devastating punch line: "Truly, I say to you, there will not be left here one stone upon another that will not be thrown down."[49] Judgment was coming.

No, Jesus did not ask his questions into a timeless vacuum. The circumstances and people of his time affected what he said and did. And that time—filled with brutal oppression, venality, and a yearning for true freedom—is much like our own. May we allow his questions to engage our attention, shock us when necessary, and force us to grapple with truth, even today. For Jesus remains on an urgent errand, with judgment looming for us, too. Do we have ears to hear?

Suggested Reading

Bruce, A. B. *The Training of the Twelve*. 4th ed. New Canaan, CT: Keats, 1979.

Coleman, Robert E. *The Master Plan of Evangelism*. Old Tappan, NJ: Spire Books/Revell, 1964.

McQuilkin, J. Robertson. *Understanding and Applying the Bible: An Introduction to Hermeneutics*. Chicago: Moody, 2009.

Perrin, Nicholas. *Lost in Transmission: What We Can and Cannot Know about the Words of Jesus*. Nashville: Thomas Nelson, 2007.

Wright, N. T. *Jesus and the Victory of God*. Minneapolis: Fortress, 1996.

Discussion Questions

1. How does an accurate understanding of the world in which Jesus lived help us understand him?
2. In what way is first-century Palestine like, and unlike, our world today?
3. In what ways does Jesus fit into his context? In what ways does he transcend it?
4. How do you read the Bible?
5. Describe an outstanding teacher you have had. What made him or her great?
6. What are some of the functions of a question?
7. What intrigues you about the questions Jesus asked?

3

His Authority

*"How can someone enter a strong
man's house and plunder his goods,
unless he first binds the strong man?"*

Mention the word "exorcist" to the average American and you're liable to conjure up disturbing images from a certain 1973 horror movie. Mention it to an African Christian, however, and you are much more likely to get a knowing look, or a story.

For years, Esther, a young woman from Tanzania, wanted to attend religious schools but was unable. The cause was neither poverty nor a lack of academic giftedness. Instead, it was demonic oppression, according to an article in the *Africa Theological Journal*. Christian leaders eventually decided that it was time to do an exorcism on Esther. The year was 1982. When the time for the ceremony arrived, they sang several Christian songs and read more than a half a dozen religious texts describing exorcisms.

At that point, those gathered heard what they identified as demonic voices coming from Esther's mouth, crying out, "We are being burned! We are being burned!" Then came the words, "We are going out!"

Esther was declared delivered, and she needed no more help. An author reporting her case noted, "Exorcism brings both spiritual and bodily or material blessings to the individuals and society. Due to such blessings, the church should see to it that exorcism is done whenever the need arises."[1]

We will examine more closely the clash of the two kingdoms in chapters 23 and 24, but here we focus first on a key battlefront: Jesus's authority over demons and what it means in today's world, particularly in Asia, Africa, and Latin America, where his authority is taken quite literally. As historian Philip Jenkins notes, "In North America, . . . ideas of exorcism and deliverance appear bizarre or fanatical to outsiders or to secular observers, whereas they fit quite logically into conventional assumptions in many newer churches outside North America."[2]

Whatever we may think in the secular West, the need for exorcism arises frequently in Africa—and indeed across large swathes of what Jenkins calls the global South. According to Jenkins, "Overwhelmingly, global South churches teach a firm belief in the existence of evil and in the reality of the devil."[3]

Of course, such ideas were taken for granted in Jesus's day.

Spiritual Realities

The first-century world in which Jesus lived was a religious mosaic. Pagan deities by the hundreds were worshiped in the Roman Empire, with Caesar given official preeminence. The Jews, of course, were strict monotheists, followers of Yahweh, who revealed himself to the patriarch Abraham two millennia before, to Moses, to David, and to a long line of prophets who proclaimed his word. Unlike the pagans, the Jews firmly believed (when they were not lapsing into idolatry, as they did many times during their history) that God reigns supreme. And yet, according to the same Hebrew Scriptures that teach monotheism, this God has an adversary, and so do we. His name is Satan, or Lucifer, and some call this fallen angel the devil. (The word *devil*, in fact, means *adversary*.) This adversary leads a kingdom that seeks to undermine and ultimately overthrow God's rule, whether we believe it or not. But if we doubt, we will find ourselves arguing with Jesus.

Skeptical scholar Marcus Borg notes, "But whatever the modern explanation might be, and however much psychological or social factors might be involved, we need to recognize that Jesus and his contemporaries (and people in premodern cultures generally) thought that people could be possessed by a spirit or spirits from another plane. Their worldview took for granted the existence of such spirits."[4]

We who would investigate Jesus as a great teacher, prophet, and lover of humanity must face the fact that he shared this worldview. The ministry of Jesus, in fact, brought the conflict between God's kingdom and Satan's out into the open. Clinton Arnold, a professor of New Testament, says, "From the very beginning of his public ministry, Jesus both spoke of and demonstrated the nature of the conflict with the opposing kingdom. He was drawn into the struggle the moment he began proclaiming the kingdom of God in the synagogue of Capernaum."[5]

Indeed, Jesus was a teacher, and much more. He was a liberator, and not just in the one-dimensional, secular sense we are familiar with today. When Jesus began his ministry, he announced, paraphrasing the words of the ancient prophet Isaiah, that he had come to "proclaim liberty to the captives and recovering sight to the blind, to set at liberty those who are oppressed, to proclaim the year of the Lord's favor."[6] But his was far from simply a ministry that met only physical needs. The spiritual and the physical went together.

And the crowds knew it. "And he went throughout all Galilee, teaching in their synagogues and proclaiming the gospel of the kingdom and healing every disease and every affliction among the people," who "brought him all the sick, those afflicted with various diseases and pains, those oppressed by demons, epileptics, and paralytics, and he healed them."[7] Yes, Jesus cared about physical needs, but he also fought against spiritual afflictions, without confusing the two.[8] It was a package deal.

In this we see that Jesus, unlike the religious action figures sold at Wal-Mart, is not infinitely bendable, able to assume whatever postmodern pose we give him. He is not the pious, otherworldly, and slightly effeminate savior of so much religious art. No, his hands are rough, even cracked, with exertion. He has stared evil and suffering in the face, seized them by the scruff of the neck, and lived to tell about it. As the crowds who watched him work exclaimed, "What is this? A new teaching with authority! He commands even the unclean spirits, and they obey him."[9] (No, Jesus was not the only Jewish exorcist at the time, as the New Testament acknowledges, but his authority was in a class by itself.)[10]

Of course, Jesus's religious enemies saw the same mighty works and came up with a different explanation, attributing them to Beelzebul (related to the ancient word *Baal*), a popular name at the time for Satan: "He casts out demons by the prince of demons."[11] Talk about the politics of personal destruction—or demonizing an opponent.

A House Divided

Jesus would have none of it, and several of his questions confront such hardened unbelief. Matthew and Luke present his response from two slightly different but complementary angles.

Matthew reports:

> Then a demon-oppressed man who was blind and mute was brought to him, and he healed him, so that the man spoke and saw. And all the people were amazed,

and said, "Can this be the Son of David?" But when the Pharisees heard it, they said, "It is only by Beelzebul, the prince of demons, that this man casts out demons." Knowing their thoughts, he said to them, "Every kingdom divided against itself is laid waste, and no city or house divided against itself will stand. And if Satan casts out Satan, he is divided against himself. *How then will his kingdom stand? And if I cast out demons by Beelzebul, by whom do your sons cast them out?* Therefore they will be your judges. But if it is by the Spirit of God that I cast out demons, then the kingdom of God has come upon you. *Or how can someone enter a strong man's house and plunder his goods, unless he first binds the strong man?* Then indeed he may plunder his house. Whoever is not with me is against me, and whoever does not gather with me scatters.[12]

At first glance, there is a surface plausibility to the Pharisees' charge that Jesus was working with Beelzebul. What better way to draw in the unsuspecting, uneducated crowds than by performing false miracles of deliverance? Since the Jews were constantly looking for signs to validate a message, why not give them some? Then, when they are hooked, you can deceive them with your lies. Perhaps Jesus was working in league with the devil to divert the people from the true path as laid out by the established religious leaders?

Such an analysis, of course, misjudges the characters of both Satan and Jesus. The works Jesus did to roll back Satan's kingdom (today we might call them miracles)—giving people back their minds, bodies, freedom, and families—were demonstrations that the heavenly kingdom was on the move. Satan, with nothing but hatred and contempt for humanity, never yields his possessions willingly. Like all dictatorships, Satan's kingdom advances only by controlling and consuming others, not by creating anything of its own. Satan's sterile but aggressive empire can only feed off the enslaved lives of others. In Jesus, God was taking them back—by force. In 1858 Abraham Lincoln understood this truth, borrowing the words of Jesus to make the point that slavery and freedom cannot coexist: "A house divided cannot stand."[13]

The Spirit's Power

Then Jesus asks, "*And if I cast out demons by Beelzebul, by whom do your sons cast them out?*"[14] In other words, "If Jesus's adversaries claim that he exorcises demons with satanic power, then it logically follows that exorcisms performed by their colleagues are accomplished by Satan as well."[15] While these adversaries may be able to smear Jesus out of pure malice, they cannot do so by condemning what their allies, true "sons" of Israel, also do.

Jesus's acknowledgement that others could break demonic strongholds illustrates that the Spirit's power was (and is) available to more than just him. In fact, as we just saw in chapter 2, Jesus called his disciples to do the same works he did. This includes confronting the powers of darkness.

On one mission, Jesus sent into ministry not just his inner circle of apostles but seventy-two of his followers, "two by two, into every town and place where he himself was about to go." When they came together for a time of debriefing, the seventy-two "returned with joy, saying, 'Lord, even the demons are subject to us in your name!'" Jesus was hardly surprised, telling his charges, "I saw Satan fall like lightning from heaven. Behold, I have given you authority to tread on serpents and scorpions"—symbols of the satanic kingdom—"and over all the power of the enemy, and nothing shall hurt you."[16] That power of the Spirit, activated in the name—or authority—of Jesus, was too much for the devil and his minions. It still is.

Power Encounters

Jesus's next question—"*Or how can someone enter a strong man's house and plunder his goods, unless he first binds the strong man?*"[17]—is a raw assertion of his superior power and authority. Yes, Satan is a "strong man," striking fear into the hearts of mortals. But Jesus is far stronger, able to tie the devil up and loot his house at will. No wonder healing and deliverance ministries are central to so many churches in the global South, who must confront multiple powers and "competing claims to faith."[18]

But Satan and his hosts are far from the only cause, or even the main one, of human suffering. As the first book in the Bible notes, thorns, thistles, sweat, and death are—for now—normal parts of our world. These natural evils are permitted by God himself, and are not necessarily the direct work of Satan.[19] Thus, it makes no sense to attribute all pain and problems to evil forces, though the Bible certainly acknowledges that they may cause some suffering, such as in the case of a faithful Jewish woman bound for eighteen years by a "disabling spirit."[20]

But it is not healthy to look for the proverbial demon behind every bush. Sometimes all we can know from a disaster—the crumpled bridge in Minneapolis, a collapsing tower in Siloam that killed eighteen people in Jesus's day, the murder of some worshiping Galileans by the Romans—is not the ultimate cause, but our response.

Jesus asks the crowds, "*Do you think that these Galileans were worse sinners than all the other Galileans, because they suffered in this way? No, I tell you; but unless you repent, you will all likewise perish. Or those eighteen on whom the tower in Siloam fell and killed them: do you think that they were worse offenders than all the others who lived in Jerusalem? No, I tell you; but unless you repent, you will all likewise perish.*"[21] Suffering forces us to take stock. And no one gets a completely free pass.

I know this from painful personal experience.

Authority amid Suffering

My birth on August 1, 1961, two months early, did not go well. Only three pounds and eleven ounces, I beat the odds and survived. But for the rest of my life I would carry the burden of cerebral palsy. Through the years I have often asked "Why?" and it was hard not to feel resentful. Most of the time I felt like an inferior, an outsider, afraid of rejection. And sometimes I was rejected. My *why* questions went unanswered and usually tied me up in emotional knots.

And yet, borrowing a phrase from Paul,[22] this thorn in the flesh has kept my outsized ego at least partly in check and prompted me to search for a God I will never fully understand. I'd also like to think that people with disabilities soften the sharp edges of society, teach us patience and humility, force us to look upward, and pull us away—if only temporarily—from our besetting narcissism.[23]

Indeed, while Jesus has the authority to deliver people from demons, death, and disease, sometimes he chooses not to, for his own good reasons. Sometimes he lets us in on those reasons. The late Tony Snow, the former White House Press Secretary, battled recurrent cancer, which eventually killed him. Yet he called the disease an "unexpected blessing":

> The moment you enter the Valley of the Shadow of Death, things change. You discover that Christianity is not something doughy, passive, pious, and soft. Faith may be the substance of things hoped for, the evidence of things not seen. But it also draws you into a world shorn of fearful caution. The life of belief teems with thrills, boldness, danger, shocks, reversals, triumphs, and epiphanies.[24]

One day, Jesus's disciples asked, "Rabbi, who sinned, this man, or his parents, that he was born blind?" The Lord said that the man's blindness presented a divine opportunity, "that the works of God might be displayed in him."[25] Such hard-won blessings will continue for all of us until this world is remade, when God "will wipe away every tear from [our] eyes, and death shall be no more, neither shall there be mourning nor crying nor pain anymore, for the former things [will] have passed away."[26] While healing and deliverance should not surprise those who follow the healer from Galilee, neither should their opposites.

Global South Realities

In the meantime, Christians in the global South and elsewhere are doing what they can to bring the light of Christ's kingdom into this present darkness, just as Jesus healed the lame, gave sight to the blind, cast out demons, and preached good news to the poor. Defeating the ugly shadows of life with the light of his in-breaking kingdom, Jesus showed the way, and many are following.

Jenkins points out that the struggle against evil forces often accompanies healing ministries, with global South Christians "seeing both as forms of deliverance."[27] Truly, much of the rest of the world sees little problem in lumping together Jesus's authority over demons *and* disease—an authority that continues to this day.

Jenkins notes that an emphasis on healing is integral to the growth and spread of Christian churches through Asia, Africa, and Latin America. "Across the global South, healing ministries have been critical to the modern expansion of Christianity, much as they were during the conversion of Western Europe following the collapse of the Roman Empire. And today, as then, it is all but impossible to separate healing of the body or mind with spiritual deliverance." He continues,

> Healing is an integral part of the narrative of conversion and salvation, and accounts of healing represent a large proportion of literature and testimony among African and Asian Christians. In a tribal community in the Philippines, for instance, an evangelist reports the experience of a new convert: "Very soon, a neighbor quietly asked him if this new God could heal his dying child. Badol laid his hand upon the motionless baby and prayed in the name of Jesus who had given life to her. The next Sunday, the entire family, with the now recovered baby, joined the church. . . . The villagers regularly asked him to pray for the sick, and most of them were healed miraculously. About fifteen years later, everyone in Papasok serves this new God who can heal the sick."[28]

Now we Westerners, with our precise, scientific, Enlightenment worldview, can raise a number of questions and objections. Perhaps the child would have gotten well anyway. Perhaps this is a case of the power of suggestion or a variant of the placebo effect (though it is hard to see how a baby could be susceptible). Maybe the evangelist is lying or exaggerating to enhance the stature and finances of his ministry.

And aside from all that, even those who are inclined to believe such reports may—like me—feel uneasy about relying on God in such situations when he seems to do so little of this kind of healing in our own experience.[29] Further, won't an overreliance on the supernatural authority of Jesus undermine a people's needed embrace of modern advances in science, medicine, and sanitation? For example, isn't it dangerous to believe in the power of witches to curse when *everyone knows* that a small, unseen virus transmitted through sexual intercourse or dirty drug needles *really* causes AIDS?

First, Jenkins notes that Christian belief in personal evil—and Jesus's authority over it—actually promotes a community's health because it treats "older notions of spiritual evil seriously," bringing them out into the open, where they can be dealt with.[30] Missionaries and other outsiders sometimes report that while people in the global South give lip service to our scientific diagnoses of their problems, their animistic worldview remains largely untouched. Often they will not confide in us or avail themselves of our cures if they do not believe we respect them. Borg notes that many cultures believe in demonic possession and exorcism.[31] Denying this fact will not make it disappear.

According to Jenkins, "Jesus's superiority to traditional healers gives churches an added weapon in the continuing contest with pagan and primal faiths, to which some Christians resort in times of crisis."[32]

Besides laying the groundwork for healthy relationships between Western-ers and non-Westerners, Jenkins lists other benefits of respecting the spiritual worldview of people in the global South: the discrediting of pagan spiritual professionals who charge exorbitantly for their services; the undermining of false charges of witchcraft; the liberation of people, such as the Dalits of India, from "the weight of history, ancestry, and accumulated sins"; relief from curses or taboos; and acceptance of the biblical principle of individual responsibility.[33]

But what of the tangible benefits of science? Doesn't belief in the miracu-lous undermine the scientific method of the laboratory? Not if you look at how Christians actually live. Jenkins suggests that most global South fol-lowers of Jesus "work strenuously to suppress fraudulent claims and bogus miracles, and they view alleged miracle healers with great suspicion. . . . Most churches, likewise, do not prevent their followers from seeking West-ern-style medicine where this is available and affordable—two conditions that are all too rarely met. . . . For most, too, healing is understood not in terms of curing specific ailments, but of offering a holistic, comprehensive treatment of ills."

He quotes an observer of Pentecostal churches in Latin America, who notes, "This option [healing] is embodied in practice by a Jesus who touches, heals and saves the sick, thus restoring them to physical health, reintegrat-ing them into their society and giving them a chance to develop a spiritual and a family life. In restoring them to health he also gives them back their dignity."[34]

However, we cannot ignore the uncomfortably large presence of religious frauds who seek ill-gotten riches off the ignorance and desperation of the needy masses. For example, a pastor from Ghana was arrested in Uganda after reportedly attempting to smuggle in a "miracle machine" that he used "to de-liver electric current on unsuspecting worshippers during church service[s]."[35] Author Michael Cuneo takes a devastating look at shady prosperity preachers and supposed miracle-workers in the United States.[36]

We have to ask: does the presence of charlatans discredit the whole idea of deliverance ministry? If so, then we will need to jettison every other area of human life riddled with crooks: the investment industry, credit card companies, psychological counseling, and the clergy, just to name four.

Western Wariness

So what's a skeptically inclined Westerner to do with all this? Should he or she write off as mere outdated superstition the numerous biblical accounts of Jesus's authority over disease and the demonic and the multiplying reports worldwide of outbreaks of divine power? To do so, I believe, will leave us not with a pristine Jesus, freed from superstitious encrustations, but no Jesus. We cannot understand him without them. As Borg acknowledges, a "remarkably high percentage" of Synoptic accounts of Jesus in Galilee involve the miraculous.[37] Remember, too, that the miracles validated Jesus's teachings in the eyes of the people. No miracles, no teaching. To strip Jesus of his authority in one realm is to strip him of his authority in all realms.

So unless we are prepared to dismiss Jesus as a fraud, we must come to terms with his supernatural authority. The question is how.

Living Supernaturally

While we Westerners are justifiably proud of our scientific advances—remembering that many outstanding scientists have been Christians[38]—perhaps our largely secular mindset has blinded us to a wider world in which God acts to display his power and advance his rule. As philosopher J. P. Moreland admits, "we Evangelicals are often too quick to dismiss healing, demonic deliverance, miracles, and prophetic words of knowledge and wisdom. Fortunately, there has been a growing consensus among evangelical New Testament scholars that certain biblical themes provide a mandate for the Spirit's miraculous power that makes such a dismissal unnecessary and unbiblical."[39]

And indeed the Protestant evangelical community is far from monolithic on the subject of the miraculous. Citing New Testament scholar Wayne Grudem, Moreland describes four streams in the Christian community: (1) *cessationists*, those who believe miraculous gifts ended with the apostles; (2) those who are *open but cautious*, but think the miraculous is not important for evangelism and discipleship; (3) *Third Wave* Christians, who believe the miraculous is important for the life of the church; and (4) the *Pentecostal/charismatic* movement, which accepts miraculous gifts but emphasizes speaking in tongues.[40]

For me,

- if Jesus healed the sick and cast out demons;
- if he told his disciples to heal and cast out demons using the authority of his name;
- if he told them to teach us to obey all he commanded them;[41]
- if he said his followers would do "greater works" than he;[42] and

- if the church is growing and has always grown through the use of his miraculous authority;

then, as difficult as this subject is to understand or as shocking as the implications may be, we must, at a minimum, accept the miraculous as a normal—if not common—part of the Christian life, knowing that God always has the final say. Of course, belief in the supernatural authority of Jesus is no guarantee everything will work out as we wish. Paul, after all, prayed three times for his thorn to be removed but was denied, told that God's power is made perfect in weakness.[43] And yet we can and should expect that God is willing and able to work wonders to advance his cause, using his followers to feed the hungry, heal the sick, cast out demons, and raise the dead.

I confess this kind of faith is often beyond me. While I can intellectually assent to what the Bible teaches and the supernaturally driven growth of churches in the global South, it is another thing to step out in faith and live as if Jesus's supernatural authority is really present. To get there, Moreland, who has moved from being a cessationist to a member of Third Wave evangelicalism, counsels that we read good books in this area (I provide a short list at the end of this chapter), learn from credible people who are involved in these kinds of ministries, allow people in your circles to share their experiences, and make learning about the miraculous an intentional part of your missionary program.[44]

I would just add two things: First, put yourself in positions where you will have to exercise your spiritual muscles. Faith never grows if it is not tested. Second, keep the focus on Jesus, not on the demonic. Make spiritual warfare just one aspect of your discipleship, neither ignoring the kingdom of darkness nor allowing it to take over your faith—knowing that Jesus's authority is far greater than Satan's. As C. S. Lewis said so well:

> There are two equal and opposite errors into which our race can fall about the devils. One is to disbelieve in their existence. The other is to believe, and to feel an excessive and unhealthy interest in them.[45]

Suggested Reading

Cuneo, Michael. *American Exorcism: Expelling Demons in the Land of Plenty.* New York: Doubleday, 2001.

Jenkins, Philip. *The New Faces of Christianity: Believing the Bible in the Global South.* Oxford and New York: Oxford University Press, 2006.

Kiely, David M., and Christina McKenna. *The Dark Sacrament: True Stories of Modern-Day Demon Possession and Exorcism.* San Francisco: Harper One, 2007.

Moreland, J. P. *Kingdom Triangle: Recover the Christian Mind, Renovate the Soul, Restore the Spirit's Power.* Grand Rapids: Zondervan, 2007.

Discussion Questions

1. What reasons are there for seeing the Gospel narratives of Jesus's supernatural authority as factual accounts of what happened during his ministry?
2. Why was the clash between the kingdom of God and the kingdom of Satan so pronounced during the time of Jesus?
3. What was the source of Jesus's authority over demons, disease, and death? Why might it continue today?
4. Is it easier to believe in divine healing or divine exorcism? Why?
5. Why do people in the West so quickly dismiss the existence of the supernatural, but people in Asia, Latin America, and Africa remain open to it?
6. What are some dangers that accompany belief in demons?
7. How can we become better informed about these issues?

4

His Humanity

"How many loaves do you have?"

Classic Car Night is a fixture during Friday summer evenings in the Chicago
suburb where I live. My family gets to mingle with hundreds of others in
our city's quaint downtown while we ogle an assortment of cool-blue Bel-Air
sedans with their long tailfins; red, rag-top Mustangs; and kit cars of every
description, all to the beat of classic rock 'n' roll. It's a time to exhale from a
stressful week and maybe grab some cotton candy from a street vendor or a
monster cone from the locally owned ice cream shop, which still has a painted
copper ceiling. It's a time to remember. And a time to forget.

But sometimes forgetting what ails us is not possible, even here. One evening several years ago, as my wife, kids, and I crossed Main Street amid the
throngs, my foot snagged on the uneven pavement, and my momentum carried
me down with a *thud*, my cane clattering loudly as it slipped from my hand.
Angrily refusing all offers of help from the able-bodied around me, I scrambled
up and over to the sidewalk as quickly as I could, with yet another bleeding
scrape on my knobby knee, with dirt covering my hands.

Mortified, I retreated to the parking lot and our van—cursing the embarrassment, and myself. As I waited for my family to finish up without me, forgetting all God's blessings and kindnesses, I dredged up my usual fury at him
for allowing my cerebral palsy. I accused him of many things, including not
knowing the humiliation of what it felt like to stumble and fall so publicly.

Then the truth struck me: Jesus knew *exactly* what it felt like. More than likely, Jesus stumbled and fell on the Via Dolorosa. At the very least, the day he was crucified, weakened from abuse, he was unable to carry his cross. The hands that had healed others, the legs that had walked on water, were useless in the sight of the world, and a bystander was pressed into service to carry the crossbeam to Golgotha.[1] Indeed, Jesus knew all about my struggles. Mortification—death—was no alien concept to this man.

Continuing Debate

Jesus Christ is the most hotly debated figure in history. As we have seen, opinions were all over the lot in the days he walked the earth. Some called him a tool of the devil. Others called him a prophet, or Elijah, or simply a good man. Roman soldiers mockingly called him the King of the Jews.[2] Others, confronted with a majesty they had never encountered, called this Jewish rabbi someone from beyond our world.

The debate has not died down over the centuries. In the first two centuries after the founding of the Christian church, a group called the Gnostics questioned whether Jesus was in fact a human being at all. Gnosticism was a direct descendant of the philosophy called Platonism, which holds that "being in the flesh is not worth celebrating [and] the flesh [is] an inconvenient impediment that someday, when the body lies in the grave, will be overcome."[3] Believing that matter is evil, or at least not as important as spirit, those who held to Gnosticism suggested that Jesus only *appeared* to be a man. One variant is called Docetism (from a Greek word meaning "appear").

Of course, Gnosticism has its adherents even today. Scholars such as Karen King assert that the four canonical Gospels we have today—Matthew, Mark, Luke, and John—were merely the survivors in a battle for control with other, equally valid accounts of the life of Christ. Some of these documents, popularized by sensationalistic books such as *The Da Vinci Code*—including the so-called Gospel of Thomas, the Secret Gospel of Mark, the Gospel of Mary, and the Gospel of Peter—present a radically different Jesus than the one portrayed in the New Testament. The Jesus in these writings seems utterly unlike us, detached from the world and even the people around him, eager to shed the material world and return to heaven.

Because many other authors, better qualified than I, have ably refuted these claims (including Darrell Bock in *Breaking the Da Vinci Code* and Lee Strobel in *The Case for the Real Jesus*), I will not do so here. Instead, suffice it to say that the case for these apocryphal Gospels is thin indeed. New Testament scholar Gary Burge lists three main problems: (1) their naming is misleading; (2) their dating is speculative; and (3) their theological framework is utterly foreign.[4]

(Oddly, while Dan Brown in *The Da Vinci Code* relies on the pseudo-Gospels as a key pillar in his novel, the Gnostic, spiritualized Jesus they present is completely different from the merely human Jesus he posits. In fact, many recent and sensational claims about Jesus—including those found in *The Jesus Dynasty* and *The Jesus Family Tomb*—receive little support from the non-canonical Gospels that present alternative "Christianities" of supposedly equal value with orthodox Christianity. Of course, that inconvenient fact has done little to slow sales by publishers more eager to make a buck than to advance knowledge of the early church.)

As Gnosticism began to wane, the developing church had to respond to a new challenge. This one questioned not Christ's likeness to us, but his unlikeness. We will consider Jesus's identity more fully in chapter 6, but I mention these historical developments to provide context for our current examination of Jesus's questions highlighting his humanity. As you can see, the theological battles fought centuries ago never really end. They simply reappear in new guises.

Equal and Opposite Errors

Just as C. S. Lewis pointed out the existence of "two equal and opposite errors" in thinking when it comes to Satan—either to disbelieve or to obsess—so we are prone to "two equal and opposite errors" when it comes to Jesus Christ. These are to believe that he is (1) merely a human being like us, to the exclusion of any supernatural attributes, or (2) a spiritual being unlike us at all, to the exclusion of any natural, human characteristics. In responding to the challenges in new garb posed by *The Da Vinci Code* (that Jesus is mere human) and the Gnostic gospels (that Jesus is not human), we must be careful not to go beyond what the biblical text says. His questions, part of that text, can point us in the right direction.

Much biblical scholarship of the past several centuries has been "questing" to find the "historical Jesus"[5]—a Jesus, in other words, who conforms to our everyday experience, who is an enigmatic religious leader but nothing more, whose questions stay tucked away safely in the first century where they cannot challenge us in the twenty-first. This is a Christ who can do little, either good or bad. And he is widely believed in today.

Unfortunately, in our zeal to respond to the current mindset and protect the reputation of Christ, too often we have swung to the other extreme, of de-emphasizing his humanity. At Christmas we sing, "Away in a Manger." One line is revealing: "The cattle are lowing, the baby awakes, but little Lord Jesus, no crying he makes"—as if Jesus was not like every other baby crying for sustenance or a fresh diaper. But Christianity is not a new form of Gnosticism. That is, Jesus did not simply *appear* to be a man whose true identity was somehow veiled in flesh.

Most popular depictions of Christ I've seen emphasize the spiritual Christ over the physical Jesus. They show stereotypical (and likely inaccurate) blond hair, parted down the middle; neatly trimmed beard and fingernails; a spotless white robe; a serene, almost cultish smile on his face; and clean leather sandals picked up on sale last week from Shoe Carnival. If these Jesuses worked with rough-hewn wood and walked the gritty trails of first-century Palestine, they're not letting on. The main character of the *Jesus of Nazareth* movie seems ethereal, detached, unemotional—in short, Gnostic.

Some of the legendary pseudo-gospels attempt to fill in gaps from the biblical record, which is silent about most of Jesus's childhood and early adulthood. They present a young superbeing who curses enemies, restores birds back to life, and generally uses his powers for trivial or selfish ends. In novelist Anne Rice's admirable work, *Christ the Lord: Out of Egypt*, Jesus is a miracle-worker. The opening scene, told in Jesus's voice, recounts how he cursed a nasty and violent neighbor boy and then raised him back to life: "Salome shot forward and whispered in my ear, 'Just make him come alive, Jesus, just the way you made the birds come alive!'"[6] And he obliges. These works present not a boy in a real family, but a young Harry Potter learning the sorcerer's craft.

Concerning Docetism, the ancient heresy that Jesus Christ only *appeared* to be a man, scholar Stephen J. Nichols comments, "Even today it manages to find mild expression in the tendency to view Jesus as sort of floating six inches off the ground as he walked upon the earth."[7]

When I was a young Christian, I thought that life was somehow easier for him. Intending no disrespect, I reasoned that his supernatural qualities trumped his humanity. In short, in my heart of hearts I believed—though I would never have admitted it—that Jesus, when you got right down to it, was using his supernatural powers whenever things got tough and essentially *faking* his humanity. I knew that if I had been in his sandals, that's what *I* would have done.

And I would have been in good company. Even the great C. S. Lewis allowed his Platonist outlook to color his Christology. Discussing the meaning of Christ's self-giving death, Lewis revealingly writes:

> I have heard some people complain that . . . "it must have been so easy for him." Others may (very rightly) rebuke the ingratitude and ungraciousness of this objection; what staggers me is the misunderstanding it betrays. In one sense, of course, those who make it are right. They have even understated their own case. . . . If I am drowning in a rapid river, a man who still has one foot on the bank may give me a hand which saves my life. Ought I to shout back (between my gasps) "No, it's not fair! You have an advantage! You're keeping one foot on the bank"? That advantage—call it "unfair" if you like—is the only reason why he can be of any use to me.[8]

With all due respect to Lewis, I don't believe that Jesus kept "one foot on the bank." No, Jesus kept both feet planted in the river. Life was not easy for him. Jesus wept, expressed amazement, felt fear seize him and joy overwhelm him, suffered in temptation, learned obedience, and experienced grief and desolation as acute as a human being ever has. As the prophet Isaiah foretold, he was "a man of sorrows."[9] Nichols states, "the Bible presents Christ as hungry, thirsty, and tired. As the ultimate testimony to his full humanity, the Bible presents him as dying on a cross."[10]

The Risk of Relationships

It also presents him, just like us, as living with imperfect knowledge of those around him. On earth he was constantly checking the spiritual temperature of specific people. Why? Because he didn't always *know*. In fact, while the New Testament portrays Jesus as sometimes knowing the hearts of friends and acquaintances in a way only a supernatural being could,[11] this is far from an unbreakable rule. A careful look at Jesus's interactions with others reveals the unsettling truth that he seems to have been continually surprised by the lack of faith or spiritual discernment in others.

One of the hallmarks of our humanity is relating to other human beings. We belong not just to ourselves, but to our families, our nations, our religions, our God. We are created for relationship, both to give and receive. Jesus was involved in real relationships, too. He was not play-acting.

When Jesus was twelve, after a Jewish holiday, Jesus stayed in Jerusalem while his family unwittingly headed back without him in a caravan to Galilee. Much like the movie *Home Alone*, after three days of frantic searching, Joseph and Mary discover the boy in the temple, conversing with the teachers of the law. "Son," his mother says (and you can almost hear the exasperation and relief in her voice), "why have you treated us so? Behold, your father and I have been searching for you in great distress."

Jesus seems genuinely surprised. "*Why were you looking for me?*" he asks. "*Did you not know that I must be in my Father's house?*"[12] This is not a smart-alecky or defensive question meant to shift the blame for their distress back on them. No, the boy Jesus can't fathom why they wouldn't have known that he is right where he is supposed to be. Like our human experience, the people around him were a constant source of both joy and frustration. Why? Because he didn't know the outcome in advance. "*Are you the teacher of Israel and yet you do not understand these things?*" he exclaimed to Nicodemus one night. "*If I have told you earthly things and you do not believe, how can I tell you heavenly things?*"[13] To the father of a boy convulsed by demons, Jesus asks, "*How long has this been happening to him?*"[14]

Think about your greatest thrill in life. For me, it was when I discovered that a beautiful, intelligent, and godly woman freely chose to love me, after I had experienced one romantic disappointment after another. She didn't have to, and I wasn't sure that she would. God knows I didn't deserve it. Part of the joy I experienced—and continue to feel—comes from the sheer surprise of it all. Now imagine that God had told me that the young woman I was thinking of asking out would say yes, that we would get married, that we would be married for many years, that we would have three children (a girl and two boys), that we would argue over certain issues, that we would face challenges unique to us, and so on, down to the last detail.

Do you think such foreknowledge might take some of the fun and excitement out of our relationship? Of course. Part of living is simply not knowing what is around the next corner. Why bother to unwrap your Christmas presents if you already know everything that is under the tree?

One time as he walked along the road, Jesus was interrupted by the loud cries of a man named Bartimaeus: "Jesus, Son of David, have mercy on me!" While many in the crowd were telling Bartimaeus to shut up, Jesus stopped, asking, "*What do you want me to do for you?*" He asks the same question of James and John, who had come to him seeking a favor.[15] Another time, he waded into a dispute, asking, "*What are you arguing about with them?*"[16] Jesus wasn't acting, merely allowing himself to be quoted for posterity. This was a real question to a real person, the start of a real relationship. Not knowing demonstrates the authenticity of his human nature.

It's similar with disappointments. While I have experienced many, the one that almost hurt the most was relatively minor. It came from a fellow believer, a Bible study leader who acted petty toward me, showing little forgiveness when I admittedly let him down. His reaction came as a crushing surprise. Because of it I learned that I am expected to keep my commitments—and that leaders don't always lead well. But if I knew in advance what his response would be, I no doubt would have acted differently to head it off—and neither one of us would have had that opportunity for growth.

When Jesus stands before Pontius Pilate, and a Roman execution for sedition looms large, the procurator asks him, "Are you the King of the Jews?" Jesus is not concerned with saving his own skin, but learning whether this brutal Roman official might be a spiritual seeker, one in whom the seed of faith is likely to grow. "*Do you say this of your own accord,*" he asks, "*or did others say it to you about me?*"[17] Jesus genuinely wants an answer *because he doesn't know*.

No Divine Trump Card

The New Testament speaks of Jesus making "himself nothing, taking the form of a servant, being born in the likeness of men . . . being found in human form."[18] In my earlier days as a Christian, I tended to view Jesus as only in the *form* of a man—not a real man; in the *likeness* of a servant—not a real servant.

It was almost as if he were saying, "I know it looks as if I am a human male, and I am, but if I ever get into a jam, I can call on my supernatural powers at any time, and everything will be fine."

There are at least two problems with this view. The first is simply that it doesn't do justice to the text. With the words "form" and "likeness," the author, Paul, is not giving Jesus an escape clause from being a human. Paul is emphasizing his humanity. Jesus has the same form we do; he is like us.

A second problem with believing that Jesus could pull out his supernatural trump card whenever he wanted to is that doing so was the first temptation of Satan during their confrontation in the wilderness. With Jesus weakened from forty days of fasting, the devil mockingly tells him, "command this stone to become bread."[19] In other words, stop acting like a man, with all the pain and limitations that go along with it. Act like the special being you say you are, serve yourself first, don't be like *them*. Take the easy way out. But Jesus says No. He is living by God's Word, not his own, day by day. Jesus refuses to play the trump card. As Paul would later say, he "did not count equality with God a thing to be grasped."[20]

Later, Jesus emphasizes to the doubting that he takes his cues from his heavenly Father, leaving himself open to Another's agenda for each day: "The Son can do nothing of his own accord, but only what he sees the Father doing. . . . For the works that the Father has given me to accomplish, the very works that I am doing, bear witness about me that the Father has sent me. . . . My teaching is not mine, but his who sent me. . . . I declare to the world what I have heard from him."[21]

Jesus lived each day according to the will of God. This was anything but safe. Think about the fact that after praying all night, Jesus selected Judas, his future betrayer, to be one of his disciples.[22] *This* was his answer to prayer? According to John 6:64, Jesus knew that Judas would betray him "from the beginning." Yes, at times he *did* know what would happen—such as his coming death on the cross[23]—but at other times Jesus appears to be going from one situation to another, variously amazed, amused, or angry.

And as we clearly saw in chapter 3, Jesus was not an all-powerful magician; he did his works in the power of the Spirit. Even in the temptation narratives, Christ followed his Father's will under the promptings of the Holy Spirit.[24]

- Jesus was "led up by the Spirit into the wilderness to be tempted by the devil."[25]
- "The Spirit immediately drove him out into the wilderness."[26]
- "And Jesus, full of the Holy Spirit, . . . was led by the Spirit in the wilderness for forty days, being tempted by the devil."[27]

Again, during his earthly life Jesus is at the disposal of God, living each day in his service, whatever the outcome.

The Intermediate Times

Jesus, as true man, lived on the edge. We see that not only was he at times ignorant of the spiritual condition of those around him, he was sometimes uncertain of the details of his life, as his questions reveal. After delivering a demon-possessed man by the Sea of Galilee, he encounters a woman with a long-term physical disability. Amid the throng, with faith and a touch of desperation, she touches his clothing, expecting to be healed—and she is.

> And Jesus, perceiving in himself that power had gone out from him, immediately turned about in the crowd and said, "*Who touched my garments?*" And his disciples said to him, "You see the crowd pressing around you, and yet you say, '*Who touched me?*'"[28]

Jesus embodied both supernatural power and human limitations. In John 11, when Lazarus dies, we see one of many paradoxes of Scripture concerning Christ's humanity. On the one hand, despite the desperate pleas of Lazarus's sisters, Jesus allows his friend to expire. Martha tells him, almost accusingly, "Lord, if you had been here, my brother would not have died." Yet Jesus also knows in advance that he will ultimately raise Lazarus back to life, telling Martha, "Your brother will rise again."

But in the intermediate time, Jesus does not even know where Mary and Martha have buried their brother, asking, "*Where have you laid him?*" God knew, but Jesus didn't.

We see a similar paradox at work in the miraculous feedings of the four thousand and the five thousand.[29] As we observed in chapter 2, the apostle records Jesus asking Philip where they are to buy enough bread to feed the crowds "to test him, for he himself knew what he would do." And yet Mark quotes Jesus as also asking, "*How many loaves do you have?*"[30]

Again, while Jesus knows the ultimate outcome, he doesn't know all the intermediate steps. To a blind man he intends to heal Christ asks, "*Do you see anything?*"[31] While the result is not in doubt, the path that gets him there is shrouded.

How like us—who as fellow human beings live in the intermediate times between now and the not yet! Like Jesus, we choose to trust God's announced plan to call a people to himself, to be with us through thick and thin, to cause all things to work together for our good, and to bring us safely to his heavenly kingdom.[32] While all these promises are not in doubt for Christians, there are no guarantees about the day-to-day details of our lives—the intermediate times.

One more question reveals the depths of Jesus's humanity. Hanging on the cross, bleeding to death, and abandoned, Jesus cries out, "*My God, my God, why have you forsaken me?*"[33] I used to view this cry as a self-conscious quoting of Psalm 22:1, as if Jesus were saying, "Here I am on the cross fulfilling a prophecy of King David from a thousand years ago. This is irrefutable evidence that I am indeed Israel's Messiah."

While I believe Jesus knew the prophecy, he wasn't engaging in what Sunday-schoolers call a "sword drill" to show off his Bible knowledge. Instead, I see him sharing in humanity's anguish, doubt, and separation from God. With his question, Jesus wasn't scoring a theological debating point; he was suffering.

Followers of Christ down through the ages have experienced the same spiritual suffering. Even Mother Teresa spoke of "this terrible sense of loss—this untold darkness—this loneliness—this continual longing for God—which gives me that pain deep down in my heart.—Darkness is such that I really do not see—neither with my mind nor with my reason.—The place of God in my soul is blank."[34]

Jesus understands our humanity from firsthand experience. Whatever temptations, trials, and pain—even disability—we face, he faced. The result: "For we do not have a high priest who is unable to sympathize with our weaknesses, but one who in every respect has been tempted as we are."[35]

Suggested Reading

Evans, Craig A. *Fabricating Jesus: How Modern Scholars Distort the Gospels.* Downers Grove, IL: InterVarsity, 2006.

Hodges, Andrew G. *Jesus: An Interview Across Time: A Psychiatrist Looks at Christ's Humanity.* Grand Rapids: Kregel, 2003.

Nichols, Stephen J. *For Us and for Our Salvation: The Doctrine of Christ in the Early Church.* Wheaton: Crossway, 2007.

Strobel, Lee. *The Case for the Real Jesus: A Journalist Investigates Current Attacks on the Identity of Christ.* Grand Rapids: Zondervan, 2007.

Discussion Questions

1. How do you understand Scripture's teaching about Jesus's humanity?
2. Which do you think is a bigger challenge to Christian faith: attacks on Christ's supernatural identity or on his human nature?
3. Why is an understanding of both essential for a healthy Christian life?
4. How does not knowing all the results in advance enhance your life?
5. How does Jesus's reliance on the Father and the Holy Spirit apply to your life? How does it not?
6. What is the biggest challenge your human limitations pose for you?
7. How does this chapter encourage you to keep going?

5

His Mission

*"Why do you not know how to
interpret the present time?"*

Brian McLaren was having lunch with a well-known scholar at a Chinese restaurant in Tyson's Corner, Virginia. As McLaren was eating his hot-and-sour soup, the scholar remarked, "You know, most evangelicals don't have the foggiest notion of what the gospel is." Considering himself an evangelical, McLaren hesitated, so the scholar bored in, like Jesus, with a question: "What would you say the gospel is, Brian?"

McLaren replied with the stock evangelical answer defining the gospel—a Greek word in the New Testament meaning "good news"—as Christ's substitutionary death on the cross for our sins and our receiving this gift by faith. The scholar then stated (and I can only surmise that there was a note of triumph in his voice), "That's what most evangelicals say."

Taking the bait, and seeking to fill the unsettling silence that followed, McLaren replied, "Well, then, what would you say the gospel is, if it's not that?"

"The kingdom of God is at hand," the scholar said emphatically. "That was Jesus's message. Don't you think we should let Jesus tell us what the gospel is?"[1]

That simple conversation began McLaren on a "quest," he says, that has led him to reject his old belief that the kingdom of God is about "heaven after you die." Instead, he says, paraphrasing Jesus, "the kingdom of God is here now, available to all! This is the reality that matters most. Believe this good news and follow me."[2]

We'll discuss the kingdom in chapter 24 and the afterlife in chapter 25. But for now, suffice it to say that McLaren is spreading his "secret" understanding of a this-worldly Jesus far and wide, almost certainly reacting against the super-spiritualized Jesus still taught in so many churches today:

> This revolutionary image of Jesus didn't come to me in Sunday school as a boy; there, Jesus was a nice, quiet, gentle, perhaps somewhat fragile guy on whose lap children like to sit, or he was a fellow in strange robes who held a small sheep in one arm and always seemed to have the other raised as if he were hailing a taxi. The revolutionary image of Jesus didn't come to me in adult church either; there, Jesus was someone whose main job was to die so my sins could be forgiven and I could go to heaven (no small thing, of course!), of great value "in my heart" and outside of this world and history, but not terribly important as a public, historical, present factor in relation to the status quo or the powers that be.[3]

So is McLaren right, like so many today, to downplay issues of sin, of heaven, of hell? Is the gospel of the kingdom mainly about setting things right in this world? Is the core of Christ's mission to be found more in his life than in his death? Jesus's questions—supplemented by the insights of those he taught[4]— will help us find out.

"Back Off"

In the last chapter we observed how Jesus, as man, did not selfishly perform miracles for himself, nor did he always know what was around the next corner. We see both limitations of his humanness in an incident in the small city of Cana in Galilee, shortly after Jesus had selected his disciples to follow him. A wedding was going on—we don't know whose—and Jesus, his disciples, and his mother, Mary, were invited to the festivities, which lasted several days. We shouldn't wonder at this; weddings were community affairs. We sometimes lapse into thinking of Jesus, Mary, and the disciples as mere (but awesome) religious icons, chastely removed from the sufferings and joys we ordinary people experience. This episode should disabuse us of that idea. It occurred after Jesus had chosen his disciples, but before he had begun his public ministry.

At such a wedding, perhaps the most important event a person would ever be a part of, the wine flowed freely as one of the symbols of God's blessing and abundance. It was not BYOB, and there were no cash bars back then. The hosts were responsible for the wine. It was expected that guests would have plenty to eat and drink. To run out of either would be a mortifying *faux pas* before the whole community, where everyone knew everyone.

Mary seems to share a special bond with the families who have organized it. We can guess this because the unthinkable—through poor planning, excessive drinking on the part of some, or stinginess—has happened, and Mary immediately finds Jesus amid the crowd. Using perhaps a plaintive tone and a pleading look, Mary says simply, "They have no wine."

Jesus's reply to his mother is curt and to the point, to say the least: "*Woman, what has this to do with me? My hour has not yet come.*" A commentator paraphrases his question like this: "How can this affair concern me?"[5] Jesus seems surprised by her implied request. He has not come into the world to fix every problem that crops up in human relationships, no matter how much stress people may experience. He has a larger, more important mission in life—a mission that hasn't even officially started yet. It sounds as if he is politely saying, "Mother, back off."[6]

Ignoring Open Doors

While the instinctive reaction of this supposedly meek and mild man is to deny her request, I think I understand at least a bit where he is coming from. In my own life, I have applied for many jobs—most of which, thankfully, I never got. Sometimes my reason for applying has been boredom with a current job or simply a desire to "move up" and make more money. One time when I was in high school there was an opportunity to sell newspaper subscriptions over the phone. The position appealed to me because (1) I liked newspapers; (2) the job was in an office environment with no travel required; and (3) selling over the phone seemed like an easy way to pick up some extra cash.

I quit, chagrined, within a week.

I discovered that people really didn't like to be interrupted at home by my sales pitch. Worse, I took each angry response and rejection personally. While others thrived in this kind of position, at the end of each shift I felt like I had been kicked in the stomach. Finally, I was a mediocre salesman at best. After I resigned, I didn't even ask the newspaper for my small paycheck. I figured I hadn't earned it anyway.

But I picked up something much more valuable: the insight—not always applied even today—that just because I have an opportunity to do something doesn't mean I should. There is more to discovering what you ought to be doing than simply walking through every open door. Other factors to consider include understanding your basic temperament, gifts, and interests. Skip those opportunities that don't seem to be a good fit and pursue those that do. Unless you receive direct evidence to the contrary, assume that your gifts and opportunities will work in harmony, and work to develop those gifts for God's glory.

Of course, there are other factors. Raw need is certainly one. Sometimes a job simply must be done, and there is simply no one else to do it—gifted or otherwise. Moses stepped into such a leadership vacuum. When God called him to lead the Hebrews out of Egyptian slavery, he protested, "I am slow of speech and of tongue."[7] In other words, he didn't have the gifts to stand up to Pharaoh. But the need for freedom was undeniably there, and Moses was God's man.

That brings up another factor: God's particular calling, or vocation, on a person's life. Gifts are one thing, needs another (including the need to pay for your next meal). Your calling at a particular time in life may or may not match your gifts. But if God calls you to do something, then do it in faith—not in yourself, but in him who calls.

When considering our options, we must never forget our calling. Albert Einstein was an obscure patent clerk until he discovered his calling in physics. Abraham Lincoln was a successful attorney in Springfield, Illinois, who simply kept running for office until he wound up as one of the most improbable (and greatest) presidents in American history. God called Moses to lead the Israelites out of Egypt, and Moses tried to make excuses, saying he was not particularly gifted for the job. But God brushed the excuses aside, asking: "Who has made man's mouth? Who makes him mute, or deaf, or seeing, or blind? Is it not I, the Lord? Now therefore go, and I will . . . teach you what you shall speak."[8] The key issue, then, is not gifts, but calling. Find yours.

A Sense of Timing

Jesus certainly had this sense of vocation in mind when he rebuffed his mother, saying, in effect, "This isn't my job." His hour (Greek *hora*, elsewhere translated as *time* or *moment*) to perform such feats had not arrived. He was not talking about clock time, but timing. Scholar Walter Elwell gives the sense: "The Bible . . . regards time as a created sphere in which God's redemptive plan is actualized."[9] It was not the proper time to begin working miracles. Perhaps Jesus was not yet ready to begin drawing crowds because he wanted more one-on-one time with his disciples. Or maybe other events had to fall into place first. Regardless of the reason, he did not want to begin his public ministry now. Matthew Henry puts it this way: "For every thing Christ did, and that was done to him, he had his hour, the fixed time and the fittest time, which was punctually observed."[10] Jesus did not act haphazardly; he was on a mission.

And yet at the end of this vignette, we see Jesus change his mind and quietly turn a copious amount of water into the needed wine (the best, in fact): blessing the festivities, providing a well known but subtle sign of his messiahship,[11] and causing his disciples—but not the crowds yet—to believe in him.

Interpreting the Signs

But Jesus would not keep his mission a secret for long. Later, Jesus challenged the crowds, like John the Baptist, to understand that judgment was near. But unlike the man wearing the strange clothes, Jesus was to be the one who would be executing that judgment:

> "I came to cast fire on the earth, and would that it were already kindled! I have a baptism to be baptized with, and how great is my distress until it is accomplished! *Do you think that I have come to give peace on earth?* No, I tell you, but rather division. For from now on in one house there will be five divided, three against two and two against three. They will be divided, father against son and son against father, mother against daughter and daughter against mother, mother-in-law against her daughter-in-law and daughter-in-law against mother-in-law."
>
> He also said to the crowds, "When you see a cloud rising in the west, you say at once, 'A shower is coming.' And so it happens. And when you see the south wind blowing, you say, 'There will be scorching heat,' and it happens. You hypocrites! *You know how to interpret the appearance of earth and sky, but why do you not know how to interpret the present time?*"[12]

There's that word *time* again. It is a quickly closing door of opportunity that, like Jesus's questions, demands a response *now*. This is not the time to kick back in our easy chairs and relax. There is no coasting, no neutrality. We must decide.

We sentimentally call Jesus the Prince of Peace, and this is surely right and good, as the Bible does the same.[13] But it is not just any kind of peace, nor peace at any cost, nor peace to the exclusion of other virtues such as justice, nor peace without limit—not in our fallen world. While certainly Jesus called peacemakers blessed,[14] he didn't deny the fact that sometimes interpersonal peace is impossible.

In the instance above, Jesus says following him can bring ugly division in our families, which normally are supposed to provide love, mutual support, protection, and room to grow. Certainly many who decide to follow the Prince of Peace experience turmoil in their relationships. For example, many a Muslim has faced ridicule, ostracism, and even death—at the hands of family members, no less—for naming Christ as Lord and Savior. For others, the stakes are lower, but still painful. Think of a young man raised in a secular home who feels duty-bound, now that he is a Christian, to warn his parents of God's judgment on sin. His impassioned pleas are met with a raised eyebrow, or stony silence. Is he a fanatic?

Other relationships can also go by the wayside, despite our best efforts. Think of the teenaged girl who no longer believes she should engage in drinking parties and premarital sex and who is then labeled a prude by her former friends. In our pluralistic climate, think of the pressure pastors and leaders such as Franklin Graham experience at public events to pray not in the name of Jesus but instead in the (generic) name of God.

Despite all the praise he receives from those who don't follow him, Jesus is a divisive figure. Those who speak his name face opprobrium—think of all the public ridicule a campaigning George W. Bush received in 2000 after naming Jesus as his favorite philosopher. While Martin Luther King and Gandhi are universally hailed in death, a risen Jesus still divides. Fascinating, since they derived much of their inspiration from him. Perhaps Jesus had a different kind of peace in mind.

In this passage, Jesus warns his listeners to take note of the special time in which they live. The Greek word translated as "time" here is *kairos*, which "refers to a definite point of time especially appropriate for a given undertaking." *Kairos* is not simply a religious concept. When the Allies decided to roll back Nazi tyranny in Europe, they didn't choose just any old time to land in Normandy, as if one day was as good as another. No, troops and supplies had to be painstakingly positioned. Hitler's generals had to be misled about the location and timing of the attack. D-Day had a special *kairos*. Likewise, the invasion of Christ into our sin- and Satan-dominated world had its own *kairos*. It was "a decisive momentary unveiling of the eternal."[15]

Thus, time for Jesus is not the succession of seconds, minutes, and hours into an infinite future. It is special, charged with purpose. With his question, it is as if he is saying to the crowd (and to you and me), "Don't you *get* it? This moment will never come again. It will change your eternal destiny. Don't miss it! If you can track the ordinary signs of earthly life with care and precision, why can't you recognize the momentous thing happening right *now*, in your midst? Is it because you don't want to?"

A Focus on the End

The four Gospels give anything but a balanced, purely chronological account of Jesus's life. While they provide solid eyewitness testimony concerning the man from Galilee, they make no effort to cover everything. Instead, they focus on certain aspects as with a zoom lens, while barely mentioning, or even skipping, large swathes of material we might find interesting. Matthew and Luke invest a lot of space covering the births of John the Baptist and Jesus. Then all of the Gospels, save Luke, skip Jesus's growing up years entirely. (Luke, you will recall, recounts only his meeting with teachers of the law in the Jewish temple and his return home with his parents.) These four short books don't cover the estimated three-year public ministry of Christ in exhaustive detail. As John freely admits near the end of his book, "Now Jesus did many other signs in the presence of the disciples, which are not written in this book, but these are written so that you may believe."[16]

No, they focus on the end, the final week in Jerusalem, and its aftermath. Matthew devotes eight of his twenty-eight chapters to Jesus's confrontations with the authorities, his final instructions to his disciples, his arrest and trial, his execution on a Roman cross, and reports of his resurrection. Mark covers the same events with six of his sixteen chapters. Luke does it in six of his twenty-four chapters, John in ten of his twenty-one chapters. The Bible says the risen Jesus appeared to his disciples over a forty-day span, so adding it all together we have a total of forty-seven days of special focus for the Gospel writers. This compressed period represents only about .004 percent of the approximately twelve thousand days Jesus walked this earth, yet to the disciples it was paramount. It was God's time.

Jesus's mission, in one sense, was multifaceted. He said he came to call sinners, to fulfill the Law and the Prophets, to divide, to judge, to save the lost, and to testify to the truth.[17] But we see the main focus in a scene of Jesus and the disciples heading into dangerous territory.

After a narrow escape from the Jewish authorities, Jesus decides to return to Jerusalem, into the teeth of the opposition.[18] The scene is told beautifully in the old-fashioned Bible translation used by Matthew Henry:

> And they were in the way going up to Jerusalem; and Jesus went before them: and they were amazed; and as they followed, they were afraid. And he took again the twelve, and began to tell them what things should happen unto him, saying, Behold, we go up to Jerusalem; and the Son of man shall be delivered unto the chief priests, and unto the scribes; and they shall condemn him to death, and shall deliver him to the Gentiles: And they shall mock him, and shall scourge him, and shall spit upon him, and shall kill him: And the third day he shall rise again.[19]

Instead of shrinking from this fate, Jesus embraces it, saying: "the Son of Man came not to be served but to serve, and to give his life as a ransom for many."[20] Boiling down his mission into a single sentence, Jesus says he came to die—and to die for others.

Limited Time

His disciples are shocked by his determination: "Rabbi," they fairly stammer, "the Jews were just now seeking to stone you, and are you going there again?" Jesus knows his time is short, answering their question with one of his own: "*Are there not twelve hours in the day?* If anyone walks in the day, he does not stumble, because he sees the light of this world. But if anyone walks in the night, he stumbles, because the light is not in him."[21]

Elsewhere Jesus called himself the light of the world.[22] But with his question he reminds the disciples that his time on earth is limited—that the light is going out. His followers must make the most of this opportunity to be with him, because it is quickly passing. In another place he answers a question about the identity of his forerunner with one that clearly shows the trouble ahead: "*And how is it written of the Son of Man that he should suffer many things and be treated with contempt?*"[23]

When Jesus and the disciples get to Jerusalem, Jesus the man feels the enormity of what he is about to do. "Now is my soul troubled. *And what shall I say? 'Father, save me from this hour'? But for this purpose I have come to this hour.*"

Then he spells out the purpose of the *hora*: his death on the cross: "Now is the judgment of this world; now will the ruler of this world be cast out. And I, when I am lifted up from the earth, will draw all people to myself." Later, he tells the crowds, as he just reminded the disciples, "The light is among you for a little while longer. Walk while you have the light, lest darkness overtake you. The one who walks in the darkness does not know where he is going. While you have the light, believe in the light, that you may become sons of light."[24]

But despite all this, the disciples are still slow to grasp his mission. As he gathers with them for a last meal before he is handed over to the powers that be, Jesus says, "A little while, and you will see me no longer; and again a little while, and you will see me." Seeing their confusion, in gentleness he draws them out with a question. "*Is this what you are asking yourselves, what I meant by saying, 'A little while and you will not see me, and again a little while and you will see me'?*"

Then he tells them plainly that he will die—and after that he will rise.

Truly, truly, I say to you, you will weep and lament, but the world will rejoice. You will be sorrowful, but your sorrow will turn into joy. When a woman is giving birth, she has sorrow because her hour has come, but when she has delivered the baby, she no longer remembers the anguish, for joy that a human being has been born into the world. So also you have sorrow now, but I will see you again and your hearts will rejoice, and no one will take your joy from you.[25]

Fulfilling the Scriptures

Even then the disciples cannot (or will not) believe what is about to happen. How can their leader, master, hope, and friend leave them? God's anointed cannot die. Probably still grasping at dreams that a this-worldly kingdom must be inaugurated to drive out the Romans and purify Israel, their obstinate hearts remain darkened.

Later that night, the mob—wielding swords, clubs, and torches—closes in. In desperation Peter, one of Jesus's inner circle, grabs his own sword and takes a wild swing at the bondservant of the high priest. Jesus sternly rebukes Peter and his faulty understanding of the mission:

> Put your sword back into its place. For all who take the sword will perish by the sword. *Do you think that I cannot appeal to my Father, and he will at once send me more than twelve legions of angels? But how then should the Scriptures be fulfilled, that it must be so?*[26]

Again we see Jesus's understanding of his mission as a fulfillment of Scripture.[27] His death is no tragic accident befalling an idealistic religious reformer, cutting a promising ministry short. Jesus *must* die. Despite what the new proponents of so-called kingdom theology may say, his mission cannot be confined to this earth, because he was not confined to this earth.

In chapter 1 we saw John the Baptist pronounce Jesus not as a great teacher, healer, exorcist, or miracle worker. No, he is "the Lamb of God who takes away the sin of the world!"[28] In the Hebrew Scriptures, of course, the lamb is an innocent sacrificial substitute that bears the people's sins so they can find peace with God. Jesus is the ultimate substitute, the ultimate Lamb.

"Christianity is a rescue religion," John Stott says. "It declares that God has taken the initiative in Jesus Christ to deliver us from our sins. This is the main theme of the Bible."[29] Indeed, Stott will get no argument from the apostle Paul, who met the risen Christ and had his life utterly transformed, moving from persecutor to proclaimer.[30] For Paul, the meaning of the gospel, the good news, was crystal clear, fulfilling the Hebrew Scriptures. And it wasn't about an earthly kingdom. As he told the new church in Corinth,

> Now I would remind you, brothers, of the gospel I preached to you, in which you stand, and by which you are being saved, if you hold fast to the word I preached to you. . . .
>
> For I delivered to you as of *first importance* what I also received: that Christ died for our sins in accordance with the Scriptures, that he was buried, that he was raised on the third day in accordance with the Scriptures, and that he appeared to [Peter], then to the twelve. Then he appeared to more than five hundred brothers at one time, most of whom are still alive, though some have fallen asleep. Then he appeared to James, then to all the apostles. Last of all, as to one untimely born, he appeared also to me.[31]

The death, burial, and space-time resurrection of Jesus are of "first importance." This does not mean the other things he said and did are of *no* importance. But they are less important in the single plan of God. Jesus's mission was prioritized. Some things were more important than others. The same is true for us. Without priorities, everything settles into a mushy equality, with nothing more important than anything else. Jesus had priorities, and so must we. This is a hard truth for those of us who want to keep our options open, but time is short. We must choose.

Think of Jesus's mission this way. Jesus's miracles, teaching, and presence in the world—as wonderful as they are in elevating our lives and thinking—could not atone for even one human sin. But his death on the cross—as awful and unfair as it was—was indispensable in bringing us peace with a holy God. Without his death, his perfect life would only condemn us as moral failures. It is his death that conveys to us the benefits of his life.

After seeing the resurrected Christ, Peter finally understood it, asserting, "For Christ also suffered once for sins, the righteous for the unrighteous, that he might bring us to God."[32] Yes, for many people believing that Jesus's "main job was to die so my sins could be forgiven and I could go to heaven" sounds trite and simplistic. Somehow this is not revolutionary enough for these wisdom seekers.

And yet in their quests to find secret messages from a revolutionary Jesus, such scholars overlook the revolutionary open secret contained in the Word of God—a secret available to all but accepted only by a "foolish" few. Paul states ironically,

> For the word of the cross is folly to those who are perishing, but to us who are being saved it is the power of God. For it is written:
>
> > "I will destroy the wisdom of the wise,
> > and the discernment of the discerning I will thwart."
>
> . . . For since, in the wisdom of God, the world did not know God through wisdom, it pleased God through the folly of what we preach to save those who believe. . . . For the foolishness of God is wiser than men, and the weakness of God is stronger than men.[33]

To a group of Jewish "wise men," Jesus declared, "unless you believe that I am he you will die in your sins."[34] So according to Jesus, his main task was to die for our sins; our task is to believe. In fact, if what Jesus said about his mission is true, our eternal destiny hangs in the balance.

What kind of person can make such demands? And what kind of person can rescue us from our sins? To answer these questions about the identity of Jesus, we turn to the next chapter.

Suggested Reading

Dever, Mark. "Nothing But the Blood." *Christianity Today*, May 2006, 28–33.

Piper, John. *Fifty Reasons Why Jesus Came to Die*. Wheaton: Crossway, 2006.

———. *The Future of Justification: A Response to N. T. Wright*. Wheaton: Crossway, 2007.

Stott, John. *Basic Christianity*. Downers Grove, IL: InterVarsity, 2006.

Discussion Questions

1. What is the gospel?
2. What are some of the this-world applications of the gospel?
3. Why do so many scholars balk at traditional, orthodox interpretations of the gospel?
4. What kind of peace did Jesus come to bring?
5. How can Jesus's understanding of time inform our own?
6. How can Jesus's sense of calling affect our own?
7. Do you see yourself as a sinner in need of God's rescue?

6

His Identity

"Who do you say that I am?"

Sir Leigh Teabing sits down with Sophie Neveu to tell her the "truth" about Jesus Christ, something she never learned in Sunday school. The Bible we have today, Teabing asserts, is "a product of man [that] has evolved through countless translations, additions and revisions." The church's understanding of the deity of Christ did not come about until the Council of Nicea, about three hundred years after his death. "At this gathering," Teabing tells the breathless Sophie, "many aspects of Christianity were debated and voted upon . . . [including] the divinity of Jesus. . . . Until that moment in history, Jesus was viewed by his followers as a mortal prophet . . . a man . . . Jesus's establishment as the 'Son of God' was officially proposed and voted on by the Council of Nicea."

"Hold on," Teabing's listener replies with incredulity. "You're saying that Jesus's divinity was the result of a vote?"

"A relatively close vote at that."[1]

Yet there are few contemporary scholars who are willing to cast a vote for Dan Brown's fanciful scenario. As Robert M. Bowman and J. Ed Komoszewski state, "More than one scholar has demonstrated that *The Da Vinci Code* shares more in common with conspiracy theories than with sober historical analysis, yet its message continues to resonate with contemporary culture."[2]

It's true; all the unsupported, shoddy history and theology in Dan Brown's book has had an effect, forcing many ordinary people who are not biblical scholars to doubt whether the New Testament accounts clearly point to Christ as someone much more than just a man.[3]

"The facts are very much otherwise," according to Bowman and Komoszewski. To take just one of their examples: the practice of giving Jesus divine honors—of religious, spiritual devotion to Jesus—was an established, characteristic feature of the Christian movement within the first two decades of its existence. This is strong evidence that the deity of Christ was an established, early doctrine of the church, which, after all, had a large contingent of fiercely monotheistic Jews. Larry Hurtado, professor of New Testament at the University of Edinburgh, describes the emergence of devotion to Jesus as "a veritable 'big bang,' an explosively rapid and impressively substantial development in the earliest stage of the Christian movement."[4]

So who is right? One thing is for sure, the answer matters: "belief in the deity of Jesus—his unique status among human beings as God in the flesh— implies that Jesus is the only way for people to be properly related to God."[5] And Jesus's questions can help us discover the all-important answer.

Who Is Jesus?

We have come a long way in our attempt to answer this section's question, "Who Is Jesus?" We have seen that he expects his followers to live in total dedication to him (chapter 1). His questions, asked in a particular context, nevertheless have timeless power today as they draw men and women to follow him (chapter 2). Jesus is a wonder worker in the natural and supernatural worlds (chapter 3). Though he possessed great power and insight, Jesus was not an incomprehensible and aloof spirit, but a human being, subject, like us, to many of life's uncertainties (chapter 4). And although Jesus did good deeds and taught life-changing truths, he came mainly not to show us a better way (though he certainly did that), but to die on the cross for our sins (chapter 5).

The present chapter, the final one in this section, will put the finishing touches on the portrait of Jesus that his questions have been painting for us. They will force us to grapple with history's most enigmatic and compelling figure, one who draws people from every nation, tongue, tribe, and time. As the first-century Jewish historian Josephus exclaimed, "Jesus . . . was a doer of startling deeds, a teacher of people who received the truth with pleasure. And he gained a following both among many Jews and among many of Greek origin."[6] The questions in this chapter will go a long way toward showing us why.

Egocentric?

Universally hailed as meek and mild, the man Jesus was intensely interested in knowing what others thought of him. The Synoptic Gospels all record him basically asking the disciples the same question, "*Who do people say that I am?*" Then Matthew, Mark, and Luke record the all-important follow-up question: "*But who do you say that I am?*"[7] No false humility for Jesus. He evidently agreed with John the Baptist, who said (as we saw in chapter 1), "He [Jesus] must increase, but I [John] must decrease."[8] But it wasn't an insecure egotism that caused Jesus to be so concerned with what others thought of him. Rather, it was a profound altruism. Last chapter we heard him say, "unless you believe that I am he you will die in your sins."[9]

So what kind of "he" is Jesus—one who demands our unreserved belief and who controls our eternal destiny? The traditional Christian answer, of course, is that Jesus is God. And certainly the earliest Christians, who were strict monotheists, didn't think this man was egocentric, nor that worshiping him was blasphemous.

Marcus Borg, however, conflates "Jesus as God" talk with the ancient heresy of Docetism—assuming that if Jesus were divine then necessarily he would only have *appeared* to be human. For Borg, this would mean Jesus was "not really one of us."[10] Evangelical theologian Millard Erickson acknowledges that the deity of the man Jesus Christ is one of the most controversial—and crucial—Christian doctrines. "It lies at the heart of our faith," Erickson insists. "For our faith actually rests on Jesus's actually being God in human flesh, and not simply an extraordinary human, albeit the most unusual person who ever lived."[11]

Dropping Hints

Jesus's questions can help us sort out whether he was simply an extraordinary man—or God in the flesh. Like someone playing a parlor game, Jesus dropped a lot of hints. Facing determined opposition in Jerusalem from the religious power brokers, Jesus graciously warned them of their approaching doom via a parable. Then he capped it off with a question with which they would be familiar, taken directly from Psalm 118:

Have you never read in the Scriptures:

> *"The stone that the builders rejected*
> *has become the cornerstone;*
> *this was the Lord's doing,*
> *and it is marvelous in our eyes"?*[12]

By referring to the ancient Hebrew Scriptures, Jesus was pointing to his foundational (and long anticipated) role in the religious life of the nation— despite their opposition. Here was no mere prophetic reformer. He was soon to topple the entire religious system that had put them at the top.

Another time, observers asked Jesus why his disciples did not fast when those of John and the Pharisees did. Jesus answered their question with one of his own, which again pointed to his unique status within Judaism: "*Can the wedding guests fast while the bridegroom is with them?*"[13] Jesus is saying that something new has arrived, and that this new thing is all about him. The disciples are the guests; he is the main event—but one that will eventually come to end.

Though he was an unparalleled figure by any definition, Jesus didn't mind appealing to others for endorsements. For example, the Galilean presents as a witness in his defense David, Israel's greatest king, who ruled the nation during its Golden Age a millennium before. This of course was natural, since one of the names for Israel's messiah was "Son of David." The nation's kings—and especially David—were considered to be in special relationship with God and in some sense to be sons of God. This dynamic can be seen in Psalm 2, which David wrote. It speaks of the Lord's "anointed"—an appellation that Bible scholars say can apply to an earthly king as well as to the long-awaited Messiah, who comes to inaugurate the consummation of God's rule.

This dual understanding of messianic predictions is of a piece with the rest of the Hebrew Scriptures. Many prophecies in the Old Testament have an immediate application as well as a future one. Such is the case with this royal psalm. Speaking for God, it states, "As for me, I have set my King on Zion, my holy hill." Then it goes on to quote Israel's king and Messiah:

> I will tell of the decree: The LORD said to me, "You are my Son;
> today I have begotten you.
> Ask of me, and I will make the nations your heritage,
> and the ends of the earth your possession."[14]

Truly the Son of David is an exalted figure, worthy to possess the nations. As this psalm ends, the nations are warned: "Kiss the Son, lest he be angry, and you perish in the way; for his wrath is quickly kindled. Blessed are all who take refuge in him."[15]

Indicating its appropriateness, Jesus responded to the Son of David title, but he also questioned his listeners to get them to think more deeply about it. One day he used it to get them to consider Psalm 2 more carefully, not allowing them to fall back on more comfortable and less challenging interpretations:

> Now while the Pharisees were gathered together, Jesus asked them a question, saying, "*What do you think about the Christ? Whose son is he?*" They said to

him, "The son of David." He said to them, *"How is it then that David, in the Spirit, calls him Lord, saying,*

> *'The Lord said to my Lord, "Sit at my right hand,*
> *until I put your enemies under your feet"'?*

If then David calls him Lord, how is he his son?"[16]

Jesus was hinting that the psalm ultimately applied not to David, but to someone immeasurably greater—himself. We will return to this theme later in the chapter.

Another time, some Pharisees accused his disciples of breaking the Sabbath "no work" law by plucking grain. The law of Sabbath observance, of course, was given to help humanity, not curse it, which Jesus's accusers evidently had forgotten. The ancient world did not know of respite from labor in its desperation to provide for daily needs. The command to Israel to obey God by doing no work on the Sabbath, then, was actually an invitation to trust in Yahweh's loving care. So Jesus answered their misguided indictment with a question, followed by a statement asserting his lordly right to authoritatively interpret and act on the God-given Jewish day of rest, which is enshrined as the second of Yahweh's Ten Commandments.

> *"Have you never read what David did, when he was in need and was hungry, he and those who were with him: how he entered the house of God, in the time of Abiathar the high priest, and ate the bread of the Presence, which it is not lawful for any but the priests to eat, and also gave it to those who were with him?"* And he said to them, *"The Sabbath was made for man, not man for the Sabbath. So the Son of Man is lord even of the Sabbath."*[17]

Jesus was not only greater than Israel's great poet-warrior king; he surpassed even the Sabbath in importance.

His Acts

What other clues can we find that will lead us to the identity of Jesus? Certainly if Jesus is God, then it would be reasonable to assume that he should act like God. We have seen many down through history claim to be God, or God's Son—including Jim Jones and Sun Myung Moon. But their acts and character fall far short of matching the deeds we would expect of God.

We have seen that Jesus worked mighty miracles by the power of the Spirit, such as healing the sick and casting out demons. But miracles don't force anyone to believe. Jesus's representatives also performed such acts in his name without claiming divinity for themselves—although on at least one occasion they were mistaken for Greek gods.[18] In fact, the performance of miracles was no guarantee that people would draw the right conclusions about Jesus and his followers. So at several key junctures Jesus would pause after a miracle and ask if people had gotten the point.[19]

Often the objects of Jesus's instruction were his disciples, those he was training to carry on the work after he was gone. The New Testament records two occasions when Jesus miraculously fed the crowds.[20] Some time later, the disciples began discussing the fact that the little band had nothing to eat.

> "Why are you discussing the fact that you have no bread? Do you not yet perceive or understand? Are your hearts hardened? Having eyes do you not see, and having ears do you not hear? And do you not remember? When I broke the five loaves for the five thousand, how many baskets full of broken pieces did you take up?" They said to him, "Twelve." "And the seven for the four thousand, how many baskets full of broken pieces did you take up?" And they said to him, "Seven." And he said to them, "Do you not yet understand?"[21]

Much like the Israelites, who grumbled despite the manna God provided during the Exodus fourteen hundred years before, the disciples here doubted God's provision in Jesus for their needs. Did they not know who he was? Did they not yet understand?

Once he returned home to Capernaum, and the crowds came pouring in to see him. It was standing room only. Suddenly four men carrying a paralytic showed up, but they could not get near Jesus. But where there is a will, there is a way, and they took the outside stairs to the top of the house and began digging through the flat, thatched roof. Once they made an opening big enough, they lowered the unfortunate friend down into the house. Jesus, touched by their faith and friendship, looked down on the paralytic and spoke to a need even greater than the one for physical healing: "My son, your sins are forgiven."

The scribes were shocked at what they considered Jesus's blasphemy, knowing rightly that only God can forgive sins. Jesus read their minds (or perhaps just their faces) and quickly asked,

> "Why do you question these things in your hearts? Which is easier, to say to the paralytic, 'Your sins are forgiven,' or to say, 'Rise, take up your bed and walk'? But that you may know that the Son of Man has authority on earth to forgive sins"—he said to the paralytic—"I say to you, rise, pick up your bed, and go home." And he rose and immediately picked up his bed and went out before them all, so that they were all amazed and glorified God, saying, "We never saw anything like this!"[22]

The question forces the listeners to face Jesus's identity. Anyone can *say* he or she has the authority to forgive someone's sins, and the claim cannot be checked. But backing it up with an unmistakable display of divine power lends real credibility to the message. And Jesus did.

While some have tried to undermine it, the famous "trilemma" of C. S. Lewis still demands an answer from each of us who believes Jesus was a good enough teacher to get his message across to those who walked with him:

> Christ says that He is "humble and meek" and we believe Him; not noticing that, if He were merely a man, humility and meekness are the very last characteristics we could attribute to some of His sayings.
>
> I am trying to prevent anyone from saying the really foolish thing that people often say about Him: "I'm ready to accept Jesus as a great moral teacher, but I don't accept His claim to be God." That is the one thing we must not say. A man who was merely a man and said the sort of things Jesus said would not be a great moral teacher. He would either be a lunatic—on a level with the man who says he is a poached egg—or else he would be the Devil of Hell. You must make your choice: Either this man was, and is, the Son of God: or else a madman or something worse. You can shut Him up for a fool, you can spit at Him and kill Him as a demon; or you can fall at His feet and call Him Lord and God. But let us not come up with any patronizing nonsense about His being a great human teacher. He has not left that open to us. He did not intend to.[23]

In the introduction we first encountered Jesus stilling a storm. Now we turn to a similar episode of the man from Galilee again controlling the laws of nature. At night, Jesus walks on the water, greatly frightening the disciples, who are stuck in their boat amid a storm and not at all expecting a display of supernatural power. But ever-impulsive Peter asks Jesus to allow him to also walk on the water—and he does, for a time.

> But when [Peter] saw the wind, he was afraid, and beginning to sink he cried out, "Lord, save me." Jesus immediately reached out his hand and took hold of him, saying to him, *"O you of little faith, why did you doubt?"* And when they got into the boat, the wind ceased. And those in the boat worshiped him, saying, "Truly you are the Son of God."[24]

While the disciples initially doubted, they came to the only logical conclusion possible under the circumstances: Jesus is the Son of God, and worthy of worship. And note that Jesus does not disabuse them of their understanding. Jesus *acts* like God because he *is* God. He was, and is, worthy of our faith and worship.

Jesus's divinity was not decided at some church council three centuries later. With apologies to Sir Leigh Teabing, it was an unavoidable fact. Bowman and Komoszewski point out that throughout the New Testament Jesus shares the honors due to God, the attributes of God, the names of God, the deeds of God, and the seat of God's throne.[25]

But deeds are not enough without a character to match.

His Character

One day Jesus was telling the Jewish crowds that they were not rightly related to God. "Truly, truly, I say to you, everyone who commits sin is a slave to sin." The crowds retorted, "Abraham"—the patriarch of the nation—"is our father. . . . We have one Father—even God."

Jesus's reply is stinging, and not at all PC: "You are of your father, the devil. . . . Because I tell the truth you do not believe me." To prove he is truthful, Jesus clinches his riposte with two questions: "*Which one of you convicts me of sin? If I tell the truth, why do you not believe me?*"[26]

In our day it's common for political candidates to pay for "opposition research" to dig up dirt on their competitors. In the 1980s, while seeking the Democratic presidential nomination, Senator Gary Hart challenged a curious press to prove he was involved in an affair. When embarrassing photos taken on a boat called the *Monkey Business* came to light, Hart's presidential aspirations were sunk. The lesson? Those involved in flagrant immorality should never invite scrutiny of their private lives. In this instance, though, Jesus invites his opponents to dig up any dirt on him they can find, but they come up empty. They are silent, because Jesus—like God—never sinned.[27] As Peter later testified, "He committed no sin."[28] Thus he is a believable, trustworthy guide.

Next we come to a paradoxical question of Jesus. A moral and very prominent man in the community (one text calls him a "ruler") who scrupulously tries to obey the commandments as he understands them runs up to Jesus with the sixty-four-thousand-dollar question: "Good Teacher, what must I do to inherit eternal life?" Before answering the question, Jesus focuses on the adjective—"good": "*Why do you call me good? No one is good except God alone.*"[29] Since Jesus already takes for granted his own goodness (in fact, sinlessness) and performs acts only God can do, what can he possibly mean here?

Certainly one likely interpretation that fits all the evidence: he is attempting to shake up this man—who actually believes he can *earn* eternal life. The man erroneously thinks he must *do* something to gain eternal life, as if it is a commodity to be bought. But Jesus here warns that he will never be good enough to pull it off, for only the pure in heart will see God,[30] and Jesus seems to indicate that the man is not nearly as holy as he thinks he is.

Then we turn to the personal pronoun. "Why do you call *me* good?" Jesus asks. Jesus seeks to bring the man's sinful condition into sharp relief. In one sense, to call Jesus merely *good* is to bring him down to our own level: "Jesus is good, yes; but so am I." The truth is, Jesus is without peer. Yes, Jesus is good, but he is much more than that, and much more than we are. We add nothing to his goodness. Why do we, who are utterly evil, think we can call Jesus good, as if we have the moral authority to pronounce anything meaningful about him? That's like me, who labors in the pool three times a week to stave off old age, calling Michael Phelps a good swimmer. It may be an accurate statement, but so what?

Further, Bowman and Komoszewski note that Jesus "may have been asserting that goodness is ultimately found in God alone,"[31] and the man's outward piety was a pale imitation at best. In Matthew's recounting, the man stresses the good deeds required for life, and Jesus responds, *"Why do you ask me about what is good?* There is only one who is good."

Jesus's question forces the man—and us—to consider the implications: Only God is good—truly good. Jesus is good. Therefore, Jesus is God, and his pronouncements about eternal life are binding.

A Greater Witness

Jesus also claims a unique relationship with God the Father—divine sonship. It is true that Israel was in a sense God's son,[32] and that the Jewish kings were also sons of God.[33] But we have seen that Jesus claimed an intimate father-son relationship with God that scandalized his contemporaries. And his awareness of this relationship started early. As we saw in chapter 4, when he was a boy of twelve, Jesus became separated from his family in Jerusalem. After several gut-wrenching days of frantic searching, Joseph and Mary finally found him—conversing in the temple with the teachers about God's law. *"Why were you looking for me?"* Jesus asks. *"Did you not know that I must be in my Father's house?"*[34]

After he is grown, Jesus tells the crowds that those who trust in him are eternally secure. Then he adds a statement designed to shock these first-century monotheists into thinking about his identity: "I and the Father are one." When they pick up stones to kill him for blasphemy, Jesus defends himself by quoting from the Old Testament:

> Is it not written in your Law, "I said, you are gods"? If he called them gods to whom the word of God came—and Scripture cannot be broken—do you say of him whom the Father consecrated and sent into the world, "You are blaspheming," because I said, "I am the Son of God"?[35]

If human beings made in God's image can metaphorically be called gods, then what, Jesus asks, is the problem with me calling myself God's Son?

The night he was to be handed over to his enemies, Jesus gives his disciples some last-minute instructions and encouragement that they are secure in his and God the Father's love. "Let not your hearts be troubled," he says. "Believe in God; believe also in me." As if that is not clear enough for them, Jesus adds, a few sentences later, "I am the way, and the truth, and the life. No one comes to the Father except through me. If you had known me, you would have known my Father also. From now on you do know him and have seen him."

Then Philip expresses profound confusion, blurting out, "Lord, show us the Father, and it is enough for us."

This is too much for Jesus. You can almost hear the frustration in his voice that, even at the eleventh hour, they still don't grasp his identity.

> *Have I been with you so long, and you still do not know me, Philip?* Whoever has seen me has seen the Father. *How can you say, 'Show us the Father'? Do you not believe that I am in the Father and the Father is in me?*[36]

Seeing Jesus is like seeing the Father.

Later that night, as Jesus is betrayed to the religious authorities, Peter whips out his sword and takes a wild, desperate swing at the servant of the high priest. As we saw in chapter 5, immediately Jesus rebukes him, saying, "*Do you think that I cannot appeal to my Father, and he will at once send me more than twelve legions of angels?*"[37] Jesus here claims that he is the Son of God, with immediate access to tens of thousands of angels.[38] But his task is to die for our sins, and so die he must. And did.

After the End

But Jesus didn't stay dead. On the third day, he rose again, and his questions continued. As his disciples huddle together, the risen Lord suddenly stands before them. Not expecting a physical resurrection, they think he is a spirit. So he shows them his hands and feet and asks, "*Have you anything here to eat?*"[39] They gave him—likely with trembling hands—a piece of fish, and Jesus ate it. The God-Man had come back, physically, our penalty paid (chapter 5), his divinity proven beyond all doubt. Soon he would return to his Father, leaving the disciples to carry on his work. But why was it necessary—*contra* Marcus Borg—that Jesus be both man (chapter 4) and God (chapter 6)? The old Puritan theologian Stephen Charnock put it this way:

> He hath something like to man, and something like to God. If he were in all things only like to man, he would be at a distance to God: if he were in all things only like to God, he would be at a distance to man. He is a true mediator between mortal sinners and the immortal righteous One. He was near to us by the infirmities of our nature, and near to God by the perfections of the Divine; as near to God in his nature, as to us in ours; as near to us in our nature, as he is to God in the Divine. Nothing that belongs to the Deity, but he possesses; nothing that belongs to the human nature, but he is clothed with. He had both the nature which had offended, and that nature which was offended.[40]

We have one more question to consider about Jesus's identity before moving on to section 2, "How Do You Follow Him?" It was asked of Saul of Tarsus on the way to Damascus. The book of Acts, which chronicles the growth and spread of the early church, describes the vicious Jewish leader Saul as "still breathing threats and murder against the disciples of the Lord." Then, on the road to Damascus, "suddenly a light from heaven flashed around him. And falling to the ground he heard a voice saying to him, '*Saul, Saul, why are you persecuting me?*' And [Saul] said, 'Who are you, Lord?'"

Then came the fearful, half-expected words: "I am Jesus, whom you are persecuting."[41] The question indicates that the one who rose again and ascended into heaven still identifies personally with the people he has left behind. To persecute them is to persecute their Lord. Though the Son of God has returned to heaven, leaving all his temporary earthly limitations behind, he never really left. The ascended Jesus remains mystically united with his people, who are called to make disciples until he returns. "All authority in heaven and on earth has been given to me," Jesus said. "I am with you always, to the end of the age."[42]

Suggested Reading

Bock, Darrell L., and Daniel B. Wallace. *Dethroning Jesus: Exposing Popular Culture's Quest to Unseat the Biblical Christ*. Nashville: Thomas Nelson, 2007.

Bowman Jr., Robert M., and J. Ed Komoszewski. *Putting Jesus in His Place: The Case for the Deity of Christ*. Grand Rapids: Kregel, 2007.

Frame, John M. *The Doctrine of God: A Theology of Lordship*. Phillipsburg, NJ: P&R, 2002.

Discussion Questions

1. What evidence do we have that Jesus was considered to be God well before the Council of Nicea?
2. Is there an inherent contradiction between Jesus being both God and man? Why or why not?
3. What questions of Jesus support his divinity?
4. How can we reconcile the meekness of Jesus with his deity?
5. Which three aspects of Christ presented here support his deity? Why are they important?
6. Why is the doctrine of Christ's deity important?
7. Why is Christ's continuing presence with the believer vital for the Christian life?

How Do You Follow Him?

7

Relationship with Him

"Why are you weeping?"

Norman Rockwell's well-known painting from 1943, "Freedom from Want," presents a classic vision of an extended family gathered around the table to celebrate a bounteous holiday feast. While lack of food is still a problem for too many in the United States, for most people the major want is not in the belly. More and more Americans are starving instead for significant relationships.

In 2006, the *American Sociological Review* published a disturbing study, "Social Isolation in America." Researchers Miller McPherson, Lynn Smith-Lovin, and Matthew E. Brashears reported a "remarkable drop" in the size of people's core network of confidants—those with whom they could talk about important matters.[1]

As of 2004, the average American had just two close friends, compared with an average of three in 1985. Those reporting no confidants at all jumped from 10 percent to 25 percent. Even the share of Americans reporting a healthy circle of four or five friends had plunged from 33 percent to just over 15 percent.

Increasingly, those whom we consider close friends—if we have any—are household members, not people who "bind us to community and neighborhood." Our wider social connections seem to be shriveling like a turkey left for too long in the oven.

"You usually don't expect major features of social life to change very much from year to year or even decade to decade," Smith-Lovin, a sociologist at Duke University, told the news media.

Some may contend that the trend is no big deal, because the population is growing older and more racially diverse, and these demographic groups usually have smaller networks where friendships form. However, the nation's increasing level of education, the study says, should more than offset those factors (because, it argues, education often brings more social contacts). Yet our isolation has increased, leaving us at higher risk for a host of physical, social, and psychological ailments.

Certainly, the pressure to isolate ourselves is longstanding. Back in the 1960s, cultural critics Simon and Garfunkel noted the temptation to fall into what is now innocuously called cocooning: "I've built walls, a fortress deep and mighty, that none may penetrate. I have no need of friendship; friendship causes pain. It's laughter and it's loving I disdain."[2]

Created to Relate

Still, human beings were created for relationships. Everywhere you go, you see people talking into cell phones or texting one another: at school, at work, on the road, on vacation, even at church. People young and old want to connect, to build relationships in our hectic and hurried society. How else can you explain the popularity of websites such as Facebook and MySpace—where we can reach across the relational void and tell complete strangers intimate details about ourselves?

One of the things that made the television show *Seinfeld* so intriguing to viewers was the utter freedom the characters had to just burst in on each others' lives, completely unannounced. They may not have had much of significance to talk about, but George, Elaine, Kramer, and Jerry had *access*.

This desire for relationships, though hard to satisfy, is perfectly natural and good. God created us not to be isolated individuals, but to have significant relationships with others. God *wants* us to have good friends. The Bible tells us indirectly that the one God himself exists in a relationship of Persons we call the Trinity: Father, Son, and Holy Spirit.[3] When God placed the man in the Garden of Eden, he also placed a woman, because "it is not good for the man to be alone."[4]

Where Are You?

But there is a much deeper friendship that many people overlook. God himself dwelled with Adam and Eve in an intimate and joyful relationship, a relationship that was ruptured only by their sin. Genesis 3:8–9 says, "And they heard the sound of the LORD God walking in the garden in the cool of the day, and the man and his wife hid themselves from the presence of the LORD God among the trees of the garden. But the LORD God called to the man and said to him, 'Where *are* you?'"

Down through the centuries, God still asks, "Where are you?" In the time of Moses, God told the Israelites to build a tabernacle, a place to worship him. As Exodus 25:8 says, "let them make me a sanctuary, that I may dwell in their midst."

Later, God allowed the temple to be destroyed because of the unfaithfulness of his people. But he never stopped seeking to restore our broken relationship with him. As we saw in the previous two chapters, he came to earth as a man, Jesus Christ, so our relationship could be restored. John 1:14 says, "And the Word became flesh and dwelt [literally, *pitched his tent*] among us." And this desire to repair that relationship springs not from any lack on God's part, nor any attractive moral perfection on ours, but simply from his loving heart. As Paul noted, "but God shows his love for us in that while we were still sinners, Christ died for us."[5]

Other Religions

For all their wondrous architecture and surprising insights into the human condition, the world's other great religions have nothing like this idea of God seeking intimacy with created beings. India has 330 million gods who are worshiped and appeased twenty-four hours a day. But most Hindus will tell you that the highest reality, Brahman, is impersonal and without attributes. Much of Hindu religion is a striving for morality and spiritual discipline so that one can escape the wearying karmic cycle of death and rebirth and death. This presumed escape for good Hindus is not into the arms of a loving heavenly father, but a surrendering of personality in which the soul becomes one with Brahman, "much as a drop of water is dropped into the ocean."[6] What relationships can a religious system by itself produce and nurture, when the basis of such relationships—personality—is categorically denied?

Buddhism, an offshoot of Hinduism, tries to steer a "Middle Way" for devotees between indulgence and asceticism. Buddhists do this through the disciplined adoption of right views, goals, speech, conduct, lifestyle, efforts, awareness, and concentration.[7] While there are several schools, one of the key beliefs of Buddhism, according to scholar Terry Muck, is that all of reality is conditioned and impermanent. Another is that the individual self is a construct of historical and cultural forces. These forces must be overcome to achieve "enlightenment."[8] Again, if personality is not lasting, what hope is there for relationships?

And what of Islam? While the God of Islam is mighty and merciful, he is wholly other. Scholar of Islam Warren Larson notes that in the Muslim religion,

> God's mercy is subordinate to his sovereign power and subject to his ironclad will. One cannot but conclude therefore that divine love in Islam is reciprocal and why most Muslims cannot say: "God is love." In Islam, God is all-powerful and distant, not personally involved with people. Essentially, he says, "Some to heaven, some to hell and I care not." Heaven depends on a divine fiat; he makes an arbitrary decision. In fact, not one of Allah's ninety-nine names suggests he is longing and willing to save us. In Islam, God has the power, but apparently lacks the will to save lost, helpless sinners.[9]

Thus we see that the world's great non-Christian religions have no answer for man's persistent quest, his driving thirst, to relate with the divine. Christianity does; and the highest, clearest expression of this is seen in Christ. As John Stott says, "There is a thirst that none but Christ can satisfy. There is a thirst that none but he can quench. There is an inner emptiness that none but he can fill."[10] Now we will turn to the questions Jesus asked that shed light on his desire to relate to us—and for us to be in a right relationship with him.

A Man Born Blind

This desire for loving relationship often comes through loud and clear in Jesus's conversations with people with disabilities. Jesus said, "Blessed are the poor in spirit,"[11] and few things in life remind you of your spiritual poverty and drive you to pray as much as a physical disability. While it is not always true, a physical handicap often dispels the illusion that we are in control of our lives. Pain and disappointment force us to ask questions that the able-bodied too often put off. Disability encourages us to look away from ourselves and up to God. Not surprisingly, Jesus often used disability to build bridges with people.

One day he came upon a man who was known to have been blind from birth.[12] The disciples voiced a commonly held prejudice of the day: "Rabbi, who sinned, this man or his parents, that he was born blind?" They wanted a pat theological answer that would comfortably explain the man's pitiful condition. No doubt they also were seeking reassurance that such a fate wouldn't befall them or their loved ones.

Note the question was *who* sinned, not even *whether* someone sinned at all. They assumed that a life of disability was just punishment for sin. Few people today, who know some of the scientific reasons for handicaps, would draw that conclusion. But don't be too hard on the disciples. We're not really much more compassionate. Sometimes it seems as if our own age—with all its commitment to curb cuts and handicapped parking—actually suffers from the same kind of fear and loathing when it comes to disabled people. As author and activist Joni Eareckson Tada has said, "People have a fundamental fear of disabilities."[13]

Jesus told the disciples that their focus—seeking someone to blame for the man's blindness—was all wrong. They were asking the wrong question: Who sinned? The key actor in this man's suffering was not the blind man, but God. "It was not that this man sinned, or his parents," Jesus said, "but that the works of God might be displayed in him."

Then Jesus gave his followers a gritty object lesson in what those works might look like: He stooped, spat on the dusty ground, and made mud with his saliva. Next he scooped up some of the mixture with his fingers and rubbed it like a salve on the man's eyes. Then he told the blind man to wash it off in the nearby Pool of Siloam. The man, probably with a mixture of excitement and fear, bumped his way to the centuries-old spot where Hezekiah's water tunnel emerged from the city wall in Jerusalem.[14] A few minutes later, no doubt, he came running back, eyes shining.

But unfortunately the story does not end at this happy climax. Jesus had healed the man on the Sabbath, which the Jewish leaders said was prohibited work. Seeking to discredit the new movement, they ejected the man from the local synagogue for standing up for Jesus. This effectively blacklisted him from much of the community's life—a devastating blow in first-century Israel. Then we have this remarkable scene:

> Jesus heard that they had cast him [the formerly blind man] out, and having found him he said, "*Do you believe in the Son of Man?*" He answered, "And who is he, sir, that I may believe in him?" Jesus said to him, "You have seen him, and it is he who is speaking to you." He said, "Lord, I believe," and he worshiped him.[15]

Jesus, aware of what happened, sought out the man and engaged him on a personal level. And he went for the spiritual jugular, asking not whether his eyes worked or whether he would be able to find a new "church home." No, Jesus's main concern was whether the man, who had received his physical sight, had also received his spiritual sight. Jesus was asking, "Do you know me?"

The man, sensitized through his experience as a living object lesson, but reviled as a base sinner by the religious intelligentsia—"born in utter sin," they said—was ready to commit to a life-giving relationship with the Lord. Even today Jesus reaches out to the downtrodden and despised, asking the same basic question: "Do you believe?" The poor in spirit will answer, as the formerly blind man did, "Yes." Do *we* also have eyes to see, to relate to Jesus in faith?

Blind and Lame

On another occasion, the relationship came *before* the healing. Jesus and his disciples were walking near Jericho, accompanied by a crowd. A blind man by the side of the road heard the commotion and began shouting out one of Jesus's most well known messianic titles. "Son of David!"[16] he persistently, desperately roared above the din, "have mercy on me!"[17] Jesus stopped, had the blind man brought to him, and asked the most obvious question in the world: "*What do you want me to do for you?*" Now Jesus could not have failed to notice that the man was blind—and to know that the man wanted to be healed. So why would he ask the question?

As a father of young children, I think I have at least a partial answer. Often I know what my kids want before they ask, whether it be a certain kind of breakfast cereal, a toy, or simply my undivided attention. But does this mean I mechanically supply the need immediately, without being asked? Not at all. Part of the joy in our relationship is the actual *relating* with one another. I allow my children to tell me their needs in their own words. Their unique facial expressions, verbal formulations, and dependence on their father bring me delight. Once, when I shared the last sips of my soda with one of my boys, he said with real satisfaction, "That was my first taste of Pepsi." It doesn't sound like much, but such interactions bring joy.

I see that dynamic at work in this scene. After Jesus asks the blind man to clearly state his request, there is no doubt that it will be fulfilled. "[The blind man] said, 'Lord, let me recover my sight.' And Jesus said to him, 'Recover your sight; your faith has made you well.' And immediately he recovered his sight and followed him, glorifying God." Jesus rewards the man's trust with divine healing. The relationship, brought out by the question, both precedes and follows the miracle. The man knew Jesus and, because of that knowledge, followed. The miracle, compared to his real need for relationship, is almost incidental.

Similarly, as we saw in chapter 4, with desperate faith, a woman with a long-term discharge of blood came up behind Jesus and touched the fringe of his clothing—and was instantly cured. But this felt need was not the main point for Jesus.

> And Jesus, perceiving in himself that power had gone out from him, immediately turned about in the crowd and said, "*Who touched my garments?*"[18]

In a sense, the question was unnecessary. The healing had already taken place. What more needed to be said? Others required his attention, didn't they? But Jesus wants details, and he painstakingly stops his busy schedule to get them. Jesus desires to know the person who has exercised such trust in him. In the midst of a brutally taxing ministry, he's willing to spend time with a woman everyone else has overlooked. The Gospel of Mark reports,

And he looked around to see who had done it. But the woman, knowing what had happened to her, came in fear and trembling and fell down before him and told him the whole truth. And he said to her, "Daughter, your faith has made you well; go in peace, and be healed of your disease."[19]

Another follower gained? Yes, and more than that—a friend, even a daughter. Those who follow Jesus are brought into a family relationship with the Lord of heaven and earth. "*Who is my mother, and who are my brothers?*" Jesus asks. "Whoever does the will of my Father in heaven is my brother and sister and mother."[20]

Of course, Jesus sometimes bestowed his gifts on those who were not ready to follow him. By the Sheep Gate of the temple in Jerusalem, Jesus comes upon a man who had been lame for thirty-eight years.[21] Just imagine that for a minute: What were you—or your parents—doing thirty-eight years ago? I was a kid who had recently been mainstreamed from a special school for the disabled into a regular public elementary school. When I think of all the struggles, joys, and challenges I have faced in those intervening four decades— college, career twists, marriage, grad school, children, multiple moves—I can hardly believe it. You can probably say the same. *That* is how long this man, by another ancient pool, called Bethesda, had been in this difficult condition. Waiting hopelessly for a miracle by the pool, the man was an anonymous lump among many other anonymous lumps.

Jesus strikes up a conversation by asking the man, "*Do you want to be healed?*" Again, a seemingly obvious query, but the man fumbles it, complaining that he is not agile enough to get into the pool ahead of his fellow disabled competitors. With the solution standing before him, the invalid focuses only on his problems, rattling off a litany of excuses as to why he cannot be healed. Like many of us trapped in a naturalistic worldview, the man's tiny universe has no room for God's power. But that doesn't stop Jesus, who is intent on performing another sign, another act of mercy, on the Sabbath.

Instead of explaining all this to him, Jesus simply cuts to the chase, ordering him, "Get up, take up your bed, and walk." The man didn't know Jesus from Adam, but he heard the divine command and obeyed without question. Unfortunately, the Jewish legalists caught up with this former invalid and accused him of breaking the Sabbath for the crime of carrying his pallet— apparently unmoved that he had been miraculously healed. They also wanted to know who was guilty of healing him.

Later, Jesus found the man—note who is still taking the initiative in this relationship—and warned him enigmatically to "sin no more, or something worse may happen to you." I don't know whether this indicates that the man's disability was the result of sin. Surely some disabilities are (think of people injured by drunken drivers). In one sense, it doesn't really matter. As in the case of the man born blind, Jesus's focus is not on the past, but on the future.

But the man quickly ran (presumably using his strengthened legs) straight to the religious authorities, with whom he apparently wanted to curry favor, to rat out Jesus. I guess that his heart still wasn't right, and the opportunity for further relationship was lost. It's a hard truth: not all whom Jesus blesses will respond in faith. Think of the multitudes who seemingly start well in their Christian lives, but whose zeal is choked out by the cares of this world or burned by the heat of persecution. The fact that you spoke with Jesus once is no guarantee that you will not go spiritually deaf. As in *The Polar Express*, only those with faith can hear the jingling of the Christmas bell. Do we *want* to be healed?

Relating beyond the Grave

Jesus's commitment to relationships continues beyond the grave. One of his most heroic followers was Mary of Magdala in Galilee. Jesus had cast seven demons out of her, and she in turn followed him all the way to the cross, even when the male disciples—Peter most conspicuously—denied him and fled. Then after Jesus's crucifixion, she and some other women came to the tomb to finish his corpse's preparation for the grave. But on Sunday morning, a confused and distraught Mary Magdalene stands weeping outside Jesus's open and empty tomb, wondering who has moved his body.

> She turned around and saw Jesus standing, but she did not know that it was Jesus. Jesus said to her, "*Woman, why are you weeping? Whom are you seeking?*" Supposing him to be the gardener, she said to him, "Sir, if you have carried him away, tell me where you have laid him, and I will take him away." Jesus said to her, "Mary." She turned and said to him in Aramaic, "Rabboni!" (which means Teacher).[22]

Again, Jesus knew perfectly well why she was crying and whom she was seeking. She thought she had forever lost her teacher, redeemer, and friend. There was no need to ask. But he asked anyway.

Jesus was gently engaging this woman who had stood by him for months, if not years. I suppose he could have simply said, "Mary, open your eyes! It's me, *Jesus*! No need to weep now!" He could have short-circuited her grief, but he didn't. He asked questions that forced her to acknowledge her loss while simultaneously pointing her to a world-shattering hope. And in fact God is often found at life's low points. John Newton's conversion began during a horrific storm at sea. Charles Colson and Jonathan Aitken, two convicted and disgraced former government officials, found Christ while in prison. I found him while struggling to find lasting relationships and a reason to live. Jesus doesn't always rescue us from hard times; he meets us in them.

Later that day, two emotionally crushed disciples were trudging the seven miles from Jerusalem to a village called Emmaus. A stranger appeared and began walking alongside them.

And he said to them, "*What is this conversation that you are holding with each other as you walk?*" And they stood still, looking sad. Then one of them, named Cleopas, answered him, "Are you the only visitor to Jerusalem who does not know the things that have happened there in these days?" And he said to them, "*What things?*"[23]

The inquisitive stranger, of course, was Jesus. Again, he was allowing his friends to process their grief so that they would be prepared for the glorious news of his resurrection. We Christians often talk about having a "personal relationship with Jesus." But do we allow *him* to personally relate to *us*, to walk next to us in our sorrows and triumphs, asking his probing questions along the way?[24] And do we walk beside others who are suffering with the same kind of patient gentleness?

Then, waiting to reveal himself at dawn on a beach in Galilee, Jesus calls out to his weary and discouraged disciples, "*Children, do you have any fish?*"[25] Again, Jesus knows the answer. He was not looking for information, but for relationship.

And now we come to Simon Peter, who tried to inaugurate the kingdom with a sword and—when that failed—denied his Lord three times during the night. After the resurrection, Jesus is walking along the beach with Peter, who is to be pillar of the early church.

When they had finished breakfast, Jesus said to Simon Peter, "*Simon, son of John, do you love me more than these?*" He said to him, "Yes, Lord; you know that I love you." He said to him, "Feed my lambs." He said to him a second time, "*Simon, son of John, do you love me?*" He said to him, "Yes, Lord; you know that I love you." He said to him, "Tend my sheep." He said to him the third time, "*Simon, son of John, do you love me?*" Peter was grieved because he said to him the third time, "Do you love me?" and he said to him, "Lord, you know everything; you know that I love you." Jesus said to him, "Feed my sheep. Truly, truly, I say to you, when you were young, you used to dress yourself and walk wherever you wanted, but when you are old, you will stretch out your hands, and another will dress you and carry you where you do not want to go." (This he said to show by what kind of death he was to glorify God.) And after saying this he said to him, "Follow me."[26]

Here Peter, who denied Christ three times, is given the grace to affirm his love three times. But it is a severe grace. As Peter follows Jesus, he will be led to his own cross. Following Jesus, relating to him who for love took our sins upon himself, is no mere walk on the beach. Jesus calls us, known or unknown, great or small, to carry our own cross. But the promises of his presence more than make up for the burdens of the Christian life.

And while we have not seen Jesus face to face as his disciples did, we have God's promise in the Bible, "I will never leave you nor forsake you." It's a relationship we can count on—both now and for eternity.

Why? Because God is a God of relationship. As Revelation 21:3–4 says, "And I heard a loud voice from the throne saying, 'Behold, the dwelling place of God is with man. He will dwell with them, and they will be his people, and God himself will be with them as their God. He will wipe away every tear from their eyes, and death shall be no more, neither shall there be mourning nor crying nor pain anymore, for the former things have passed away.'"

Suggested Reading

Holladay, Tom. *The Relationship Principles of Jesus*. Grand Rapids: Zondervan, 2008.

Piper, John. *Desiring God: Meditations of a Christian Hedonist*. Sisters, OR: Multnomah, 1986.

Stafford, Tim. *Personal God: Can You Really Know the One Who Made the Universe?* Grand Rapids: Zondervan, 2008.

Stott, John. *Why I Am a Christian*. Downers Grove, IL: InterVarsity, 2003.

Discussion Questions

1. Why are so many people starving for significant relationships?
2. Why does the God of the Bible work so diligently to relate to us?
3. How is Christianity different from other world religions in this regard?
4. What are some ways we can come alongside hurting people?
5. How do physical needs and spiritual needs relate?
6. What should we do when people reject our attempts at relating to them?
7. What is the hope of relationships for the Christian?

8

Faith in Him

"Do you believe?"

Christine and I, having been married for about a year, were part of a church-based group sharing behind the Iron Curtain what we knew of Jesus Christ. Daily we were on the streets and in the parks outside the walls of the ancient city of Krakow. The Polish people we met were bright, thoughtful, and articulate. But steeped in the rigid Roman Catholicism most were born into, and targeted with atheist propaganda, these people—students, mostly—didn't know that they could have a relationship with God by trusting in Christ and his finished work on the cross. They mostly believed that God's favor is earned through good works and acts of piety. Patiently we explained our experience with the gospel—that God's love is a gift that can be earned only through faith.[1] Explaining such rich theological concepts to complete strangers was difficult work, made tougher because of the language and culture barriers.

But we had a dedicated helper—a university-educated translator who accepted us as friends with open arms. He was a self-described cultural Catholic with little personal experience of actually believing his beliefs. In fact, he was wracked with doubts. But as he listened to us, he began to wonder if religion might be more than a human institution.

One day he asked if we would sit down to answer his own religious questions, which were numerous. With a basic understanding of apologetics and evangelism, but feeling a duty in our short time there to reach out only to those who were genuinely searching, we wanted to gauge his spiritual interest before investing this amount of time.

So I asked our translator what I thought was a probing question: "If I answer all of your intellectual objections satisfactorily, will you become a Christian?"

"Yes," he said simply and directly. So one by one we examined his objections and doubts concerning the divinity of Christ, the trustworthiness of the Bible, and other issues. While I am no expert in such matters, I thought I handled the conversation quite well, if I do say so myself. Over two hours later, we sat back, mentally exhausted. I spoke first.

"Did I answer all of your intellectual objections to the Christian faith?"

"Yes," he admitted.

"Do you want to become a Christian?"

Our translator's unexpected answer floored me: "No."

"Why not?" I fairly demanded of him. "No" was not part of our bargain!

"I'm not ready to make a commitment."

That day I learned a valuable lesson. Faith in Christ is much more than intellectual assent. It is a matter of trust, a thing of the heart. That has been driven home to me the last few years. We have seen a confident resurgence of atheism in the public square, exemplified, for example, by Sam Harris in his *Letter to a Christian Nation* and Richard Dawkins in *The God Delusion*.

While multitudes of good Christian responses have been published, I wrote a little column explaining why Christianity makes sense to me. I briefly listed ten things that help me believe, such as the existence of beauty, the apparent fine-tuning of the universe for humanity, the honesty of the Bible about its sinful leading figures, and the freedom and prosperity that have generally followed the spread of Christianity.[2] It was all pretty basic stuff, and I made no proof claims.

The scores of responses by atheists to the column were interesting. "Is that the best you've got?" one fairly screeched in an online comment. Others, equally unmoved, chortled that I had proven nothing, offering their own alternative explanations to the data I had presented. Of course, just from my experience with my Polish translator friend, I knew going in that you cannot prove Christ, any more than you can prove love. Yet that doesn't mean they are unreal or unimportant—far from it. As a wise man stated two millennia ago: "without faith it is impossible to please [God]."[3] Not surprisingly, Jesus was keenly interested in the faith of those he encountered.

Questions of Belief

Over and over Jesus asked variations of "Do you believe?" The Greek word usually translated *believe* is *pisteuo* in the New Testament. It is also rendered in English as *to have faith in, to trust in, to commit to,* and *to rely on.*[4] Thus, New Testament belief involves casting one's lot, entrusting one's life, to someone else. It means living with abandon.

The apocryphal story is sometimes told of the tightrope walker standing at Niagara Falls, his line stretched out like a thread over the roaring waters. To the watching crowd he asks, "How many of you believe I can safely make it across?" Without hesitation, all of the onlookers shout encouragement or raise their hands. Then the man fixes his eyes on the audience and says mischievously, "Now who among you will trust me to carry you across the falls?" The people are suddenly silent. All that can be heard is the cascading torrent. *That* kind of cast-your-lot-with-me faith can be dangerous.

But it was a dangerous faith Jesus sought—and still does.

- To the man born blind, he asks, *"Do you believe in the Son of Man?"*[5]
- To Martha, who is grieving over the inexplicable death of her beloved brother, Jesus says, "I am the resurrection and the life. Whoever believes in me, though he die, yet shall he live, and everyone who lives and believes in me shall never die. *Do you believe this?"*[6]
- Moments later, Jesus tells the assembled mourners to open the tomb of Lazarus, whose body has been decomposing for four days. In a classic understatement, Martha reminds him that the corpse will have an "odor." Jesus answers, *"Did I not tell you that if you believed you would see the glory of God?"*[7]
- To his confused and anxious disciples during the Last Supper, Jesus tells of God the Father's love and his own intimate relationship with the first person of the Trinity. The disciples, relieved by his "plain speaking," blurt out, "Now we know that you know all things . . . we believe that you came from God." Knowing that severe tribulation is ahead for all of them, Jesus asks, *"Do you now believe?"*[8]

Faith in the New Testament is not about approving a course of action, signing off on a memo, or hoping for the best. It is about life and death. It is about blindness being cured, men being raised from the dead, the horrid forces of entropy at work in every life (in or out of the tomb) being reversed, and suffering being faced with confidence and peace. Do we *believe* in spite of it all? Belief in Jesus is not a cold, scientific acceptance of the unavoidable, for such faith saves nothing and no one. As another wise man noted of this kind of lifeless belief, "Even the demons believe—and shudder!"[9]

John Stott likens saving faith to opening the door of your life:

> You can believe in Christ intellectually and admire him; you can say your prayers to him through the keyhole (I did for many years); you can push coins at him under the door to keep him quiet; you can be moral, decent, upright and good; you can be religious; you can have been baptized and confirmed; you can be deeply versed in the philosophy of religion; you can be a theological student and even an ordained minister—and still not have opened the door to Christ. There is no substitute for this.[10]

Continuing Faith

Of course, such belief is not a one and done. The door must remain open. A faith that saves is a faith that continues. Jesus's questions probe the sincerity of our faith through all of life's ups and downs. Will we trust him despite the hardships that inevitably come our way, or will we grow discouraged or angry and walk away? Have we really cast our lot with him? Times of suffering will tell. This doesn't mean we will never doubt, however. Doubt is a normal part of every healthy life, but this does not give us license to wallow in it.

We cannot ignore our doubts, but must continually overcome them. When Jesus walks on the water toward his boat-bound disciples, Peter steps out to join him. But when Peter looks not at Jesus but at the stormy weather, he begins to sink like a rock beneath the wild waves. Instead of stroking his impetuous disciple's self-esteem ("Gee, Peter, you made it pretty far and couldn't be expected to do better"), Jesus saves him with a questioning rebuke: "*O you of little faith, why did you doubt?*"[11]

Such questions sting like salt spray on a bitter day. They throw any quaint notions of "Jesus meek and mild" into turmoil. By assuming that faith—not doubt—is to be the default setting for every Christian, they force us to doubt our doubts. And as we do, may we worship the master of creation, saying with the awe-struck disciples, "Truly you are the Son of God."[12]

No one is exempt from Jesus's searching questions about faith. To the mourners for the daughter of Jairus, Jesus asks, "*Why are you making a commotion and weeping?*"[13] Such words sound harsh to our postmodern ears (doesn't he understand our *grief*?), but only if we forget who is asking them. The Lord of Life is among us even now, ready to bring life from death in response to the smallest indication of faith. "*Do you believe that I am able to do this?*"[14] Jesus asks two blind men—and us. *Do* we?

Yet Jesus understands our doubts. To the doubting disciples he allows that they may have faith as inconsequential as a tiny grain of mustard—and yet God can use that speck to work his wonders.[15] To a father who has confessed less than full faith in Jesus's ability to deliver his demon-possessed boy, the Lord provides healing anyway.[16] Talking about God's ability to provide, Jesus gently reminds his followers, "*which of you by being anxious can add a single hour to his span of life?*"[17] God will provide, so don't stress.

When Prayers Go Unanswered

And yet we must face the fact that not every prayer is answered according to our desire. Some must simply wait. After spitting on the eyes and laying his hands on a blind man at Bethsaida, the Lord asks, "*Do you see anything?*" Quavering, the man replies, "I see men, but they look like trees, walking."[18] Imagine for a moment being in this man's sandals: The Healer has come, has attempted a cure, and then wants to know whether it took—and you have to tell him that your vision is still blurry! Everyone else seems to be healed with a word, with a touch, instantly.[19] Why not *you*? Are you really a worse sinner than the rest, as you have long suspected? What's wrong with your faith?

When I was a new Christian, back in high school, some fellow believers excitedly invited me to a tent meeting at their church. A famous "faith healer" was coming to town, and I was urged to go. While I don't think they promised that this man would definitely heal me of my lifelong cerebral palsy, the implication was pretty obvious (at least to me). Alone, I wrestled with the decision. Jesus's question—"*Do you want to be healed?*"[20]—was especially relevant. Yes, I wanted to be free of my disability and the ever-present sense of isolation it brought, and the humiliations, large and small, that were its children. But what if I went and *nothing happened*? A son of the Enlightenment, I was still new to the faith and had great skepticism about miracles breaking through into our clockwork world—and still do.

Yet the risk of staying home seemed greater than the risk of going, so I drove to the church, not telling my parents the precise purpose of the meeting. (We were a non-churchgoing family, except for me.) As I sat there under the tent, I saw others in the congregation go forward, have this man pray over them, and then fall backwards as he forcefully touched them on their foreheads (thankfully, helpers were always there to catch them). This was the sign they had been "healed."

So up I went, and soon I stood unsteadily before the faith healer. I can't remember what he said, but it was something about God's power. Then he put his right hand on my forehead, and I felt—what?—a slight impetus, a push. I fell backwards, and as I collapsed into the arms of a waiting attendant, I heard the faith-filled murmur of the audience.

Of course, I soon discovered I wasn't healed, and I immediately sought to make sense of what had happened. Was my belief in healing wishful thinking? Was the faith healer a fraud? Was God real? As I stood off by myself at the end of the evening, I tried to understand it all. "Lord," I prayed silently, "if I am truly healed, please let me know." Then suddenly I felt something like a wave, but not a wave, wash over me. It was not an emotion I could have worked up, and it was not a push. For a moment I was enveloped in a state of love, serenity, and peace that was more personal and profound than anything I have ever experienced. When it was over, I found myself sitting safely and comfortably in a folding chair I hadn't noticed was there.

I took this incident as a sign that my healing, if not immediate, would be coming soon. But as the days of waiting stretched into weeks, months, and years, I faced doubt, disappointment, and occasional devastation. Was my faith defective? Or was God a sham? Was the experience at the end of the revival meeting of God—or the devil?

I'd like to have an easy answer for what happened, but I don't. For a time my faith in Christ was shaken. But, like the blind man who received partial healing, now I'm willing to trust even while my vision remains blurred.

First, I believe that, in God's eyes, I *am* being healed of my main handicap, which is a sinful heart. I can see increasing love for God and others in the nitty-gritty of my life. Like the young man who was lowered to Jesus for healing but who first received attention for a deeper need,[21] I now realize that some things take priority over physical wholeness. Besides the spiritual strengthening I have experienced because of my disability, my children are also growing in ways I could not have expected when I fell back into that folding chair. They are more loving and accepting of people with differences, whether those differences be Down syndrome or another ethnicity.

And second, my disability brings God glory in ways my healing never could. As I seek to make my way through life, not doing anything particularly heroic, people often tell me they see God at work. They are encouraged not by my wholeness but by my brokenness. I overcome this affliction bit by bit, daily. When my weakness is ultimately and completely overcome, in the resurrection, God will get a thousand times more glory. I see my disability as a normal part of life in a fallen world. One day what has fallen, including my physical body with all its imperfections, will be restored. The book of Romans says,

> the sufferings of this present time are not worthy to be compared with the glory that is to be revealed to us. For the creation waits with eager longing for the revealing of the sons of God. For the creation was subjected to futility, not willingly, but because of him who subjected it, in hope that the creation itself will be set free from its bondage to corruption and obtain the freedom of the glory of the children of God.[22]

Right now creation is trapped in a bitter "bondage to decay," and us with it. Those with disabilities feel this enslavement to entropy more keenly than most. One day, perhaps sooner than you think, creation—including my body—will be set gloriously free, to the everlasting praise of God. Yes, God could heal me now, but for some mysterious reason he chooses not to. Because of that delay, the celebration will be that much greater when "the perishable puts on the imperishable."[23] Is *that* worth the wait? I think so, but no one ever said delayed gratification is easy. Just ask a kid waiting to tear open his packages on Christmas morning.

When God Says "No"

Other prayers, however, are turned aside. We don't always get what we ask for. Sometimes this is because the time is not right. Other times the request is not worthy. James, the brother of the Lord, reminds us, "you do not have because you do not ask," and "you ask and do not receive, because you ask wrongly, to spend it on your passions."[24] Sometimes, mercifully, the answer is no.

"*What do you want?*" Jesus asks the mother of two disciples. Hearing that she desires for them to sit beside him with special honor in the kingdom, Jesus is polite, but direct: "to sit at my right hand and at my left is not mine to grant, but it is for those for whom it has been prepared by my Father."[25] The answer is no. What must the woman have thought as her prayer was turned aside? While bold, persistent faith can move our heavenly Father to grant our requests,[26] sometimes it takes more faith to keep going when the loving answer comes back, "No."

Despite the confident assurances of well-funded faith healers and other religious charlatans that if you just have "enough faith" then God, like a genie, will take care of your every wish, we all know, if we are honest, that it doesn't always work that way. And would we really want it to? Can a God who is obligated to his creatures, always rushing about fulfilling our whims, really be trusted to order heaven and earth rightly and to secure our salvation? This is not the God of Scripture, who says, "For as the heavens are higher than the earth, so are my ways higher than your ways, and my thoughts than your thoughts."[27] We cannot expect to understand this God all the time, and that's okay. We take some things on faith, as we ought.

Delighting the Lord

Of course, exercising this kind of faith—and *exercising* is certainly a meaningful word when it comes to belief—is not and should never become a dry, dusty legalism, a dutiful gritting of the teeth, something Christians do because we *have to*. Jesus was variously amazed, amused, and touched by the expressions of faith he encountered. Do we really think he would be less so in his glorified state?

Of the Roman centurion he exclaimed, "I tell you, *not even in Israel* have I found such faith!"[28] A repentant woman he assured, "Your faith has saved you; go in peace."[29] We have the same opportunity to delight our Lord and receive his blessing by the way we respond in faith. When some penny-pinching bean-counters denigrate the lavish, faith-filled act of a woman anointing Jesus's head with a flask of the first-century equivalent of Chanel No. 5, he briskly defends her, saying, "Leave her alone. *Why do you trouble her?* She has done a beautiful thing to me."[30] We have no business dousing the faith of anyone. Jesus apparently values extravagance for him more highly than responsible "stewardship."

When we exercise such extravagant faith, we open the door to new opportunities to see the Lord at work. When Jesus approached the soon-to-be-disciple Nathanael for the first time, he referred to the man's guileless character. When

Nathanael asked Jesus how he knew him, the Lord answered cryptically, "when you were under the fig tree, I saw you." While we don't know what else Jesus saw in this brief flash of divine omniscience, it was enough to convince Nathanael, who exclaimed, "Rabbi, you are the Son of God! You are the King of Israel!" Jesus, no doubt pleased with this sudden burst of faith, replied with a question and a commitment: *"Because I said to you, 'I saw you under the fig tree,' do you believe?* You will see greater things than these."[31]

Jesus loves even small expressions of genuine faith, and promises to reward them with even greater displays of his glory. Before my daughter was old enough to go to school, she heard about a terrible earthquake that killed tens of thousands of people in India. She had recently made a commitment to follow Christ and as an expression of her faith gave all of her money—six dollars and change—to a Christian relief agency to help alleviate the suffering. Did my daughter's compassionate expression of faith do all that much for the victims? Perhaps not. But somewhere in heaven Jesus marked down in his ledger the faithful gift of a child—perhaps next to his entry about the destitute widow who "put in more than all of them."[32] We don't know what my daughter's reward will be, any more than we know how Jesus rewarded the nameless widow. What we do know is that such acts do not go unnoticed, or unrewarded.

Practical Atheists

And yet so seldom do we act as if God and his promises are true. Like Peter, we take our eyes off the Savior and look at the howling winds of our lives— and we begin to sink. Jesus asks us, *"How many loaves do you have?"*[33] We see the immense needs around us and our own feeble resources and answer, "Not enough." We are insensate to the spiritual possibilities of faith. We are practical atheists, living as if God doesn't exist. Is this why so many today are tempted by atheism, because they see so few Christians living as if Jesus Christ is alive? After his resurrection, he asked his doubting disciples, *"Why are you troubled, and why do doubts arise in your hearts?"*[34]

He asks us the same. Looking back on my life, I can clearly see God's acts in my life: My marriage and the births of our three children were clearly *divine* gifts. God has used me repeatedly to help and encourage friends in their career paths. I have felt his presence in the midst of difficult personal struggles in ways that defy an easy materialistic explanation. Christ has used my words and example to bring hope and strength to audiences around the world. Facing thoughts of worthlessness and suicide as a teen, I am now an eyewitness to God's powerful, life-giving love.

And yet each day I wake up with the question: will I trust God today, or doubt him? For me, at least, trusting God is very much a case of "what have you done for me lately?" Jesus walks on water for me but then, seeing my persistent struggle to believe, feels compelled to ask, *"Where is your faith?"*[35]

A former pastor of mine, Kent Hughes, always encouraged the congregation to "believe what you believe." That's sometimes easier said than done—but it is indispensable to a faith-filled Christian life. Unfortunately, like the disciples, we are dull spiritually, our minds and hearts bound to this world.

Blind Faith

After Jesus had miraculously fed thousands—with plenty to spare—on two occasions, he told the disciples, "Beware of the leaven of the Pharisees and Sadducees."[36] Now they should have been familiar with this metaphor; he had already reminded them how the kingdom, like yeast, spreads thoroughly once it has been introduced.[37] Jesus appears to be saying in this instance that a little evil can go a long way. But the metaphor about the yeast of his opponents' teaching eluded his followers, their minds still reeling from the feeding miracles. They wondered: Where are we going to get more bread? Will Jesus come through again? Then Jesus gets what I can only describe as frustrated. His questions come rapid fire:

> *O you of little faith, why are you discussing among yourselves the fact that you have no bread? Do you not yet perceive? Do you not remember the five loaves for the five thousand, and how many baskets you gathered? Or the seven loaves for the four thousand, and how many baskets you gathered? How is it that you fail to understand that I did not speak about bread?*

This lack of faith plays out on several levels. First, the disciples lack spiritual *perception*. Having seen Jesus already meet their material needs in the past, they somehow fail to see that he is still present and that his love never fails. It's as if they are saying to their Lord, "Jesus, I know you supplied our need once, but I'm not quite sure you'll do it again." As time passes, their faith wavers.

Robertson McQuilkin, chancellor of Columbia International University, coined a statement that has stuck with me for two decades: "Let me get home before dark." McQuilkin's prayer was to get to the end of his life with his faith intact—because not everyone does.

Second, their *memory* has failed—figuratively, if not literally. We forget what God has done for us. This can happen in the sheer busyness of life; we are simply too harried—even by legitimate ministry—to recall all that God has done. That's why I like the annual church calendar, which highlights the key acts that God has done to secure our salvation, everything from the incarnation to the pouring out of the Holy Spirit. Further, God in the Old Testament repeatedly reminded the Jewish people about his saving acts through Scripture and through the Jewish festivals. They then replayed that history over and over. We need such reminders to keep our faith strong.

The same thing happens when Christians take communion, which is a picture of what God has done for us in Christ. Remembering the Lord's practical care in the past helps us face today—and tomorrow—with confidence. Some Christians find that writing down not just prayer *requests*, but also prayer *answers*, can be faith-building. Remembering is an act of faith.

Third, because they lacked sufficient faith, they *failed to understand* Jesus's deeper point. Their brains had hit a spiritual brick wall. Because Jesus asks us to love him with our mind,[38] this is a grievous failure. When we lack such insight, we cannot progress in our relationship with Christ. Our discipleship becomes stagnant. Like spiritual babies, we can digest only simple teachings—milk, not solid food.[39] The media scribe who said that believing Christians are "poor, uneducated, and easy to command" didn't understand basic discipleship. Jesus expects us to honor him with our minds. But if we refuse to approach him in an attitude of faith, our intellect will not lead us to ultimate truth. Think back to my translator in Poland. Head and heart go together in the Christian life, but heart must close the deal.

An Awake Faith

Faith, though so simple even a three-year-old can exercise it, nevertheless requires adult perseverance. As the mobs are about to close in and put him on the cross, Jesus goes to the Garden of Gethsemane to pray. He takes his three closest disciples—Peter, James, and John—to do something simple: prayerfully "watch."[40] Yet the stress and the late hour are too much for them, and they fall asleep—not once, not twice, but three times.

Jesus chides the leader, Peter: "*Simon, are you asleep? Could you not watch one hour?*" And later he asks the group: "*Are you still sleeping and taking your rest?*" God promises a future rest for his children,[41] but right now the battle rages, and we must remain alert. As the apostle Paul says, "the hour has come for you to wake from sleep. For salvation is nearer to us now than when we first believed."[42]

Football players risk serious injury every second they are on the field. Former center Bill Curry has said they must give 100 percent at all times, not merely to win, but to survive. For players who covet the respect of their teammates, loafing is not an option.[43] If undivided devotion is the norm in the world of sports, where new champions are crowned every year, how much more should it be so for faithful disciples of Jesus Christ, who seek an ultimate prize? Let's keep our faith awake.

Suggested Reading

Little, Paul E. *Know Why You Believe*. Downers Grove, IL: InterVarsity, 1968.

Packer, J. I. *Knowing God*. Downers Grove, IL: InterVarsity, 1973.

Strobel, Lee. *The Case for Faith Visual Edition*. Grand Rapids: Zondervan, 2005.

Discussion Questions

1. Can a person be reasoned into the kingdom of God? Why or why not?
2. Why is faith supposed to be the default setting for the Christian?
3. What then are we to do with honest doubts?
4. How does prayer figure into the faith-doubt equation?
5. How does remembering what God has done strengthen our faith?
6. How do mind and heart work together in bringing a person to faith?
7. Why does faith delight Jesus, and how can you delight him today?

9

Discipleship Directed by Him

"What are you seeking?"

He was not a general, a diplomat, an attorney, or an athlete. He was not anything that the world would consider great. Dietrich Bonhoeffer was a young pastor, and not a notably successful one, by the world's standards. A theologian, he was single-minded, but he was not simple. While many others in the clergy were co-opted by the National Socialist Party, or simply cowed into inaction or silence, Bonhoeffer spoke boldly against what he saw as a godless ideology. As Nazi tyranny spread across his native Germany, friends spirited the pastor out of the country out of concern for his safety. But he couldn't stay away.

"I shall have no right," he said, "to participate in the reconstruction of Christian life in Germany after the war if I do not share the trials of this time with my people. . . . Christians in Germany will face the terrible alternative of either willing the defeat of their nation in order that Christian civilization may survive, or willing the victory of their nation and [thereby] destroying our civilization. I know which of these alternatives I must choose; but I cannot make this choice in security."

Casting his safety aside, the pastor returned to Germany. He had decided the Christian thing to do was work for the overthrow of the vicious Nazi regime. But on April 5, 1943, the Gestapo arrested him in his parents' home and shipped him off to prison and various concentration camps. As the liberating Allies closed in, on April 9, 1945, the thirty-nine-year-old pastor was hung without trial, by special order of Heinrich Himmler.[1]

While Bonhoeffer's remains have never been found, his legacy lives on. In perhaps his greatest work, *The Cost of Discipleship*, the young pastor wrote, "When Christ calls a man, he bids him come and die."[2]

Counting the Cost

Such disciples, willing to die, are too rare these days. Non-Christians sometimes rightly criticize contemporary evangelicals for a certain shallowness not just in our worship services, but in our lives. Yet those who would follow Christ are bidden to come and die. Are we willing? Or is Jesus just the means to a happier, more satisfying life? Too many of us reach for the crown without taking up the cross.

The story is told of a man who stood up in a church service and began loudly proclaiming, as he walked down the aisle, that he was Jesus Christ. From his pulpit the minister shrewdly answered, "Then show me the nail prints in your hands." There were none, of course. But what about us?

Those who would be little Christs—*Christians*—will bear the marks of suffering. We will resemble Jesus not just in word, but also in deed. As Jesus said, "A disciple is not above his teacher."[3] So if Jesus suffered, we will suffer. Referencing his impending death, Jesus asked his disciples: "*Are you able to drink the cup that I drink, or to be baptized with the baptism with which I am baptized?*"[4] We cannot escape the fact that one of our callings as Christian disciples is suffering. It's guaranteed.[5]

As we observed in chapter 2, Jesus the rabbi was seeking disciples who would pass on his teachings. But it was more than that. His followers were to become *like* him. Unlike the students of other rabbis, they were to be judged not by their eventual independence as teachers in their own right, but by their faithfulness to him, both to his teachings and to his example. Jesus was "a man of sorrows, and acquainted with grief,"[6] and those who follow him will experience their own sorrows and griefs.

Don't come to Christ if you want an easy life. Relationships, through no fault of your own, may be strained or severed. You may lose out on certain "business opportunities." People may think you have gone off the deep end. You may be called upon to speak up when everyone else is silent, or to serve those who have no intention of paying you back.

But if you want to be like him, by all means, come. Just know that it won't be easy—but it will be worth it. Suffering builds character in ways a life of ease never could. Jesus never sugarcoated this hard truth. In fact, with penetrating questions he urged his would-be followers to first count the cost.

> Now great crowds accompanied him, and he turned and said to them, "If anyone comes to me and does not hate his own father and mother and wife and children

and brothers and sisters, yes, and even his own life, he cannot be my disciple. Whoever does not bear his own cross and come after me cannot be my disciple. *For which of you, desiring to build a tower, does not first sit down and count the cost, whether he has enough to complete it?* Otherwise, when he has laid a foundation and is not able to finish, all who see it begin to mock him, saying, 'This man began to build and was not able to finish.' *Or what king, going out to encounter another king in war, will not sit down first and deliberate whether he is able with ten thousand to meet him who comes against him with twenty thousand?* And if not, while the other is yet a great way off, he sends a delegation and asks for terms of peace. So therefore, any one of you who does not renounce all that he has cannot be my disciple."[7]

Once while in college I sat down to lunch with a close friend. I was burdened that he did not know God and determined to share with him the good news of eternal life and his need to repent and believe. Though I was nervous, the conversation went well. I patiently explained to my friend that, according to the Bible's standards, we all are sinners who need God's forgiveness. I told him that God freely offers him the gift of eternal life—not through anything he can do, but solely because of Christ's death and resurrection. My friend's only task was to believe this and receive Christ as Lord and Savior. No muss, no fuss, right?

My friend, though he didn't know much about the Bible, knew it wasn't quite that simple. And while I firmly believe that salvation is by faith, not by works,[8] my friend was right. A fairly typical college student, he liked to drink, sometimes to excess. He asked me if he would have to stop getting drunk if he became a Christian. I carefully allowed that while there are no moral hoops we must jump through before we exercise faith, after he became a Christian, it was entirely likely that the Lord would convict him that drunkenness is unhealthy and wrong, and that he would have to (indeed, want to) give it up.

My friend counted the cost that day—and decided the price was too high. Like the rich young man,[9] he went away, if not exactly sorrowful, still unwilling to give Jesus everything. To my knowledge, a quarter-century later, he remains outside the kingdom. While you or I might gasp at his shortsightedness, we at least have to give him credit: he counted the cost.

Have *we?* Are there any nail prints in our hands? People "accept Jesus" today—a popular but unbiblical term—for many reasons: their friends have done it; their parents want them to do it; they want to date someone in the church; they want to make business contacts; they are lonely and confused; they admire the man from Galilee. But many who make such a "decision" haven't grappled with the cost of discipleship, that it involves not only life, but death. The heat of persecution burns up their spindly spiritual roots; the cares of this world strangle their initial interest.[10]

One of my friends has a teenaged son who struggles with a bipolar disorder that causes him to experience tremendous mood swings that must be regulated by medication. The struggle has worn down this young man, who has been a professing Christian for many years. In his pain he has begun to rage at his family and at God. His suffering surprises him. It is an understandable but flawed view. Why are we so surprised by suffering, when Jesus himself suffered?

I wonder whether expectations were more honest in prior eras. The famous "Serenity Prayer," attributed to theologian Reinhold Niebuhr, was penned with suffering in mind. In it the author clearly exhibits trust in God whatever happens, honestly grappling with the cost of discipleship:

> God, give us grace to accept with serenity
> the things that cannot be changed,
> courage to change the things
> which should be changed,
> and the wisdom to distinguish
> the one from the other.
> Living one day at a time,
> enjoying one moment at a time,
> accepting hardship as a pathway to peace,
> taking, as Jesus did,
> this sinful world as it is,
> not as I would have it,
> trusting that you will make all things right,
> if I surrender to your will,
> so that I may be reasonably happy in this life,
> And supremely happy with you forever in the next.
> Amen.

So before we decide to "accept" Jesus, perhaps we ought to consider carefully his question: "*What are you seeking?*"[11] If we are seeking *him*, we will receive him, and a lot more besides—including suffering.

Serving Others

But suffering, while integral to discipleship, is not the last word. Suffering by itself can make us self-centered, because we focus only on our pain. But suffering with our eyes on Jesus gives us hope.[12] One way to keep our eyes on him while we suffer is to serve others. Instead of constantly being on the receiving end of help, we give it. And regardless of whether we wish to serve, service is not optional for the disciple. Jesus did not say, "If you have all of your needs met first then you can serve others." Instead, he says, "It is more blessed to give than to receive."[13] If we want to be blessed, we must give. We are to avail ourselves of this difficult blessing regularly—even when we suffer.

One day Jesus's disciples were arguing about which was the greatest. They apparently hadn't gotten the servanthood memo. So he gave them one, showing how the kingdom turns the world's value system on its head, in that those who are the greatest are the servants:

> The kings of the Gentiles exercise lordship over them, and those in authority over them are called benefactors. But not so with you. Rather, let the greatest among you become as the youngest, and the leader as one who serves. *For who is the greater, one who reclines at table or one who serves? Is it not the one who reclines at table?* But I am among you as the one who serves.[14]

Jesus would poignantly illustrate this brand of service at the Last Supper, just before the ultimate act of self-giving, his sacrificial death on the cross. In the upper room Jesus wraps himself in a towel—the humble garb of a slave—and washes his disciples' filthy feet. Then he drives the object lesson home with another question:

> When he had washed their feet and put on his outer garments and resumed his place, he said to them, *"Do you understand what I have done to you?* You call me Teacher and Lord, and you are right, for so I am. If I then, your Lord and Teacher, have washed your feet, you also ought to wash one another's feet. For I have given you an example, that you also should do just as I have done to you. Truly, truly, I say to you, a servant is not greater than his master, nor is a messenger greater than the one who sent him. If you know these things, blessed are you if you do them."[15]

Dangerous Discipleship

Such discipleship holds nothing back. It trusts the one who calls us and relates to us in love, and who calls us to follow, even to the cross. Such discipleship is dangerous. It forces us to live with abandon. That abandon is not confined to some airy spiritual realm, either. It is eminently practical. When Jesus said to count the cost, he wasn't being purely metaphorical.

One day Jesus told his disciples a curious parable about a dishonest business manager. The man, who knew he was about to be fired, settled his master's outstanding accounts for pennies on the dollar. The motive was not vindictiveness toward his employer, but so that these debtors would be grateful and take care of the steward when he lost his job. "The master," Jesus said, "commended the dishonest manager for his shrewdness." Then Jesus urged them to be as faithful with the money God entrusts to them as the manager was shrewd with his master's. The reason is not because money is so important, but because it ultimately isn't.

> One who is faithful in a very little is also faithful in much, and one who is dishonest in a very little is also dishonest in much. *If then you have not been faithful in the unrighteous wealth, who will entrust to you the true riches? And if you*

*have not been faithful in that which is another's, who will give you that which
is your own?* No servant can serve two masters, for either he will hate the one
and love the other, or he will be devoted to the one and despise the other. You
cannot serve God and money.[16]

A number of key discipleship principles surface in these questions. (1) We are
called to be faithful managers of *God's* money. Thus, it is to be spent ultimately
with *him* in mind. (2) Financial wealth can be unrighteous, or worldly (Greek
adikos).[17] While money can and should be used for God's glory (and our good),
too often it draws us away from God. As Paul said, "For the love of money is
a root of all kinds of evils. It is through this craving that some have wandered
away from the faith and pierced themselves with many pangs."[18] (3) There are
"true riches" that are more important and lasting than our financial assets.
(4) There is a definite link between how we spend (God's) temporary riches
and how much of these true riches we will receive as a reward. In this regard,
we do well to recall martyred missionary Jim Elliot's famous dictum: "He is
no fool who gives what he cannot keep to gain what he cannot lose."[19]

Yet in a high-tech economy measured in trillions of dollars, too often we
Christians give the equivalent of our pocket change and keep the rest for
ourselves. According to groups such as empty tomb inc., most professing
Christians give 3 percent or less to church-related causes.[20] While investing
to purchase an easy retirement never seems to end, giving to world missions
so that the unevangelized can enter God's rest scrapes by on relative crumbs.
As former Columbia International University President George Murray has
asked, "If missionaries are willing to go without financial equity to get the
gospel out, should we consider going without equity in order to help send
them?"[21]

These are excruciating questions that demand an honest response. When
my wife and I, fresh from our challenging but faith-building Christian grad
school experience, moved to our quaint (and largely God-fearing) Midwestern
community, we didn't think we had a problem with materialism. Aside from
our aging car, our financial wealth was measured in three digits. We didn't have
much, and we didn't much care. We had each other, and we had a call.

But then the homes, automobiles, and upscale lifestyles of the good Christian people we were getting to know started to register. Envy—at least my
own—started to take root. Quickly, our spacious two-bedroom apartment
became too small. It was a "bad investment" since we were just "throwing
our rent money away." So, earning two incomes, we discovered we qualified
to buy a nice three-bedroom townhome. Thrilled, we did, and our costs immediately shot up. (To be fair, so did our tax deduction.) Later, however, as
kids came along, we found that we "needed" a home with a real yard. So we
bought a modest raised ranch close to a good school, and our housing budget
leaped again. Yet, still comparing ourselves with our undeniably wealthier

neighbors, I continue to speak wistfully of the space and amenities we *don't* have. I suspect that I always will.

There are many reasons for our good-natured greed and coy covetousness. I believe it boils down to one thing: unbelief. We don't believe that God is (1) the ultimate source of joy, or (2) willing and able to meet our needs (and maybe just a little bit more). Such unbelief (which we will examine more fully in chapter 16) undeniably is a spiritual issue. Paul labeled greed as basic idolatry,[22] and so it is, because greedy people, to borrow a phrase, "exchange the truth of God for a lie, and worship and serve created things rather than the Creator."[23]

Yet while Jesus asks his disciples to be *faithful* with money—to trustingly share his wealth with others for his glory and their own ultimate reward—he does not end there. He also promises to provide. After telling his disciples that they are to follow his example and serve others, Jesus reminds them of an earlier episode when he sent them out on their own to minister. Unlike most short-term mission teams that go out today with extensive planning and resources, the apostles went with nothing. "*When I sent you out with no moneybag or knapsack or sandals,*" he asks, "*did you lack anything?*" They said, "Nothing."[24]

They lacked *nothing*.[25] Neither will we, but learning this lesson often takes time. Despite my bouts with greed, God has continued to supply all of our family's needs. We have faced modest or nonexistent incomes over two decades of marriage, multiple jobs and moves, three children, unexpected expenses, and the loss of a job. Yet we have never lacked homes, automobiles, food, and clothing—everything needed to live and serve him in the places to which he has called us. No, it hasn't always been easy, but the Lord has amply rewarded what little faith we have. Other disciples no doubt could say the same.

Fiery Followers

Our faithfulness to Jesus is primarily a response to his faithfulness to us. It does not stand on its own, but responds to his clear demonstration of love. And it is a passionate faithfulness. Our following of Jesus is never meant to be a dry, dusty obligation. We do not check Jesus off our list of daily chores. His love ignites our love and consumes our lives, which are to be sacrificed for his glory.[26] As John said, "We love because he first loved us."[27]

Jesus expects his disciples to demonstrate fervent commitment to him, as both salt and light. We are to be present in the world, adding the righteousness that it lacks. "*You are the salt of the earth,*" he stated in the Sermon on the Mount, "*but if salt has lost its taste, how shall its saltiness be restored? It is no longer good for anything except to be thrown out and trampled under people's feet.*"[28] Disciples who lose their saltiness are good for nothing. Jesus expects us to work hard in the world, not sit locked away in ivory towers. While there is a place for contemplation, thought, and prayer, the disciple never forgets ministry. Work is a mark of a true disciple. The word *disciple*, after all, is related to *discipline*.

Martin Luther sparked the Protestant Reformation after realizing he could never be good enough to earn God's favor, which comes as a gift. Yet this realization did not make him stop working for God. It made him realize his place of service was much wider. Leaving the monastery, he knew that Christian discipleship was not the call of a special few, but the gracious responsibility of all, whether butcher, baker, or candlestick maker. "Luther's return from the cloister to the world was the worst blow the world had suffered since the days of early Christianity," Bonhoeffer said. "The renunciation he made when he was a monk was child's play compared with that which he had to make when he returned to the world."[29]

Intimacy with Jesus

And yet following the King is a joyful vocation. And it is an *individual* joy. While many in recent years have rightly criticized the individualistic approach to God of American evangelicalism ("Just me and Jesus"), there is a significant element of truth in it. Jesus's call is always an individual call.

After Andrew left John the Baptist to follow Jesus, he quickly told his brother Simon and brought him to the man from Galilee. Jesus immediately sized up the impulsive fisherman, asking, *"So you are Simon the son of John? You shall be called Cephas."*[30] Cephas, which is Aramaic for *rock* (Peter is the Greek form), referenced something essential in the man's character, but which was not all that developed or evident to those around him. He would be a solid and fearless leader of the new Jesus movement.

Of course, Peter had his failings along the way: he sought to put himself first, punish those who blocked his way, and run from Christ's holiness. Speaking of rocks, Peter hit rock bottom the night Jesus was betrayed, denying his Lord three times. Emotionally unstable, Peter was hardly the rock Jesus made him out to be. Sometimes he seemed more like shifting sand. Yet through it all God was working to mold Peter into a rock of faith.

After the resurrection, the Lord returns to the beginning, reminding Peter three times of his initial call, canceling out each of his disciple's denials: *"Simon, son of John, do you love me more than these? . . . Simon, son of John, do you love me? . . . Simon, son of John, do you love me?"*[31] Each time Peter affirms his love for Jesus.[32] In this scene, we see that forgiveness is always available to the disciple, even for the worst sins.

Afterward, Peter became the rock Jesus always knew he would be, fearlessly standing up to the religious leaders who ordered him to shut up. "Whether it is right in the sight of God to listen to you rather than to God, you must judge," Peter proclaimed with the apostle John in Jerusalem, "for we cannot but speak of what we have seen and heard."[33] Peter was now a rock indeed.

Jesus calls us all individually. We won't all take the path that Peter took, but we will take one marked out especially for us.[34] Jesus tells Peter the path will lead to his own cross, and indeed church tradition indicates that Peter was crucified upside down for his faith. Our paths may or may not lead to martyrdom. But they will be just what we need to fulfill Jesus's individual call on our lives.

Then Peter turns and sees John, blurting out, "Lord, what about this man?" Jesus answers this question with a question of his own: "*If it is my will that he remain until I come, what is that to you? You follow me!*"[35]

None of My Business

Frankly, it is none of my business what Jesus has planned for his other disciples. And it doesn't really matter. They may experience more suffering than I do, or less. More money, or less. More fame, or less. That is all up to him. My task is not to compare myself with other disciples, but simply to follow him, wherever he leads.

While you may decide to follow in a full stadium or as part of a people group movement, you must pick up your cross alone. But Jesus, as with Peter, knows what he is doing. He knows what twists and turns our paths will take. He sees where we will fail him, where we will serve him, and he walks with us, quick to forgive, always ready to pick us up off the ground. As with Peter, Jesus knows his own special name for us, and one day we will know it, too. "To the one who conquers," Jesus says, "I will give him a white stone, with a new name written on the stone that no one knows except the one who receives it."[36]

Suggested Reading

Bonhoeffer, Dietrich. *The Cost of Discipleship*. New York: Macmillan, 1963.
Fernando, Ajith. *The Call to Joy and Pain: Embracing Suffering in Your Ministry*. Wheaton: Crossway, 2007.
Hughes, R. Kent. *Disciplines of a Godly Man*. Wheaton: Crossway, 1991.

Discussion Questions

1. In what ways is being a disciple of Jesus Christ like death?
2. How does suffering confirm our calling as disciples?

3. Why is service so important for the follower of Christ?
4. Why are we to have our money at the Lord's disposal, and what are some practical ways to make this happen?
5. What can you do when feeling spiritually dry?
6. What keeps you from working hard for Jesus Christ?
7. How do you suspect your call as a disciple differs from all other calls?

10

Lordship under Him

"Will you lay down your life for me?"

To keep your sanity, sometimes it seems as if parenting is all about establishing routines with the children. The official evening routine for our kids goes something like this: finish homework and room cleaning, help set the table, eat dinner and engage in conversation during the meal, put dishes away, get nightclothes on (without playing with toys), eat dessert, brush teeth, have story time, pray, go to bed (and stay there).

One night, however, our six-year-old son was having trouble following the routine. He kept getting sidetracked by his Legos, no matter how many times I reminded him to get back on the routine. Becoming frustrated, but not wishing to have a full-scale confrontation (read "shouting match, followed by crying"), I decided to take a softer approach, hoping he would see the error of his ways. I called him aside and asked, "Don't you think it's important to obey your father?"

My six-year-old gave me a sincerely thoughtful look, paused as he considered the question, and then said, "Not really." It was probably the most honest thing he had uttered all day. Obedience, to him, was an optional extra.

Obedience Essential

Last chapter we began to look at the life of a disciple. It is a joyous calling, but a demanding one. It requires, at a bare minimum, obedience. John, known as the disciple whom Jesus loved,[1] records Jesus saying, "If you love me, you will keep my commandments. . . . Whoever does not love me does not keep my words."[2] Later John emphasizes the point: "Whoever says 'I know him' but does not keep his commandments is a liar, and the truth is not in him."[3]

Obedience is an essential mark of discipleship. It is not an unpleasant add-on to the Lord's ministry of love, but a necessary response to it. "The obedience he demands," John Piper notes in *What Jesus Demands from the World*, "is the fruit of his redeeming work and the display of his personal glory."[4]

A couple of decades ago, evangelicals sparred over the issue of "lordship salvation." When people come to Christ, what part do works of obedience play in their salvation? On one side was John MacArthur, who argued that Christian discipleship involves the understanding that one will follow Jesus not just as Savior, but also as Lord. On the other was Zane Hodges, who argued that salvation is "absolutely free," that since we are declared righteous apart from our works, we don't have to live obedient lives to be saved.[5]

If two such accomplished theologians of good will cannot come to an agreement on this vital matter, then who am I to enter the fray? Well, if fools rush in where angels fear to tread, then consider me a fool. I cannot say *when* someone who trusts in Christ must begin the life of obedience, but I can say that one whose life is characterized by *dis*obedience should have *no* assurance of his or her salvation. Jesus is, after all, the *Lord* Jesus.

And *Lord* is not just some fancy title. According to theologian John Frame, the New Testament word for "Lord" when applied to Jesus, *kyrios*, is the same word that the translators of the Septuagint used for Yahweh, the main and most personal Old Testament name for God.[6] Yahweh is Lord; Jesus is Lord. And being the divine Lord, or ruler, Jesus deserves our worshipful obedience.

Doing Someone Else's Thing

Despite the modern desire to "do your own thing," obedience—doing someone else's thing—is entirely appropriate in some contexts. The bookstores, for example, are filled with titles extolling leadership—but the very concept of leadership means that some must follow—in other words, do someone else's thing. And people actually don't mind following great leaders, who draw the best out of them. Think of the late Vince Lombardi, who demanded excellence and yet evoked awe and respect—even love—from his players.

Lombardi came to the one-win Green Bay Packers before the 1959 season, telling his downtrodden men that they would have to work to be the best, and it would involve pain: "Dancing is a contact sport" Lombardi said. "Football is a hitting sport." And hit they did, devotedly following Lombardi's demanding coaching philosophy. In three years, the Packers won the first of numerous world titles. "He made you a believer," former player Willie Davis said. "He told you what the other team was going to do, and he told you what you had to do to beat them, and invariably he was right." Forrest Gregg, who later became a coach himself, noted, "When Lombardi said 'sit down,' we didn't look for a chair."[7]

And how great a leader is Jesus? Doesn't *he* deserve our devoted service? When you think about it, obedience is the only appropriate response to Christ's lordship, a fact Jesus noted when he asked his disciples, "*Why do you call me 'Lord, Lord,' and not do what I tell you?*"[8] If we call Jesus "Lord," we are obligated to obey him. The two concepts go together. He is Lord; we obey our Lord. And yet we often fail to do so.

On the night Jesus was betrayed, he warned the disciples of their impending separation from him. Ever-impetuous Peter promised he would willingly die for Jesus. Knowing this man named Peter, who was far from being a rock,[9] Jesus penetratingly asked, "*Will you lay down your life for me?*" The distressing answer was one neither wanted to hear: not yet.[10] Some followers of Jesus, however, get it.

Monica Sierra seemingly had it all. Elected as the youngest circuit court judge in Florida's Hillsborough County, she drove a Mercedes and enjoyed a $145,000 salary and all the perks that came with her position. But in November 2007 she announced she was taking a three-month unpaid leave to volunteer at a mission agency that provides humanitarian and spiritual aid in several refugee camps in the Middle East.

But then, after her hiatus was over, Sierra, forty-one, announced an even more radical step. On February 1, 2008, she resigned from the bench—one year before completing her first term—to pursue full-time ministry among refugees. Friends and family—who had sacrificed much to get her elected— were stunned. No longer able to count on her six-figure income, Sierra said she would rely on donations to the small mission agency she works with, as well as her own savings. Sierra told *The Tampa Tribune* she had no choice but to act in "obedience to his direction," adding: "I have to trust that the Lord knows better than I do."[11]

He does.

Whose Likeness?

Does Jesus have the right to ask us to make such radical changes? Isn't that just a bit *extreme*? Only if you fail to recognize his rights as *Lord*. If we are all free agents who come to Jesus for advice or a spiritual pick-me-up, then the concept of his lordship makes no sense. But if we go to Jesus hungry, looking for the bread only he can supply, then we have no other option. We must get our marching orders from him, not from someone else.

"We do not make the call," Tim Stafford writes. "We cannot tell anyone that Jesus wants him or her to go somewhere that death awaits. To forfeit a career, to sell all and give it to the poor—it is not for us to put such expectations on another human being. Only Jesus can."[12] A story from Jesus's ministry will illustrate why.

One day when Jesus was in Jerusalem, the scribes and chief priests asked him a trick question—one of many such attempts. These questioners wanted him to say whether the Jewish people should pay taxes to their oppressors. If he said yes, he would be discredited in the eyes of the people. If no, then Pontius Pilate would likely throw him in prison as a rabble-rouser or traitor to the empire.

Jesus asked to see a denarius, a coin worth about a day's wage for a laborer. *"Whose likeness and inscription does it have?"* Jesus asked, probably turning the coin over in his hands as he spoke. Not perceiving the trap he had set for them, his would-be accusers blurted out, "Caesar's," leaving themselves vulnerable. Then Jesus delivered the verbal knockout: "Then render to Caesar the things that are Caesar's, and to God the things that are God's."[13]

The message was crystal clear to any Jew who knew his Bible, and Scripture was the specialty of the scribes and chief priests. If that which is stamped with Caesar's image belongs to Caesar, then those things stamped with God's image—namely, men and women[14]—belong to God. And Jesus is God the Son. His identity is stamped into us more indelibly than our DNA. The Lord Jesus owns us as surely as Caesar laid claim to a denarius.

Jesus is Lord because he created us, yes. But he is Lord in other ways, as well. We will examine the facets of his lordship that his questions force us to confront.

Examining the Facets

Lord of the Sabbath: Jesus and his disciples are walking through a field on the Sabbath.[15] Hungry, they pluck and eat some grain. The Pharisees, who evidently were walking along with them, waiting to be scandalized, complained to Jesus: "Look, your disciples are doing what is not lawful to do on the Sabbath." According to Deuteronomy 23:25, of course, it *was* lawful for the needy to glean small amounts from a neighbor's field. This was because God's law encouraged the people of God to be generous and to share with the poor.

The Pharisees undoubtedly knew this, but assumed that such otherwise lawful acts of necessity were illegal on the Sabbath, the day of rest. According to Puritan commentator Matthew Henry, "plucking and rubbing the ears of [grain] on that day was expressly forbidden by the tradition of the elders, for this reason, because it was a *kind of reaping*."[16] And "reaping," being a form of work, was forbidden. Or at least that's what they thought.

So Jesus mercifully uses questions to show them they are ignorant of their own Scriptures.

Have you not read what David did when he was hungry, and those who were
with him: how he entered the house of God and ate the bread of the Presence,
which it was not lawful for him to eat nor for those who were with him, but
only for the priests? Or have you not read in the Law how on the Sabbath the
priests in the temple profane the Sabbath and are guiltless?

Had they not *read* their own Scriptures? Such a question hit these men, who
prided themselves on their extensive biblical knowledge, like a slap in the face.
Then Jesus tells them to get their spiritual priorities in order.

I tell you, something greater than the temple is here. And if you had known what
this means, 'I desire mercy, and not sacrifice,' you would not have condemned
the guiltless. For the Son of Man is lord of the Sabbath.

Christ's lordship allows him to interpret the law as God intended, and his lordship not only brings obligation; it brings freedom, too. Here, a disciple is free
under God's mercy to eat. God's mercy trumps the critics' misguided desire
for (someone else's) sacrifice. In this we see that some obligations are more
important than others. A healthy disciple does not give every commandment
the same weight. Depending on the circumstances, we may safely dispense
with a lesser commandment to follow a greater one. For example:

- Go ahead and set aside your quiet time by the lake to rescue a drowning
  man.
- Even break the speed limit, if by so doing you can get him to the
  hospital.

And matters of the heart—character over naked obedience—come first.
We can make these distinctions because Jesus is Lord of the Sabbath—and
over every other religious regulation.

For example, one day the collectors of the half-shekel temple tax—"an
annual levy on Jewish males between the ages of twenty and fifty for the
support of the temple"[17]—came to Peter in Capernaum, nervous or perhaps
fearful over what his master, Jesus, might say. Jesus had spent much of his
ministry overturning the narrow religious conventions of the day. Perhaps
Jesus, who at the age of twelve had called the temple "my Father's house,"[18]
and who evidently was quite touchy when financial matters became enmeshed
with temple worship,[19] would balk at paying the tax? Not wanting a verbal
confrontation, the collectors did the safe thing and asked Peter, "Does your
teacher not pay the tax?" Peter reflexively said, "Yes," and then went looking
for Jesus, just to make sure.

And when he came into the house, Jesus spoke to him first, saying, "*What do*
you think, Simon? From whom do kings of the earth take toll or tax? From

their sons or from others?" And when he said, "From others," Jesus said to him, "Then the sons are free."[20]

Tax shelters are nothing new. In that day—and often still in ours—those close to power escaped the heavy obligations imposed by government. In the first century, Caesar would no more tax his sons than he would tax himself. Our hopeful modern notions of equality would have had little traction in the ancient world. The powerful protected their own; the burdens always fell on "the little guy." That's just the way it was, and Jesus recognized (but did not endorse) this state of affairs.

But then he used this brutal earthly fact of life to share a spiritual truth: Jesus, as Son of the heavenly king, is exempt from any obligations for the upkeep of his Father's house. Jesus's followers, who are closer to him than flesh and blood,[21] are also in the clear. Yet while law will have no hold on the Lord's disciples, grace may compel them to act generously anyway. But no matter; the Lord will provide.

> However [Jesus said], not to give offense to them, go to the sea and cast a hook and take the first fish that comes up, and when you open its mouth you will find a shekel. Take that and give it to them for me and for yourself.

Lord of Creation: Such absolute lordship also brings courage. As we saw in the introduction, Jesus slept like a baby during a fearsome storm on the lake. Nothing on earth could shake his confidence. The disciples, however, cried out, "Save us, Lord; we are perishing." His question—*"Why are you afraid, O you of little faith?"*—speaks to the doubter in each of us.[22] The Lord of Creation speaks, and the storm disappears. But even if he remains silent and the storm continues, he is still Lord.

I am reminded of the passage in the Book of Daniel when Shadrach, Meshach, and Abednego were threatened with imminent death in a specially constructed human incinerator because they refused to worship a golden idol of Nebuchadnezzar. The three express trust in God's ability to save them—and even more trust if he doesn't: "If this be so, our God whom we serve is able to deliver us from the burning fiery furnace, and he will deliver us out of your hand, O king. But if not, be it known to you, O king, that we will not serve your gods or worship the golden image that you have set up."[23]

When the tsunami inexorably rolls toward us, when the hurricane roars, when the tornado twists a path of devastation through our neighborhood, do we trust the Lord's omnipotence? Do we trust his goodness? If Jesus is Lord of Creation, we can rest assured that nothing will happen outside of his plan—and sleep soundly, whatever happens.

Lord of Human Need: While Jesus is in Nazareth, "his own city," some people bring him a young man confined to his bed because of paralysis. Though many Christians today gravitate toward meeting physical needs before (or instead of) addressing people's need for a Savior,[24] not so with Jesus here. "Take heart, my son," Jesus says. "Your sins are forgiven."[25] Some scribes present concluded that Jesus had committed blasphemy, correctly noting that only God can forgive a person's sins. Jesus, reading their minds, asks them two penetrating questions: "*Why do you think evil in your hearts? For which is easier, to say, 'Your sins are forgiven,' or to say, 'Rise and walk'?*"[26]

First, the scribes even thinking that Jesus blasphemed is evil. It shows a cold-heartedness that obstinately refuses to acknowledge the spiritual dawn breaking out all around them. Second, Jesus seems to be implying, talk is cheap. It's one thing to *say* you forgive sin; it's another entirely to demonstrate the power of divinity—and thus the *right* to forgive sin. Jesus backs up his talk by moving from the paralytic's spiritual need to his physical need. He can take care of both, because he is God.

Jesus is able to meet every need today, even those needs of which we are only dimly aware. One of my children is learning in her public school that human beings have physical, mental, emotional, and social needs. This is true enough, as far as it goes. But this approach is too secular—it acts as if our spiritual needs do not exist or are inconsequential.

Yet it is often true—though not always—that those who have their spiritual houses in order also have other needs met. I am reminded of the second stanza from "Come, We That Love the Lord," an old hymn by Isaac Watts: "Let those refuse to sing who never knew our God; But children of the heav'nly King may speak their joys abroad." Those who have Jesus experience joy and healing that are simply unavailable to others.

That certainly was the case with John Wesley, who preached the gospel and saw whole impoverished communities respond not just with faith, but with a stewardship approach to their redeemed lives that brought tangible economic benefits.[27] When people become Christians in areas where other religions dominate, they are often accused of converting through unethical "inducements," such as promises of food or jobs. Often what really happens is that they learn of their dignity and worth as children of God and begin doing the things—working, planning, saving, and sharing—that spark economic gains in their communities. And as new members of the Christian body, they become part of a network whose members look out for one another in love. This is not bribery or coercion; it is a sign of the kingdom of God.

Those who have their spiritual priorities straight sometimes overcome mental illness through the power of God's Spirit. Think of those souls in the New Testament who were freed from the power of demons and then sat "at the feet of Jesus, clothed and in [their] right mind."[28] Sometimes those who trust Christ find great relief for their emotional and social isolation via the Spirit's power and the loving community of God's people.

No, spiritual healing is no guarantee of healing in our finances or our mental makeup. There are many poor and broken Christians in this world, and as Jesus said, he came for such people. As we saw in chapter 8, sometimes our full restoration is only begun in this world and awaits the future consummation of all things. But it is the essential *first step*, as Jesus demonstrated with the paralyzed young man.

A Graceful Obedience

So if Christ the Lord owns us, what are we to do? Revel in our freedom and in his grace, yes. But we also must do the work to which he calls us. "His yoke is easy," Stafford notes, "though it remains a yoke."[29] One day, via a parable, Jesus urges his listeners to act like servants waiting for their master's return, which could come at any time. "You also must be ready," Jesus warns, "for the Son of Man is coming at an hour you do not expect."[30] Perhaps trembling, Peter asks if the parable applies to the disciples or just to the crowds. Jesus doesn't answer directly, but the message is clear enough:

> *Who then is the faithful and wise manager, whom his master will set over his household, to give them their portion of food at the proper time?* Blessed is that servant whom his master will find so doing when he comes. Truly, I say to you, he will set him over all his possessions. But if that servant says to himself, "My master is delayed in coming," and begins to beat the male and female servants, and to eat and drink and get drunk, the master of that servant will come on a day when he does not expect him and at an hour he does not know, and will cut him in pieces and put him with the unfaithful.[31]

In this passage, we cannot overlook the glorious truth that those who are obediently working when Jesus returns will be amply rewarded. But neither can we skim over the plain fact that those who aren't will be punished—because they show by their deeds that they have no faith.

While we are saved by grace through faith,[32] if we are not following Christ as our Lord, then we have legitimate grounds to question the genuineness of our faith—and the time to do that is now, *before* he returns. Those who have true faith will *work*. No works, no faith; no faith, no salvation. As Bonhoeffer said, "Only he who believes is obedient, and only he who is obedient believes."[33]

But like the half-shekel temple tax, Jesus supplies what we need in order to obey. It is all grace. As Augustine prayed, so must we: "Command what you wish, but give what you command."[34] The Lord gives what he requires. Bonhoeffer said of this costly grace,

> Such grace is *costly* because it calls us to follow, and it is *grace* because it calls us to follow *Jesus Christ*. It is costly because it costs a man his life, and it is grace because it gives a man the only true life.[35]

All Christ's gifts are pure grace, worth more than all our effort. And while rewards are promised to all faithful disciples, we shouldn't ever demand them as our due. We cannot earn his salvation, and Jesus owes us nothing. Jesus asks:

> Will any one of you who has a servant plowing or keeping sheep say to him when he has come in from the field, "Come at once and recline at table"? Will he not rather say to him, "Prepare supper for me, and dress properly, and serve me while I eat and drink, and afterward you will eat and drink"? Does he thank the servant because he did what was commanded? So you also, when you have done all that you were commanded, say, "We are unworthy servants; we have only done what was our duty."[36]

God owes us *nothing*. We can *never* earn Christ's favor. We can put *no* claim on him with our works, however many they are. But isn't this good news? We are motivated not to legalistically earn God's favor—because we can never do that—but to glorify and please him, because he already loves and serves us. This focus directs our eyes to God, where they belong. As Kent Hughes says, "legalism is self-centered; discipline is God-centered."[37]

We are in a relationship of love, not fear, with the Lord of all.

Suggested Reading

Galli, Mark. *Jesus Mean and Wild: The Unexpected Love of an Untamable God*. Grand Rapids: Baker, 2006.
Piper, John. *What Jesus Demands from the World*. Wheaton: Crossway, 2006.

Discussion Questions

1. Why does our culture make it so hard for people to obey others?
2. What are some examples of healthy obedience? Unhealthy obedience?
3. What is the relationship between belief and obedience?
4. Why does Jesus require our obedience?
5. What are the consequences of both obedience and disobedience?
6. Does following Christ as Lord bring freedom? How?
7. How does Jesus help us to obey?

11

Prayer According to Him

*"And will not God give
justice to his elect?"*

Nicolae Ceauşescu and his wife, Elena, might not have invented the term "iron fist." But certainly they perfected its application during twenty-four years of merciless, tyrannical rule in Romania. In 1966 the new communist dictator, without the confining checks and balances that a liberal democracy affords, was free to indulge his delusions of grandeur in this inconsequential slave state in Eastern Europe. Ceauşescu looked about him and saw a small country, certainly one not worthy of his greatness. He would make it a big one, one way or another.

In 1966 he hatched a plan that was brutally simple—to increase Romania's population from 23 million to 30 million by the year 2000. Deciding that the problem was too few births, Ceauşescu made pregnancy a virtual state policy. Romania, largely Christian by heritage, had become an Orwellian world in which the government almost quite literally was in people's bedrooms. "The fetus is the property of the entire society," Ceauşescu announced. "Anyone who avoids having children is a deserter who abandons the laws of national continuity." Contraception was banned, the infant mortality rate exploded, and a thriving abortion black market developed.[1]

The country's Soviet masters didn't care about Ceauşescu's evil whims, or their consequences, just as long as order was kept and the money flowed uninterruptedly to Moscow. Like most communists before him, however, Ceauşescu saw the church as an enemy to his grandiose plans. As we have seen, Christianity says Jesus—not Marx, Lenin, Hitler, or Ceauşescu—is Lord.

So among his many other sins, Ceauşescu cracked down on the churches. Romania was one of the Soviet bloc's "most oppressive and cruel regimes," notes the Operation World prayer guide. "Under Communism, manipulation and control of the churches was oppressive, with severe persecution for those who refused to submit."[2] Consistent prayer went up for the oppressed Romanians by Christian brothers and sisters around the world. But at the time you could be forgiven for wondering if Romania would remain a picture of George Orwell's *1984*—a boot stamping on a face forever.

Yet as the mighty Soviet empire began to unravel in 1989, Nicolae and Elena Ceauşescu were unable to escape God's finger of judgment. In mid-December, protests over government mistreatment of László Tőkés, a dissident priest, began in the western city of Timişoara. Then citizens, whom authorities counted on to act like sheep, complained about a lack of bread. Unrest and violence spread and intensified over the next ten days. Ceauşescu's troops responded brutally, enraging citizens who had been under the boot long enough.

Finally, demonstrators converged on Ceauşescu's palace in Bucharest. The dictator and his wife tried to flee (hoping to take large stashes of money with them), but members of the military who had joined the revolution hunted them down. A secret tribunal quickly found the unholy pair guilty of genocide and other crimes against the state. Then Nicolae and Elena, who had enjoyed absolute power, were treated like common thugs: summarily executed, their bullet-riddled bodies displayed for all to see on national television. A once enslaved people poured into Romania's drab streets on December 25, not to mourn, but to celebrate.[3]

It is a scene that has been repeated down through the centuries: Hitler and Saddam cowering in underground bunkers as liberating forces move in; Nebuchadnezzar losing his lordly bearing and eating grass like an ox for seven years; Alexander the Great felled by a mosquito; a fat despot stabbed by a left-handed swordsman; a drunk Belshazzar reading the writing of judgment on the wall, "Mene, Mene, Tekel, and Parsin"; a proud Herod eaten by worms with the echoes of sycophantic crowds still ringing in his ears. Scripture and history show there is no long-term job security for tyrants and persecutors of God's people. As the Psalmist said, "He who sits in the heavens laughs; the Lord holds them in derision. Then he will speak to them in his wrath, and terrify them in his fury."[4]

An Absent Father?

And yet sometimes God followers can feel abandoned and forgotten. When one persecutor is mowed down, another arises to take his place. The Jews

endured centuries of slavery in Egypt before Moses was stopped in his dusty
tracks by the sight of a bush unconsumed by a strange, heavenly fire; Jesus
hung on a Roman cross as the people he came to save taunted him, and his
own disciples hid in the nooks and crannies of Jerusalem; a megalomania-
cal dictator in North Korea who is called "Dear Leader" has thrown tens of
thousands of Christians into brutal prison camps from which few ever return;
in some Muslim-majority nations, such as Saudi Arabia, conversion to Christ
is an offense punishable by death; worldwide, an estimated 200 million Christians potentially face interrogation, arrest, and death for their faith.[5] As the
Psalmist also said bitterly,

> Yet for your sake we are killed all the day long;
> we are regarded as sheep to be slaughtered.
>
> Awake! Why are you sleeping, O Lord?
> Rouse yourself! Do not reject us forever!
> Why do you hide your face?
> Why do you forget our affliction and oppression?[6]

God both delivers his children and forces them to wait; he cares for them
and often seems absent; he stands for justice but sometimes injustice reigns.
In Jesus's day, of course, the Jews—God's chosen people—were enslaved by
Rome. God's call does not guarantee insulation from the world's injustices.
It is into this paradox that Jesus asks questions that force his followers, then
and now, to think deeply about prayer to their heavenly Father.

The Unjust Judge

> And he told them a parable to the effect that they ought always to pray and not
> lose heart. He said, "In a certain city there was a judge who neither feared God
> nor respected man. And there was a widow in that city who kept coming to
> him and saying, 'Give me justice against my adversary.' For a while he refused,
> but afterward he said to himself, 'Though I neither fear God nor respect man,
> yet because this widow keeps bothering me, I will give her justice, so that she
> will not beat me down by her continual coming.'" And the Lord said, "Hear
> what the unrighteous judge says. *And will not God give justice to his elect,
> who cry to him day and night? Will he delay long over them?* I tell you, he will
> give justice to them speedily. *Nevertheless, when the Son of Man comes, will
> he find faith on earth?*"[7]

This parable has been difficult for God's people to understand ever since
Jesus spoke it. Is God, like the judge, unjust and uncaring? Must we wear
him out to get what we need? Is that why we must wait for his answers to our
prayers? Perhaps this uncertainty is why Luke, under divine inspiration, felt it

necessary to spell out the point up front: that Christ's disciples "ought always to pray and not lose heart." Why might this be so? Simply because we are continually tempted to quit. That temptation presents itself not because we quickly see God answer our prayers, but precisely because so often we don't. Much of church history is before Christmas Day.

Jesus asks whether God will delay long over his people; sometimes it seems as if the answer is "yes." Bible scholar Walter Elwell notes a "point of tension" in this parable: "if justice is received so quickly, why would anyone give up in prayer?" He answers his own question by saying, "Perhaps the vindication will not seem to be quick at all for people on earth, but will be agonizingly slow—so slow that they may give up on prayer, concluding that God is not just, that he does not punish the wicked and vindicate those who long for justice."[8]

Such reasoning, while seemingly rational, evidences a lack of faith. Jesus warns against this mindset. One who decided to take that route is New Testament scholar (and former evangelical) Bart Ehrman, author of *God's Problem: How the Bible Fails to Answer Our Most Important Question—Why We Suffer.* "I realized I couldn't explain any longer why there could be such pain and misery in the world that was supposedly ruled by an all-powerful and loving God," Ehrman says. "So I became an agnostic."[9]

This parable, and Jesus's questions, can help us see that while a loving and all-powerful God may allow injustice to continue, evil does not get the final word. Any evaluation of suffering that fails to account for this two-sided reality is incomplete at best, misleading at worst. It impugns the character of God and downplays the significance of our being in his family.

Even a cursory look at the parable shows differences between God and the judge. They are not synonymous. This is, after all, a parable and not an allegory. Parables impart a main spiritual lesson. Each element of a parable does not necessarily "stand for" something else, as is the case with an allegory.

Noting that the judge is far from an exact representation of God, Puritan commentator Matthew Henry draws the contrast between the unjust (and seemingly all-powerful) judge—who must be cajoled and pestered to do the right thing—and God: (1) the widow was a stranger, but we are God's "elect," or chosen people; (2) she was just one person, but God's people who pray in agreement about a matter are many; (3) she came to a judge who didn't care for her, but we come to a loving Father; (4) she came to an unjust jurist, but we come to a righteous Judge; (5) she came to the judge on her own business, but we come to God on his; (6) she had no one to plead her cause, but we have Christ as our advocate; (7) she had no promise or encouragement, but we have God's promise that he will answer; (8) she could approach the judge only at certain times, but we can seek him "day and night"; (9) she provoked the judge with her requests, while we please God with ours.[10]

God is both Judge and Father, both fearsome and approachable, depending upon our relationship with him. In this parable—and in Jesus's probing questions—we see the juxtaposition. If we look at only one side of his character, his holiness for example, we see a harsh, unapproachable taskmaster seeking only our obedience and unconcerned with our welfare. We can never measure up to such a lawgiver. "Performance is such a high standard," Tim Keller says, "the strain is unsupportable."[11]

If we look only at God's love, on the other hand, we are tempted to see God as a celestial Santa Claus continually passing out goodies, but who is unwilling or unable to protect his children.

Theologian J. I. Packer says many people look at God's character sentimentally. "Speak to them of God as a Father, a friend, a helper, one who loves us despite all our weakness and folly and sin, and their faces light up; you are on their wavelength at once," Packer says. "But speak to them of God as Judge, and they shake their heads."[12]

But is this juxtaposition really so hard to understand? As a father, I do sometimes find it difficult to display both holiness and love for my children. They need to see both a commitment to do right and a loving nature from their father. However, some evenings after work, when I am worn down from each day's tasks, they see a grumpy, legalistic taskmaster. But I have no such trouble exercising love and law together when my kids' welfare is threatened. When they need the protective love of their father, both holiness and love come together naturally, as in this parable—and if you're giving them trouble, you'd better watch out.

A History of Judgment

In earlier ages, history was interpreted through the lens of the Christian faith. Great universities were founded for the glory of God and the equipping of his church. History was seen as moving in a definite direction, the consummation of all things in Christ. Paul notes in Romans that

> the creation itself will be set free from its bondage to decay and obtain the freedom of the glory of the children of God. For we know that the whole creation has been groaning together in the pains of childbirth until now. And not only the creation, but we ourselves, who have the firstfruits of the Spirit, groan inwardly as we wait eagerly for our adoption as sons, the redemption of our bodies.[13]

We knew, on the authority of Scripture, that history was going somewhere, because God was actively guiding it until Christ's return. Then, as Enlightenment values spread, the West forgot its heritage.

History no longer seemed to have a definite goal (other than the assumed steady improvement and eventual exaltation, without God, of humanity).

Time morphed into a succession of random, chaotic events. Faith on God's earth was slipping away. We no longer could see God as the Lord of history, punishing evildoers and vindicating the righteous in the end. If God existed, he didn't concern himself much with daily events. Perhaps he would bring the play to a close one day, we thought, but he didn't concern himself with the day-to-day scenes.

Talk about an incentive to lose heart in prayer! Evangelical Christians, long expelled from the academies they had founded, accepted these ground rules and studied and presented history as if God were absent, or irrelevant.

That's why Jerry Falwell's comment that the September 11 terror attacks were evidence of God's judgment stirred such derision—even hatred—among both the common man and the elites. To suggest that God is angry to the point of judging national sins such as abortion and homosexual conduct, they seemed to be saying, is not just ontologically wrong, but bad form. Echoing the serpent in the Garden, they seemed to ask, "Has God *really* said?"

Reflecting on 9/11, Steven J. Keillor, an adjunct professor at Bethel University, notes in his book *God's Judgments* that God indeed "uses historical events to punish collective, national evil."[14] As we saw in chapter 2, John the Baptist and Jesus stepped into a context where national judgment loomed. The forerunner preached, "Who warned you to flee from the wrath to come?"[15] As Keillor says, "John the Baptist 'prepared the way' by warning that the coming One would bring a sifting-out mishpat," or judgment, separating the righteous from the unrighteous.[16]

Jesus, rather than attempting to disabuse his followers of the common notion that God would come as Judge, instead stokes it in this parable. Appealing indirectly to God's character, Jesus drives the point home, asking, *"And will not God give justice to his elect, who cry to him day and night? Will he delay long over them?"*[17]

God judged Jerusalem for its hard-hearted unbelief in that generation,[18] causing it to fall to the Romans in AD 70, and the Romans to the barbarians less than four centuries later. While God's judgments may have tarried by human standards because of his kindness,[19] they were brutally quick and final when they came. And we need to keep in mind that such judgments in history are mere foretastes of the final judgment to come.[20]

And it *will* come. As Paul said to the suffering church in Thessalonica, "God considers it just to repay with affliction those who afflict you, and to grant relief to you who are afflicted as well as to us, when the Lord Jesus is revealed from heaven with his mighty angels in flaming fire, inflicting vengeance on those who do not know God and who do not obey the gospel of our Lord Jesus."[21]

And note that Jesus, depicted often as meek and mild, encourages his people to keep praying for justice—evil people getting what they deserve—though it seems to be delayed. To oppose God's justice is to insult and oppose the righteous Judge. All that is wrong one day will be set right, and we are encouraged to pray regularly for that day.

Relentless Prayer

Prayers of request, of course, seek both more and less than simple justice. Our daily needs are also important to our Father. Because we are finite, we naturally seek help from the infinite. Rugged individualism has no place in biblical faith. We are utterly dependent on God to supply what we need. Acknowledging this fact is not weakness; it is realism. And Scripture commends us for sticking with it.

In prayer, persistence is a virtue. But like all virtues, it doesn't come easily. Ask committed believers what spiritual obligation is most difficult, and many will say prayer. That is certainly true for me. While we exclaim that prayer is a delight because we are communicating with our loving heavenly Father, in the day-to-day marathon that is real life, too often prayer is drudgery. God not only doesn't seem to answer; he doesn't seem to hear. As Matthew Henry notes from across the centuries, "it is a hard thing to pray well."[22] Given that fact, how can we (1) keep going, (2) know that we are praying the right things, (3) know that we are being heard, and (4) know that God will answer? Perhaps this is why the disciples sought Jesus's insights on prayer.

> Now Jesus was praying in a certain place, and when he finished, one of his disciples said to him, "Lord, teach us to pray, as John taught his disciples." And he said to them, "When you pray, say:
>
> > 'Father, hallowed be your name.
> >   Your kingdom come.
> > Give us each day our daily bread,
> > and forgive us our sins,
> >   for we ourselves forgive everyone who is indebted to us.
> >   And lead us not into temptation.'
>
> And he said to them, *"Which of you who has a friend will go to him at midnight and say to him, 'Friend, lend me three loaves, for a friend of mine has arrived on a journey, and I have nothing to set before him'; and he will answer from within, 'Do not bother me; the door is now shut, and my children are with me in bed. I cannot get up and give you anything'?* I tell you, though he will not get up and give him anything because he is his friend, yet because of his impudence he will rise and give him whatever he needs. And I tell you, ask, and it will be given to you; seek, and you will find; knock, and it will be opened to you. For everyone who asks receives, and the one who seeks finds, and to the one who knocks it will be opened. *What father among you, if his son asks for a fish, will instead of a fish give him a serpent; or if he asks for an egg, will*

give him a scorpion? If you then, who are evil, know how to give good gifts to your children, how much more will the heavenly Father give the Holy Spirit to those who ask him!"[23]

After Jesus teaches the essentials of prayer in this shortened version of what we call the "Lord's Prayer,"[24] he again encourages his disciples to persevere. And he illustrates this (again) with a contrast. If a mere human being who would be greatly inconvenienced can be persuaded to help us in time of need, how much more can an omnipotent God be trusted? ("How much more" is a theme we will revisit in chapters 15 and 26.)

Those who ask will receive; those who seek will find; those who knock will find the door opened. If earthly fathers can be trusted to provide good things for their children, how much more can our heavenly Father be relied upon? We pray in expectation because we trust in the love and character of God.

And yet questions remain: Why does a loving God, who could fulfill our requests in an instant, often delay so that we must keep on asking, seeking, and knocking? Why must we come to him over and over again? We don't usually have to ask a friend repeatedly for help. If he is a friend, once is enough. And if our children ask for something to eat, we don't make them beg. Why is it different with God? Why does he so often engineer circumstances so that we don't get what we so desperately want?

And let's be honest: sometimes we ask and do *not* receive; we seek and do *not* find; we knock and the door remains *closed*. A disconsolate C. S. Lewis wrote after his beloved wife, Joy, died, "go to Him when your need is desperate, when all other help is vain, and what do you find? A door slammed in your face, and a sound of bolting and double bolting on the inside. After that, silence. You may as well turn away."[25]

What then? What good is perseverance when God clearly is not answering? I believe Jesus tells us to be relentless in prayer not so that we can get what we want, but so that we can get what *God* wants. Persistent prayer doesn't change God; it changes us. I believe it does three main things.

1. *Persistent prayer changes our view of God.* In the passage above, Jesus assures us that our heavenly Father knows our requests and will answer them. But as a Father, he reserves the right to answer them as he sees fit. He is a Father, not a Butler. Note also that his answers may not track exactly with what we have requested. He has promised not to give us merely what we want, but exactly what we need.

God is our Father, but he has a bigger agenda than my life, liberty, and pursuit of happiness. The Bible tells us that God is on a mission to save people, to build his kingdom, to display his glory among the nations. But the world and its people are desperately sick and in rebellion against his good rule. For now, Satan is active. This is not heaven. While we may be privileged, here and there, to enjoy a foretaste of the life to come, we are not promised endless bliss in this one. To borrow an idea from JFK, we should ask not what our God can do for us, but what we can do for our God. As Jesus said: "Thy kingdom come, thy will be done."

It is hard to pray this way, but necessary. Jesus, after all, prayed (unsuccessfully) that the cup of suffering might pass from him. Should we be surprised when it comes around to us? We need God's wisdom and power to pray this way. At the end of his *Confessions*, Augustine of Hippo makes the point that ultimately only God can help us grasp his perspective:

> What human can empower another human to understand these things? What angel can grant understanding to another angel? What angel to a human? Let us rather ask of you, seek in you, knock at your door. Only so will we receive, only so find, and only so will the door be opened to us.[26]

2. Persistent prayer changes us. As I have struggled with the problem of seemingly unanswered prayer, I have concluded that too often I have had the wrong focus. I have been fixated on what I have asked for, as if God's main task is to make me happy. And if God were to always give me what I want, when I want it, let's face it, I *would* be happy. But should my momentary happiness be his chief concern? I think not.

While the analogy quickly breaks down, I have found my own role as a dad instructive as I think about my heavenly Father. When my daughter started attending her middle school a mile from our home, she thought the distance was too far to walk. And indeed navigating through the ice, snow, and wind can be difficult on cold Midwestern winter days.

Her mother and I, however, firmly believed that walking is good for her, both physically and spiritually. It built her endurance, taught her discipline, and showed that her parents do not run an unlimited taxi service awaiting her beck and call. She saw walking, however, as a needless impingement of her freedom and complained nearly every morning when a ride was not forthcoming. I didn't expect her to understand why I didn't give in to her emotional pleas. But I hope one day she will be a more mature young woman who is physically fit, disciplined, less self-centered—and thankful for when she does get a ride.

Perhaps God the Father has similar goals in mind when we don't get the answers we expect. His refusal to answer indicates not a lack of love, but a fatherly compassion to give us what we really need. At some point when we pray, we will need to accept, however painful, the "no" of God, trusting that he has an unknown "yes" in mind.

First, however, we need to understand that acceptance is not a copout. It's not giving God an escape clause to shore up our own shaky faith. Just as perseverance comes from trusting in God's fatherly heart for his children, so does acceptance. Donald G. Bloesch notes that biblical prayer has a place for both importunity and submission:

It is both wrestling with God in the darkness and resting in the stillness. There is a time to argue and complain to God, but there is also a time to submit. Biblical faith sees submission to the will of God coming after the attempt to discover his will through heartfelt supplication. Prayer is both a pleading with God that he will hear and act upon our requests and a trusting surrender to God in the confidence that he will act in his own time and way. But the confidence comes only through the struggle.[27]

3. *Persistent prayer changes our requests.* As we ask and do not receive, our heart is, little by little, imperceptibly softened. I have asked for many things that I haven't received during the course of my life: a new car, a new relationship, a new job. At the time, my requests seemed to be the most urgent things in the world, and I would hunger for them like a homeless man in a posh subdivision.

But after it became clear that I would not get that for which I so persistently asked, I would become spiritually depressed. Hadn't Jesus encouraged me to keep on asking, keep on seeking, keep on knocking? What then was the use? But as I look back through the lens of increased maturity, I can sometimes see why my prayers went unanswered: God had already provided transportation; that young woman was a bad personality match; that job did not fit my skills and would have foreclosed the opportunities I have now. And when I consider all that God *has* provided, I would not trade my life for anyone else's. Any small change then would immeasurably have altered the good life I have now. As I pray, I'm starting to trust that maybe Father really *does* know best.

I have a friend who was injured in an auto accident not of his doing. My friend ran up several thousands of dollars worth of rehabilitation bills for his back. My friend has persistently, and prayerfully, tried to get the other driver and his insurance company to own up to their responsibility to pay for his legitimate medical expenses. But they stonewalled him every step of the way. My friend attempted to speak with them, but his calls were not returned. He tried mediation, and they seem determined to take the case to trial, where prospects for a settlement in his favor were poor. My friend, like the widow seeking justice, prayed regularly for relief and enlisted my prayer and that of others for a just resolution. Yet the impasse dragged on, month after month. Eventually, he had to accept his heavenly Father's mysterious "no."

I asked him how God not answering his prayer affected his faith. My friend said he is trusting that God has a bigger purpose in this incident, though he does not know what it is. He is learning, through God's silence, to look out not just for his own good, but for God to accomplish something he never would have thought of—or asked for. His prayers, and his faith, are getting larger.

Jesus, after pointing out that even evil earthly fathers can be relied upon to give their children what they need, makes a curious statement: "how much more will the heavenly Father give the Holy Spirit to those who ask him!"[28]

Why did the Holy Spirit slip into a conversation about earthly needs? Perhaps it's because ultimately what we need, whether we ask for him or not, is the Holy Spirit, the third person of the Trinity, the Lord and Giver of life.

We need the Spirit to quicken, comfort, and empower. We need the Spirit to help us pray when we have reached the end of our rope. The Holy Spirit is our ultimate good and our helper to get us there. He meets our deepest needs, even when our lesser ones go unmet. He is ultimately what we should pray for, and the one who helps us to pray. I don't often start out praying for the Holy Spirit; but in my best moments, that's where I end up.

Matthew Henry says it well:

> We must ask for the Holy Spirit, not only as necessary in order to our praying well, but as inclusive of all the good things we are to pray for; we need no more to make us happy, for the Spirit is the worker of spiritual life, and the earnest of eternal life.[29]

Lord, teach us to *pray*.

Suggested Reading

Keillor, Steven J., *God's Judgments: Interpreting History and the Christian Faith*. Downers Grove, IL: InterVarsity, 2007.

White, John. *Daring to Draw Near: People in Prayer*. Downers Grove, IL: InterVarsity, 2008.

Discussion Questions

1. Why do you think people today doubt whether God judges in history?
2. How might we know whether particular events reflect God's judgments?
3. How and why does Jesus encourage us to persevere in prayer?
4. What things keep us from persevering in prayer?
5. How should we respond when, after praying about a matter for a long time, the answer from God seems to be "no"?
6. Have you seen God enlarge your prayers?
7. Why does Jesus promise that God will give the Holy Spirit to those who ask?

12

Priorities Given by Him

"For what does it profit a man
if he gains the whole world and
loses or forfeits himself?"

Someone in the crowd said to him, "Teacher, tell my brother to divide the inheritance with me." But he said to him, *"Man, who made me a judge or arbitrator over you?"* And he said to them, "Take care, and be on your guard against all covetousness, for one's life does not consist in the abundance of his possessions." And he told them a parable, saying, "The land of a rich man produced plentifully, and he thought to himself, 'What shall I do, for I have nowhere to store my crops?' And he said, 'I will do this: I will tear down my barns and build larger ones, and there I will store all my grain and my goods. And I will say to my soul, Soul, you have ample goods laid up for many years; relax, eat, drink, be merry.' But God said to him, 'Fool! This night your soul is required of you, and the things you have prepared, whose will they be?' So is the one who lays up treasure for himself and is not rich toward God."[1]

While "self-actualization" is no longer the buzzword it once was, its influence is felt far and wide in Western society. We all belong to the cult of self-esteem, perpetually seeking to prop up our feelings about ourselves. Everyone gets a trophy nowadays.

After failing to show for a mandatory morning practice, Chris Duhon, a professional basketball player, was asked why he had left his floundering team the night before a crucial road game to enjoy a contest involving his alma mater halfway across the country. The player said the year had been going so poorly that he needed to rebuild his "self-esteem" with some of his friends. His shorthanded teammates, however, were forced to carry on the game without him—and lost.[2]

C. S. Lewis may have warned us of an "excessive and unhealthy interest" in the demonic. Perhaps he should have warned us of an excessive and unhealthy interest in the self. Or maybe he did, and we weren't paying attention.

Certainly there is a place for self-regard in the Christian life. The Bible tells us we are made in God's image,[3] fearfully and wonderfully made,[4] co-laborers with God,[5] and future judges of the angels.[6] Jesus died for us, so we are worth an immeasurable amount to God the Father. As the old saying goes, "God made me, and God doesn't make junk."

But there is a difference between biblical self-regard and idolizing the self. And that difference leads us to either heaven or hell. Jesus calls those who selfishly lay up treasure for themselves and are not rich toward God "fools"—not intellectually challenged, but morally bankrupt. He refuses to get involved in the ugly, petty squabbles over money and property that frequently surface among family members when someone dies. He's interested in much more valuable treasure: our very souls.

As we have looked at the questions Jesus asks about following him in this section of the book, we have pondered covetousness. But being rich toward the God who seeks a relationship with us (chapter 7) involves more than money—much more. It involves our very being. Chapter 8 pointed out that faith is not mere belief or intellectual assent. It is casting our lot with God and trusting him through the darkness. Chapter 9 describes discipleship as involving suffering and service while we wait confidently for God to provide our needs. Chapter 10, on Christ's lordship, points out that obedience is essential to Christ followers, but reminds us that our obligations bring true freedom. Chapter 11, on prayer, gives the reassuring promise that God watches over his people and will provide what we most need.

Death Before Life

Yet his loving provision for us is not a spiritual get-out-of-jail-free card. In this chapter, we return to a theme we considered in chapter 9: death. "I came that they may have life," Jesus said, "and have it abundantly."[7] Granted; but the bright, abundant living he offers comes with a shadow. Jesus's followers must walk through the valley of the shadow of death before we can reach the sunlit mountains of life. As Bonhoeffer said, "When Christ calls a man, he bids him come and die."[8]

This truth shines with awful clarity one day in Caesarea Philippi, where Jesus prays and then asks his disciples to identify who he is. As we saw in chapter 6, our understanding of Jesus's identity is all-important. It is such a pivotal scene that Jesus's biographers Matthew, Mark, and Luke recount it, each emphasizing many of the same (and some slightly different) details.[9]

Matthew quotes Peter as saying Jesus is "the Christ, the Son of the living God." Mark calls him "the Christ, the Son of God." Luke economizes Peter's words as simply "the Christ of God." As we look at Jesus's questions embedded in the incident, for brevity I will condense and combine the three accounts into one, interspersing them with my comments.[10]

> And he strictly charged and commanded them to tell this to no one, saying, "The Son of Man must suffer many things and be rejected by the elders and chief priests and scribes, and be killed, and on the third day be raised."

After commending his impetuous disciple, the Lord tells his men the uncomfortable implications. In the revolutionary first-century climate, with Israel under the thumb of Rome, such a title for Jesus would provoke the powers that be and call down their wrath—as indeed it eventually did. *Christ*, or *Messiah*, as we have seen, was a political title. For the Jews, it designated the coming one who would overthrow their oppressors. For the Romans, it indicated a challenger to imperial power.

And indeed, some angry Jews called for revolt and were crushed for it, including Theudas and Judas the Galilean.[11] No wonder Pilate acted against his conscience to execute the Lord after the Jewish leaders cried out, "If you release this man, you are not Caesar's friend. Everyone who makes himself a king opposes Caesar."[12]

With more ministry ahead, Jesus told his men to keep the truth about his identity quiet—for the time being. Interestingly, at this moment Jesus names the elders, chief priests, and scribes, but he does not mention here the actual perpetrators of his death—the Romans. But that will come. Jesus does, however, mention his coming resurrection, although the disciples are unwilling or unable to absorb this good news, in shock, as they must be, at hearing about his coming death.

> And Peter took him aside and began to rebuke him. "Far be it from you, Lord! This shall never happen to you." But turning and seeing his disciples, he rebuked Peter and said, "Get behind me, Satan! For you are not setting your mind on the things of God, but on the things of man."

Rebuking the Lord

First, imagine the temerity of Peter to even consider *rebuking* the Lord. There is no other incident recorded in the Gospels in which the disciples reprimand Jesus. Perhaps Peter is guilty of being "more spiritual" than Jesus. It's easy to see how this could happen.

His love for Jesus was real. When the risen Lord asked Peter the third time about his commitment, *"Simon, son of John, do you love me?"* the response was unequivocal: "Lord, you know everything, you know that I love you."[13] Here Peter could not bear to think of the Christ, the Son of God, suffering and dying. His rebuke seems to assert that he knows better than Jesus, that such pain should never touch God's Anointed. Is this merely a theological disagreement, to be resolved for Peter by more careful study of the Scriptures?

I think there is more going on here. Notice that Jesus now rebukes Peter, but using the name of the archenemy of God and humanity. This is not an academic debate. It is spiritual war. Jesus sees Peter's words as a temptation straight from hell for him to shirk his mission, which we concluded in chapter 5 was to die for our sins. But Peter says he knows better, that suffering and death "will never happen to you."

Perhaps what he meant was that this ignominious fate will never happen to *me*. When Peter signed up, no one told him that death was a part of the bargain. Joining the Messiah was supposed to be about glory and the sunlit slopes, not suffering and the shadow of death. Jesus then tells Peter that his disciple is focusing on his own priorities for security, success, and happiness—not God's. It is a temptation we all face: to seek God for what we can get, not for what we can give.

Taking Up Our Cross

> Then Jesus told his disciples, "If anyone would come after me, let him deny himself and take up his cross and follow me. For whoever would save his life will lose it, but whoever loses his life for my sake will find it. *For what will it profit a man if he gains the whole world and forfeits his life? Or what shall a man give in return for his life?"*

Now Jesus spells out the priorities for "anyone" who would "come after" him. They involve (1) denying yourself, (2) taking up your cross, and (3) following him. Doing just one is not an option. Two out of three isn't good enough. The operative word here is "and." We can't simply deny ourselves and follow him; we must also take up our cross. Neither can we just take up the cross and follow. We must do all three: deny, take up, *and* follow. Those who follow Jesus do not self-actualize; we self-deny. We don't "look out for No. 1"; we look out for him. We don't set our minds on selfish, worldly things; we set our minds on the things of God.

Then the Lord mentions the cross that *all* true disciples must bear. In fact, as we saw in chapter 9, it is an *individual* cross; for a follower, it is "his" (or her) cross. Not that Christians glory in our own death; far from it. It is never easy to take up our cross. Death never comes without pain, and we do not enjoy it. Jesus tells us to carry our cross *precisely because* death is so hard. Like all living things, we don't seek death, but life.

However, increasing numbers of militant Muslim mothers celebrate the deadly martyrdoms of their children and even blow themselves up in their twisted attempts to honor Allah. "We love death," Osama bin Laden has said. "The U.S. loves life. That is the big difference between us."[14] This Islamist embrace of death and murder is not only unnatural and perverted; it is un-Christian. Militant Muslims take their lives for Allah's cause; Jesus gave his life for God's. The Lord attended weddings and funerals, built friendships, and participated in the warp and woof of our existence. He recognizes that life is good, but calls his disciples to a higher life that can only be attained by dying to this one. And it is a death to self, not a wanton murder of others.

Now death on a Roman cross was the worst of ignominies for a Jew. Not only was crucifixion at the hands of Israel's pagan oppressors acute and prolonged, but it was seen as a sign of God's disfavor: as the ancient Scripture said, "Cursed is everyone who is hanged on a tree."[15] This is what following Jesus means: it is a walk unto death. Hinting at his coming execution, Jesus tells his men that they must also walk their own Via Dolorosas.

Yet while it is a universal call, it is a particular cross. No two crosses are alike. Peter was physically crucified for his Lord. John suffered a spiritual crucifixion on Patmos. But both men carried crosses.

Yet those who lose their life for Jesus will truly find it, because, as Bonhoeffer said, he is the source of the only true life. When letting go of this life for Jesus, the sacrifice is minuscule in view of all we stand to gain. A life of faith is certainly not boring. After learning that he had cancer (which would eventually kill him), Tony Snow felt "an inexplicable shudder of excitement, as if a clarifying moment of calamity has swept away everything trivial and tinny, and placed before us the challenge of important questions."[16] That is life—real life—in the midst of death.

Life and Death

Then Jesus lays out the alternatives: life and death. With his queries he urges his would-be disciples to not only count the cost of following him, but also to count the *greater* cost of *not* following him.

"*For what does it profit a man to gain the whole world and forfeit his life?*" Ever since the Declaration of Independence, Americans have been on a mad dash for "life, liberty, and the pursuit of happiness." And we have largely succeeded, if these three goals are attained through freedom, wealth, and leisure. Americans routinely tell pollsters that they are "happy," or even "very happy." And make no mistake: life, liberty, and happiness are good—but only if they are directed at the right things. They should be seen not as goals in themselves, but as means to even greater goals. Left to themselves, they turn our hearts inward, making our horizons small and our thoughts suffocatingly selfish. (Perhaps our hedonistic bent is why so many self-reported "happy" citizens are on mood-altering medications.) But as stepping stones to serve God and humanity, they move us beyond ourselves and catch us up into God's grand story to redeem and restore all of creation.

This question juxtaposes *gaining* the whole world and yet *losing* your life or self. Seen in this light, focusing solely on our own happiness—seeking to gain our life—ultimately will bring only misery and loss in the end. "To seek to secure one's own life in selfish disregard of its spiritual dimension is finally to lose it," says H. D. McDonald; "while to lose it for Christ's sake is to save it."[17] We've already heard from missionary martyr Jim Elliot, who said, "He is no fool who gives what he cannot keep to gain what he cannot lose."[18] Instead of vainly trying to *gain* the whole world—whether in packets of money, fame, power, or relationships—we ought to be giving away these things we cannot keep to gain God's eternal rewards, starting with their *sine qua non*, our own life or self.

"Life" in this case that Jesus references is much more than mere physical existence; it is the Greek word *psyche*, "the animating principle of life . . . a person's self."[19] Even a mocking Satan knows that life is man's paramount possession. "Skin for skin!" he snarled at the Lord when Job refused to curse God after the loss of all his possessions. "All that a man has he will give for his life."[20] Unfortunately, too often we short-sighted humans trade our lives for mere possessions—what we cannot keep.

The 1980s-era bumper sticker "He who dies with the most toys wins" is a bald-faced lie. Grasping at what we (or others) have is a sucker's bet, because what we acquire at the cost of our life must inevitably slip through our fingers. "John D. Rockefeller was one of the wealthiest men who ever lived," Randy Alcorn says. "After he died someone asked his accountant, 'How much money did John D. leave?' The reply was classic: 'He left . . . *all* of it.'"[21]

Selling Our Soul

"*Or what shall a man give in return for his life?*" This second question, looking at the issue from a slightly different angle, focuses not on *gaining* the world, but on attempting to *regain* one's life. It assumes that life is far more valuable than all that this world has to offer. It may also be that the person has already sold his or her soul for the things of this world and is having a major case of buyer's remorse. Not only has the focus on the things of this world failed to satisfy, it has cut the hapless soul off from the source of true life. Talk about bait and switch! At the beginning of the chapter we looked at Jesus's story of a rich man who lost it all—both the things of this world and, ultimately, his very soul. Being rich only toward self is the ultimate stupidity.

Jesus told a second story of misdirected wealth and another unnamed rich man.[22] It is commonly known as "The Rich Man and Lazarus." Curiously, only the poor man is named. Why did the rich man go unnamed? Perhaps because those who seek to save their life not only lose it, but lose their very identity as well. The story serves as a warning to those of us who are rich by the world's standards—and that includes nearly everyone in the West. Maybe the wealthy man is unnamed because he stands for *us*.

In the story, the rich man "was clothed in purple and feasted sumptuously every day." The poor man, Lazarus, was perpetually hungry and "covered with sores." He subsisted on the crumbs that fell from the rich man's table. Apparently the rich man would not even lift a finger to help his unfortunate compatriot. Are we similarly stingy, giving only our crumbs to the destitute around us, seen and unseen?

Then a great reversal occurs. First Lazarus dies, then the rich man. Angels carry Lazarus to live with the righteous patriarch Abraham, while the rich man ends up in Hades, where he is "in torment."

"Father Abraham," he pleads across the "great chasm" between them, "have mercy on me, and send Lazarus to dip the end of his finger in water and cool my tongue, for I am in anguish in this flame." At this point the rich man has no hope he can actually give *anything* in exchange for his life, for he has nothing to give. He is just hoping for a little relief. But the answer is no. His fate is sealed. Dante envisioned a sign before the gates of hell: "Abandon hope, all ye who enter here." Surely he had this awful story in mind. The one who seeks to save his life will lose it—irretrievably. If we are like the rich man, who had everything in this world and nothing—not even a drop of water—in the next, we will be unable to give anything to regain our souls.

Standing for Jesus

> For whoever is ashamed of me and of my words in this adulterous and sinful generation, of him will the Son of Man also be ashamed when he comes in the glory of his Father with the holy angels.[23]

Jesus then answers the unasked but all-important application question: how do we know whether we have the right priorities, whether we are focused on the things of humanity or God, whether we are saving our lives now (only to lose them later), or losing them now (only to gain them later)? The answer is deceptively simple. Are we willing to stand for Jesus? Are we willing to be martyrs—literally, witnesses—for the Lord?

Tim Stafford tells the story of a Sri Lankan Christian going by the name of Bernard.[24] This young man—"slight, almost delicate in his appearance"—was swept up in the island nation's ethnic and religious violence. In 1998 the Buddhist government threw Bernard, who was studying to be a pastor, into prison on suspicion of aiding the Hindu Tamil Tiger rebels. For two days Bernard was beaten and threatened with execution. Instead, his captors put him in an eight-by-eight-foot room with forty other men. "I shared Jesus Christ with many people," Bernard told Stafford. "It was a good place to tell about Jesus." Eventually Bernard was sent to a rehab center/prison. There he and two other Christians actively witnessed about Christ to their fellow prisoners, and a number of them became Christians.

But someone else complained, and the captain called Bernard in, demanding to know who had given him the authority to lead the group. "I said that God gave me the authority," Bernard said. "He made me kneel down on the floor, and he beat me." The new converts were also beaten.

"We were very glad of this, because of Christ," Bernard said. "It was a very useful experience for me. I learned how to communicate with people, how to counsel." Eventually he was released. Not all who follow Christ are.

Zia Nodred was another Christian who didn't seek to save his life. Blinded as an infant in Afghanistan when a doctor prescribed the wrong medicine, Zia was an outstanding linguist who first heard the gospel while listening to Christian radio. One day this Muslim young man was speaking with Betty Wilson, whose husband, J. Christy Wilson Jr., was pastor of the international church in Kabul (which was later destroyed by militants in 1973). Zia wanted her to explain the meaning of the substitutionary atonement of Christ, which he had heard about on the radio. (Most Muslims believe that Jesus did not really die on the cross.)

Later, Zia confided to her that he had accepted Jesus while listening to the radio. She asked whether he knew his life was at risk, because Islamic law calls for the death penalty for apostates. "I have calculated the cost," Zia replied, "and am ready to die for Christ, since he has already died for me on the cross."

Before escaping to Pakistan to avoid persecution from militant Muslims, Zia helped translate the New Testament into Afghan Persian. Warren Larson of the Zwemer Institute for Muslim Studies notes Zia's powerful ministry to Afghan refugees in Pakistan, where he evangelized Muslims "boldly and brilliantly."

But in 1988, Zia was coaxed back into Afghanistan under false pretenses. There the feared Afghan warlord Gulbuddin Hekmatyar kidnapped, tortured, and murdered Zia. "It is reported that his tongue was cut out," Larson says, "because he refused to stop speaking for his Lord."[25]

Living and Dying

But what of those of us who are not called to physically die for Jesus? And let's face it: that's most of us. How are *we* to serve as martyrs, as *living* witnesses to our Lord? How are we to lose our lives so that we may save them?

In one sense, losing our lives in this way isn't something we *do*; it's something we *are*. The apostle Paul considered his entire way of life before Christ, all his self-righteous striving, as pure loss.[26] He had died with Christ, only to find his life—this time, his *true* life. Paul didn't die with Christ through sheer force of will, either. Such a death is not something we can work up. Like our salvation, it is a gift we gratefully receive.

Jesus has told us to set our minds on the things of God, not on the things of this earth. Paul tells us the same thing, reminding us of the encouraging news that the death Jesus requires has already been achieved for us. Our part is not so much to kill our earthly self, but to live as though we were already dead. Yet we are to live not in death, but in what comes after death—resurrection. Jesus was raised; because of that, *we* will be raised.

Entropy teaches that things break down and die. But death is not the final reality for us. Death is real, but it is not our destination. We have already been raised in *God's* eyes, and one day we will be raised in the *world's* eyes. And we are to live today in light of this already-and-not-yet reality.

This resurrection life begins by setting our minds on the things of God. Hear Paul's words to the fledgling church in Colossae:

> If then you have been raised with Christ, seek the things that are above, where Christ is, seated at the right hand of God. Set your minds on things that are above, not on things that are on earth. For you have died, and your life is hidden with Christ in God. When Christ who is your life appears, then you also will appear with him in glory.[27]

Both Jesus and Paul end up at the same place in this matter—the second coming. The most powerful incentive to getting our priorities right, to losing our life so that we may find it, is understanding that this life is not the end. Most people in our secular society don't have the problem of being "so heavenly minded that they're no earthly good." The bigger problem is that we have too many people who are so earthly minded that they're no heavenly good.

Most of us deal with death by ignoring it, by hoping it will not visit our address. But suppressing this truth will not make it go away. It is said that nothing is more certain than death and taxes. That's only half true: some people successfully avoid the taxman, but none escape the Grim Reaper. Going through life without a backward glance at death shows that our teleology is flawed. *Star Trek II: The Wrath of Khan* got it right when Captain Kirk said, "How we deal with death is *at least* as important as how we deal with life."

Are we ready to die so that we may truly live? For what does it profit a person if she gains the whole world and loses or forfeits herself?

Suggested Reading

Alcorn, Randy. *The Treasure Principle: Discovering the Secret of Joyful Giving*. Sisters, OR: Multnomah, 2001.

Augustine. *The Confessions*. Translated by Sister Maria Boulding. Hyde Park, NY: New City Press, 1997.

Discussion Questions

1. Why is storing up things for ourselves foolish?
2. Is following Christ easy or hard?
3. How are the crosses that Christians carry the same? How might they be different?
4. What are some of the excuses we use to keep from dying to self so that we can live for God? How much water do they hold in the light of eternity?
5. Do you stand for Jesus when it is unpopular, inconvenient, or dangerous? Name an example.
6. How do we set our minds on heavenly things when all we see are earthly things?
7. How do we begin to live the resurrected life?

Where Is Your Thinking?

13

Discernment for Him

"What do you think?"

Bible-believing Christians have received fierce criticism from the liberal cultural elites for their supposed intellectual deficiencies. During the 2008 presidential primaries, one of the leading candidates offended many by describing a large section of disaffected voters as those who "cling to guns or religion"—as if religious belief is a sign of an intellectual or character flaw.

Evangelicals themselves have looked at their intellectual achievements in American society and sometimes found them wanting. "The scandal of the evangelical mind is that there is not much of an evangelical mind," historian Mark Noll has charged, saying Bible-believers have "largely abandoned the universities, the arts, and other realms of 'high' culture." Evangelicals have "failed notably in sustaining serious intellectual life."[1]

Such sour assessments would be unwelcome surprises to our spiritual ancestors, who saw loving God with all of our minds as a specifically Christian calling.[2] Sociologist Rodney Stark notes that the West advanced beyond all contemporary societies, scientifically and politically, not in spite of the Christian religion, but because of it. "The West is said to have surged ahead precisely as it overcame religious barriers to progress, especially those impeding science," Stark says in his groundbreaking book, *The Victory of Reason*. "Nonsense. The success of the West, including the rise of science, rested

153

entirely on religious foundations, and the people who brought it about were devout Christians."[3]

Stark calls several historical witnesses to the compatibility of the Christian faith with reason. One is Augustine of Hippo. "Heaven forbid that God should hate in us that by which he made us superior to the animals!" Stark quotes Augustine as exclaiming. "Heaven forbid that we should believe in such a way as not to accept or seek reasons, since we could not even believe if we did not possess rational souls." Clement of Alexandria stated, "Do not think that we say that these things are only to be received by faith, but also that they are to be asserted by reason. For indeed it is not safe to commit these things to bare faith without reason, since assuredly truth cannot be without reason."[4]

Stark lists four main reasons why the West was won by people of faith: (1) the development of faith in progress within Christian theology; (2) this faith in progress being translated into technological and organizational innovations; (3) theology-inspired reason leading to political states that allowed individual freedom; and (4) the application of reason to commerce, leading to capitalism.[5]

As we saw in chapter 7, the other world faiths cannot provide mankind with personal access to God. Stark asserts that they also fail the rationality test. He notes that only Christianity developed theology—defined as "*formal reasoning about God*"—as "a sophisticated, highly *rational* discipline."[6] He says,

> The emphasis is on discovering God's nature, intentions, and demands, and on understanding how these define the relationship between human beings and God. The gods of polytheism cannot sustain theology because they are far too inconsequential. Theology necessitates an image of God as a conscious, rational, supernatural being of unlimited power and scope who cares about humans and imposes moral codes and responsibilities on them, thereby generating serious intellectual questions.[7]

No wonder Jesus says we are to love God with our minds.[8] Anyone studying his questions, of course, will realize that they presuppose that people are rational beings able to reason out problems and connect on an intellectual level with this "conscious, rational, supernatural being of unlimited power and scope."

Jesus asks questions, of course, not because he is playing semantic games, but because he knows we can think them through and provide answers. He asks not in order to supply some lack in his understanding of an issue, but in ours. A good number of Jesus's questions assume and encourage not blind faith—though at times he does simply demand our trusting obedience—but discernment and a rational discipleship. "*What is written in the Law?*" Jesus asks. "*How do you read it?*"[9]

Back when IBM was the undisputed heavyweight champion of the computer world, the company had a simple slogan: "Think." Likewise, Jesus's questions call on us to do nothing less than use our God-given gray matter in his service.

God's Character

Jesus asks us to think as we consider God's character. Illustrating the idea that God cares about seemingly insignificant little children, he introduces the parable of the lost sheep with simple questions: "*What do you think? If a man has a hundred sheep and one of them has gone astray, does he not leave the ninety-nine on the mountains and go in search of the one that went astray?*" Just as it would be unthinkable for the man to simply shrug his shoulders over the lost sheep and say, "Oh, well," so it is inconceivable to the thoughtful disciple that God does not care about children: "So it is not the will of my Father who is in heaven that one of these little ones should perish."[10]

In the chapter on prayer, we saw God's generous heart contrasted with our sometimes-miserly character. Jesus draws us out of our self-absorbed fears that God will not answer our prayers with his question, "*What father among you, if his son asks for a fish, will give him a serpent; or if he asks for an egg, will give him a scorpion?*" The answer, once pondered, is obvious: "If you then, who are evil, know how to give good gifts to your children, how much more will the heavenly Father give the Holy Spirit to those who ask him!"[11]

If Jesus's questions show us the kindness of God, they also force us to thoughtfully face his severity. As we have seen, if people simply refuse to obey the truth right in front of them, eventually the Lord's judgment will come.[12] God's patience is great, but it is not endless, and this goes for nations as well as for individuals. In Jerusalem, just before his Passion, Jesus speaks of impending judgment for the nation of Israel, whose leaders rejected him and attributed his work to Satan (even as many Jews believed in him and became his disciples).

"Daughters of Jerusalem, do not weep for me, but weep for yourselves and for your children," Jesus told those mourning for him on his way to the cross. "*For if they do these things when the wood is green, what will happen when it is dry?*"[13] This judgment came in AD 70, when the Romans destroyed the city, scattering the Jewish people to the four winds.

Jesus tells the parable of the tenants, which describes the leaders' wicked misuse of the master's vineyard—the vineyard being a well-known allusion to Israel. The parable recounts the master sending a series of servants to collect his harvest from the tenants. But one after another they abuse and kill his emissaries. Finally he sends his son, whom they murder. Clearly, Jesus has in mind his own impending death. This brings special force to his question,

"When therefore the owner of the vineyard comes, what will he do to those tenants?"

The question is enough. Jesus doesn't need to pronounce judgment on the leaders; they do it themselves, answering, "He will put those wretches to a miserable death and let out the vineyard to other tenants who will give him the fruits in their seasons." And they understood his gracious warning: "When the chief priests and Pharisees heard his parables, they perceived that he was speaking about them."[14]

Opposing the Kingdom of Darkness

God's judgment extends beyond humanity to the angelic realms.[15] In the *Star Wars* myth, the dark and light sides of the Force are equal in power, and trouble only comes when they get out of balance. In biblical thinking, the kingdom of darkness and the kingdom of light, while opposed to one another now, are vastly different in power. For a time God allows Satan and his minions to traverse the earth and work evil within certain divinely proscribed limits.[16] But as Martin Luther asserted in "A Mighty Fortress," Satan's ultimate "doom is sure."

We see this clearly in the life of Christ and in his questions.[17] Here we will focus on the questions that compel our understanding of the truth that God and Satan are not equal. When Israel's leaders attribute Jesus's work to Satan or Beelzebul, the Lord's questions—presented from a number of angles—invite them to see the absurdity of their position.[18]

- *"And if Satan also is divided against himself, how will his kingdom stand?"*[19] Jesus asks. Translation: Satan's kingdom only advances through domination. Anyone being released from the devil's spiritual slave state cannot but undermine his power.
- *"And if I cast out demons by Beelzebul, by whom do your sons cast them out?"*[20] Jesus expands on the first point by pointing out that divine power is available to all God's followers, which Jesus's critics can clearly see.
- *"How can Satan cast out Satan?"*[21] Though cunning, the devil is unable to voluntarily weaken his grip on human lives, even temporarily. This reminds me of totalitarian states that ease up on their populace and then find themselves confronted with revolution. For Satan to loosen his grip even once is to invite the destruction of his kingdom. Satan is too insecure for that.
- *"Or how can someone enter a strong man's house and plunder his goods, unless he first binds the strong man?"*[22] There is no doubt that Satan is a "strong man," but Jesus has authority over him because he is stronger.

Satan will not give up his goods voluntarily, but he can be plundered by Christ. This happens every time someone is freed from demonic possession or turns from the kingdom of darkness to the kingdom of light.

Grasping these truths, using the minds God has provided us, gives us confidence in the face of evil. We know God's kingdom is greater and that Satan is on the run, the sand in his hourglass quickly running out. And Jesus can use us to rout him from his strongholds in this world. As David said,

> For it is you who light my lamp;
> the LORD my God lightens my darkness.
> For by you I can run against a troop,
>   and by my God I can leap over a wall.
> This God—his way is perfect;
> the word of the LORD proves true;
>   he is a shield for all who take refuge in him.
>
> For who is God, but the LORD?
> And who is a rock, except our God?—
>   the God who equipped me with strength
>   and made my way blameless.
> He made my feet like the feet of a deer
> And set me secure on the heights.[23]

Walking and Talking

Theologians today are known to argue over whether theology is narrative or propositional. That is, is theology primarily a story, or is it a systematic collection of truths? Do we know God primarily by his acts or by his words? The best answer is probably both/and, not either/or. These two kinds of truth often work together. Sometimes Jesus's questions tease out our capacity for critical thinking by asking us to evaluate what he has just demonstrated. They cause us to put into words what our eyes have just seen.

While truth is propositional (God is three-in-one, human beings are sinners, etc.), it is not *only* propositional. It is also lived out. To possess a truth without walking in that truth is inconceivable to the biblical authors. "Blessed is the man," the Psalmist observes, "who walks not in the counsel of the wicked . . . nor sits in the seat of scoffers; but his delight is in the law of the LORD, and on his law he meditates day and night."[24] The law—verbal communication— affects how we live and touches our hearts and minds. We receive the truth and act on it with our whole lives, not just with our cognitive abilities. We meditate on it. We turn it over in our minds until it becomes a part of us. The verbal interprets the nonverbal. That is what Jesus's questions accomplish.

During the Last Supper, Jesus gives his disciples a vital object lesson and then a diagnostic question to check their comprehension. In this case, he even supplies them with the answer, wanting to make sure they "get it."

> When [Jesus] had washed their feet and put on his outer garments and resumed his place, he said to them, *"Do you understand what I have done to you?* You call me Teacher and Lord, and you are right, for so I am. If I then, your Lord and Teacher, have washed your feet, you also ought to wash one another's feet. For I have given you an example, that you also should do just as I have done to you. Truly, truly, I say to you, a servant is not greater than his master, nor is a messenger greater than the one who sent him. If you know these things, blessed are you if you do them."[25]

Jesus asks a similar question after presenting a series of parables: *"Have you understood all these things?"*[26] The question here is not about raw obedience, but understanding. God cares about our *minds*.

Truth by Analogy

Like the parables, Jesus's questions enable us to see some deeper truth by analogy. An analogy presents "a meaning that is similar, but neither identical nor totally different."[27] For example, when telling people that his ministry will expose the secret things of their hearts, Jesus asks a seemingly absurd question with only one possible answer: *"Is a lamp brought in to be put under a basket, or under a bed, and not on a stand?"* The light is, of course, to be set up in a place where it can illuminate the dark places. Thus, Jesus follows up his question with a penetrating aphorism: "For nothing is hidden except to be made manifest; nor is anything secret except to come to light. If anyone has ears to hear, let him hear."[28] Jesus is here, and he will expose our dark secrets.

Here is another analogy Jesus presented with a question. After telling the crowds that judgment is coming and that following him will bring not peace but division, he warns them that they are failing to understand the present time, or *kairos*.[29]

> When you see a cloud rising in the west, you say at once, "A shower is coming." And so it happens. And when you see the south wind blowing, you say, "There will be scorching heat," and it happens. You hypocrites! *You know how to interpret the appearance of earth and sky, but why do you not know how to interpret the present time [kairos]?*[30]

Their priorities are wrong. They study the weather, which comes and goes, but this moment, this opportunity to align oneself with God's purposes, will never come again—and yet people don't use their brains to evaluate these unique circumstances and make the right decision. It is damnable ignorance.

Such attitudes are just as prevalent today. People study the stock market, the weather, the baseball box scores, how to land a good job, and many other subjects, some more worthy, some less. But they expend few or no brain cells on the most important matters: Is there a God? What is he like? What does he require of us? How do we get into heaven and stay out of hell?

There are answers, of course. To take just one example, in 1966 *Time* magazine published a cover with the stark question, "Is God dead?" The article examined a theological movement declaring that God is dead. Ironically, philosophical arguments in support of the existence of God have enjoyed a stunning renaissance in the academy since 1967, when Alvin Plantinga wrote *God and Other Minds: A Study of the Rational Justification of Belief in God.*[31]

But do we take the time and trouble to familiarize ourselves with these arguments? Or do we simply go on with our lives, listening to talk radio, going to sales, trading in our old vehicle for a shiny new model? Do we spend our life on what won't last, or do we make a rational decision to focus on matters vital to our eternal existence? French philosopher Blaise Pascal said the most rational thing you can do is to choose to believe in Christ in the face of doubt, because the punishment for being wrong is so slight (the loss of nothing) and the promised gain for being right is so grand (eternal life).

But I believe evidence for the Christian religion is available to any open mind, making faith not blind, but eminently reasonable.[32] Certainly God's Spirit is indispensable in this process,[33] and many Protestants, including theologian Karl Barth, have held that genuine knowledge of God by natural, unsaved man is impossible because our minds are warped so completely by our total depravity.[34]

And yet Jesus treats us as rational creatures, saying, "If anyone's will is to do God's will, he will know whether the teaching is from God or whether I am speaking on my own authority."[35] No, intellectual belief is not decisive, but you can't have true discipleship without it.

Words and Deeds

Another analogy (and analogy presupposes a person's ability to see both the similarities and the differences in the comparison): speaking in the Sermon on the Mount (which is full of analogies), Jesus says that we must keep our guard up against false religious teachers.

> Beware of false prophets, who come to you in sheep's clothing but inwardly are ravenous wolves. You will recognize them by their fruits. *Are grapes gathered from thornbushes, or figs from thistles?* So, every healthy tree bears good fruit, but the diseased tree bears bad fruit.[36]

Healthy or diseased, productive or weedy, the fruit reveals the nature of the tree or vine. Certainly Jesus's question here has been confirmed countless times in church history. Bad doctrine, or erroneous orthodoxy, leads to bad living, or erroneous orthopraxy. Whether we are observing the Jim Jones cult, a polygamous group in Texas, or other aberrant sects that claim to possess the true faith, their walk reveals their talk. While no group follows God's truth perfectly, of course, those that start off on the wrong foot doctrinally quickly end up in a ditch—and often in sexual sin. Those who evaluate these groups with a thoughtful and critical eye will see them for what they are: diseased trees.

Orthopraxy, with a heart warmed by faith, is very much on Jesus's mind when he tells the parable of the two sons. Jesus opens and closes the parable with questions:

> *What do you think?* A man had two sons. And he went to the first and said, "Son, go and work in the vineyard today." And he answered, "I will not," but afterward he changed his mind and went. And he went to the other son and said the same. And he answered, "I go, sir," but did not go. *Which of the two did the will of his father?*[37]

Obviously, the first. Jesus was telling his opponents to think critically about what their eyes were showing them about his ministry. Like the first son, the tax collectors and prostitutes—who had denied God by their very choice of profession—were entering the kingdom. Meanwhile, the chief priests and elders—who ostensibly had said yes to God by their vocations—ultimately denied him by rejecting Jesus.

When asked, "Who is my neighbor?" by a man wishing to lighten the responsibility of actually loving his neighbor, Jesus does not give a dry, theoretical answer. Instead, he tells the story of the good Samaritan, who acted in a neighborly way to a Jewish man who had been mugged. Two Jewish leaders in the story, meanwhile, had ignored the man's plight.

"*Which of these three, do you think, proved to be a neighbor to the man who fell among the robbers?*" Jesus asks. Unable to even spit out the word *Samaritan*, the man replies, "The one who showed him mercy." Jesus then produces the killer application, "You go, and do likewise." Orthodox words must produce orthodox deeds.[38]

Reason Plus Faith

As we have seen, rationality without faith only takes us so far. One night Nicodemus, a member of the Pharisees (a group often hostile to the Lord), comes to Jesus to get more information: "Rabbi, we know that you are a teacher come from God, for no one can do these signs that you do unless God is with him."

Jesus cryptically tells the timid but questioning religious leader that, though he is on the way spiritually, he is not there yet: "unless one is born again, he cannot see the kingdom of God."

Nicodemus, operating purely on a rational level, then asks incredulously: "How can a man be born when he is old? Can he enter a second time into his mother's womb and be born?" Jesus answers curtly that the new birth is of the Spirit, and a dumbfounded Nicodemus blurts out, "How can these things be?" Jesus then provides him with a brief gospel presentation, interspersed with questions urging Nicodemus to think:

> Are you the teacher of Israel and yet you do not understand these things? Truly, truly, I say to you, we speak of what we know, and bear witness to what we have seen, but you do not receive our testimony. If I have told you earthly things and you do not believe, how can you believe if I tell you heavenly things? No one has ascended into heaven except he who descended from heaven, the Son of Man. And as Moses lifted up the serpent in the wilderness, so must the Son of Man be lifted up, that whoever believes in him may have eternal life.[39]

We see Jesus telling Nicodemus to grasp the analogy between earthly and heavenly things. Here the Lord seems disappointed, even frustrated or surprised, that a teacher of Israel has no spiritual sensitivity to these analogies, that his rationality is unguided by his faith. We need to beware the same danger in our own lives.

Jesus often checks up on his disciples' rational/spiritual sensitivity with questions.

- "Can a blind man lead a blind man? Will they both not fall into a pit?"[40]
- "Why do you see the speck that is in your brother's eye, but do not notice the log that is in your own eye? How can you say to your brother, 'Brother, let me take out the speck that is in your eye,' when you yourself do not see the log that is in your own eye?"[41]
- "Do you not understand this parable? How then will you understand all the parables?"[42]
- "Then are you also without understanding? Do you not see that whatever goes into a person from outside cannot defile him, since it enters not his heart but his stomach, and is expelled?"[43]
- "Can the wedding guests fast while the bridegroom is with them?"[44]

Sometimes perfectly rational people switch off their minds when it comes to matters of faith. Perhaps it is the scientist who stands in awe before the ancient immensity of the universe who has no curiosity over who made it.

But what could be more important than knowing whether there is a supreme being, and what this being is like? Isn't ignoring this ultimately irrational? Certainly God's existence cannot be proven with scientific precision, but a lack of such proof does not negate the need to investigate the evidence available both from special revelation (God's Word) and general revelation (God's world, see Rom. 1:18–20).

Many have found that their most serious objections melt away like ice on a summer day when the light of reason and an open heart are trained on them. Christian apologetics can help, even in our supposedly postmodern age. Presenting the evidence for Christian faith allows people to exercise their critical thinking, which opens the door to an exercise of faith. "It is the broader task of Christian apologetics, including natural theology, to help create and sustain a cultural milieu in which the gospel can be heard as an intellectually viable option for thinking men and women," Christian philosopher William Lane Craig writes. "It thereby gives people the intellectual permission to believe when their hearts are moved."[45] No, all truth is not propositional and logical. But we won't get far in the Christian life without using our minds.

Planning to Believe

We can learn much of the spiritual realm through the sanctified use of our minds. For example, planning and priorities, which don't seem very "spiritual," are in fact vital to the Christian life.

> Now great crowds accompanied him, and he turned and said to them, "If anyone comes to me and does not hate his own father and mother and wife and children and brothers and sisters, yes, and even his own life, he cannot be my disciple. Whoever does not bear his own cross and come after me cannot be my disciple. *For which of you, desiring to build a tower, does not first sit down and count the cost, whether he has enough to complete it?* Otherwise, when he has laid a foundation and is not able to finish, all who see it begin to mock him, saying, 'This man began to build and was not able to finish.' *Or what king, going out to encounter another king in war, will not sit down first and deliberate whether he is able with ten thousand to meet him who comes against him with twenty thousand?* And if not, while the other is yet a great way off, he sends a delegation and asks for terms of peace. So therefore, any one of you who does not renounce all that he has cannot be my disciple."[46]

Forget about being "poor, uneducated, and easy to command." Christ wants thinking disciples. Choosing to follow him with your mind is the most rational thing you can do.

Suggested Reading

Plantinga, Alvin. *God and Other Minds: A Study of the Rational Justification of Belief in God*. Ithaca, NY: Cornell University Press, 1990.

Stark, Rodney. *The Victory of Reason: How Christianity Led to Freedom, Capitalism, and Western Success*. New York: Random House, 2005.

Discussion Questions

1. Why are evangelicals caricatured as "poor, uneducated, and easy to command"? How accurate is this characterization?
2. Why does Christianity have a rich heritage of reason as a Christian duty?
3. In what ways is reason not strictly rational?
4. How does propositional truth relate to other kinds of truth?
5. How does reason relate to character?
6. Why is reasoning by analogy so important to the Christian?
7. How do we sometimes use reason to sever us from a life of faith?
8. How does reason sort through the evidence of general and special revelation?

14

Self-examination for Him

"Why do you ask me?"

Bible-believing Christians face criticism in Western society, not only for their presumed intellectual deficiencies, but also for their moral ones. Barna Group researchers David Kinnaman and Gabe Lyons report that many young people distrust Christians. "Outsiders consider us hypocritical—saying one thing and doing another—and they are skeptical of our morally superior attitudes," Kinnaman and Lyons write in their book *unChristian*. "They say Christians pretend to be something unreal, conveying a polished image that is not accurate."[1]

While it is easy for non-Christians to unfairly stereotype those they don't understand, we have to admit that at least sometimes they are right. Ron Sider's book *The Scandal of the Evangelical Conscience* carries the provocative subtitle *Why Are Christians Living Like the Rest of the World?* The book documents the fact that despite our professions of faith and high moral standards, many of us—when it comes to moral issues such as divorce—do not live all that differently from the rest of society.[2]

And even those of us who do manage to keep our standards must face the fact that we sometimes are putting on a show, making ourselves look better than we really are. During a Q&A session at a conference for young people called Passion 2007, a student asked one of the speakers, author and pastor

John Piper, how he stayed so humble. Piper responded to the query, like Jesus, with a question: "How do you know I'm humble?"[3]

How do we know this, even for ourselves? Such knowledge is elusive for sin-scarred human beings, who are quick to overlook our faults and God's holy standards. Such self-assessment, if done honestly, is a recipe for humility. As pastor C. J. Mahaney says in his book, *Humility: True Greatness*, "Humility is honestly assessing ourselves in light of God's holiness and our sinfulness."[4]

Jesus's questions of self-examination force us to dig deep into our souls. Jesus asked the self-righteous Pharisees, who were satisfied with outer appearances and unchanged hearts: "*Did not he who made the outside make the inside also?*"[5] When allowed to do their work, these questions peel away the upper layers of our polished, religious exteriors, allowing the festering sores of our hypocrisy and self-absorption to be healed when exposed to the life-giving breeze of the Spirit. In C. S. Lewis's classic Narnia tale, *The Voyage of the Dawn Treader*, the self-absorbed Eustace is turned into a dragon, symbolizing his selfishness and greed. Only when the great lion Aslan, who symbolizes Christ, painfully slices off Eustace's scaly epidermal layers is the boy set free to follow. Like the Word of God of which they constitute a part, Jesus's questions are "living and active, sharper than any two-edged sword, piercing to the division of soul and of spirit, of joints and of marrow, discerning the thoughts and intentions of the heart."[6]

Self-Deception

Jesus, of course, was not shocked by hypocrisy. He confronted it at every turn, and graciously tried to tear it off of his opponents—not to win an argument, but to save their souls. Here we will examine those questions that bear directly on people's need for self-examination.

Hypocrisy is revealed when mere religiosity confronts the light of true holiness. In the chapter on the Lord's identity, we saw how the religious establishment tried to trap him into a no-win situation by asking whether the Jews should pay taxes to Rome. Mark's Gospel peers into Jesus's heart to show us our own: "But knowing their hypocrisy, he said to them, '*Why put me to the test?*'"[7] They did so not because they wanted an answer, but because they were playing a deadly religious game.

Sometimes we can play this game so much that we don't even realize it. Here's a word of advice: Don't play games with Jesus. If you are weary and heavy-laden, by all means, go to him.[8] He will be waiting. But don't use him to hypocritically score cheap religious points. He isn't interested in playing along with your self-deception.

"We are all capable of believing things which we know to be untrue," George Orwell said in 1946, "and then, when we are finally proved wrong, impudently twisting the facts so as to show that we were right. Intellectually, it is possible to carry on this process for an indefinite time: the only check on it is that sooner or later a false belief bumps up against solid reality, usually on a battlefield."[9]

Reality may be delayed, but it is never denied. After demonstrating his identity through word and deed to the hypocritical Pharisees over and over, they come demanding yet another sign. Jesus asks, "*Why does this generation seek a sign?*" And his answer is ominous, for them and us: "Truly, I say to you, no sign will be given to this generation."[10]

We see religious hypocrisy throughout the arrest and trial of Jesus. And this is no surprise. Hypocrisy is indispensable if religious leaders are to kill the greatest religious leader who ever lived. When the soldiers come to arrest him at Gethsemane, Jesus asks his betrayer, "*Judas, would you betray the Son of Man with a kiss?*"[11] To the crowd that had come to arrest him, he asks, "*Whom do you seek?*"[12] and "*Have you come out as against a robber, with swords and clubs?*"[13]

At Jesus's illegal late-night trial,[14] the religious authorities are interrogating him.[15] The charges against Jesus are three: (1) he had threatened to destroy the temple, (2) he had claimed to be God's Son, and (3) he had incited the people against Caesar.[16] The high priest asks Jesus about his disciples and teaching. According to Jewish law, the only accusers allowed at a trial are witnesses to the alleged crimes, and in this case the witnesses' testimony against Jesus does not agree.[17] So the high priest seeks incriminating testimony from the lips of Jesus himself, who refuses to play along.

> I have spoken openly to the world. I have always taught in synagogues and in the temple, where all Jews come together. I have said nothing in secret. *Why do you ask me?* Ask those who have heard me what I said to them; they know what I said.[18]

Sending the high priest back to the rules of evidence, Jesus exposes his hypocrisy. Acting like the protector of God's law, the high priest subverts it in a mad quest to silence this upstart. The high priest's question masks the fact that this is a kangaroo court. "Why do you ask *me*?" Jesus asks in return. It is a question he also asks us.

Jesus does not brook hypocrites. The Lord sees past our facades, under our skin, and into our heart. Our religious titles mean nothing without a life to match. (In fact, they can make us even more culpable.) We cannot use him to oppress others or consolidate our power. Jesus hates it when any pastor, bishop, elder, priest, cult leader, or televangelist takes advantage of his position to exploit his flock. Flowing robes or an impressive, large congregation, a bestseller or a popular radio program cannot conceal a heart stained with sin.

People who blindly follow such leaders don't get off the hook, either.

> When [the Lord] had said these things, one of the officers standing by struck Jesus with his hand, saying, "Is that how you answer the high priest?" Jesus answered him, *"If what I said is wrong, bear witness about the wrong; but if what I said is right, why do you strike me?"*[19]

When one of the officers at the trial defends the honor of the high priest by hitting Jesus (a legal and moral transgression), the Lord graciously asks him a probing question about his own failure to live up to the light he has. We too are responsible. We cannot say, as some of the Nazi guards did, that we were "just following orders." It didn't work at Nuremburg, and it won't work for us on Judgment Day. Sometimes I get discouraged when I see the multitudes following false religions or cult leaders. I become even more discouraged, however, when I see people who have access to God's true revelation, as this officer did, misusing that access to harm others.

Yet this question—*"Why do you strike me?"* (echoed later in the risen Lord's question, *"Saul, Saul, why are you persecuting me?"*[20])—is somehow oddly encouraging. From the greatest to the least, people are free moral agents made in the image of God, responsible for their choices and acts. We are not mindless zombies but consequential moral agents. Our choices matter. We *matter*. Would we really wish it to be any other way?

Of course, we do not all bear the same moral responsibility for our choices. We are responsible according to the light we have. The Jewish leaders, for example, apparently bore more responsibility for the death of Christ than did Pontius Pilate, even though it was Pilate who actually ordered the execution. They had more light. Jesus tells Pilate before the crucifixion, "You would have no authority over me at all unless it had been given you from above. Therefore he who delivered me over to you has the greater sin."[21] Our culpability is not uniform. But we are *all* responsible. Rather than reach for the speck in someone else's eye, we must learn to remove the log in ours.

> *Why do you see the speck that is in your brother's eye, but do not notice the log that is in your own eye? Or how can you say to your brother, "Let me take the speck out of your eye," when there is the log in your own eye?* You hypocrite, first take the log out of your own eye, and then you will see clearly to take the speck out of your brother's eye.[22]

We are not robots. God has given us the freedom, by his power, to obey. But confronting our responsibility and guilt requires thoughtful self-examination, the kind Jesus's questions force on us.

Spiritual Nearsightedness

Often Jesus encountered people who were living only according to a shallow interpretation of the rules, unable to make further moral progress. They knew they shouldn't murder but didn't realize that the heart of murder is hatred; they knew adultery is wrong but didn't see the connection with lust; they grasped the permissibility of divorce but not the sanctity of marriage.[23] Repeatedly he told them a surface approach to godly living is insufficient for living a life that reflects God's mercy, justice, and love. We must think more deeply and get at the heart of the matter.

We know from looking around us that surface living is not enough. We need to grapple with the complexity of life, both physical and spiritual. We see the grandeur of creation, and also its brutal ugliness. We see the wonder of birth and the pain of abortion, the grace of a tiger and the dismembering of its prey. We must explain these facts of earthly life that seem in conflict— and so it goes with spiritual life. To discover a deeper explanation for how everything fits together requires our careful thought.

Sometimes we are guilty of judging by appearances. We see the businessman with the spacious home and three-car garage and judge him more successful than we are. We do not see the infidelities, large and small, that undermine his marriage and will one day bring him to spiritual, social, and financial ruin. We see the family raising the child with Down syndrome, wondering why God is punishing them and silently praising this same God for not giving us that cup of suffering. We do not see the unadulterated joy of this child in the everyday, nor the godly character being built, brick by brick, into the hearts of his parents and siblings—character that will prepare them for all that this life and the next have to offer. We are trapped by our spiritual nearsightedness when judging by appearances. Looking only at what we can see, we miss what God is really up to. We need to put on spiritual spectacles.

Working on the Sabbath

Some in the Jerusalem crowd are mystified—upset, really—that Jesus has the temerity to heal a man on the Sabbath. Doesn't this supposed prophet know that work is only allowed Sunday through Thursday? They are unable to see the deeper truths even in the law in which they trust. "*If on the Sabbath a man receives circumcision, so that the law of Moses may not be broken,*" Jesus asks, "*are you angry with me because on the Sabbath I made a man's whole body well? Do not judge by appearances, but judge with right judgment.*"[24]

Judging with right judgment requires making moral distinctions. Not every moral issue carries equal weight. "Woe to you, scribes and Pharisees, hypocrites!" Jesus thundered. "For you tithe mint and dill and cumin, and have neglected the weightier matters of the law: justice and mercy and faithfulness."[25]

Some sins are judged more harshly than others. Sometimes the law of love requires that we set aside one aspect of God's law to fulfill a more important one. The law said, for example, that people with leprosy were unclean and could not be touched, and there was a perfectly good reason for this seemingly harsh rule—the protection of the community from an outbreak of disease. Lepers had to keep their distance and, because of their much-feared affliction, were treated as tragic pariahs.

One day, however, in one of the cities of Galilee, a man "full of leprosy" fell on his face before Jesus. "Lord," the man said in a determined voice, "if you will, you can make me clean." It was an audacious, desperate request—topped only by Jesus's response. "And Jesus stretched out his hand and touched him, saying, 'I will; be clean.' And immediately the leprosy left him."[26]

Jesus could have healed the man without touching him, as he did for the servant of a faithful Roman centurion.[27] This would have done the job while fulfilling the letter of the law. But Jesus was doing something more important: restoring the man's soul and his position in the community. Jesus also disregarded the Mosaic injunction not to have contact with the dead when he went up to a funeral procession and touched the bier, compassionately raising a widow's only son.[28]

Grasping these kinds of distinctions requires careful thought. While there are many good things Christians should do to extend God's compassion to a hurting world and promote his glory, some are more important than others, and the more important duties come first. For example, people are more important than other obligations, even those mandated by God's Word. As God says in the book of Isaiah, required religious performance is damnable presumption without a heart and life to match:

> What to me is the multitude of your sacrifices?
>   says the LORD;
> I have had enough of burnt offerings of rams. . . .
>
> Bring no more vain offerings;
>   incense is an abomination to me. . . .
> When you spread out your hands,
>   I will hide my eyes from you;
> even though you make many prayers,
>   I will not listen;
>   your hands are full of blood.
> Wash yourselves; make yourselves clean;
>   remove the evil of your deeds from before my eyes;
> cease to do evil,
>   learn to do good;
> seek justice,
>   correct oppression;
> bring justice to the fatherless,
>   plead the widow's cause.[29]

Man-made Rules

Which is more important to us, checking off our compliance with basic rules, or seeking to live out God's compassion daily? Often we don't have to choose—but not always. Do we limit our witness and effectiveness by slavishly following someone's cramped interpretation of God's law—no movies, drinking, or dancing—rather than, like Jesus, seeking to minister to those around us? Jesus was to be found on the mean streets of his day, in the bars, and in the psych wards. So must we.

Another man-made rule that made first-century Jews blind to larger truths prohibited people from swearing by the temple concerning a business debt, but not by the gold in the temple. According to this interpretation, "The Temple and the altar provide no surety, therefore, and make oaths in their name meaningless. But a creditor might well claim the gold dedicated by his debtor on the altar."[30]

Jesus, however, says those involved in the business deal had forgotten who is watching over the transaction. "*For which is greater*," Jesus asks, "*the gift or the altar that makes the gift sacred?*"[31] According to commentator Walter Elwell, "the whole view is flawed, for it takes no account of God—who gives the temple and its contents their meaning."[32] Again, we live our whole lives—not just our religious lives—*coram deo*, before the face of God. We cannot wall off one part of it—perhaps the business portion—from him. God expects holistic obedience.

We see the same principle at work when Jesus tells the crowds that slavish scrupulousness with regard to Jewish dietary restrictions cannot give us a pure heart or a clear conscience before God. Would that it were that simple!

> And he called the people to him again and said to them, "Hear me, all of you, and understand: There is nothing outside a person that by going into him can defile him, but the things that come out of a person are what defile him."[33]

We cannot look on the outside. We cannot judge by appearances. We must go deeper. In fact, as author and psychologist Larry Crabb said, "Our Lord reserved his harshest criticism for people who made denial into a trademark. The Pharisees specialized in looking good. They managed to preserve their image by defining sin in terms of visible transgressions and then scrupulously adhering to the standards they established. Their source of joy was the respect of others, and they found effective means of gaining it."[34] Even Jesus's disciples, who should have known better, were shocked by Jesus's demand for inner righteousness. Jesus sets them straight with a couple of penetrating questions.

> And when he had entered the house and left the people, his disciples asked him about the parable. And he said to them, "*Then are you also without understand-*

ing? Do you not see that whatever goes into a person from outside cannot defile him, since it enters not his heart but his stomach, and is expelled?" (Thus he declared all foods clean.) And he said, "What comes out of a person is what defiles him. For from within, out of the heart of man, come evil thoughts, sexual immorality, theft, murder, adultery, coveting, wickedness, deceit, sensuality, envy, slander, pride, foolishness. All these evil things come from within, and they defile a person."[35]

The inward look is indispensable for the Christian, not because we enjoy the process of navel-gazing, but because we are such deep-seated sinners.

Gazing on Sin

Many of us, however, are skilled in self-deception. I am one of them. There was a point in my career when I believed I desperately needed some recognition—both for personal and professional reasons. Personally, I was doubting my calling and effectiveness and needed some reassurance that I was in the right place. Professionally, I was experiencing one discouragement after another and I thought the recognition would bolster me in my place of work. Seemingly from God, several of my articles were entered in a national contest. If I won (or at least put in a very good showing), perhaps the pressure would be relieved. I was competing against Christian journalists from across the country but didn't pray too much for their success. It was all about me.

The contest results came in during a particularly tough time at the office, and my awards were modest, to say the least. Instead of being happy for the winners, I was crushed and embarrassed by my seeming mediocrity. The results depressed me for the better part of a weekend, and the letdown drained me both physically and emotionally. Why had I failed so miserably? Wasn't I cut out for this line of work? The self-doubt tormented me.

Then the spiritual fog began to clear when my wife told me, in effect, to snap out of it. I began to reflect on a couple of vital facts about my career that were true whether some fellow journalist I didn't even know thought my work was good or not. (1) God had put me in my place of service not to win awards but to help people and to provide for my family—and by his grace I undeniably had been able to do both. (2) My skills, however good or bad, were gifts from God and not things to exult or despair over. They are given, as Paul says, "for the common good,"[36] not for my selfish image boosting. They are to be used with thankfulness for God's kingdom. Boasting or crying over them is inappropriate. As Paul also said, "by the grace of God I am what I am."[37] Examining our sinful motives for even good things can be excruciatingly hard.

As Crabb says in his book *Inside Out,*

Fallen man has taken command of his own life, determined above all else to prove that he's adequate for the job. And like the teen who feels rich until he starts paying for his own car insurance, we remain confident of our ability to manage life until we face the reality of our own soul. Nothing is more humbling than the recognition of (1) a deep thirst that makes us entirely dependent on someone else for satisfaction and (2) a depth of corruption that stains everything we do—even our efforts to reform—with selfishness. To realistically face what is true within us puts us in touch with a level of helplessness we don't care to experience.[38]

Jesus's questions force us to thoughtfully face our inner corruption, for only as we face it can we forsake it. In the previous chapter we observed Jesus on his way to the cross exhorting the crowds in Jerusalem to critical thinking by asking why they don't "know how to interpret the present time."[39] His presence brings crisis and means a break with old ways. In the next breath, Jesus warns by analogy that, just as a smart person would settle with a legal adversary rather than risking losing in court and going to jail, it is time for them to reconcile with God, with whom the stakes are incalculably higher. This crisis of the soul—which we all face—requires careful thought. Do we really understand our predicament before God? Jesus's question is meant to slap us in the face: "*And why do you not judge for yourselves what is right?*"[40]

It is a frightening measure of humanity's sinfulness that Jesus, our sinless Creator and Redeemer who spoke the words of eternal life, engendered not only hatred, but—even more damning—indifference. At the home of a Pharisee named Simon, Jesus contrasted his host's indifference with the overflowing gratitude of a "woman of the city, who was a sinner." Telling the Pharisee a parable about a moneylender who forgave two debts of unequal sizes, Jesus asked, "*Now which of them will love him more?*" The implication: the Pharisee who did not come to Jesus for pardon was not forgiven. To drive home the point, he directed Simon's gaze to the grateful woman of the streets, asking, "*Do you see this woman?*" Frighteningly, there is no indication that the self-satisfied Simon ever similarly repented.[41]

As the apostle John noted rather incredulously, "He was in the world, and the world was made through him, yet the world did not know him. He came to his own, and his own people did not receive him."[42]

There is no cause to blame the Jews exclusively for the death of Jesus. We *all* turned our backs on him. If you don't believe this, look at today's world. Would Jesus's light be welcomed into our internet chat rooms? Our places of work and professional backstabbing? Our affairs? Our genocides? Our apathies? Our petty indulgences? Just as we all ate the fruit, so we all murdered Jesus.

Used to hearing our reflexive words of honor, today the Lord still asks, "*Why do you seek to kill me?*"[43] We see Jesus's matchless words and deeds and praise him as a prophet, as a revolutionary, as a defender of women and the poor, as a holy man. But Jesus asks for more. As God incarnate, one with the Father, Jesus demands our everything—and we pick up stones to silence him. "*I have shown you many good works from the Father,*" Jesus says; "*for which of them are you going to stone me?*"[44] As he also noted, "And this is the judgment: the light has come into the world, and people loved the darkness rather than the light because their deeds were evil."[45]

This sinful desire for darkness over light is true whether we call ourselves followers of God or not. And such religiously rooted sinfulness is a special abomination to Jesus. One day the mother of his disciples James and John approaches the Lord with a request. Keep in mind that Jesus has just told his followers that he will be condemned to death, mocked, flogged, and crucified.

The grasping woman—and we all have seen parents like her—apparently wasn't listening and has nothing but blind ambition for her boys as she kneels before the Lord. His question ought to have brought her up short: "*What do you want?*" Breathtakingly, the mother's answer is not about bringing in Christ's kingdom, but about what recognition James and John will receive: "Say that these two sons of mine are to sit, one at your right hand and one at your left, in your kingdom." Audacity doesn't begin to describe what she wants. As we saw previously, the answer to this unworthy request was a curt no.[46]

We may chuckle at her chutzpah. We might be better off, however, asking ourselves the same question: what do *we* want out of Jesus? We all are naturally repulsed at Christians who use their faith as a means to gain wealth, power, and recognition. God is not a divine butler, and Jesus gave up all he had to save us from our sin. Now it's quite true that God's blessings for his children are many, and he always gives far more than we deserve. But John Piper has rightly said the real reward of the Christian life is not some bestowal of divine blessings, but God himself: "God is the gospel."[47] Paul blasted those "depraved in mind and deprived of the truth [who suppose] that godliness is a means of gain."[48] Such an attitude is not a harmless peccadillo but evidence of a deep, inward depravity.

Paul the devoted religious man had to face his own depravity, for one of the questions of the risen Lord ("*Saul, Saul, why are you persecuting me?*"[49]) plunged him into a painful season of self-examination. When Paul emerged from it, he willingly and completely abandoned his self-righteousness "because of the surpassing worth of knowing Christ Jesus my Lord."[50] John Calvin had it right when he said: "It is evident that a man never attains to a true self-knowledge until he has previously contemplated the face of God, and come down after such contemplation to look into himself."[51]

Are we ready to encounter the risen Lord on the road and examine our own hearts?

Suggested Reading

Mahaney, C. J. *Humility: True Greatness*. Sisters, OR: Multnomah, 2005.
Sider, Ron. *The Scandal of the Evangelical Conscience: Why Are Christians Living Like the Rest of the World?* Grand Rapids: Baker, 2005.

Discussion Questions

1. Why are evangelicals so often called hypocrites?
2. How can we root out the hypocrisy in our lives?
3. Do you believe in a hierarchy of moral issues? Why or why not?
4. In what ways do we keep faith too simple?
5. How do we move below a surface-level approach to righteousness?
6. Do you *feel* like a sinner? Does this matter?
7. How is God the best reward for the Christian?

15

Overcoming Anxiety for Him

*"Which of you by being anxious can
add a single hour to his span of life?"*

Despite September 11, 2001, and the periodic economic woes common to all industrialized societies, Americans live in the most prosperous, powerful, and safe nation in the history of the world. And yet they worry as if the world is falling apart.

The National Institute of Mental Health (NIMH) says that 40 million American adults experience anxiety disorders.[1] Stress, sleep disorders, mental illness, and other conditions linked to our anxiety run rampant in Western society. We worry about our weight, our cholesterol and triglycerides, the size or appearance of our sexual organs, whether we will save enough for retirement (remember the TV ad where the grown son sends his aging parents back into the work world with the cheery words, "Get out there and make me proud"?), our kids' grades (and whether they will be able to go to Harvard and get a job that will enable them to take care of us in our old age), whether we will survive cutbacks at work, and on and on.

Something is wrong with our thinking, because our mental pictures do not correspond to the world as it is. We're anxious. Anxiety is a "state of uneasiness and distress about future uncertainties; apprehension; worry." It suggests not an objective reality of danger but "feelings of fear and concern detached

175

from objective sources, feeding themselves, as it were."[2] A lot of times, FDR's words of comfort during the Depression ring true: "The only thing we have to fear is fear itself."

The NIMH has a name for our affliction: Generalized Anxiety Disorder. The malady is "characterized by chronic anxiety, exaggerated worry and tension, even when there is little or nothing to provoke it." Those with GAD "can't seem to shake their concerns. Their worries are accompanied by physical symptoms, especially fatigue, headaches, muscle tension, muscle aches, difficulty swallowing, trembling, twitching, irritability, sweating, and hot flashes."[3] A quick Google web search turns up 190 million hits for anxiety, and another 63.1 million for worry.[4]

Despite all our blessings and against our better judgment, we find it nearly impossible to obey Jesus's command to "not be anxious for tomorrow."[5] Sometimes we put our negative mental state on autopilot. Anxiety is our default mode. We think; therefore we worry. But Jesus's questions can help our thinking better reflect reality, even here.[6]

Perfectly Rational Fear

But this chapter is not about having a positive mental attitude in the face of real problems. Some of our fears are perfectly rational (I lost my job in the recession of 2009). I am reminded of a humorous tagline from a poster: "Just because you're paranoid doesn't mean they're *not* out to get you."

A positive mental attitude, as helpful as it might be in some contexts, is defenseless against a machete. Joel N. was a traveling evangelist from Zambia who led a church in Zimbabwe when he, along with tens of thousands of others, had to flee the country, run by the dictator Robert Mugabe. Joel ended up in South Africa, where those who initially welcomed him turned on him with murderous intent. Amid anti-immigrant rioting, Joel was forced to flee the shantytown where he had been staying and was uncertain whether or when to return.

"I still have that fear," Joel told *Christianity Today*, "because you don't know who is going to stab you in the back. You don't know who is going to befriend you, who is going to kill you."[7] Anxiety can be a perfectly rational place to be on a human level (but whether we are to live there is another matter).

The truth is, sometimes they *are* out to get us. Suffering is real—and sometimes it is on purpose. We must face that fact, but without fear. Jesus commanded us to love our enemies, recognizing that we *will* at times have enemies. As Paul said, "Indeed, all who desire to live a godly life in Christ Jesus will be persecuted."[8] Jesus knew this first hand, and he tried to prepare his disciples for the hard truth that oppression is a natural part of discipleship.

Fearing God

The sunny days of walking with Jesus to the applause of the crowds would soon be replaced with a lonely, gloomy stumbling toward a cross. *"Can you make the guests of the bridegroom fast while he is with them?"* Jesus asks. "But the time will come when the bridegroom will be taken from them."[9] But this knowledge is not meant to paralyze us with fear, but to face our coming calamities with confidence. One day Jesus takes his disciples aside from the crush of the crowds and says:

> I tell you, my friends, do not fear those who kill the body, and after that have nothing more that they can do. But I will warn you whom to fear: fear him who, after he has killed, has authority to cast into hell. Yes, I tell you, fear him! *Are not five sparrows sold for two pennies?* And not one of them is forgotten before God. Why, even the hairs of your head are all numbered. Fear not; you are of more value than many sparrows.[10]

Actually, in this instance he tells us that we must indeed fear *someone*. Fear *will* come, no matter what. Fear is a fact of any thinking person's existence. But it matters supremely what the object of our fear is. Jesus says that since we are going to fear anyway, it makes more sense to fear God, not man.

God-fear is perfectly rational. "Nothing in all creation is hidden from God's sight," the writer of Hebrews says. "Everything is uncovered and laid bare before the eyes of him to whom we must give account."[11] That kind of fear (Greek, *phobeomai*), elsewhere rendered in the New Testament as *worship*, *terror*, and *reverence*,[12] is entirely justified, given God's absolute authority to take our lives both now and for eternity. We will learn more about judgment and hell in chapter 22, but for now it is enough to know that we don't stroll into the presence of the Lord of heaven and earth lightly, without a care in the world. If we are smart, we will enter like the Cowardly Lion in *The Wizard of Oz*, on our knees.

Yet this holy fear provides the right life balance for the Christian. While the secular man, as we saw in chapter 2, fears everything, the properly thinking Christian fears only God. This is the right priority. Fear God, and you don't have to fear anything else. When you come to Christ, you are progressively freed from the fear of man. As David prayed, "preserve my life from dread of the enemy."[13]

Before I was a Christian, I was in bondage to what other people thought of me, particularly with regard to my disability. *Did I look foolish? Clumsy? Dorky? Would anyone care to see beneath my exterior and really appreciate me as a person?* Now I mainly care what God thinks.

Yes, occasionally the old fear of people returns, until I remind myself that God has accepted me, no matter what, and it is his opinion and friendship that count. And I have discovered that many of the things I had unsuccessfully grasped at from others for so long—love, friendship, respect—are becoming mine now that my fear is starting to be directed toward God alone. This makes sense.

Paradoxically, people who fear God exude confidence. They learn to take their eyes off of themselves and become attractively other-centered. With matters settled between themselves and the Lord of the universe, they have the emotional space and energy to care for others without fear.

Actually, they don't so much *learn* to stop thinking about themselves and focus on others. Rather, they are so busy thinking about God that they don't have *time* to worry about themselves. Such people will look you in the eye, listen attentively without trying to steer the conversation back to themselves, and offer to help in any way they can. I'm not there yet, but I'm walking the path. Little by little, and not all at once, in my middle-aged years I am beginning to experience the awesome truth of Jesus's command and promise to "seek his kingdom, and these things will be added to you."[14]

As the old hymn "How Firm a Foundation" puts it:

> Fear not, I am with thee; O be not dismayed,
> For I am thy God, and will still give thee aid.
> I'll strengthen thee, help thee, and cause thee to stand,
> Upheld by My righteous, omnipotent hand.[15]

Inestimable Value

Now, following Jesus's advice to fear only God, we come to his intriguing question: *"Are not five sparrows sold for two pennies?"*[16] The Greek actually says "two assaria," which were Roman coins made of copper and together were worth about one-eighth of a day's wage for a laborer.[17] It would take, in other words, roughly half an hour's worth of work to earn enough to buy a sparrow at the market. A day laborer could earn enough to buy a sparrow without breaking a sweat. And yet, Jesus assures his disciples, God remembers each sparrow individually.

If we are to think rightly, we must look up—at the birds. But what do sparrows have to do with the preceding command to fear God, not man? Simply this: if we cast our lot with God, he will not forget us, no matter how insignificant we may appear. In fact, Jesus assures his fearful disciples, God knows the very number of hairs on our heads. That's intimacy beyond our wildest dreams. He made us. Nothing about us or our disheveled lives surprises him. God has things under control and can be trusted completely in the face of any difficulty.

Even for the disabled, who are often considered to be worth less than birds in today's culture. Stephanie Hubach is the mother of Timmy, a child with Down syndrome. She has struggled with the anxiety, depression, bewilderment, and brokenness that her son's chromosomal condition has brought. But she has also seen God bring light to what many consider to be an unremittingly dark path.

"Disability is essentially a more noticeable form of the brokenness that is common to the human experience—a normal part of life in an abnormal world," Hubach writes. "It is just a difference of degree along a spectrum that contains difficulty all along its length. Due to God's common grace, no one exists in the extreme of complete brokenness. Due to the fall, no one enjoys the extreme of complete blessing. We all experience some mixture of the two in every aspect of our humanity."[18]

God has the mixture just right for each of us to seek him and show forth his glory: neither too much blessing to make us forget him; nor too little to make us curse him.[19]

This question about sparrows, which touches on our inestimable value in God's eyes, follows his commands not to fear man but God, and it is followed by one more command not to be afraid: "Fear not," Jesus still says to us, "you are of more value than many sparrows." Thinking about this fact, straight from the lips of Jesus, gives unshakeable courage.

In the Sermon on the Mount, Jesus again touches on things avian. "Look at the birds of the air," he says; "they do not sow or reap or stow away in barns, and yet your heavenly Father feeds them. *Are you not much more valuable than they?*"[20] The answer is obvious.

Fearing the Future

Sometimes, however, our primary fear isn't from without but from within. We know God is both powerful and good and can protect us from others, but we are anxious about ourselves. Somehow we think we still have the power to mess things up. We fear that we cannot provide for ourselves, that we can get into messes that even God cannot clean up, knots that even he cannot untie. Ultimately we think our well-being, and that of our families, is up to us, and such thinking paralyzes us.

> Therefore I tell you, do not be anxious about your life, what you will eat, nor about your body, what you will put on. For life is more than food, and the body more than clothing. Consider the ravens: they neither sow nor reap, they have neither storehouse nor barn, and yet God feeds them. *Of how much more value are you than the birds! And which of you by being anxious can add a single hour to his span of life? If then you are not able to do as small a thing as that, why are you anxious about the rest?* Consider the lilies, how they grow: they neither toil nor spin, yet I tell you, even Solomon in all his glory was not arrayed like one of these. *But if God so clothes the grass, which is alive in the field today, and tomorrow is thrown into the oven, how much more will he clothe you, O*

you of little faith! And do not seek what you are to eat and what you are to drink, nor be worried. For all the nations of the world seek after these things, and your Father knows that you need them. Instead, seek his kingdom, and these things will be added to you.[21]

Blinded by what passes for reality, we become transfixed with *our* lives, *our* bodies, *our* spans of life—as if we are autonomous, untethered free agents trying to get through a dangerous world as best we can. Or we fear that, no matter what God has promised in his word, we are somehow different, that even if the Lord can keep chaos at bay for other believers, he cannot or will not do so for us. We fear that somehow or other our mistakes are special and beyond the power and reach of God. This is sinful conceit.

We forget to whom we belong. "Once God takes us into covenant with himself," J. I. Packer and Carolyn Nystrom write, "as he does the moment we put faith in Christ and are born again by the Holy Spirit, our relationship to God is of child to Father and sheep to shepherd, and that means that the Father, the Son, and the Spirit will hold us fast and not let go of us, even if in moments of madness or sadness, or just plain badness, we stray into the wilderness of sin and death."[22]

After introducing the disciples to sparrows, Jesus moves on to ravens. Just as we are of more worth to God than the sparrows for which he cares, so we are more valuable than the ravens that he feeds. If God feeds *them*, he will feed *us*.

God's care is not theoretical. It is intensely practical. Remember that God used ravens to feed Elijah, his depressed and frightened prophet.[23] God is not playing games, promising and not delivering. His care involves real, physical stuff—such as food.

When I was unexpectedly laid off from my job and groping to regather the shards of my shattered career, our church and other Christians came through. Friends across the street picked up low-cost groceries for us at their church. Another bought and installed more memory for our ailing computer. Others prayed, took us to lunch, pointed us to job leads, and helped with faxes and resumes. Some gave us money—frequently and anonymously. I felt carried along by their prayers and practical expressions of concern.

God's family was our family, too. As Jesus said, "And everyone who has left houses or brothers or sisters or father or mother or children or lands, for my name's sake, will receive a hundredfold and will inherit eternal life."[24]

Then come the clinching questions. Even if we choose to disregard the truth that God is for us, Jesus points out the utter futility of anxiety, asking, "*Who of you by worrying can add a single hour to his life?*"[25] If Jesus's positive, spiritual encouragement to trust God fails, then Jesus is not afraid to get brutally honest. And the honest truth is this: Anxiety doesn't work. It never has, and it never will. "*Since you cannot do this very little thing, why do you worry about the rest?*"[26] Anxiety says, "My fate is in my own hands. It is all up to me." With that kind of thinking, no wonder we remain wide-awake at three in the morning!

Not only does anxiety fail to produce any positive results for us. It often does the opposite, draining us of life itself. Those who are anxious over debt, for example, are at higher risk of ulcers or digestive tract problems, migraine headaches, severe anxiety, severe depression, heart attacks, muscle tension, losing their temper, and having trouble sleeping or concentrating.[27] Worry kills.

Author and counselor Bob Phillips tells the story of a man who met Death on the way to a far country. Death told the man he was going to kill ten thousand people in a city, and he went on. Later the man met Death going the opposite way and pointed out that he had heard that seventy thousand had perished. "I only killed ten thousand people," Death responded. "Worry and Fear killed the others."[28]

We *cannot* control life, so we *should not* worry. Of course we are called to plan and work, but we must leave the results to God. This is because the results, no matter what "self-made" Americans may believe, are ultimately out of our hands. The best-laid plans of mice and men can fail, while God's providence can bring us to unimaginable (and undeserved) heights. We are not in control of our lives—and that's okay.

In fact, our lack of control means we should worry not more, but less. Children have little to no control, yet few display symptoms of GAD. They have the least control, and probably the fewest worries. There's a reason babies sleep like babies. Without the crushing burden of responsibility, they don't have a care in the world. Children have their problems, of course. They are not immune to bullies, bad parents, or disease. As they get older, the stress of school or relationships can rob them of their sleep and wipe the smiles off their faces. But the norm for most kids, who live at the pure mercy of others, is joy. Perhaps this is one reason Jesus tells us we must "become like little children" to "enter the kingdom of heaven."[29] Worry, which is evidence of misplaced self-reliance, has no place in God's kingdom. We can control *nothing*. The King will provide.

Looking Down

To drive home the point of God's unimaginable concern for his children, Jesus next tells us to look down, turning from his high-flying avian creations to the humble grass beneath our feet. Jesus points out how our heavenly Father provides wildflowers to decorate the ground more beautifully than Solomon in all his glory.[30] As this simple yet profound act demonstrates, God's provision is extravagant, promiscuous, sovereign, unasked for, and free. God is not a miser seeking to hoard his goodness. It is in his very nature to share his best, to hold nothing back.

No wonder Jesus exclaims a rhetorical question, *"But if God so clothes the grass, which is alive in the field today, and tomorrow is thrown into the oven, how much more will he clothe you, O you of little faith!"*[31] Such grace, illuminated for us by creation, calls for awe-filled expressions of worship, as when David blurted out in sheer wonder:

> When I consider your heavens,
> the work of your fingers,
> the moon and the stars,
> which you have set in place,
>
> what is man that you are mindful of him,
> the son of man that you care for him?
>
> You made him a little lower than the heavenly beings
> and crowned him with glory and honor.[32]

Meditating on these facts should bring great assurance. Even if we don't receive everything we *want*, we will get everything we truly *need*—God himself. "What, then, shall we say in response to this?" Paul asked, reflecting on God's plan of salvation. "If God is for us, who can be against us?"[33]

Persistent Anxiety

That should be the end of the matter, but it isn't. Over and over the Bible tells people who should know better not to be anxious.

- "It is in vain that you rise up early and go late to rest, eating the bread of anxious toil; for he gives to his beloved sleep."[34]
- "Say to those who have an anxious heart, 'Be strong; fear not! Behold, your God will come with vengeance, with the recompense of God. He will come and save you.'"[35]
- "He [who trusts the LORD] is like a tree planted by water, that sends out its roots by the stream, and does not fear when heat comes, for its leaves remain green, and is not anxious in the year of drought, for it does not cease to bear fruit."[36]
- "Therefore I tell you, do not be anxious about your life, what you will eat or what you will drink, nor about your body, what you will put on. *Is not life more than food, and the body more than clothing?*"[37]
- "When they deliver you over, do not be anxious how you are to speak or what you are to say, for what you are to say will be given to you in that hour."[38]

- "Do not be anxious about anything, but in everything by prayer and supplication with thanksgiving let your requests be made known to God."[39]

But we naturally turn to worry rather than to God. Why? Yes, there is much to legitimately fear in this sin-scarred world in which the devil is constantly on the prowl. The night we sent one of our sons on his first overnight church camping trip, a late-spring tornado ripped through a Boy Scout camp in the next state and killed four young men and injured dozens more. You can be sure I regularly checked the weather reports. Our son returned home on schedule, but this did not lessen our grief for the parents of the boys who didn't—or our protective parental instinct.

I must confess that, whether for reasons of history, genetics, or choice, anxiety is my natural default mode. Much as I try to project an image of quiet confidence, a lot of my inner life is characterized by fear. I get anxious about how I will look. I fear heights. I'm afraid I won't be able to meet a particular challenge. I even get anxious when writing a chapter about anxiety!

And I suspect I'm not all that different from most people. Partly, anxiety represents a perfectly natural response to perceived threats. The fight-or-flight response to danger is deeply imprinted on our humanity. And let's face it: those who live without fear often find themselves without their health or their lives. Living without due concern for the consequences of your actions will buy you a quick ticket to the hospital or cemetery. That's why so many teens die from alcohol overdoses or reckless driving: they believe (wrongly) that they are invincible. The anxious person, however, sees himself as completely vincible, as it were.

And Jesus, far from denying the frailty and danger of the human condition, affirms it. Not only that, he takes it upon himself, day by day, month by month, year by year. He takes it upon himself and gets mockery, slander, arrest, torture, and death for his trouble. As we saw in the introduction to this book, Jesus has the serenity amid life's storms that only trust in one's heavenly Father can bring.

> And when [Jesus] got into the boat, his disciples followed him. And behold, there arose a great storm on the sea, so that the boat was being swamped by the waves; but he was asleep. And they went and woke him, saying, "Save us, Lord; we are perishing." And he said to them, "*Why are you afraid, O you of little faith?*" Then he arose and rebuked the winds and the sea, and there was a great calm. And the men marveled, saying, "What sort of man is this, that even the winds and sea obey him?"[40]

Jesus's question remains: why are we afraid, O we of little faith? If he can rebuke the winds and the sea, what is there to fear? The answer: absolutely nothing. Think about it.

Suggested Reading

Packer, J. I., and Carolyn Nystrom. *Guard Us, Guide Us: Divine Leading in Life's Decisions*. Grand Rapids: Baker, 2008.

Phillips, Bob. *Overcoming Anxiety and Depression: Practical Tools to Help You Deal with Negative Emotions*. Eugene, OR: Harvest House, 2007.

Discussion Questions

1. Why do so many Westerners feel anxious? Do you?
2. Is anxiety a sin, a disease, or a mental malady? Does it make a difference?
3. Why is it so hard for Christians not to be afraid?
4. How do Jesus's questions address our anxiety?
5. Does God's promise that he knows us and will provide for us constitute a guarantee of health and wealth?
6. Why can we know God is for us, no matter what? What difference ought this knowledge make?

Why Is Character So Vital?

16

Unbelief Rejects Him

"Why do you not understand what I say?"

Tolerance is king in pluralistic America—except when it comes to the New Atheists. They are anything but tolerant when talking about Christianity. Christopher Hitchens, a pundit who wrote *God Is Not Great: How Religion Poisons Everything*, gratingly equates belief in Jesus Christ with Islamic radicalism. Hitchens pontificates, "Many of the teachings of Christianity are, as well as being incredible and mythical, immoral." Scientist Richard Dawkins suggests that believers "just shut up."[1] Sam Harris, meanwhile, is busy writing letters to Christians to tell them how wrong-headed they are. The New Atheists are having the time of their lives, and the undiscerning American marketplace is rewarding them handsomely.

But when it comes to unbelief, Hitchens, Dawkins, and Harris are strictly minor leaguers.

Consider an incident from two millennia ago. Jesus's friend Lazarus has been rotting in a cave tomb for four days.[2] His two sisters, Mary and Martha, are devastated, and not just because their baby brother died. Even more painful, from their perspective, was that Jesus hadn't come in time to heal his friend. The corpse is wrapped up, beginning to stink. The stone is rolled over the entrance to the tomb, the mourners assembled. It is at this hopeless moment that Jesus arrives, seemingly too late. Even the carpenter from Galilee is overcome with emotion, groaning, and weeping, at the human despair all around him.

Yet the one who called himself "the resurrection and the life" does not allow decay and death to have the last word. On his order, the stone is rolled away. "Lazarus," Jesus says in front of the tomb, "come out." His simple command fires like a laser into the black burial chamber, piercing the death wrappings and plunging into the decomposing, ice-cold heart of his friend, bridging the secret and infinite distance between life and death. Somewhere, somehow, Lazarus hears the irresistible order and obeys. Like a mummy he emerges with his hands and feet bound, his face covered by a death shroud. Yet Lazarus is alive, in fact more alive than he's ever been, and many who see the sign with their own eyes believe.

But only *many*. The others go looking for Jesus's Pharisaical enemies. I can almost imagine these reluctant witnesses saying, "Houston, we have a problem." They report the miracle to their masters, not to win them to faith in Christ, but like East Germans informing on their neighbors to the Stasi, to figure out a way to maintain their privileged positions.

"What are we to do?" the huddled Pharisees and chief priests ask. "For this man performs many signs. If we let him go on like this, everyone will believe in him, and the Romans will come and take away both our place and our nation." Note carefully the order. Rather than repent and believe in the face of a divine miracle, the religious leaders are more concerned with their positions. They decide the only thing to do is kill Jesus. Then the chief priests, seeing the throngs coming out to see both Jesus and Lazarus, decide to murder the raised man, too.

This kind of unbelief is major league. It takes more faith to reject God than to embrace him. Faced with evidence that the universe had a beginning, many atheist astronomers postulate an endless string of universes so that the miracle of this one won't seem so special.

"The believers in miracles accept them (rightly or wrongly) because they have evidence for them," G. K. Chesterton observed. "The disbelievers in miracles deny them (rightly or wrongly) because they have a doctrine against them."[3] It is not a matter of honest intellectual doubt or seeking more evidence before you come to a decision. Those are the kinds of faith struggles common to most people. They are normal, natural, even healthy. We should respond with love, patience, and facts to someone who doubts, gently helping him or her to see the truth, both in our texts and in our lives.

Unbelief is not doubt, however. Unbelief is a calculating, hard-hearted rejection of evidence, whether it be intellectual, physical, historical, or spiritual. It is seeing the clear work of God and turning away. Worse, it is seeing Jesus's work by the Spirit and attributing it to Satan. Such unbelief is damnable.[4] And how could it not be? The damned unbeliever is only receiving what he has requested. Such unbelief is a form of spiritual blindness. "The light shines in the darkness," the apostle John said, "but the darkness has not understood it."[5] It is a matter not of wrong thinking, but of bad character. And it is nothing new.

The Apostle of Belief

"[Jesus] came to his own," said John, seeing the hard hearts of his people, "and his own people did not receive him."[6] John experienced this kind of unbelief firsthand, just weeks after Jesus's resurrection (which the authorities also amazingly tried to cover up[7]). John and Peter are entering the Jerusalem temple at the hour of prayer when a disabled man by the gate asks for money—no doubt hoping that either their heightened religious sensibilities (or just good, old-fashioned guilt) will prompt their largesse before they enter God's house. It's a strategy many others have copied down through church history.

The man gets less than he bargained for—and much more. "Silver or gold I do not have," Peter answers, "but what I have I give you. In the name of Jesus Christ of Nazareth, walk." Peter grasps the beggar by the hand. The man's ankles and feet are instantly strong, and he leaps to his feet, shouting praises to God. The crowds have seen the man before, as one who was lame, and are completely dumbfounded. They come running to Peter and John at Solomon's Colonnade. Peter, the leader of the fledgling church, speaks up, with John no doubt listening to his once-timid fellow disciple and taking notes.

"Men of Israel," Peter preaches, "why does this surprise you? Why do you stare at us as if by our own power or godliness we had made this man walk? The God of Abraham, Isaac and Jacob, the God of our fathers, has glorified his servant Jesus."

Did this miracle, did these convicting words and the ones that followed, change the minds of the Jewish leaders? Did these opponents say, "Hey, another miracle, this time performed through the Nazarene's followers; maybe there is something to this Jesus movement"? Not at all. Instead, they hauled Peter and John before the Sanhedrin and asked again by what name the miracle was performed, though they already knew the answer. The leaders, hearing what they didn't want to hear, that it was done in Jesus's name, the only name "under heaven given to men by which we must be saved," remained impervious to the evidence.

"What are we going to do with these men?" the leaders finally ask themselves in bewilderment. (Apparently they hadn't thought of repentance and faith.) "Everybody living in Jerusalem knows they have done an outstanding miracle, and we cannot deny it. But to stop this thing from spreading any further among the people, we must warn these men to speak no longer to anyone in this name."[8]

Think about this the next time someone tells you there is not enough evidence to believe in Jesus Christ. Judging from these incidents, there will never be enough for the defiant unbeliever—Jew or Gentile, Protestant, pagan, Catholic, or atheist. But that *doesn't* mean that there is no evidence.

John could be called the apostle of belief. The New Testament uses *pisteuo*, the Greek word for *believe*, 241 times. John, either in his Gospel or in his epistles, uses the word fully 55 times.[9] And no wonder. Belief is core to biblical faith. The miraculous signs told of in his book, John says, "are written that you may believe that Jesus is the Christ, and that by believing you may have life in his name."[10]

Belief is the goal, because it leads to life. Therefore, the converse—unbelief—is what we must avoid, because unbelief leads to eternal death. Perhaps that is why Jesus asked some of his most searching questions about unbelief, many of them recorded by John. These severe queries paradoxically bring hope, however, because they admit the possibility that unbelief—by God's grace—can be turned into faith, that death can be replaced with life.

Wrong Focus

One Sabbath while in Jerusalem, Jesus heals a paralyzed man who had been disabled for thirty-eight years.[11] Opponents claim Jesus has violated the law, and Jesus counters with a shocking answer—that he is equal with God and thus has the authority to interpret the law. In essence, Jesus says, "You have no authority to judge me. In fact, I am *your* Judge." Then he diagnoses their spiritual condition, concluding with a question:

> But I know that you do not have the love of God within you. I have come in my Father's name, and you do not receive me. If another comes in his own name, you will receive him. *How can you believe, when you receive glory from one another and do not seek the glory that comes from the only God?*

Theirs is not an intellectual problem, a matter of differing biblical interpretations between people of good will who read the sacred text differently. It is a question of character. At its core, unbelief is never a matter of the head. It is a matter of the heart. Their indefensible conclusion—that Jesus is a fraud, a lawbreaker—is inevitable, given the state of their hearts, which are lushly religious but barren of the love of God: either love for God or love from God. Instead of focusing vertically, on the Judge, they look only horizontally, at other unbelievers, in order to reinforce their culpable unbelief.

This kind community-enforced unbelief is in no way exclusive to Jesus's day. It can be seen in every age. Muslims in Asia effectively block the witness of Christians in their communities by threatening to execute those who convert to Christ. Jewish leaders deny religious freedom by labeling as traitors those among their brethren who embrace Jesus as their Messiah. In the smug secular atmosphere so ubiquitous on many college campuses, tenured professors calmly and clinically tear apart the faith of students who decide to follow hard after the Savior.

Unbelief is usually not an individual decision. It is a group project. Unbelief finds safety in numbers. Unbelievers are not really happy unless they convert others to their own godlessness. Ever wonder why the New Atheists are so intent on winning converts?

The ancient Hebrews spoke often of group guilt. Americans, however, tend to focus on individual rights, particularly those enshrined in the Bill of Rights. This is generally good, especially because the concept of the worth, dignity, and rights of the individual emerged from the Christian worldview. As the Declaration says, "We are endowed by our Creator with certain unalienable rights."

But focusing narrowly on unalienable individual rights obscures our view of the greater whole. We belong not only to ourselves, but also to our families, our communities, our nations, and our world. We have not only rights to be protected and exercised, but also responsibilities to be discharged. Fathers have responsibilities to their wives and children, to lead and protect. Citizens must pay taxes and be forces for their communities' well-being through voluntary associations such as the Rotary Club or becoming a Big Brother or Sister for a young person. Sometimes we are called into military service. Other times we see a natural disaster on television and seek out ways to help.

Adam, though created perfect, was incomplete alone.[12] We were created for community, designed to flourish in the company of others. And the Christian is called to be a part of something much bigger than himself or herself—the church, the Body of Christ. We not only have privileges as adopted children of the King, but also responsibilities to him, and to one another. Christianity was not designed for individualists. Others have said that there are no Lone Ranger Christians. One of Bonhoeffer's best-loved books is titled simply *Life Together*.[13] Many have noted the interesting fact that the Bible begins in a garden and ends in a city. We will have rest, but I'm not so sure about solitude.

Jesus certainly understood the communal aspects of faith.

- He traveled with his family to worship in Jerusalem.
- He selected twelve disciples to be with him and to carry on the work when he was gone.
- When he was tempted in the Garden of Gethsemane, Jesus called his closest companions over to watch and pray.
- When the kingdom is consummated, he will preside over a communal feast with followers from every tongue, tribe, and nation.

But Jesus also understood the communal aspects of unbelief. We Americans often think of our decisions as purely our own, not recognizing how much peer pressure, fashion, literature, and media shape us—and often not for the good. Jesus's questions remind us that most groupthink is not good for faith.

"But to what shall I compare this generation?" Jesus asks the crowd in a scene we encountered in chapter 1, discussing another John, the Baptist. "It is like children sitting in the marketplaces and calling to their playmates, 'We played the flute for you, and you did not dance; we sang a dirge, and you did not mourn.'"[14] While the kingdom indeed belongs to children,[15] it does not belong to these kinds of children, who, perpetually critical, sit around in the marketplace while others work, never satisfied, always bored. They neither mourned their sin when John came nor celebrated the advent of Jesus. A spiritually indolent group, they gladly walk "in the counsel of the wicked," stand "in the way of sinners," and sit "in the seat of scoffers."[16] No answer is ever good enough for them. As Jesus asks in astonishment after performing so many miracles to little effect, *"Why does this generation seek a sign?"*[17]

The scary thing is, those who claim to be followers of Christ can be lumped in with the unbelieving generation. *"O faithless and twisted generation,"* Jesus asks, *"how long am I to be with you and bear with you?"*[18] He exclaims this not to Pharisees, but to his own disciples, who had not the faith to cast out a certain kind of demon.

Jesus compared them to unbelievers, apparently scandalized by their lack of belief. What would Jesus say of you or me? Do we have the faith expected of a disciple? One thing is sure: we cannot strengthen our faith if we do not exercise it. God help us to say, "I do believe; help me overcome my unbelief!"[19]

Responsible Sinners

Without God's grace, we are spiritually unable to believe. "You brood of vipers," Jesus says to another crowd of unbelievers. *"How can you speak good, when you are evil? For out of the abundance of the heart the mouth speaks."*[20]

Like an expert prosecutor, Jesus resorts to blunt questions to warn a crowd whose members are sure of their right standing with God instead of their actual condition: unable to hear God's Word.

> They answered him, "Abraham is our father." Jesus said to them, "If you were Abraham's children, you would be doing what Abraham did, but now you seek to kill me, a man who has told you the truth that I heard from God. This is not what Abraham did. You are doing what your father did." They said to him, "We were not born of sexual immorality. We have one Father—even God." Jesus said to them, "If God were your Father, you would love me, for I came from God and I am here. I came not of my own accord, but he sent me. *Why do you not*

understand what I say? It is because you cannot bear to hear my word. You are of your father the devil, and your will is to do your father's desires. He was a murderer from the beginning, and has nothing to do with the truth, because there is no truth in him. When he lies, he speaks out of his own character, for he is a liar and the father of lies. But because I tell the truth, you do not believe me. *Which one of you convicts me of sin? If I tell the truth, why do you not believe me?* Whoever is of God hears the words of God. The reason why you do not hear them is that you are not of God."[21]

An inability to hear the words of God does not mean we are not responsible. While our spiritual hardness is a condition, it is also a choice—a responsible choice. God's punishments prove that we are accountable for the choices we make. "The sinner sins," R. C. Sproul notes, "because he chooses to sin, not because he is forced to sin. Without grace the fallen creature lacks the ability to choose righteousness. He is in bondage to his own sinful impulses."[22] Or, as the Protestant Reformers put it, we are totally depraved, spiritually dead, and unable to bring ourselves to God. To repeat an old theological adage: we are not sinners because we sin; we sin because we are sinners.

Taking Offense

Christians take comfort in Jesus's statement that he is the bread of life, a permanent, living fulfillment of the manna that came from God to feed his people in the wilderness. But when Jesus first said he was giving his flesh for the world, his opponents didn't take comfort. They took offense. And so did his own disciples.

> When many of his disciples heard it, they said, "This is a hard saying; who can listen to it?" But Jesus, knowing in himself that his disciples were grumbling about this, said to them, *"Do you take offense at this? Then what if you were to see the Son of Man ascending to where he was before?* It is the Spirit who gives life; the flesh is of no avail. The words that I have spoken to you are spirit and life. But there are some of you who do not believe." (For Jesus knew from the beginning who those were who did not believe, and who it was who would betray him.) And he said, "This is why I told you that no one can come to me unless it is granted him by the Father."[23]

The reason the disciples took offense lay not in the doctrine, but in their own hearts. They wanted to rule, sitting at Jesus's right hand and on his left in his kingdom.[24] But they didn't want to get there the Jesus way.

Jesus's sacrificial death for the sins of the world was God's Plan A *before* Eve ever gave Adam the fruit. It was not some emergency response to a world spun horribly out of control. It was ordained from the foundation of the world[25] and predicted in various ways in the Hebrew Scriptures. The disciples should have recognized this central event in salvation history but didn't. Their response was disturbingly like that of unbelievers. They were ready to dominate but not to die.

Jesus reminds them their offense is misplaced because his death is inextricably linked with his post-resurrection ascension. The gore and the glory are two sides of the same coin. You cannot have one without the other. In fact, the one *leads to* the other. No wonder Paul could later say with full conviction about his Lord: "And being found in appearance as a man, he humbled himself and became obedient to death—even death on a cross! Therefore God exalted him to the highest place and gave him the name that is above every name."[26]

For those true disciples still struggling with what they have just heard, Jesus understandingly points out that his words are spiritual truth only perceivable by those with spiritual eyes. Faith is a gift to be received, not a work to be done. Paul said, "For it is by grace you have been saved, through faith—and this not from yourselves, it is the gift of God—not by works, so that no one can boast."[27]

No wonder Jesus (quoted again by John) says to Nicodemus, "I tell you the truth, no one can see the kingdom of God unless he is born again."[28] What if, despite our religious credentials, we find we do not have faith, that we cannot see the kingdom of God? Some will walk away, of course. "From this time many of his disciples," John observed, "turned back and no longer followed him."[29]

So do we resign ourselves to fatalism, assuming that if God chooses whom he wills that there is nothing we can do? Many caricature the doctrine of predestination in this way: if salvation is foreordained, then why try to follow God? But Jesus puts the onus on us, asking the twelve disciples, "*Do you want to go away as well?*"[30] What do they want to do? Then he follows up with a balancing question, indicating his sovereign control of their free choices: "*Did I not choose you, the Twelve? And yet one of you is a devil.*"[31] Our choices are our own, but God is still in control.

Our task, however, is not to figure it all out, but to follow. What do *we* choose—death without Jesus or life with Jesus? What do we *want* to do?

Spiritual Wandering

I have had dark nights of spiritual wandering. Sometimes the faith has just seemed too difficult, the hypocrisy and venality of other Christians too much to bear, or the Bible too opaque. At times opposition or misunderstanding from friends and family was too painful. Christian restrictions over my personal life seemed onerous. Some people worried that I had become unbalanced, and perhaps I had. Perhaps I *was* in a cult, as a trusted authority figure once charged.

Plus, the seemingly carefree approach to life of those unconcerned with pleasing God attracted me. As Billy Joel once said, "The sinners are much more fun." And there were lots of *other* ways of looking at the divine, weren't there? What made me sure *I* was right? Why not continue going to church, but not take the following Jesus part *too* seriously?

And for a time I strayed, attempting to fill the empty place in my soul with the approval of others. It was easy, so far from home and without deep roots in a Christian community. When in Rome, the adage goes, live as the Romans do. Surrounded by pagans in my college dorm (actually, lapsed Protestants, Catholics, and Jews), I began to live like a pagan. I watched my new friends revel in debauchery of every kind, smiling and saying nothing to them. I allowed my mind to wander into areas that were clearly the devil's territory, and the experience felt scary, fun, and oddly liberating. Like many young people on the University of Florida campus, I became drunk more than once, and I laughed at the sad antics of a young man named Spike, who displayed what I now realize are signs of alcoholism.

But the smell of vomit in the morning—or anytime, actually—has a way of removing the allure of partying. A hangover can be a great reality check. But even more important, I began to notice what I had unceremoniously stuffed in my closet. My peace was gone, my sense of purpose AWOL. The joy I had felt knowing Christ was barely a memory. Rather than reveling in the promise of eternal life, I had wallowed in myself—and an unattractive self at that: in the space of a few months, I had become a silly, underachieving drunk, unthankfully spending my parents' money without a care in the world. Like the Prodigal Son, I was far from home. So much for my fun.

But God was never far from me. Walk away from God, if you can. If he has his hand on you, you will walk back. "Where shall I go from your Spirit?" the psalmist wondered. "Or where shall I flee from your presence?"[32] Despite my sinful declension, I never lost the sense of his constant presence, which has stayed with me to this day. Try as I might to wriggle free from the Lord's grasp, he would not let me go. The Bible, which had seemed so confining, became interesting again. Instead of an archaic book of myths and rules, it morphed back into a love letter from the Almighty that detailed his plan for the world and my place in it. My own thoughts about God had been the real myths.

Scripture became solid again, a rock of assurance in my sea of doubts. Sometimes we may hold the conceit that our generic musings about God are more enlightened than what is presented to us in the Old and New Testaments. And indeed, God's Word may "contain some things that are hard to understand, which ignorant and unstable people distort . . . to their own destruction."[33] The seemingly endless genealogies, the food laws, the harsh judgments I began to see afresh in the light of the cross, which was the ultimate proof of God's love for me. That love he demonstrated by leaving the shores of eternity to rescue vile sinners—including me—drowning in oceans of our own wickedness.

No Other Story

Leaving this holy narrative and attempting to construct a better one had been an utter failure. Foolishly we think there may be something better out there that will help us make sense of life, that will explain the mysteries of existence, that will give us hope and a future. Believe me, there isn't. There is no story like this one. It is the story on which all other stories are built. I could see that clearly only after I had walked away.

For the Twelve, the answer to Jesus's question—"*Do you want to go away as well?*"—is easy. "Lord, to whom shall we go?" Peter asks in response. "You have the words of eternal life."[34] While self-assessment is necessary ("Examine yourselves to see whether you are in the faith," Paul told the Corinthians; "test yourselves."[35]), our task is not to endlessly wonder whether we have been chosen. It is to choose, trusting that God will do the rest. "If you abide in my word," Jesus says, "you are truly my disciples, and you will know the truth, and the truth will set you free."[36]

So we can relax. Belief and salvation do not ultimately depend upon us and our mental acuity. Yes, we must exercise faith, but our faith springs not from ourselves but from someone who has already proven his good will toward us. "For God so loved the world," Jesus said, quoted by John in the most famous statement in Scripture, "that he gave his one and only Son, that whoever believes in him shall not perish but have eternal life."[37]

Suggested Reading

Chesterton, G. K. *Orthodoxy*. New York: Doubleday, 1908.

Flew, Antony, with Roy Abraham Varghese. *There Is a God: How the World's Most Notorious Atheist Changed His Mind*. San Francisco: HarperOne, 2007.

McKnight, Scot, and Hauna Ondrey. *Finding Faith, Losing Faith: Stories of Conversion and Apostasy*. Waco, TX: Baylor University Press, 2008.

Packer, J. I. *Evangelism and the Sovereignty of God*. Downers Grove, IL: InterVarsity, 1991.

Sproul, R. C. *Willing to Believe: The Controversy Over Free Will*. Grand Rapids: Baker, 1997.

Tucker, Ruth A. *Walking Away from Faith: Unraveling the Mystery of Belief and Unbelief*. Downers Grove, IL: InterVarsity, 2002.

Discussion Questions

1. Why are the New Atheists so aggressively taking on the Christian faith, and why are they winning such big audiences?
2. Do you ever think that if God performed a miracle, more people would believe in him? What does the Bible say about this?
3. Do you believe that unbelief is a matter of the heart, not the head? Why or why not?
4. Belief leads to life and unbelief leads to death. But how important is the object of belief?
5. What role does groupthink play in unbelief?
6. Should belief that God grants faith turn us into fatalists? Why or why not?
7. What are some things we can do to "make our calling and election sure"?

17

Compassion Models Him

*"Ought not this woman be
loosed from this bond?"*

As I sit before my computer to start this chapter, my right (good) hand is mostly covered by a thermoplastic cast that extends from the tip of my ring finger to about two-thirds of the way down my forearm. (Due to my cerebral palsy, my left hand is clumsy at best.) Typing is frustratingly slow. My right thumb, index finger, and middle finger are free to make the attempt but are greatly hindered from even this menial task by my ring finger and pinky, which are pushed forward by the cast, which is open at the top, except for a hardened portion curling between my thumb and forefinger.

Guarding my skin against irritation is a hot, sock-like sleeve that must be washed daily to avoid the sweaty stink—but a blister has developed anyway. So I cover the blister with a disposable bandage, which frequently comes loose. Securing the whole orthopedic ensemble are six Velcro straps, such as the kind my seven-year-old has on his sneakers. The doctor has told me I must keep the cast on all the time—but because of my spasticity on my left side, I cheat and remove it when going to the bathroom or taking a shower.

My hand is broken because of a freak injury at work. My erratic gait causes my arms to swing more than those for the average nondisabled person. The injury occurred when I was walking down a hallway and my hand accidentally banged against a wall. My momentum carried me forward, and I heard a sickening snap. I knew instantly that I had broken a bone. X-rays later that morning confirmed that I had a clean break of the fifth metacarpal—the bone below my knuckle that connects my pinkie to my wrist. Because this is my "good" side, I have trouble doing everything from brushing my teeth to putting on my shoes and socks. As I daily attempt to relearn the simple tasks of life, my frustration is a constant companion. Everything takes longer, including writing. This injury likely would never have happened if I were not disabled.

I understand intellectually how God has used my cerebral palsy for my good and his glory. In my saner moments, I would not trade my handicap for a complete physical makeover. I know that it is one of many things that God has used to both draw me to him and conform me more and more into his image. However, it can be hard to maintain one's "sanity" amid the day-to-day frustrations, disappointments, and heartaches that can be the lot of people with disabilities.

I remember well a certain dark day when I was a kid. I had closed myself in the upstairs bathroom, crying and muttering about the injustices of life. My dad had played tennis with my younger brother but not with me. I thought he was being completely unfair and believed that I should have equal time. From the other side of the door, my dad heard me (as I had hoped) and agreed to take me out to the tennis courts. There it quickly became obvious that I had neither the quickness nor mobility to play the game. My father hadn't been excluding me; he just knew that tennis was beyond my ability—which I learned to my embarrassment and sorrow that day.

Sometimes people are afraid to call disabled people what we are: disabled. Instead, they use a more politically correct term, such as "differently abled." What a crock.

This was a small thing, I know. Many people who don't play tennis are perfectly happy. But my life is full of such small things, whether from lost sports opportunities or the occasional broken bone. Sometimes they add up to big things. These incidents have made a cumulative imprint on my psyche. My self-esteem, rightly or wrongly, has been forever touched by my disability.

If someone had offered me a miraculous cure for my cerebral palsy while I was growing up, I would have accepted immediately, with tears of joy. I would not have said, "That's okay; my disability is building my character." I would have grabbed the opportunity like a get-out-of-jail-free card, no questions asked.

While a day is the same length for everyone, for those with disabilities, a day can seem endless. We never know what indignities or inconveniences the next twenty-four hours may bring. Maybe we will break a bone; perhaps we will learn we cannot play tennis. Perhaps we will simply be confused with someone else who has the same kind of disability, as I have many times.

While we may accept disability as a necessity for some in this fallen world, those of us who believe in Jesus are understandably eager to experience the healing that awaits us in the next.

And yet the able-bodied sometimes don't understand. They don't experience, as we do, the full contrast between current physical limitations and our promised future bodily liberation.[1] While the able-bodied usually mean well, they can be forgiven for often forgetting the daily frustrations of life for the disabled: the stumbling, the search for a handicapped parking space, the curb cut back by the dumpster or blocked by an idling SUV; the stairs without railings.

But Jesus wants us to remember. He asks us to develop compassion: a "deep feeling of sharing the suffering of another, together with the inclination to give aid or support or to show mercy."[2]

Long-term Disability

> Now he was teaching in one of the synagogues on the Sabbath. And there was a woman who had had a disabling spirit for eighteen years. She was bent over and could not fully straighten herself.[3]

We have already seen how Jesus liked to provoke his hard-hearted enemies on the Sabbath. Sometimes the provocation came from his words. Other times, it came from his works. Here it is both, and Jesus is responding to a long-term problem. And not for the first time: Mark describes a woman who has had a discharge of blood for a dozen years;[4] John of a man born blind.[5] In this incident, Luke the physician tells us that a particular, embarrassing disability has dogged a certain woman in the synagogue for eighteen years.

She has two problems: her sex and her disability. Such a person had little power or respect in the first century—seemingly cursed, alone, and yet dependent—and this one has lived under these barely tolerable conditions for nearly two decades. It's worth noting, while most people simply pass by the disabled without a thought (other than, perhaps, "Thank God that's not me"), God does not forget. He keeps a record of our sufferings.

Unlike some other infirmities mentioned in the Gospels, this one is specifically tied to demonic activity, not to the general fallenness of the world. While we may safely accept God-given trials as means to spiritual growth,[6] we ordinarily do not respond to the work of Satan with the same resignation.[7] Instead, we ought to be ready for battle, to turn back the works of the devil, to advance the kingdom of God. The Lord certainly was.

> When Jesus saw her, he called her over and said to her, "Woman, you are freed from your disability." And he laid his hands on her, and immediately she was made straight, and she glorified God.[8]

Seeing the Suffering

First, note that Jesus *saw* her. We can trust that Jesus sees *all* the invisible people, whether they are counted among the tens of millions of people around the world with disabilities, or children sold into the sex trade, or unborn Chinese girls aborted because of their sex, or Asian wives who have acid thrown into their faces by their husbands. Jesus sees it all. And, "filled with compassion,"[9] Jesus acts. He sets us free, and not just spiritually.

Here, the shackles of disability are smashed, and the woman, who has been as crooked as a boomerang for a generation, is suddenly perpendicular again. Other than telling us that this pious Jew glorified the God of Abraham, the narrative doesn't give the details of her reaction, but it is safe to assume she wore a look of joyous disbelief on her face.

Maybe she dropped to her knees in gratitude, a tear rolling down her cheek. I remember the night after my first bike ride. I wasn't a kid; I was in my thirties. Because of my disability, I had missed out on this rite of passage and remained earthbound as the neighborhood kids continually zoomed past me to destinations unknown. I could only watch them from the sidewalk.

But the night after the first ride of my life—on a three-wheeled recumbent—I was excitedly replaying my triumph with my wife. And then an odd, unexpected thing happened: I cried. Something I never thought *would* happen *had* happened. Talk about longing fulfilled! It was time to celebrate—and weep. Yes, this woman's tears are easy for me to envision.

But perhaps she simply stood up, beaming. I can see her throwing convention aside and leaping into the air for joy, as some recipients of divine healing did.[10] It doesn't really matter what she did, though. The miracle was real, the glory was God's, and now *everyone* saw. But not everyone rejoiced.

Inhumane Humans

"But the ruler of the synagogue, indignant because Jesus had healed on the Sabbath, said to the people, 'There are six days in which work ought to be done. Come on those days and be healed, and not on the Sabbath day.'"[11]

Bart Ehrmann struggles over some alleged discrepancies of the Bible. Others stumble over the doctrine of God punishing his Son in our place, claiming this would be a form of "divine child abuse." But let me tell you what I struggle with—the Bible's unsparing, unremitting depiction of human depravity, exemplified by this synagogue ruler. Others may have trouble believing a fish could swallow a man. I have more problems swallowing this man's response. Are we human beings really this callous? Talk about *inhumane*!

Demanding that this woman bear up under her infirmity even one more day than she already has betrays a breathtaking ignorance of her plight. The synagogue ruler is like those among us who complain about all the handicapped spaces that are "wasted" on the handicapped. They'd rather the disabled stay home rather than have to walk a few more yards themselves to go shopping. They are too busy to be even slightly inconvenienced, too controlled by their own agendas and schedules to lift a finger to help. Such people, obviously, have never been disabled.

Of course, hardness of heart is not the exclusive property of the able-bodied. Despite my disability, to my shame I've turned away from people with other kinds of problems. I can't count how many times I've gone quickly past the homeless, clucking all the way, or ignored someone whose disability was more evident than mine. So Jesus asks *all* of us to develop compassion. Like David in Nathan's story, *we* are the man.[12]

True Religion

To be fair, a key component of the Jewish people's covenant obligation is obedience to God's laws, and Sabbath observance is the fourth commandment in the Decalogue. On one level, one can forgive the synagogue leader for doing all in his power to keep it. The commandment certainly is not something to be trifled with. God was very clear about that:

> Remember the Sabbath day by keeping it holy. Six days you shall labor and do all your work, but the seventh day is a Sabbath to the LORD your God. On it you shall not do any work, neither you, nor your son or daughter, nor your manservant or maidservant, nor your animals, nor the alien within your gates. For in six days the LORD made the heavens and the earth, the sea and all that is in them, but he rested on the seventh day. Therefore the LORD blessed the Sabbath day and made it holy.[13]

Commendably, the synagogue ruler was trying, at least on the surface, to keep the Sabbath holy. But he had forgotten a very fundamental truth. We cannot honor God by dishonoring those made in his image. "The Sabbath was made for man," Jesus said on another occasion, "not man for the Sabbath."[14] The Sabbath, the day of rest provided by God, was never meant to be a burden, but a blessing.

> Then the Lord answered him, "You hypocrites! *Does not each of you on the Sabbath untie his ox or his donkey from the manger and lead it away to water it? And ought not this woman, a daughter of Abraham whom Satan bound for eighteen years, be loosed from this bond on the Sabbath day?"* As he said these things, all his adversaries were put to shame, and all the people rejoiced at all the glorious things that were done by him.[15]

Before Jesus launches his devastating questions like well-aimed Scud missiles, he flushes out his opponents with a single noun: "hypocrites." Their religion was an act. While the synagogue leader and the others who objected to the timing of the healing outwardly displayed their religiosity, their inward state kept them from practicing true religion, which involves caring for the vulnerable and needy, such as widows and orphans[16]—or this disabled woman. Their religion was for show only. Jesus accused the Pharisees on another occasion, "you give God a tenth of your mint, rue and all other kinds of garden herbs, but you neglect justice and the love of God."[17] Their priorities were wrong. They had no compassion.

And we are not much better. Isn't religious hypocrisy—that Christians fail to practice what they preach—still the key accusation leveled against God's people? Not much has changed, seemingly, after two millennia.

Then, arguing from the lesser to the greater as a good rabbi would,[18] Jesus fires his questions, one after the other: if they would perform "work" on the Sabbath by untying an ox or donkey to lead it to water, why would they object if a "daughter of Abraham whom Satan bound for eighteen years, be loosed from this bond on the Sabbath day"? The healed one was no beast of burden but in fact was a woman bearing God's image. Didn't *she* deserve refreshment? More than that, she was a child of the covenant, of which they too were heirs. Therefore, these fellow Jews had an even greater obligation to help her.

On top of that, as Walter Elwell observes, "the Sabbath is a particularly appropriate day to frustrate the work of Satan."[19] The Sabbath is not a day to cease from doing the work of ministry, but to do God's works of mercy all the more. The people grasp this truth intuitively and rejoice at this unbridled display of honest religion on the Sabbath.

Mercy and the Sabbath

The Sabbath, given to mankind at the end of the creation week of Genesis, points to God's ultimate rule over all of creation, and the Lord's repeated acts of divine mercy on this holy day pointed to the sudden arrival—in the person of King Jesus—of the kingdom of God. Jesus's many Sabbath miracles announced the beginning of the end. "Indeed," Elwell says, "as Jews viewed the kingdom of God as the Sabbath age (the Sabbath would crown history as it crowned creation), it was especially appropriate for Jesus to heal on the Sabbath. The healing declares and celebrates the dawn of the end."[20]

Given this context, the questions of Jesus are even more revealing of our hearts. On another Sabbath, Jesus encounters a man with a withered hand. The disciples were so impressed that the incident was recorded in all of the Synoptics.[21] While each account gives slightly different details—only Luke the physician, for example, records the fact that the man's *right* hand is affected—the main point is unmistakable.

Jesus's opponents, well aware of his penchant for healing on the Sabbath, attempt to trap him with a no-win question, asking, "Is it lawful to heal on the Sabbath?" If Jesus answers, "Yes," they will accuse him of breaking the commandment. If he says, "No," he will lose face in the sight of the people. But Jesus turns the tables on them by asking his own questions. This time, arguing from the lesser to the greater once again, he mentions not oxen or donkeys, but a beast perhaps even less valuable in the eyes of the world.

"*Which one of you who has a sheep, if it falls into a pit on the Sabbath, will not take hold of it and lift it out?*" Jesus asks. "Of how much more value is a man than a sheep!" Whether this second sentence is an exclamation or a question doesn't much matter. The response is obvious: it is not only lawful to rescue a helpless sheep; it is lawful to rescue a human being, who is worth "much more." And then Jesus expands the principle still further, saying, "So it is lawful to do good on the Sabbath." We may not only heal the sick specifically, we may do good generally.

But Mark and Luke phrase this verbal dagger of Jesus to his adversaries as a penetrating question in its own right, one we must also answer. "*Is it lawful on the Sabbath,*" Jesus asks, "*to do good or to do harm, to save life or to kill?*" This expanded wording raises the stakes for all of us. Not only is it permitted to do good on the Sabbath; it is enjoined. Not to do good when one can is tantamount to doing harm, or even destroying life. Saving lives is not a right; it is our responsibility. We cannot look away. We *are* our brothers' keeper.

Weekend Warriors

What does this mean for those of us who treat professional football or another televised sporting event, the weekend paper, or some kind of rest or recreation as a right on "our" Sundays? Must we give them all up for a grim obligation to serve others on the Sabbath? First of all, whatever the Sabbath—the seventh day of the week, Saturday—has meant to Jews, it is clear something significant happened when Jesus rose from the dead on Sunday, the first day. This paradigm-shifting event brought a new beginning, a transformation, a bursting of the old wineskins. The early church, which was largely comprised of Jews, began worshipping on Sunday, not Saturday.[22] And today the Christian church, by and large, worships on Sunday in commemoration of the resurrection.

Rather than rest at the end of a long and arduous week, our focus is indeed on recreation—literally, *re-creation*—on what has come to be known as the Lord's Day.[23]

And if Sunday is uniquely the Lord's Day, it makes sense to do the life-affirming works on Sunday that he did on the Sabbath. Honoring this transcending day not only permits us to help a dumb animal—and sheep really are dumb. It encourages us to do good, whatever the need of the moment might be. Works of mercy are signs of the kingdom, which has quietly entered history in weakness and will one day be inaugurated in power: "thy kingdom come, thy will be done, on earth as it is in heaven."

So doing good on the Lord's Day ought not be a grim legalism but a joyous opportunity to share the life of God with those who need him. Jesus was "grieved at [people's] hardness of heart" for turning what God meant for good into a life-killing legalism, so we ought not turn our own desire for obedience into an excuse for the same. I cannot tell you how, when, or how often you should do good on the Lord's Day, only that you should. Perhaps we can start by simply emulating Jesus: when we see a need on the Lord's Day, we should do what we can to meet it. Don't worry; God will help.

Such an approach can be exhilarating, and a little scary. As I was beginning to write this chapter, I became aware that a neighbor on my street is struggling with a brain tumor. (Somehow in my self-absorption I had not known this.) I felt strongly moved to reach out but didn't know what to do. I don't know this man and have little in common with him. Feeling stupid, I decided to keep it simple. On a recent Sunday afternoon I bought a small chocolate cake and, with my daughter, brought it over to the man and his wife. Seeing the brutal toll the disease and its treatment had taken on him, I awkwardly offered my help and my prayers, then left. It wasn't much, but my neighbors seemed touched, and I have been praying regularly for them. Do I feel that I have arrived with regard to the Lord's Day? Not at all. But at least I have taken a step.

Damnable Silence

Luke provides us with another test of our Lord's Day compassion.

> One Sabbath, when he went to dine at the house of a ruler of the Pharisees, they were watching him carefully. And behold, there was a man before him who had dropsy. And Jesus responded to the lawyers and Pharisees, saying, "*Is it lawful to heal on the Sabbath, or not?*" But they remained silent. Then he took him and healed him and sent him away. And he said to them, "*Which of you, having a son or an ox that has fallen into a well on a Sabbath day, will not immediately pull him out?*" And they could not reply to these things.[24]

Invited to dinner after a service, Jesus again encounters someone in need. He also faces the same hard-hearted religious legalism as before. These people could apparently eat and drink with no pangs of conscience as the suffering looked on, unhelped. Perhaps this man had even been planted in the audience as a way to show up Jesus. The question was not whether Jesus *could* heal; all knew that he could. The issue was whether he *would* heal, thereby breaking their rule on the Sabbath.

The answer was not long in coming, and Jesus did not disappoint. They were apparently not gluttons for food, but gluttons for punishment! He saw a man with dropsy, which is an illness that causes swelling in the body's tissues and cavities because of too much fluid.[25] Anyone who has experienced swelling in the hands or feet can attest to the accompanying discomfort and embarrassment. This condition was doubtless worse, and Luke describes the miracle without fanfare. Jesus simply heals the man and sends him on his way. This dispute is not about a man's healing, but about the Pharisees' unhealed hearts.

This time Jesus is the one attempting to initiate the discussion. The first question—about whether healing is permissible on the Sabbath—is his. But they don't care to have a dialogue with their dinner guest. They are too busy, like small-town prosecutors, gathering evidence.

The healing does nothing to loosen their tongues (or soften their hearts), so Jesus asks another question. Even if they care nothing for *this* man, surely they care for their own? And if they can be trusted to "break" the rule in one case, what is to prevent them from opening their hearts to a stranger? The logic of the question is impeccable. But perhaps having seen how Jesus had exposed his interlocutors before, the Pharisees are speechless. They have been caught in their own trap.

Love in Deed

The question probes our own hearts, too. If the repeated scriptural command to love your neighbor as yourself means anything, then it is a love that must be expressed in concrete deeds.[26] And the apostle John knew that the bridge between love and action is compassion, supremely illustrated by Jesus:

> This is how we know what love is: Jesus Christ laid down his life for us. And we ought to lay down our lives for our brothers. If anyone has material possessions and sees his brother in need but has no pity on him, how can the love of God be in him? Dear children, let us not love with words or tongue but with actions and in truth.[27]

Sometimes we find our neighbors, our brothers and sisters, not in the same house or city, but in faraway places. Kay Warren, the wife of *Purpose Driven* pastor Rick Warren, was used to changing the channel whenever her television brought images of evil and suffering. But Warren grasped the call to compassionate action one day when she was visiting Cambodia and was brought to Svey Pak, an area outside Phnom Penh. There Western men prey on child prostitutes as young as age 7.

"I came away from Svey Pak wounded by the pain of these young girls forced to act like grown women," Warren says. "Changing the channel could no longer be my response to evil in the world. My newfound knowledge made me ready to face it, hate it, and resist it."[28]

True love always produces compassion. And, yes, sometimes that compassion produces not a soft-hearted sentimentality but honest-to-goodness hatred—hatred of everyday evil and suffering.

There is no one right way to fight suffering and evil in God's world, a planet in which the kingdom has been promised but only partially delivered. We can oppose sex trafficking or homelessness, poverty or persecution. God's call may differ for each of us. But we cannot even begin to answer it without his compassion. And woe to us if we, like the Pharisees, remain silent.

Suggested Reading

Haugen, Gary A. *Good News About Injustice: A Witness of Courage in a Hurting World*. Downers Grove, IL: InterVarsity, 2009.

Hubach, Stephanie O. *Same Lake, Different Boat: Coming Alongside People Touched by Disability*. Phillipsburg, NJ: P&R, 2006.

Discussion Questions

1. Have you ever experienced a physical disability or know someone who has? What is it like?
2. How might disability shape the character of the person affected? How might it develop compassion in someone who is not disabled?
3. What beliefs or agenda items keep us from helping the suffering?
4. In what ways can you make the Lord's Day special?
5. Why is faith without works a dead faith?
6. How is compassion a bridge between belief and action?
7. Into what areas of service might the Lord be calling you? How can you explore this further?

18

Gratitude Honors Him

*"Was no one found to return
and give praise to God?"*

Our consumer society has yet to figure out Thanksgiving. The holiday, despite its long and proud history in the United States, sparks nothing more than a few turkey sales. Many of us would rather get right to Christmas. Peter Gomes of Harvard Divinity School says wryly, "When I saw the Christmas lights being strung up across the city streets and the Santa Clauses in the store windows at Sears, I knew that Thanksgiving could not be far away."[1]

Conditioned as we are to always want a little bit more, it's difficult to package gratitude for profit—especially because it's so hard for many to escape from America's ideal of rugged individualism. Why should we be thankful if we've done it all ourselves? Or perhaps we're just too busy. Robert Emmons, a psychologist at the University of California, Davis, sadly observes, "Nowadays, it is not so much that we are strongly opposed to gratitude on philosophical and moral grounds, but rather that we don't think about it very often."[2]

Family Feud

Ingratitude is hardly a modern phenomenon. One day Jesus encountered it while traversing what Matthew Henry calls "the frontier-country, the marches

208

that lay between Samaria and Galilee."[3] Heading south, Jesus and the disciples are going to Jerusalem, where the Lord is about to parry the determined hostility of the religious intelligentsia and where he will ultimately give his life. Jerusalem, of course, was the center of Jewish religious life. The magnificent temple of Herod brought the oppressed people great pride even under Roman occupation, giving them hope that one day God would restore the fortunes of his people under a new David. The city always bustled with festivals, economic activity, and the hint of insurrection. No true Jew could wish for anything other than the honor of God's chosen people to be restored.

The inhabitants of Samaria, of course, were not true Jews. The descendents of the region's Jewish and Gentile inhabitants following the utter defeat of the Northern Kingdom seven centuries before, the syncretistic Samaritans were a thorn in the side of any self-respecting Jew. They were a "schismatic monotheistic group similar in theology to the Jews." The Jews saw their "worship of God [as] only a veneer for underlying idolatry." They saw themselves, however, as "true Israelites in descent and worship."[4]

Such closeness married with difference sparked ugly conflict. Those searching for the roots of interreligious tensions in the Middle East might want to look at the strained first-century relationship of Jews and Samaritans. *Strained* is probably too kind a word for it.

The apostle whom Jesus loved reported matter-of-factly, "Jews have no dealings with Samaritans."[5] John notes that Jesus's opponents insulted him by calling him a Samaritan.[6]

The disciples were no better. When a Samaritan village rejected Jesus, the disciples asked for permission to call down lightning bolts to "destroy them."[7] And the feeling was mutual. History tells of a massacre of Jewish pilgrims from Galilee by Samaritans in AD 52.[8] Truly there was no love lost between these estranged cousins.

And yet Jesus was not constrained by long centuries of prejudice and hatred. While sticking to his theological convictions,[9] Jesus was able to treat a Samaritan as equally needy, equally human—and equally responsible.

On the Frontiers of Faith

> On the way to Jerusalem he was passing along between Samaria and Galilee. And as he entered a village, he was met by ten lepers, who stood at a distance and lifted up their voices, saying, "Jesus, Master, have mercy on us."[10]

During this errand through the "frontier-country," Jesus is called aside by the plaintive shouts of men afflicted with a serious skin condition that present-day translators render as *leprosy*. Bible scholars generally don't believe their disease was the same as modern-day leprosy, but it clearly fell under the unhappy strictures of the Old Testament law intended to keep communicable disease from spreading.[11] That law was strictly enforced in Jesus's day. One rabbi threw stones at lepers to make them keep their distance. Another refused to eat an egg if it had been bought on the same street where a leper lived.[12]

This condition brought a physical and spiritual quarantine that any Israelite dreaded, and those who had the disease were ceremonially unclean and banned from the larger life of the community unless a priest pronounced them cured. To enforce their own isolation, those who suffered from this illness had to shout words of warning to the healthy. It was a living death sentence.

These ten men between Samaria and Galilee knew the law. They had to; it was a matter of life and death. But they also knew something of the kindness and power of Jesus. His fame had preceded him, even in this seemingly godforsaken dead end. Surely, they must have thought, if Jesus could cure the blind, heal the lame, and raise the dead, he had the power to help them, too? They were already outcasts and had nothing left to lose, so they raised their voices in desperate hope.

Yet in doing so they implicitly acknowledged that those who seek God's help should make no demands. Theirs is a request, not a command. It is the Lord's gracious prerogative to help. "Those that expect help from Christ," Henry notes, "must take him for their Master, and be at his command."[13] These men, like so many who turn to Jesus, had no other options. And Jesus never turns away the down and out.

Divine Shyness

When he saw them he said to them, "Go and show yourselves to the priests."[14]

In this instance, the Master talked rather than touched. Why Jesus did not touch them as he had others with leprosy, I don't know. Jesus's cures were always fitting to the circumstances, and their mode varied enormously. One he spoke at a distance, raising a dead servant to life. One he spit into the dirt, rubbing the muddy mixture on a blind man's eyes. One he took a little girl by the hand in a quiet room and told her parents to give her something to eat. In this instance, however, Jesus simply tells the recipients of his grace to go to the priests, who were the first-century referees as to whether a healing had taken place. Any cure, according to the book of Leviticus, would need the equivalent of a "Good Housekeeping seal of approval."[15]

This approval was required so that the formerly suffering individual could be ritually restored to the community—and so that the community could welcome him or her back with open arms amid the assurance that the risk of contagion was past. It didn't matter whether a well-known healer such as Jesus had performed a miracle; the ten would still have to do the paperwork.

Jesus wasn't in ministry for the notoriety, and certainly not for the money. He rarely gathered big crowds to witness his acts of mercy. "Tell no one," was his common statement to those he healed. The right hand rarely knew what the left hand was doing. Here there is no show, no pomp and circumstance. There is no pronouncement of healing, no admonition, no speech, no gathering of new disciples, no marketing campaign. He simply sends them off to the priests. Here Jesus displays true humility, almost a divine shyness. Could we do the same? Or can we not resist blowing our own horns?

Trial of Obedience

And as they went they were cleansed.[16]

I am reminded of the Old Testament story of Naaman, the Syrian general who was healed of leprosy by Elisha.[17] When the prophet told Naaman to bathe in the Jordan, initially he balked. The strange task seemed silly and much beneath the dignity of this great military commander. However, a wise servant encouraged Naaman to swallow his pride and do the act in faith. He did, and healing quickly followed.

Here the ten face a similar test. Will they go to the priest who must certify their healing? How can they, since Jesus has done nothing outwardly to assure them of a cure? How can they be sure they have actually been cured?

"This," Henry notes, "was a trial of their obedience."[18] Could they have argued with Jesus instead? Certainly they could have demanded some sign or a bit of personal attention from the healer. Others—including demoniacs, the chronically ill, and the previously dead—had received it. Why not *them*? Were they less worthy of his attention?

Or could they have doubted he would actually help them? Of course; Jesus had been "amazed at [the] lack of faith" in his own hometown.[19] The trust of these outliers was in no way a given.

And the simplicity of his answer was ambiguous: "Go and show yourselves to the priests." Was Jesus merely passing the buck for their case to other religious professionals? The men might go and then discover there was no healing. What an embarrassment and disappointment that would be! Perhaps they will get there and be chagrined to discover that their illness remains—then what fools they will have been to trust a Galilean healer! And of course he would be long gone. Perhaps his words were merely a polite way of turning them down?

Or were they a simple acknowledgment that the men's request was granted, not even worth discussing? Something in the reputation of Jesus, or perhaps in the way he looked them in the eye, encouraged them that they had met, not divine indifference, but God's mercy, on the road that day.

"And as they went they were cleansed." Note the progression: "as they went they were cleansed." The obedience precedes the healing. It seems clear: no obedience, no blessing. If they had not gone, they would have remained lepers. The obedience was necessary to receive God's grace; necessary, but not sufficient. God's grace is always his choice, otherwise it would not be grace, unmerited favor.

While we can never earn God's grace, in everyday life we can short-circuit it with our own self-destructive rebellion. Robertson McQuilkin, one of my spiritual role models, always emphasized two critical aspects of the Christian life—trust and obedience—as integral to the walk of faith. Trust is one step, obedience the other. With both we move forward in the Christian life. Emphasizing one over the other will leave you, however, "hopping mad." Here the ten do both—trust and obey.

A simple application: if God calls you to obey, then obey. The blessing will come in God's good time, in God's way. But this is not the health and wealth gospel. This is the life of a disciple: "Blessed is the man . . . [whose] delight is in the law of the LORD. . . . Whatever he does prospers."[20] Sometimes the blessing comes slowly, ambiguously, and quietly. But we can't just stand there waiting for it. The blessing comes as we step forward in faith. Or, as James says, "You see that a person is justified by what he does and not by faith alone."[21]

Turning Back

> Then one of them, when he saw that he was healed, turned back, praising God with a loud voice; and he fell on his face at Jesus' feet, giving him thanks. Now he was a Samaritan.[22]

The men go as directed, and then their healing comes. We don't know how far they traveled toward the priests before it dawned on them that they were cured. We do know it could not have been a great distance, because the Samaritan who turned back is able to find Jesus, who is heading for Jerusalem. Also, apparently the disciples could hear the man's loud praising before he got to Jesus, so while he probably had not been too far off when the healing came, he had not been right next to them. I'm guessing that the return trip for this man was more than a few steps; otherwise, there is no compelling reason why the other nine would not have come, too. Going back to Jesus definitely involves a detour, a change in plans, for the patient.

Until this point, the ten lepers have acted in concert: they had lived together, they had cried out together, they had gone off together, and they had been cleansed together. Now, however, one peels off like a jet leaving the formation and heads for Jesus. Something is different: perhaps his skin is clear, or the constant itching and pain are gone. Whatever has happened, the man knows he has been blessed, and the blessing requires a response. First he sees, then he turns, then he praises.

Such a response would have been perfectly natural for a first-century Jew, of course. The Hebrew Scriptures, including the Psalms, are replete with calls to praise and thanksgiving:

- "Sing to the LORD, you saints of his; praise his holy name."[23]
- "Then we your people, the sheep of your pasture, will praise you forever."[24]
- "Enter his gates with thanksgiving and his courts with praise; give thanks to him and praise his name."[25]

The cleansed man, however, is not one of the chosen people, but that doesn't stop him. No, he retraces his steps so that he can find Jesus. Once he does, he falls at the Lord's feet and offers a heartfelt thanksgiving to the one who has healed him.

According to Emmons, "thanks" and its cognates appear in the Bible more than one hundred and fifty times, and gratitude has been a cherished virtue down through church history: "The reformationist Martin Luther referred to gratitude as 'the basic Christian attitude' and the theologian Karl Barth remarked that 'grace and gratitude go together like heaven and Earth; grace evokes gratitude like the voice and echo.'"[26] John Wesley said, "True religion is right tempers toward God and right tempers toward man. It is, in two words, gratitude and benevolence—gratitude to our Creator and supreme Benefactor, and benevolence to our fellow creatures."[27] Jonathan Edwards, in his classic work, *A Treatise Concerning Religious Affections*, notes approvingly the "gracious stirrings of grateful affection toward God."[28] These the Samaritan displayed with joy.

And then, with the Samaritan still humbly at Jesus's feet, come three pointed, rapid-fire questions, which cast a shadow over the joyous scene.

Grace and Gratitude

Then Jesus answered, *"Were not ten cleansed? Where are the nine? Was no one found to return and give praise to God except this foreigner?"*[29]

I must confess; these three questions have always bothered me. At first blush they seem to reflect a childish need for praise and recognition on the part of Jesus. Wasn't performing the miracle enough for him? Isn't doing a good deed its own reward? Why did he need to be thanked?

The scene reminds me of the immature behavior of my kids who, when they do a tiny task around the house or some small favor for a sibling, stand before me, petulantly demanding recognition. Or, if I am honest, I recall my own need to be honored for some minor task, whether it be putting dishes in the dishwasher or . . . writing a book. Is the Son of God really that petty, that insecure?

Weren't they doing what he had asked, going to the priests? And wouldn't turning back be disobedient? Additionally, going to the trouble of finding him again would take time and effort and delay their restoration to the community. Jesus would understand. They were only following orders.

Only Jesus *didn't* understand. He wanted something beyond naked obedience. He wanted them to clothe their hearts in gratitude. And after they had received a new lease on life, was this really so much to expect? "Gratefulness," Emmons notes, "is a knowing awareness that we are the recipients of goodness."[30] Didn't these men *know*?

If, as Socrates said, the unexamined life is not worth living, then surely the same goes for the ungrateful life. Ungratefulness is a form of ignorance. The nine men who did not give thanks were not only rude. They were ignorant, misaligned with the truth of the universe. We are the recipients, not the creators, of goodness. Failing to give thanks reveals our incredible ignorance of this basic fact.

Even those who are only dimly aware of God can recognize the need to give thanks. If the history of humanity reveals anything, it is that we are dependent creatures. We depend on the rain falling, the sun shining, the doctor curing, the meteor missing. Yet thankfulness is not automatic for us. I have often wondered whom the atheist thanks for a sunrise. Expressing gratitude to the cosmos for the random interactions of molecules on one's retina seems like thin gruel indeed.

Before G. K. Chesterton became a Christian, the great writer and journalist puzzled over the paradox between the magnificence of life and the supposed lack of a God to thank for it all.

> The test of all happiness is gratitude; and I felt grateful, though I hardly knew to whom. Children are grateful when Santa Claus puts in their stockings gifts of toys or sweets. Could I not be grateful to Santa Claus when he put in my stockings the gift of two miraculous legs? We thank people for birthday presents of cigars or slippers. Can I thank no one for the birthday present of birth?[31]

Chesterton's impulse toward gratitude is perfectly natural. "I have come to believe," says Emmons, "that inside of us looms a powerful need to express gratitude for the goodness we have received."[32]

A Gracious Command

John Piper wrestled with the idea that God not only desires our praise but commands it—until he started reading C. S. Lewis's essay, "A Word about Praise."

But the most obvious fact about praise—whether of God or of anything—strangely escaped me. I thought of it in terms of compliment, approval, or the giving of honor. I had never noticed that all enjoyment spontaneously overflows into praise unless . . . shyness or the fear of boring others is deliberately brought in to check it. The world rings with praise—lovers praising their mistresses, readers their favorite poet, walkers praising the countryside, players praising their favorite game—praise of weather, wines, dishes, actors, motors, horses, colleges, countries, historical personages, children, flowers, mountains, rare stamps, rare beetles, even sometimes politicians or scholars. I had not noticed how the humblest, and at the same time most balanced and capacious, minds, praised most, while the cranks, misfits and malcontents praised least. . . . I think we delight to praise what we enjoy because the praise not merely expresses but completes the enjoyment; it is its appointed consummation. It is not out of compliment that lovers keep on telling one another how beautiful they are; the delight is incomplete till it is expressed.[33]

We praise God first of all because he is worthy. Second, we praise him because it is good for us. Blessing God blesses us. It would be unloving of God not to command our praise. "God," Piper summarizes, "is the one Being in all the universe for whom seeking his own praise is the ultimately loving act."[34]

Not only us, but the universe, created by our loving Father in heaven, is itself hard-wired for praise. "The heavens declare the glory of God," David marveled; "the skies proclaim the work of his hands."[35] The declarations and proclamations of creation, to be sure, are eloquent arguments for the existence of God, but they are much more than mere apologetics; they are a primal form of praise. "Let the heavens rejoice, let the earth be glad," the Psalmist said. "Then all the trees of the forest will sing for joy."[36]

When Jesus entered Jerusalem during the last week of his earthly ministry, the crowd of disciples erupted in praise, echoing the Psalms: "Blessed is the king who comes in the name of the Lord! Peace in heaven and glory in the highest!" Some of the Pharisees, however, growled, "Teacher, rebuke your disciples!" Jesus rightly answered, "I tell you, if they keep quiet, the stones will cry out."[37] Praise is not an option. It is a joyful inevitability. The only question is whether we will add our voices to the choir.

The Least We Can Do

Once I was at a hospital. A dear loved one was on an operating table that overlooked the valley of the shadow of death. We were in the hallway, anxiously awaiting word from the doctor as to whether our loved one had survived a procedure to relieve pressure on her brain. The diagnosis had been grim: it was a tumor that likely could not be removed. As we waited, the minutes hung cruelly like hours. We dreaded seeing the surgeon approach us, and yet we had to know the outcome. The delay was excruciating. Each footfall around the corner might be bringing the news we feared, and each time it did not, I exhaled.

Finally the doctor came, but with an excited look. He told us the unbelievable: there was no tumor. The problem was caused by an infection and was treatable.

We stood there, dumbly trying to grasp what he had said. There had been, and was, no cancer. Then, the truth finally sinking in, suddenly I shouted, "Praise God!" It was no burden. Miracles demand praise, and we delight to give it in such circumstances.

When thinking of God's blessings—not just the spectacular ones that we sometimes experience, but the everyday miracles—the least we can do is say, "Thank you." We should be grateful for everything, everyday—things such as fresh air, sunshine, friendship, and marriage. Too often, we focus on what we can't have rather than what we can. Gratitude happens naturally when we see all of life—even the hard parts—as a gift.

Restorative Faith

And he said to him, "Rise and go your way; your faith has made you well."[38]

When I was a kid, my mom and dad insisted that we write thank-you notes to our grandparents and others for their generosity at Christmas. I usually complained and performed this task grudgingly. But this was a good exercise nonetheless, because it took me outside my own selfishness and made me see how much I depended on the kindness of others. "The self," in the words of Emmons, "is a very poor place to find happiness or meaning in life."[39] How much better, then, to render thanks to God, the ultimate giver, and find the lasting joy only he brings?

I wonder how the nine felt when the man, rising from his worship, finally caught up with them, telling of his grateful exchange with Jesus, who wondered why they had not returned. Or perhaps others told them later that Jesus had made them object lessons in *in*gratitude. Certainly any who were left at the time Luke included their story in his Gospel would immediately recognize themselves. They had already missed the opportunity to deepen and confirm their elation by giving thanks. Would the knowledge of their ungrateful hearts have further quenched the joy they felt at their healing?

Henry says that the grateful man received more than the other nine because "he had his cure confirmed particularly with an encomium: *Thy faith hath made thee whole. . . .* Temporal mercies are *then* doubled and sweetened to us when they are *fetched* in by the prayers of faith, and *returned* by the praises of faith."[40] The nine had their cure; the one had his cure, *plus* a relationship with Jesus.

And note that it was a hated Samaritan, and not one of the chosen people, who had exercised this faith. Spiritual advantages can be disadvantages when approaching the kingdom of God. Blessed are the *poor*.

No Excuses

Just as there are no barriers to experiencing God's grace, neither are there excuses. If we want more, we must use what we have. A thankful heart always leads to more blessings, even if we don't seem to have a lot to be thankful for. When I lost my job, I quickly realized that unemployment, as bad as it is (and it is bad), is far from the worst thing that can happen to you. I can think of two things that are worse: death and divorce. By God's grace, neither of those things has visited our home, so I can honestly count myself way ahead. While God sometimes allows those things, too, and still is good, he has not in my case, and I am thankful. That thankfulness brought us another blessing: peace.

"For everyone who has," Jesus said, "will be given more, and he will have an abundance. Whoever does not have, even what he has will be taken from him."[41] God's blessings are available to us all, if we will but take them, thankfully.

The healed man didn't remain facedown on the ground. Instead, he arose, invited by his loving Master to begin a new way of life—a thankful life. Gratitude is not only humbling; it is liberating. Truly, he who humbles himself will be exalted.[42]

Suggested Reading

Emmons, Robert A. *Thanks! How the New Science of Gratitude Can Make You Happier*. Boston and New York: Houghton Mifflin Company, 2007.

Piper, John. *Desiring God: Meditations of a Christian Hedonist*. Sisters, OR: Multnomah, 1986.

Discussion Questions

1. Do you think Western society is becoming more grateful, or less? Why or why not?
2. What significance do you see in the fact that the thankful man was a Samaritan?
3. Why did Jesus send the ten to the priests?
4. When was the last time you obeyed *before* seeing the blessing? How did it turn out?
5. Is it hard or easy for you to publicly give thanks to God? Why?
6. What are you thankful for?
7. How can you cultivate an attitude of gratitude?

19

Love Mirrors Him

"If you love those who love you,
what reward do you have?"

Eighteenth-century French philosopher Jean-Jacques Rousseau didn't struggle with what is known today as low self-esteem. Historian Paul Johnson says rather that Rousseau was in the grip of an "overpowering egoism." And indeed, his statements bear out the point. Rousseau was the self-described unique friend of mankind. "The person who can love me as I can love is still to be born," he stated without blushing. "No one ever had more talent for loving."

However, among the people who actually knew him, the verdict was considerably different. "But loving as he did humanity in general," Johnson notes, "he developed a strong propensity for quarreling with human beings in particular. One of his victims, his former friend Dr. Tronchin of Geneva, protested: 'How is it possible that the friend of mankind is no longer the friend of men, or scarcely so?'"[1]

Rousseau brings to mind another famous philosopher—one Linus Van Pelt—who is reported to have said, "I love mankind; it's people I can't stand." Love is easy to extol but much harder to put into practice.

Love and Law

Love is the ultimate test of character. The apostle Paul told us that the greatest virtue—even higher than faith and hope—is love,[2] and you would be hard-pressed to find a philosopher or poet, clergyman or politician, who would disagree. Yet love is never alone. For believers, Paul lists love, followed by joy, peace, patience, kindness, goodness, faithfulness, gentleness, and self-control as the fruit of the Spirit. Then he adds, "Against such things there is no law."[3] Indeed, the law only comes into play where love is absent. If we all loved perfectly, we would not need the Ten Commandments, because we would already be doing them instinctively. There would be no need to lock our doors, to warn our children about strangers, to take self-defense classes, or even to password-protect our computers. It is the lack of love that brings the law.

Yet the law is not meant merely to restrain our sinful proclivities, but to fan into flame the missing virtue that caused it to be given in the first place. As we will see, the law was meant to bring us back to love. In fact, love lies like a dynamic, energy-charged nucleus at the heart of God's law. The ultimate aim of the law is not mere obedience; it is loving relationship. As Paul said, "So the law was put in charge to lead us to Christ."[4]

Loving Neighbors

This book has focused mainly on the questions *Jesus* asked his contemporaries—and, by extension, what he asks *us*. But what about all the questions his hearers asked *him*? If you could stand before Jesus right now, what would you ask him? What one thing would you most like to know? Certainly there are many possibilities: questions about the nature of heaven, the meaning of life, the Christian's duty to the state, or the fate of the unevangelized.

But for me, the key question is obvious: how can I *know* that I have eternal life? Can anything be more important than this? I don't think so. Fortunately, some of Jesus's contemporaries had the presence of mind to ask this all-important question, and we can learn much by studying the answers Jesus gave them.

One day a rich man asks the Lord, "Teacher, what good thing must I do to get eternal life?"[5] The man apparently was hoping that there was one simple task he could perform to gain eternal life—one quick, clean, straightforward transaction. I can imagine his face falling when Jesus tells him to slow down. Jesus points him back to the law, saying, "If you want to enter life, obey the commandments." The man answers (quaveringly, I suspect), "Which ones?" The requirement has suddenly exploded like a moral Big Bang, and who knows where it might lead? Surely Jesus didn't mean he had to keep all six hundred–plus Old Testament regulations, did he? Doing all that is impossible!

In answer, Jesus presents him with the six commands of the Second Table, those that deal with our obligations to our fellow human beings. (He could have also directed the young man's attention to the First Table commands about our obligations to God, but apparently thought the Second Table commands would be sufficient to make his point.)

So Jesus lists them: "Do not murder, do not commit adultery, do not steal, do not give false testimony, honor your father and mother, and 'love your neighbor as yourself.'" That last one, about neighbor-love, is not actually in the Ten Commandments,[6] but it summarizes the Second Table well.[7]

"All these I have kept," the man says sincerely, apparently suffering from an acute case of self-esteem. "What do I still lack?"

"If you want to be perfect," Jesus replies, "go, sell your possessions and give to the poor, and you will have treasure in heaven. Then come, follow me."

At this seemingly new requirement, the man slinks away. Give away all his stuff? *That* wasn't supposed to be part of the deal—or was it? While the man has just said he has loved his neighbor as himself, his love really stops at his checkbook. Why? Because it isn't real love. While he has apparently obeyed the letter of the law, he fails miserably when tested by its spirit. Even the prospect of endless life with God cannot warm his loveless heart and pry open his wallet.

"Teacher," a lawyer asks Jesus another time, "what shall I do to inherit eternal life?" Apparently he had not been present when the rich man had asked Jesus that very thing. Again, by bringing the scribe back to Scripture, Jesus allows the man, who knew the law, to answer his own question. And he gives a good answer—a very good one.

> [Jesus] said to him, "*What is written in the Law? How do you read it?*" And he answered, "You shall love the Lord your God with all your heart and with all your soul and with all your strength and with all your mind, and your neighbor as yourself." And [Jesus] said to him, "You have answered correctly; do this, and you will live."[8]

The scribe knew, unlike the rich man, that love is at the center of the universe. He knew that under all the Old Testament rules and regulations is the beating heart of a loving Father. Further, he knew that we fulfill the law of God when we love. Even more, he understood that our love must be aimed not only horizontally, at our fellow sojourners, but also vertically, at God. Only those who love God and others completely and unconditionally are fit for heaven. Love, not law, is ultimate.

(On another occasion, when someone asks Jesus to name the greatest commandment, he answers with the same two, and they both involve love: love God wholeheartedly, and love your neighbor as yourself. The greatest human obligation is to love. "All the Law and the Prophets hang on these two commandments,"[9] Jesus pronounces, and no religious expert in the long ages before or since has ever contradicted him.)

These insights our scribe knows, and we must not disparage his later failure, for many sages and wise men have never traveled to such heights on the path to spiritual insight. Jesus acknowledges as much, but then moves quickly to the application: "Do this, and you will live." Eternal life, we see, is not gained simply by *knowing* the right things (though knowledge is certainly indispensable),[10] but by *doing* the right things.[11] Discussion over? Not quite.

The scribe, however, knows he has not lived a life of love. He knows what we sometimes forget: that love is much more than a "lovin' feelin'." The scribe knows that real love is active and specific, not a mushy sentimentality. But how do you *do* love?

Let's look at the context. The command to "love your neighbor as yourself" should not be read in isolation. In its original scriptural setting, the command comes at the end of a long section in Leviticus 19 that provides flesh for the bare-bones directive to love our neighbor. Jesus and the lawyer both know this context, which undoubtedly shapes the rest of their conversation. According to this passage in Leviticus, neighbor-love

- involves sharing what we have with the poor and the aliens in our midst (vv. 9–10);
- prohibits stealing and lying (vv. 11–12);
- prohibits fraud, robbery, and slow payment (v. 13);
- prohibits mocking or harming the disabled (v. 14);
- involves equal justice (v. 15);
- prohibits slander or endangering someone's life (v. 16);
- prohibits secret hate, but enjoins righteous rebuke of the guilty (v. 17); and
- prohibits revenge or bearing a grudge "against one of your own people" (v. 18, NIV).

The Hard Work of Love

Seeing this comprehensive list of societal obligations to love in concrete ways, it is easy to see why the lawyer would look for an escape clause. Love is hard work. Asking an academic question, he receives a personal challenge. Too late, the man realizes he has been trapped and desperately tries to wriggle free, like a fly in a spider web.

Perhaps he can escape the implications of the command by defining those eligible to receive his love so narrowly that, for all practical purposes, his obligation is rendered null and void: perhaps the command only applies to his fellow Jews, or even to a smaller subset of "his kind of people"?

Hence his next question: "And who is my neighbor?" In other words, the scribe wants to know whom he is obligated to love—and, especially, whom he isn't. Perhaps he has in mind the words "one of your own people" from the first part of Leviticus 19:18 (listed above). One implication of this phrase, at least for those looking to escape the command, might be that it is limited only to our own kind, that those who are *not* our neighbors need not be loved.

Such a limiting interpretation would make sense to most people. Tribes whose members fiercely love one another will, just as fiercely, attack members of other tribes because they are not part of the "in" group. As we saw in the last chapter, "Jews have no dealings with Samaritans." We do the same thing today, don't we, writing off people who espouse different politics or lifestyles, who are of other races, religions, or castes?

Jesus, however, refuses to go along with this crabbed interpretation. The command to love is not an excuse to hate. But neither does he answer this man's question directly about the identity of his neighbor. Instead, he tells a story, one of the most beloved narratives in the history of the world. It is about a traveler who has come to be known as . . . the Good Samaritan.[12]

Being a Neighbor

> Jesus replied, "A man was going down from Jerusalem to Jericho, and he fell among robbers, who stripped him and beat him and departed, leaving him half dead. Now by chance a priest was going down that road, and when he saw him he passed by on the other side. So likewise a Levite, when he came to the place and saw him, passed by on the other side. But a Samaritan, as he journeyed, came to where he was, and when he saw him, he had compassion. He went to him and bound up his wounds, pouring on oil and wine. Then he set him on his own animal and brought him to an inn and took care of him. And the next day he took out two denarii and gave them to the innkeeper, saying, 'Take care of him, and whatever more you spend, I will repay you when I come back.' *Which of these three, do you think, proved to be a neighbor to the man who fell among the robbers?*" He said, "The one who showed him mercy." And Jesus said to him, "You go, and do likewise."[13]

The question Jesus asks here is not about defining (or limiting) who our neighbor is. That information no longer matters. It is about *being* a neighbor, even to those society would say we must avoid. Again we see that love will be, *must be*, expressed in practical acts. And these acts are not to be parceled out in a miserly way only to a few people who meet our standards. No, *everyone*—of whatever ethnic background—is our neighbor, with a compelling claim on our mercy. Paul, the Jewish apostle to the Gentiles, acknowledges, "For in Christ Jesus neither circumcision nor uncircumcision counts for anything, but only faith working through love."[14] Christian faith *works* through *love*.

Acts of mercy save no one, of course—not even us. But their absence ought to be a warning sign. True faith produces love, which produces works of love.

Inevitably. No works, no faith. No faith, no works. Quoting John: "If anyone has material possessions and sees his brother in need but has no pity on him, how can the love of God be in him? Little children, let us not love with words or tongue but with actions and in truth."[15]

Loving Enemies

The scribe was not alone. In the Sermon on the Mount, Jesus directly takes on how many of his contemporaries were twisting Scripture. Their perversion of God's Word had become so common that it had morphed into a malignant tradition that turned the command to love into a license to hate. Jesus remarked, "You have heard that it was said, 'You shall love your neighbor and hate your enemy.'"[16] It was a bald-faced attempt to not only evade the command but to turn it on its head. If you didn't feel like loving someone, call him your enemy. Matthew Henry comments, "they looked upon whom they pleased as their enemies, thus making void the great command of God by their traditions."[17]

In the story of the Good Samaritan, Jesus tells us to treat all people as our neighbors, but his is not a glassy-eyed idealism. Jesus knew what real enemies were. Much of the religious establishment sought to marginalize, humiliate, undermine, and, ultimately, murder him. Yes, modeling Levitical neighbor-love perfectly, he righteously rebuked the guilty. Yet, as we have seen, he ever tried to woo his opponents, to love them as neighbors. And he calls his followers to do the same. We must not only refrain from hating our enemies; we must positively love them.

Enemy Prayer

> But I say to you, Love your enemies and pray for those who persecute you, so that you may be sons of your Father who is in heaven. For he makes his sun rise on the evil and on the good, and sends rain on the just and on the unjust.[18]

Jesus says we must love our enemies (with all that this entails; see Leviticus 19 again). In the Middle East, where grudges get handed down for generations, even millennia, the call to love your enemies is perhaps the most offensive command in the Bible. Integral to such love, of course, is forgiveness. We cannot love if we do not forgive.

But note, the requirement to forgive is not a call to gloss over the very real evil that occurs between people, in societies, and among the nations. Such forgiveness is costly. Lewis Smedes wrote, "Forgiveness happens only when we first admit our hurt and scream our hate."[19] To forgive is not to let the offender off scot-free, either. To forgive on the individual level is not to forget on the judicial level, though nations that have been torn apart by genocide often must establish processes by which sins are recognized but criminals are pardoned.

Miroslav Volf, a professor of theology at Yale who witnessed interethnic strife in his native Croatia, says forgiveness does not overturn justice. "Divine grace does not preclude justice being done," he told *Christianity Today* just days after the 9/11 attacks. "The naming of the deeds as evil and the protection of those who are innocent is extraordinarily important," Volf said. "But none of these things means we should not also seek to forgive the offender and reconcile with the offender."[20]

But Westerners who take pride in our tolerance and mercy fare little better than perennial hotbeds of ethnic strife. Racism, sexism, crime, and defamation run rampant in our nations, neighborhoods, and homes. And yet we must overcome evil not with more evil, but with good.[21] "It ain't those parts of the Bible that I can't understand that bother me," Mark Twain reportedly once said, "it is the parts that I do understand."[22] We understand on an intellectual level that we must love our enemies, but try telling this to someone who has been injured. Sometimes forgiving our enemies seems overwhelming, especially if we have been deeply hurt. Yet Jesus does not leave us here, at the base of this moral Everest, with no way to ascend.

He gives us a little-recognized tool against our own inertia: prayer. I don't know about you, but I find it nearly impossible to pray for someone without having my own heart softened, my attitudes changed. If you are having trouble loving someone, try praying for that person. Our love not only must be expressed outwardly. It must work its way inward, until our very hearts are transformed. Prayer helps in that process.

Yet prayer for an enemy is no simple task, either. Just ask Semise Aydin. In April 2007, five Muslim fanatics in eastern Turkey beat, tortured, and executed her husband, Necati, and two other men. Before their murders, the victims had to endure their fingertips being sliced and their windpipes and esophagi severed. Their crime? They were Christians interested in spreading God's Word in the mostly Muslim nation.

Necati Aydin's offense in the eyes of those who slaughtered him was particularly heinous: he had been a Muslim who had transferred his allegiance to Jesus Christ. "I have received this salvation by faith in Jesus," Aydin told his horrified family after his decision, "and there is nobody, no poverty, no hardship, no illness, no evil, no death that has the power to turn me away from my faith unto salvation." He would receive a martyr's death, leaving his wife and two young daughters behind.

"Mommy," his six-year-old daughter asked one day, "I miss my daddy so much. Can't Jesus bring him back to us?"

Her mother, Semise, groped to explain what had happened. "Esther, Jesus decided to take Daddy to heaven, to be with him," she said, trying to sound reassuring. "So we have to wait until Jesus takes us to heaven to see Daddy again."

Not too surprisingly, little Esther replied, "Well, if Daddy isn't coming back, then I want to go to heaven, too!"

Such is the painful life Semise Aydin has faced since her husband's grisly murder. "Necati's absence is a cross for me every day," she told Compass Direct News. "It's a daily stress on all of us."

Yet two days after the slaughters, Semise publicly forgave the culprits. Beyond that, love for her enemies has gone to the next level: prayer. She is praying for at least one of the fanatics to repent and believe in Jesus. She said: "That's the ultimate revenge, isn't it?"[23]

Mirror Images

But Jesus goes a step further, pointing us to the author of the commandment and to the great object of our prayers: our heavenly Father. We are to be children of our heavenly Father, doing what he does. Jesus seems to be saying, "Like Father, like son." It's true that God uniquely crafts every child; no two are exactly alike—even so-called "identical" twins have irreducible differences. Parents may have significant differences in personality, gifts, and outlook than their children.

But there are deeper commonalities. These things parents and children hold in common may not be evident at first but emerge later only after many years. The way a daughter raises an eyebrow may have an uncanny resemblance to her father; the way a son responds to stress may be an ugly approximation of his mother; the way a man disciplines his children may be a mirror image of how his dad dealt with him. While there are many ways in which we differ from our heavenly Father, we show ourselves to be his children by doing what he does.

When the Lord God passed before Moses in giving the new Tables of the law, he described himself in part as "the compassionate and gracious God, slow to anger, abounding in love and faithfulness, maintaining love to thousands, and forgiving wickedness, rebellion and sin."[24] Jesus's hearers would know this narrative implicitly, and then they would be forced to see how they measured up. God blesses the evil and unrepentant, and so must we. As Jesus asks in the parable of the unforgiving servant, *"And should not you have had mercy on your fellow servant, as I had mercy on you?"*[25]

A Rewarding Love

And if being like the heavenly Father is not enough incentive, Jesus asks four questions that bring it down to street level for his self-interested followers:[26]

For if you love those who love you, what reward do you have?

At first blush, thinking about our reward seems crass at best. Isn't doing the right thing "its own reward"? We're only doing what is required. What's reward got to do with it? Quite a lot, actually. Yes, in another part of the Sermon on the Mount, Jesus tells us to disdain earthly treasures[27]—but not for the reasons you might think. Listen to Randy Alcorn: "Consider what Jesus is saying: 'Do not store up for yourselves treasures on earth.' Why not? Because earthly treasures are bad? No. *Because they won't last.*"[28] Jesus encourages us here to work for the rewards that will last, and the quickest way to acquire them is to love and pray for our enemies.

Then Jesus leads us to another comparison, this time a negative one. While first he calls us to look up at God in an elevating comparison, now he forces us to look down, at the dregs of society.

> *Do not even the tax collectors do the same? And if you greet only your brothers, what more are you doing than others? Do not even the Gentiles do the same?* You therefore must be perfect, as your heavenly Father is perfect.

While Jesus's questions to compare ourselves with the most despised elements of society might seem insensitive, in reality they are a gracious wake-up call. Here Jesus gives no happy-talk about the inherent goodness of the lost. He says even the kindnesses of tax collectors and Gentiles are selfish and without merit before a holy God who judges the heart. He implies that such acts not only bring no reward to the dregs, but will fail to benefit those who claim to be his followers. "We cannot expect the reward of Christians," Matthew Henry notes, "if we rise no higher than the virtue of publicans."[29]

In the similar Sermon on the Plain,[30] Jesus makes the same point with slightly differing emphases. Financial matters seem to be on his mind.

> *If you love those who love you, what benefit is that to you?* For even sinners love those who love them. And if you do good to those who do good to you, what benefit is that to you? For even sinners do the same. And if you lend to those from whom you expect to receive, what credit is that to you? Even sinners lend to sinners, to get back the same amount. But love your enemies, and do good, and lend, expecting nothing in return, and your reward will be great, and you will be sons of the Most High, for he is kind to the ungrateful and the evil. Be merciful, even as your Father is merciful.[31]

Here we see again that true love *works*. It involves prosaic activities such as lending—*without* the expectation of getting paid back. When was the last time we considered making a loan that might well turn into a gift? I don't believe Jesus is condemning capitalism, which runs efficiently based largely on the expectation that loans *will* be repaid—and which teeters on the brink of collapse when large numbers of borrowers default. But he is saying that we cannot run our personal affairs strictly as a business when someone asks for help.

Just as different laws come into play in the universe at the subatomic level compared to the galactic level, so different laws can apply when the scale of our social interaction shrinks. It is not the bank's job to love our neighbor; it is *our* job. Such love is radical and costly. When I lost my job, our family was thankful for government unemployment benefits. But what touched our hearts were the many—and I mean *many*—personal gifts from fellow church members. Some had notes attached; others were anonymous. Some came by check; others were in cash. Some were large, others small. What they all shared was a commitment to love, in deed as well as in word.

Jesus's negative comparison here is to "sinners." The clear implication in this passage is that if we do no more than common, garden-variety sinners, then we can expect no more reward than they receive—which is nothing. Compared to the other sermon, in this one the incentives are reversed: first the promised reward (which will be "great"), then the promised likeness to our Most High, merciful Father.

Which incentive is greater, the reward or the likeness? Or are they different aspects of the same thing? There comes a time in life for those of us blessed enough with economic opportunity (and blessed with the brains and luck to take advantage of it) when we have all we really need in material things. What then? Perhaps when we get older the gravitational pull of our stuff gets less and less as we come to grasp how little it satisfies. At that point the gravitational pull from another world starts to take over, and we begin looking more and more in that direction, which is to say, upward. People start to matter more than they did. God matters more.

As John Piper has said, God himself—not any benefit he confers—is the gospel. "The best and final gift of the gospel," Piper writes, "is that we gain Christ."[32] Heaven is not just a place where our desires are fulfilled, our pains removed. It is where God is. We see the emptiness of lives packed with stuff but devoid of solid relationships, and a longing, maybe suppressed or beaten down for decades, begins to emerge. It is a longing for God, a longing not just to be with him, but to be like him in our character. We want to be sons and daughters of the Most High. We need nothing more, want nothing more. To be like him is more than enough.

Suggested Reading

Colson, Charles, with Ellen Santilli Vaughn. *God and Government: An Insider's View on the Boundaries Between Faith and Politics*. Grand Rapids: Zondervan, 2007.

Haugen, Gary A. *Just Courage: God's Great Expedition for the Restless Christian*. Downers Grove, IL: InterVarsity, 2008.

Shriver, Donald W. *An Ethic for Enemies: Forgiveness in Politics*. New York: Oxford University Press, 1995.

Discussion Questions

1. What does society say love is?
2. What is at the heart of the Bible's commandments?
3. What does biblical love look like?
4. How can we show this kind of love in our context?
5. How do you balance love for someone who has wronged you and the biblical call for justice?
6. What encouragements does God's Word give us to persevere in our love?
7. What might some of the rewards for loving others look like? For loving God?

What Are Some Critical Doctrines?

20

Understanding His Word

*"Is this not the reason you are
wrong, because you know neither the
Scriptures nor the power of God?"*

L isa Miller's December 15, 2008, cover story in *Newsweek* magazine, "Our
Mutual Joy," purports to lay out the biblical case for gay marriage.[1] Her
hermeneutical journey quickly goes off the rails because Miller ignores the
Bible's direct statements against homosexual acts[2] and turns instead to the
lives of its characters (never the wisest hermeneutical course, given the rough
crowd inhabiting its pages):

> Let's try for a minute to take the religious conservatives at their word and define
> marriage as the Bible does. Shall we look to Abraham, the great patriarch, who
> slept with his servant when he discovered his beloved wife Sarah was infertile?
> Or to Jacob, who fathered children with four different women (two sisters and
> their servants)? Abraham, Jacob, David, Solomon and the kings of Judah and
> Israel—all these fathers and heroes were polygamists. The New Testament
> model of marriage is hardly better. Jesus himself was single and preached an
> indifference to earthly attachments—especially family. The apostle Paul (also
> single) regarded marriage as an act of last resort for those unable to contain
> their animal lust.

Editor Jon Meacham's note defending the piece removes all doubt about media bias in this case. Dismissing all who oppose homosexual marriage for scriptural reasons, Meacham says:

> No matter what one thinks about gay rights—for, against or somewhere in between—this conservative resort to biblical authority is the worst kind of fundamentalism. Given the history of the making of the Scriptures and the millennia of critical attention scholars and others have given to the stories and injunctions that come to us in the Hebrew Bible and the Christian New Testament, to argue that something is so because it is in the Bible is more than intellectually bankrupt—it is unserious, and unworthy of the great Judeo-Christian tradition.

If believing and following the Bible is "the worst kind of fundamentalism," one wonders what Meacham thinks of the Islamic terrorists of 9/11. While I am against a rigid fundamentalism and all for an intelligent faith that graciously and thoughtfully engages with the issues of the day, there can be no solid doctrine without a firm understanding of God's Word written.

The Bible Gap

The verdict of the American people is considerably different than Meacham's. While you might think that most thinking adults see the sixty-six books of the Old and New Testaments as relics of a pre-scientific age, assented to by only backward minorities of gullible bumpkins, the numbers say otherwise. According to Frank Newport in the Gallup News Service, "About one-third of the American adult population believes the Bible is the actual Word of God and is to be taken literally word for word."[3]

However, comparatively few of us regularly read the Bible. Clearly, many people who believe the Bible is the Word of God don't bother reading it all that much.[4] Given the nagging problems confronting so many people in areas the Bible addresses—marriage, child-rearing, money, and illness, just to name a few—you would think more folks would take the time to crack open this incomparable book.

As both testaments claim, God does something when we read his Scriptures.[5] J. I. Packer and Carolyn Nystrom note that when people read or reflect upon the Scriptures, "even when they are beginners and do not as yet know the sacred text well, messages from God come through to their hearts in a way that is both startling and encouraging. Bible readers sense again and again that God is speaking significantly to them."[6]

Yet, more often than not, we keep our Bibles upon our shelves, safely zipped inside their leather covers. We believe, but we don't read. The reasons for this Bible gap could be many: a perceived lack of time, laziness, reluctance to obey what we read, fear that we will not understand, and so on. Yet this disconnect, as scandalous as it might appear, is not all that new.

Missing the Point

Jesus's era faced a similar problem. While most people did not possess their own copies of the Scriptures, they were drilled in the sacred texts starting in their youth. Ignorance was inconceivable. God's Word—the Law and the Prophets—was God's life-sustaining gift to humanity, starting with the Jews.

God's Word made clear Yahweh's requirements for life in the community under his care. In great detail it spelled out the awfulness of sin and the blessings of fellowship with him. The Word taught men how to approach God, how to avoid disaster, how to produce wealth, how to grow in wisdom, and what was ahead beyond this earthly existence. Israel knew that humanity "does not live on bread alone but on every word that comes from the mouth of the LORD."[7]

And yet, by and large, Israel disobeyed or disregarded God's Word, ultimately leading to its judgment and removal from the Promised Land by the Babylonian despot Nebuchadnezzar. God graciously returned the people to the land over the next several centuries, but something critical had been left in Babylon: the people's understanding of God's Word.

Law and Tradition

In Jesus's day, the people gamely tried to obey the Bible to win God's favor. They were much like the fundamentalists that Meacham and company mock. The scribes and Pharisees scrupulously taught the law to a people looking for freedom from the Romans, adding many human safeguards so there would be no chance that someone might transgress a commandment by accident. These were "interpretations and applications of the law of Moses, handed down from generation to generation. In Jesus's day this 'tradition of the elders' was in oral form. It was not until c. AD 200 that it was put into writing in the Mishnah."[8]

Unfortunately, these initially well-intended accretions grew up around the law and eventually smothered it. The tradition came to be seen as just as authoritative as the actual words of Scripture, kind of like a study Bible in which the line separating the sacred text from the human notes is erased. "The oral traditions developed," according to Walter Elwell, "in an attempt to prevent unwitting infringements of the Law of Moses, but they had become a burden and tended to obscure rather than illuminate the written code."[9]

Jesus was not amused. A true disciple puts God's Word first, not our interpretation of it. No matter how good or insightful an article, an institution, or a book may be, it does not carry the same binding authority as God's Word.

One such tradition, not in the Old Testament, involved hand washing as a way to avoid ceremonial defilement.[10] One day scribes and Pharisees come from Jerusalem to demand that Jesus tell them why his disciples did not follow the tradition. He quickly turns the tables on his accusers:

> He answered them, *"And why do you break the commandment of God for the sake of your tradition?* For God commanded, 'Honor your father and your mother,' and, 'Whoever reviles father or mother must surely die.' But you say, 'If anyone tells his father or his mother, "What you would have gained from me is given to God," he need not honor his father.' So for the sake of your tradition you have made void the word of God. You hypocrites! Well did Isaiah prophesy of you, when he said:
>
> > 'This people honors me with their lips,
> >   but their heart is far from me;
> > in vain do they worship me,
> >   teaching as doctrines the commandments of men.'"[11]

Jesus answers their question—why his disciples don't follow a particular tradition—with one of his own. Why do they put a tradition, as well intended as it might be, ahead of God's command? The implication: God's Word trumps human tradition. While some traditions are fine, according to Jesus, other traditions cause us to break God's commands and must be discarded.

In the instance he cites, if you had promised a certain amount of money to God, then you need not use it to support your parents. The rule was, God first, mother and father second. Sounds holy, right? It was really just a neat legal trick to escape a clear obligation to honor one's parents in practical ways.

Letter and Spirit

Understanding the letter of the law profits us nothing if we fail to grasp its spirit. Jesus is asking us to read the Bible with new eyes. He is asking us to not only know it, but also to interpret it rightly and apply it to our lives. He is calling us to a new hermeneutic, one that touches our hearts. "The goal of all Bible study," says Robertson McQuilkin, "is to apply the truth of Scripture to life. If that application is not made, all the work put into making sure of the author's intended meaning will have gone for naught."[12]

As Jesus continues this discourse, he develops the idea of finding the true heart of the law. In so doing, he brings to an end the centuries-old food laws announced to Moses, who had told the Israelites that God wanted them to eat only "clean" foods.[13] He thereby reveals another important hermeneutical principle, that of progressive revelation.

And he called the people to him and said to them, "Hear and understand: it is not what goes into the mouth that defiles a person, but what comes out of the mouth; this defiles a person." Then the disciples came and said to him, "Do you know that the Pharisees were offended when they heard this saying?" He answered, "Every plant that my heavenly Father has not planted will be rooted up. Let them alone; they are blind guides. And if the blind lead the blind, both will fall into a pit." But Peter said to him, "Explain the parable to us." And he said, "*Are you also still without understanding? Do you not see that whatever goes into the mouth passes into the stomach and is expelled?* But what comes out of the mouth proceeds from the heart, and this defiles a person. For out of the heart come evil thoughts, murder, adultery, sexual immorality, theft, false witness, slander. These are what defile a person. But to eat with unwashed hands does not defile anyone."[14]

Here Jesus implies that the food laws are temporary instructions to be done away with when people grasp their intent, which is inner holiness. The food laws provided an outward picture of an intended inner reality.

Jesus's questions help us see that biblical revelation—God's communication to humanity—is progressive. Like a good parent, God doesn't tell us everything at once; he tells us what we need to know, when we need to know it. Over time, we learn more from him. While the dietary laws were good for a certain time and place, with the coming of Christ they become outmoded, like old wineskins.[15] "*Revelation is a cumulative activity*," Packer notes. "God's revelation in Christ does not stand alone, but comes as the climax of a long series of revelatory disclosures."[16]

Here Jesus makes the seemingly simple point that a person is not defiled by what goes in (food), but what goes out (words, motivated by a sinful heart). The implication: God is more concerned with the heart than with the diet. Dietary restrictions were temporary, meant to train the people in holiness and in their commitment to Yahweh, but they were not meant to substitute for a changed heart.

Jesus was never satisfied with merely a rote understanding of Scripture, or a wooden application of its commands. Knowledge of God's Word that did not lead to a transformed heart and a holy life was less than inadequate. It was an idol that had to be smashed. "Exegesis," Professor William Larkin notes, "must include application."[17]

Purity, Inside and Out

The goal of inner change applies to other Old Testament laws. In the famous case of the woman caught in adultery, Jesus demands not only an outward purity in conformance to the law, but an inner one, too. And this demand for holiness applies not only to the hapless woman who is dragged before Jesus, but to her self-righteous accusers.

"Teacher," they demand, a chilling note of triumph undoubtedly in their voices, "this woman has been caught in the act of adultery. Now in the Law Moses commanded us to stone such women. So what do you say?" Again, Jesus's accusers are seeking to discredit him in the eyes of the crowd. They want to exploit what they see as the tension between God's law and simple human compassion. No such tension exists, as they will soon discover, for God's law is an expression of God's love. As the Psalmist says, "Steadfast love and faithfulness meet; righteousness and peace kiss each other."[18]

Under their legalistic badgering, Jesus finally stands up and says, "Let him who is without sin among you be the first to throw a stone at her." Recognizing their own guilt, one by one the accusers drop their rocks and slink away, chastened. Following this word, we would do well to reflect on our own failings, to take the logs out of our own eyes before we confront someone else's.

"*Woman, where are they?*" Jesus asks her. "*Has no one condemned you?*" The woman replies, half in shock, "No one, Lord." Without witnesses, there is no case. Will she get away with it after all? No. Jesus does not act as if the sin never happened. "Neither do I condemn you," he answers; "go, and from now on sin no more."[19]

Jesus doesn't deny the awful power and price of sin in human life. Never will we reach a place where sin loses the ability to grab us and pull us under. Yet Jesus perfectly balances truth with grace.[20] The woman has sinned, but she is now free to live without it. Jesus reminds us that the first purpose of the law is not punishment; it is restoration. Jesus understands our predicament: "For because he himself has suffered when tempted, he is able to help those who are being tempted."[21]

Knowing God, Knowing Scripture

One day the Sadducees attempt to trip up the Lord with one of their trick questions in a bald-faced attempt to deny the reality of the afterlife using the Hebrew Scriptures themselves.[22] And certainly the doctrine is not presented as clearly in the Old Testament as in the New. While there are hints of the afterlife in the former,[23] it does not come into full view until the resurrection of Jesus, who is presented as the "firstfruits of those who have fallen asleep."[24] Nevertheless Jesus does not appeal to the New Testament's coming revelation of the afterlife in his dispute with the Sadducees, but to that of the Old Testament.

Then Jesus asks his questioners a most curious question: "*Is this not the reason you are wrong, because you know neither the Scriptures nor the power of God?*"[25] If they knew their Bibles, they would know that this life is not the end. Moreover, their ignorance of the Scriptures is paired with an ignorance of God, who is the ultimate author. This is no mere coincidence. While creation shows us the power and majesty of God,[26] the Scriptures are God's primary means of self-disclosure.[27] We cannot expect to know God if we do not know his Word. Heart knowledge goes with head knowledge.

Knowledge of Scripture is necessary but not sufficient if we seek to grow as Jesus's disciples—but it *is* necessary. This will require not just devotional reading, or even daily reading, but some real work to rightly understand God's written revelation. This doesn't mean we have to learn the original languages of Scripture (though this can be helpful). We can start by simply digging into a favorite chapter or sermon text. Eventually we will want good hermeneutical tools. Besides a good study Bible, we ought to invest in a commentary, a basic text on hermeneutics, a concordance (to get the shades of meaning in the original Hebrew and Greek words), a Bible atlas, a theological dictionary, and a Bible encyclopedia.[28]

It's interesting that believers in Jesus's day had so much less to help them understand God's Word and yet most knew so much more than we do. May we faithfully learn God's second greatest gift to us, his written Word, allowing it to change our hearts.

The Link

Finally, the Hebrew Scriptures were written to point his people to the King. Over and over, Jesus appealed to his hearers' reverence for God's Word to capture their attention and clinch his argument. We have witnessed this repeatedly in the volume you are holding. But we would do well to remind ourselves how important Jesus believed the Hebrew Scriptures to be in matters of life and faith. "*Have you not read this Scripture?*"[29] he asked the doubters. "*Have you not read what David did?*"[30] he asked the skeptics. "*Or have you not read in the Law?*"[31] Had they indeed not *read*? Before cleansing the temple, Jesus asked, "*Is it not written, 'My house shall be called a house of prayer for all the nations'?*"[32] Regarding a question on marriage, Jesus replied, "*What did Moses command you?*"[33] Even as death approached, Scripture was on Jesus's lips. "*My God, my God,*" he cried from the cross, quoting Psalm 22, "*why have you forsaken me?*"[34] Jesus fully expected his hearers to know their Bibles. He certainly knew his. Jewish faith and the Word of God were inseparable. How could one know what God expected without it?

The Ultimate "Who"

But the Word was not designed to merely answer the what, when, why, and how questions, as important as those are. It was meant to draw people to the ultimate who: himself. "And the Father who sent me has himself testified concerning me," the Lord told the Jewish leaders. "You have neither heard his voice nor seen his form, nor does his word dwell in you, for you do not believe the one he sent. You diligently study the Scriptures because you think that by them you possess eternal life. These are the Scriptures that testify about me."[35]

According to Jesus, Judaism is incomplete without him. That means, as hard as it is to say it, that any Judaism this side of the cross that denies its Messiah—no matter how moral, family-oriented, or monotheistic—cannot be seen as an adequate path to the God who has revealed himself in all of Scripture. "If you believed Moses, you would believe me," Jesus told the unbelieving crowds; "for he wrote of me. *But if you do not believe his writings, how will you believe my words?*"[36]

One cannot embrace Moses while pushing away Jesus. It's a package deal. Jesus reminds his fellow Jews that those who question his authority need to remember that they aren't even following Moses. "*Has not Moses given you the law?* Yet none of you keeps the law."[37] How can they question Jesus when they haven't even bothered to obey Moses? If they have not followed the lesser prophet, how can they follow the greater one? Remember, on the mount of transfiguration, the Father made clear that Jesus is superior to Moses.[38]

These are hard words, painful words. It gives me no pleasure to say them, and I wish I could do otherwise. But I am forced to this position by the very words of Scripture, not by any animus I harbor toward Jewish people. Indeed, I resonate with Paul, the self-described "Hebrew of Hebrews,"[39] who cried out, "I have great sorrow and unceasing anguish in my heart" because of the Jewish people's rejection of Jesus as their Messiah.[40]

But given the history of Christianity's horrific outbursts of anti-Semitism—whether during the Crusades or in Germany during the time of the Nazis—it is easy to see why Jewish people take offense at this language. Too often have followers of Yeshua (the Jewish name for Jesus) persecuted his people. When I took a public stand in favor of Jewish evangelism, Yehiel Poupko, a prominent Chicago rabbi, took me to task, saying Judaism stands on its own without Jesus of Nazareth, and insisting that Jewish evangelism undermines the Jewish people.

> The Jewish-evangelical relationship is in its nascent period. We are still learning how to talk with each other and how to engage in respectful, friendly conversation about ultimate matters. The purpose of this conversation is not agreement. The basis of interfaith conversation must be mutual sacred rejection, a clear understanding of the irreconcilable differences between the faith communities. As a Jew faithful to the covenant made by God with my fathers and mothers at Mount Sinai, I reject what is most sacred to the Christian. I am prepared to die for it, as have my ancestors before me. The Christian rejects what is most sacred to me, and is likewise prepared to die for it. Only after respectful mutual sacred rejection, can we identify those beliefs that we share in common. There is aught

but the One God; God has created all of humanity in God's image; God has revealed the ways of justice, righteousness, holiness, and purity.[41]

If what is most sacred to the Jew is not the covenant with God at Sinai but the rejection of Jesus as Messiah, then we will have to agree to disagree. But never could I reject the Jews, who remain chosen and beloved of God. "As far as the gospel is concerned, they are enemies," Paul said; "but as far as election is concerned, they are loved on account of the patriarchs, for God's gifts and his call are irrevocable."[42]

So let us love and accept the Jewish people, even as we gently share with them the love of their Messiah. And let us remember that even Jesus's own followers were slow to recognize him. After the resurrection, on the road to Emmaus, two of them unknowingly told their incognito Lord of his own life and death, ending with the puzzle of the empty tomb. They did not understand the resurrection. Their ignorance and lack of faith were apparently too much for Jesus.

> And he said to them, "O foolish ones, and slow of heart to believe all that the prophets have spoken! *Was it not necessary that the Christ should suffer these things and enter into his glory?*" And beginning with Moses and all the Prophets, he interpreted to them in all the Scriptures the things concerning himself.[43]

The question is telling. If these disciples had understood their Bibles (what Christians call the Old Testament), they should have known that Christ's passion and resurrection were *necessary* parts of God's plan. They didn't, and Jesus's verdict sounds harsh: they were foolish. Ignorance of Scripture, particularly its christocentric nature, is not just regrettable. It is culpable.

Jesus not only knew the Scriptures and appealed to them; he lived them. He had said he had come not to abolish the law, but to fulfill it.[44]

- His life, death, and resurrection were foretold in the Scriptures.[45]
- As predicted in the Scriptures, he was born in Bethlehem, the city of David.[46]
- He was brought to Egypt and back, like the people of Israel.[47]
- He resisted temptation and obeyed God's law perfectly, as Israel had failed to do.[48]
- Like David, he was forsaken and rescued.[49]
- As Isaiah's suffering servant, he was punished in the place of God's people.[50]
- Jesus fulfilled all the significant Old Testament offices as Israel's ultimate prophet, priest, and king.[51]

Jesus the Key

When Peter unsheathes his sword in a misconceived attempt to defend his Lord the night he was betrayed, Jesus (as we have seen) tells him to put his weapon away. *"Do you think I cannot appeal to my Father, and he will at once send more than twelve legions of angels?"* Then he asks the clincher: *"But how then should the Scriptures be fulfilled, that it must be so?"*[52] Jesus's death *had* to be; it was foretold in the Old Testament centuries before. The Hebrew Bible cannot be fully understood apart from him.

Jesus is the key that unlocks our understanding of Scripture. And what is the purpose of Scripture? Why does God go to so much trouble to speak with us? Hint: it's not to make "fundamentalists" out of us. "The truly staggering answer," Packer says, "is to make friends with us."[53]

As we have seen, love is the purpose of law, relationship the goal of rules. God speaks because we are capable, with his help, of hearing. And if we hear, we can repent, believe, and live. So Bible reading, with the proper training and tools, is an indispensable step toward life with God. As my former pastor, Kent Hughes, was fond of saying, "It's only life or death!"

Suggested Reading

Beale, G. K. *The Erosion of Inerrancy in Evangelicalism: Responding to New Challenges to Biblical Authority.* Wheaton: Crossway, 2008.

McQuilkin, Robertson. *Understanding and Applying the Bible: An Introduction to Hermeneutics.* Chicago: Moody, 1983.

Packer, J. I. *God Has Spoken.* Grand Rapids: Baker, 1979.

Ryken, Leland. *The Word of God in English: Criteria of Excellence in Bible Translation.* Wheaton: Crossway, 2002.

Discussion Questions

1. What hindrances to Bible knowledge exist in contemporary culture?
2. What traditions do you follow that draw you closer to God's commands? Which draw you farther away?
3. What is the primary purpose of God's law?
4. How do knowledge of Scripture and knowledge of God go together?
5. How does the doctrine of progressive revelation inform our approach to Scripture?
6. How is Jesus central to Scripture?
7. In what ways is the Bible both a human and a divine book?

21

Following His Design for Marriage

"Have you not read that he . . . made
them male and female, and said,
'. . . they shall become one flesh'?"

During the last week of 2008, men and women streamed into Manhattan's dingy state Marriage Bureau to tie the knot. They came at about double the rate of most weeks, especially on New Year's Eve. Why at year's end? Their stated reasons, according to the *New York Times*, included the following:

- From a new bride: "It's easy to remember."
- From another bride: "Eight [from 2008] is a lucky number."
- "Tax reasons," another woman told the interviewer. "He has nothing; it will make a big difference." Then she turned to the groom and said, as if to reassure him: "I really do love you."[1]

Marriage used to be signified by the giving of rings, the blushing of brides, and the solemn words of a clergyman, "What God hath joined together, let not man separate." While rings are still exchanged today, brides hardly blush (nor do grooms, for that matter). God, if he is invoked at all, is mostly a comforting prop. Marriage is seen not as an awesome covenant between man and woman in the sight of God. It is an altogether optional and (if things get rough) temporary contractual arrangement between two people (opposite sexes now optional), entered lightly merely on the grounds of mutual self-fulfillment—and exited just as lightly.

If God is trotted out during the ceremony, he is depicted merely as a celestial Santa Claus meant to provide some feel-good gravitas to our people-centered pact. Once the rice (or is it bird seed?) has been swept up, God is put back in his box, to be consulted again only at the discretion of the two marriage partners, perhaps if they get around to having children. Or not.

And even those of us who call ourselves Christians, with a supposedly God-centered approach to marriage, are not all that different. Ron Sider notes: (1) evangelical Christians divorce just as often as the general population; (2) a third of evangelicals say premarital sex—what used to be known as fornication—is okay; and (3) 15 percent of evangelicals approve of adultery.[2] "The heart of the matter is the scandalous failure to live what we preach," Sider told me. "The disconnect between our biblical beliefs and our practice is just, I think, heart-rending."[3]

This do-it-yourself approach to marriage is of a piece with the larger culture. "All matters of faith and morality are now considered by a majority of Americans to be issues of mere private preference," says Al Mohler, president of the Southern Baptist Theological Seminary. "All truth is interior and privatized. This embrace of undiluted individualism underlies our current cultural confusion."[4]

But if we are thinking clearly, matrimony is about much more than just personal happiness. Matrimony, according to researchers Glenn Stanton and Bill Maier, has two primary aspects:

> Marriage always brings male and female adults together into committed sexual and domestic relationships in order to regulate sexuality and provide for the needs of daily life. Wives help men channel their sexual energy in socially productive and nonpredatory ways. Husbands help protect women from the exploitation of other males.
>
> Marriage ensures that children have the benefits of both their mother and their father, each in their distinctive and unique ways.[5]

Both church and state have a critical interest in marriage: the former because God created the institution, which is to be lived out in the redeemed and wider communities; the latter because marriage is the basic building block of society. In fact, the obligations placed upon married couples are significant, not to be taken or discarded lightly, especially for professing Christians. "Christian marriage," Kent Hughes notes, "calls for a public covenant before God, the church, the family, and the state."[6]

"Marriage is not a private matter," Hughes says. "It involves a declaration of intention and a reorganizing of relationship. The idea of a purely private marriage is a recent aberration spawned by the culture of individualism and the demise of community."[7]

Jesus versus Moses?

While it is easy to cluck at the state of marriage today, we would do well to keep in mind that things were not all that different in Jesus's time. One day the Pharisees challenged Jesus's authority by pitting him against Moses. In the last chapter—in the case of the woman taken in adultery—we saw that they tried to insinuate that the compassionate Jesus was weak on Mosaic law. In this instance, they tried to prove he was too strict. (As during his later trial before the Sanhedrin, it appears that his accusers could never settle on an effective mode of attack and get their stories straight.)[8] They asked Jesus one of their well-planned, patented, sure-fire trick questions, only to be ambushed by his own questioning, as we shall see.

Matthew and Mark take notice of the incident, each giving slightly different emphases while agreeing on the main points.[9] Because these two passages so clearly refer to the same incident, I will go against current scholarly fashion and harmonize them here. No doubt the Gospel writers selected and presented differing details in order to buttress the themes and aims of each book, and each composition should be read and appreciated on its own terms. But if we believe that the events they depicted literally happened, we should be able to carefully piece them together as we do contemporary eyewitness accounts of the same events. In this case, Matthew and Mark present a different question asked by Jesus, either reflecting that he asked two questions, or that his original question had at least two aspects. Where the overlap in details is nearly identical, I will quote from only one account. I will intersperse this narrative with my own commentary.

> And he left there and went to the region of Judea and beyond the Jordan, and crowds gathered to him again. And again, as was his custom, he taught them.

Matthew and Mark both report that Jesus and his disciples were coming from the north and had entered the region of Judea on the east side of the Jordan. Mark, the young associate of Peter, mentions that Jesus, as was his custom, taught them. Matthew the tax collector, for his part, notes that Jesus healed the large crowds that followed. This is no contradiction, of course; certainly Jesus taught and healed, and both acts of compassion—ministries of word and deed—reinforced one another.

> And Pharisees came up to him and tested him by asking, "Is it lawful to divorce one's wife for any cause?"

The wording, "for any cause," is significant. Some Bible scholars believe that a substantial number of rabbis, the Hillelites, held that husbands could divorce their wives for any and every reason.[10] This was a tremendously powerful get-out-of-jail-free card! It was known by the rabbis as the "any cause" divorce and was based on a particular interpretation of Deuteronomy, which reads:

> When a man takes a wife and marries her, if then she finds no favor in his eyes because he has found some indecency in her, and he writes her a certificate of divorce and puts it in her hand and sends her out from his house. . . .[11]

The Hillelites believed, according to David Instone-Brewer, that the phrase translated as "some indecency" goes beyond the standard interpretation of adultery to imply "another ground for divorce—divorce for 'a cause.' They argued that anything, including a burnt meal or wrinkles not there when you married your wife, could be a cause! The text, they said, taught that divorce was allowed both for adultery and for 'any cause.'"[12]

Talk about no-fault divorce—at least for the man! Mark records the question of the Pharisees more broadly:

> And Pharisees came up and, in order to test him, asked, "Is it lawful for a man to divorce his wife?"

For Mark, the emphasis here is on the permanence of marriage, not on any exceptions that might exist. So the words "for any cause" are omitted. The chief concern is first to establish the law of marriage and divorce, not to look for legalistic exceptions. Jesus, in both accounts, indeed takes the Pharisees to the law they love, and to God's gracious intent behind it.

> He answered them, "*What did Moses command you?*" They said, "Moses allowed a man to write a certificate of divorce and to send her away."

Jesus asks what Moses commanded; they answer with what he allowed. And indeed, Jesus concedes that Moses did indeed permit divorce, the legal dissolution of a marriage. But his response indicates that this permission does not represent God's highest ideal for two married people. The standard is still the expected permanence of the marital union. He leads them back to the primal Scriptures on marriage, before Deuteronomy.[13]

> And Jesus said to them, "Because of your hardness of heart Moses allowed you to divorce your wives, but from the beginning it was not so. *Have you not read that he who created them from the beginning made them male and female, and said, 'Therefore a man shall leave his father and his mother and hold fast to his wife, and they shall become one flesh'?* So they are no longer two but one flesh. What therefore God has joined together, let not man separate."

Back to the Beginning

Jesus's question here references the two foundational passages about marriage from the first two chapters of Genesis.

The first tells us the paradoxical truth that men and women are equal in dignity and yet somehow different. "So God created man in his own image," the sacred text of Genesis says, "in the image of God he created him; male and female he created them."

The second says these equally dignified yet separate beings achieve a special unity, called "one flesh," in marriage.

Hughes notes that the Genesis 2 account "is the deep well from which is drawn all biblical teaching on the covenant of marriage."[14] Marriage indeed is a covenant, not a mere contract, between not just the man and the woman, but with God as guarantor and judge. Thus it can be said that marriage always involves at least three people: the man, the woman, and God.

Steve Tracy of Phoenix Seminary says that the Hebrew word for cleave (which the ESV rather bashfully translates as "hold fast to") "is the same term used of Israel's maintaining her covenant relationship with Yahweh." Hughes adds, "The exact sense is, 'and sticks to his wife,' even as Israel was repeatedly urged to stick to the Lord in covenantal relationship.[15] Tracy continues, "When two people make marriage vows, they are making oaths not just to each other, but also to God Almighty. This is why Malachi says God is the witness that women are made wives 'by covenant' (2:14)."[16]

Sexual Faithfulness and Fruitfulness

Sticking to one's wife implies more than covenantal faithfulness, of course. It also points to sexual faithfulness. And the Genesis account of the woman being taken from the man is redolent with sexual imagery.

> But for Adam no suitable helper was found. So the LORD God caused the man to fall into a deep sleep; and while he was sleeping, he took one of the man's ribs and closed up the place with flesh. Then the LORD God made a woman from the rib he had taken out of the man, and he brought her to the man.
>
> The man said,
> "This is now bone of my bones
> and flesh of my flesh;
> she shall be called 'woman,'
> because she was taken out of man."
>
> For this reason a man will leave his father and mother and be united to his wife, and they will become one flesh.
>
> The man and his wife were both naked, and they felt no shame.[17]

Those who accuse the Bible of being anti-sex have obviously never read it! Sex, as this brief passage shows, is part of the goodness of God's created order and a sign of his blessing. There was no shame, for the man and woman were perfectly fitted for one another. Perfect intimacy was the original design—and with God in the midst of it all. Yes, sin and alienation between the sexes and with the Creator would come all too soon. Recall Adam's accusing words to God after eating the forbidden fruit: "The woman you put here with me—she gave me some fruit from the tree, and I ate."[18]

But this was never God's original intent, hence Jesus's vital words: "from the beginning it was not so." "From the beginning" is the standard; later changes are the unfortunate exceptions. Divorce was never in view at the start of human relationships when God created the man and woman for one another. The goal was a state of being called "one flesh." This state was not merely the merging that occurs during the sexual act, though that is certainly an indispensable (and, one might say, seminal) part of it.

Sexual relations not only symbolize the one-flesh state between man and woman, they cement it. While in our culture sex and intimacy have become tragically divorced (if you doubt this, check out *Sex and the Soul* by Donna Freitas for descriptions of the "hook up" culture even on a Catholic campus[19]), God's intent was that men and women experience a physical intimacy that flows out of and reinforces a spiritual intimacy that far exceeds any supposed "fun" promoted by sexual libertines today. "Sex is not peripheral to marriage," Tracy notes, "but is delicately woven into its very fabric."[20]

And in the normal course of events, children are the blessed result of this deep intimacy. While parenthood presents serious obstacles to marital intimacy, it also can draw husbands and wives closer in a sacred obligation to raise children to know and love God and their fellow humanity.

Life Changers

Little did I know on that first trip to the hospital how much our daughter and sons would change our lives. In a sense, our lives were no longer our own; they were at the beck and call of the helpless, separate little beings, curiously like us and yet distinct, whom God sent us as a result of our intimacy. This intimacy, at least for a season, gave way to a lack of intimacy. Our comfortable togetherness was torn apart by colic, 2:00 a.m. feedings, worried visits to the doctor, and other sometimes exhausting events. We were no longer our own.

And Christine and I would have it no other way. We both say that we wish we had started having children earlier, and that we had had more of them. If you want to influence others, you will never have a better opportunity than as a mom or dad. We had always enjoyed a happy marriage, but parenthood, despite its frustrations and heartaches, propelled us to heights of challenge and satisfaction that we had never dreamed of.

Much of life is like that. A toddler cannot see beyond his highchair or the sandbox. A child in elementary school sees toys as the key to happiness. A girl in middle or high school thinks she knows everything. Then come college, the first job, and perhaps grad school. Next is marriage, then children. At each stage, we think we have attained the ultimate, but there are always more blessings around the corner, if we will but receive them.

And there are many joys down that road. One day I woke up early, which usually makes me grumpy. As I got up, my restless mind turned to some ongoing disagreements with Christine. I started focusing on these unresolved issues (while somehow mentally minimizing my own faults). Before breakfast had even started my grumpiness gave way to a depressed, icy anger. I went to work with hardly a word, good or bad, to my wife, who clearly knew something was bugging me. But she didn't press.

Later that morning, she called me at the office and invited me home for "lunch." Still nursing my grudge, I hesitated. What good would it do to spend intimate time with my wife while I was upset with her? But she clearly was in the mood, and I thought anything would be better than continuing to seethe about her supposed faults. So come home I did. After we had reconnected physically, I miraculously noticed that my attitude had changed. The problems—from both of us—remained, but they seemed somehow smaller and more manageable. My affection for Christine had been rekindled, and I felt closer to her than I had in months. With our bodies we had expressed and experienced the mystery of being one flesh.

"God created people with bodies, and God declared that they were good," writes Lauren Winner. "It is sometimes hard for us modern-day Christians to grasp that central fact. Bodies are not simply pieces of furniture to decorate or display. . . . They are simply good."[21]

One-fleshness speaks of a merging not just of bodies, but also of souls, ambitions, wills, plans, and dreams. The male and female, both created in God's image, become—in a mystical but very real sense—one, more fully expressing his image in the union of their lives. "One flesh," Hughes notes, "expresses deepest intimacy. Everything is shared."[22]

Yet this intimacy takes work. Movies that present intimacy as expected, easy, or natural distort reality. There are never any sexual setbacks in television or the movies: it is always two athletes "performing" sexual feats that would daunt an Olympic gymnast. Yes, emotional, spiritual, and physical closeness are the heritage of many happily married Christian couples, and some research indicates that religiously committed couples have deeper and more satisfying relationships than their more secularized counterparts. But there are no guarantees that sex between husbands and wives, even those who "saved themselves for marriage," will always satisfy. Though the spirit may be willing, the flesh is sometimes weak indeed, especially if one's mind wanders.

Mental Purity

Jesus dealt with a lack of self-control in his day. He famously said that sexual sin, a primary sign of marital unfaithfulness, begins in the mind: "I tell you that anyone who looks at a woman lustfully has already committed adultery with her in his heart."[23] Such a high standard of purity is impossible, of course—without God's help. It's no wonder that the Pharisees questioning Jesus about divorce rebelled against God's one-man-one-woman-for-life standard.

> He said to them, "And I say to you: whoever divorces his wife, except for sexual immorality, and marries another, commits adultery." They said to him, "Why then did Moses command one to give a certificate of divorce and to send her away?"[24]

We don't lack the biblical knowledge to understand God's will about the permanence of marriage. We lack the commitment to obey it. J. R. R. Tolkien noted that faithfulness in marriage requires something that is out of fashion today: continuous self-denial. "For a Christian man there is no escape," Tolkien said. "Marriage may help to sanctify and direct to its proper object his sexual desires; but the struggle remains."[25]

Even the disciples struggled with the standard.

> And in the house the disciples asked him again about this matter. And he said to them, "Whoever divorces his wife and marries another commits adultery against her, and if she divorces her husband and marries another, she commits adultery."

That struggle comes for many because we have selfish, unrealistic expectations. Eventually the compelling puppy love subsides. This in no way means that the love is over—unless we let it die. Not only does divorce happen because of self-centeredness or suffering, but also because the grass always seems greener. "When the glamour wears off, or merely works a bit thin," Tolkien noted, "they think they have made a mistake, and that the real soul-mate is still to find. The real soul-mate too often proves to be the next sexually attractive person that comes along."[26]

Tolkien's friend, C. S. Lewis, counseled: "It is simply no good trying to keep any thrill: that is the very worst thing you can do. Let the thrill go—let it die away—go on through that period of death into the quieter interest and happiness that follow—and you will find you are living in a world of new thrills all the time."[27]

We are tempted to think that Jesus's one-man-one-woman-for-life standard is confining, as if God is withholding something good from us. In Eden the serpent exploited this kind of suspicion, asking Eve, "Did God really say, 'You must not eat from *any* tree in the garden?'"[28] We think that someone better, or at least better for us, may come along, so mentally we keep our options open. Like restless modern consumers surfing the net for the latest bargain, we believe that our lives somehow will be more fulfilled with more choices.

This approach to marriage indicates a profound spiritual myopia. While we promiscuously scan the horizon for new thrills, we neglect to cultivate our own garden. Further, we forget the wonder and privilege of our own marriages, as if we somehow *deserve* to be intimately united with a complementary image-bearer designed for our good. The truth is, given our utter selfishness, we are downright lucky to be married. "Keeping to one woman is a small price for so much as seeing one woman," Chesterton said. "To complain that I could only be married once was like complaining that I had only been born once. It was incommensurate with the terrible excitement of which one was talking."[29]

A Living Reflection

Of course, excitement barely begins to describe the import of marriage. The apostle Paul saw marriage not as just the bonding of two lives, but as a living reflection of God's covenant love for his people. While the first marriage in Genesis was a covenant involving three persons—man, woman, and Creator—Christian marriage pictures something even more profound: God's entering an unbreakable marital covenant with his people. While Israel turned her back on Yahweh repeatedly during Old Testament history, there will be no unfaithfulness when our salvation in the heavenly Bridegroom is, in a spiritual sense, consummated.

This time, the marriage will be unsullied. "I saw the Holy City, the new Jerusalem, coming down out of heaven from God," the apostle John wrote, "prepared as a bride beautifully dressed for her husband. And I heard a loud voice from the throne saying, 'Now the dwelling of God is with men, and he will live with them. They will be his people, and God himself will be with them and be their God.'"[30] Our earthly unions are meant to reflect this coming reality. If the goal of earthly marriage is mutual faithfulness for life, the goal of this greater and still more intimate bond is mutual faithfulness for eternity.

So we who are married are to conduct ourselves in the light of this dawning reality, providing a three-dimensional explication of the covenant between Christ and his church before a watching world. "Wives," the apostle commanded, "submit to your husbands as to the Lord. . . . Husbands, love your wives, just as Christ loved the church and gave himself up for her to make her holy, cleansing her by the washing with water through the word, and to present her to himself as a radiant church, without stain or wrinkle or any other blemish, but holy and blameless."[31] G. Dale Linder, the pastor who married Christine and me in a small church in north-central Florida over two decades ago, correctly noted that while it is unfashionable to talk about the wife's submission, the man's task—to die for his wife—is actually more challenging.

Marriage, then, involves much more than two people who come together to take advantage of certain financial, physical, or legal benefits. Marriage involves the Creator God blessing and protecting a one-flesh union of man and woman, who are committed to one another for life. This union is meant not just to protect women and provide a stable environment in which to raise children (as important as these tasks are), but to illustrate the oft-unseen reality of God's love for his people—both to children and to a watching world.

Have we not read?

Suggested Reading

Lewis, C. S. "Christian Marriage." In *Mere Christianity*. San Francisco: HarperSanFrancisco, 2002.

Wheat, Ed, and Gaye Wheat. *Intended for Pleasure: Sex Technique and Sexual Fulfillment in Christian Marriage*. 3rd ed. Grand Rapids: Revell, 1997.

Discussion Questions

1. Why is the contemporary divorce rate so high, among Christians and non-Christians?
2. How does the idea of *covenant* inform our view of marriage?
3. In what ways is marriage simply an arrangement between two people? In what ways is it more than this?
4. How do the creation accounts of Genesis provide a solid foundation for marriage?
5. What are the biblical exceptions given for the permanence of marriage? What ought to be done in situations of abuse or neglect? What is your basis for saying so?
6. Does the Bible promise sexual fulfillment for Christian marriages?
7. What is the link between mental and physical infidelity?

22

Fearing His Judgments

*"How are you to escape being
sentenced to hell?"*

Invited to appear on a prominent Chicago radio show, I hesitated before accepting. Colleagues who had been on this live, call-in program warned me that the host, a nonreligious Jewish man, often tries to trip up his Christian guests by asking, "Do you think I am going to hell?" He knows that it is very difficult in a face-to-face encounter for someone to verbalize the Bible's awful warnings about judgment. Plus, I would be discussing matters of faith with another guest, a learned rabbi, so I would be outnumbered.

Nevertheless, seeing an opportunity to publicly stand for my faith, I nervously accepted the offer and began weighing possible responses to "the question." A simple "yes" was too blunt and left out the grace of God, but every alternative I considered was overlong and convoluted, likely to crumble to dust in the pressure of live radio. Finally, the day of the interview, I came up with what I thought was a probing question of my own and prepared to lob it back at the host. And I did.

My answer went something like this: "If Jesus is truly the Lord and Savior of all, and heaven contains all those who will worship and adore him for all eternity, the real question is, 'Will you *want* to be there?'" The question of my interlocutor, after all, is not mine to answer. Only he can decide where he wants to go after death; I have no power to send him one place or another. My question, I believed, would put the onus where it properly belonged, on these two friends, to decide whether they want to be a part of the only heaven there is—or its only alternative. Applying the verbal *coup de grace*, I thought, I quoted C. S. Lewis, who perceptively said that "the doors of hell are locked on the *inside*."[1]

Ignoring the Inevitable

Sadly, though I was able to regurgitate this answer despite some on-air interruptions, the conversation quickly moved to other topics. These men, unmoved, dealt with the ultimate issue—where we will end up when we die—the way most moderns do, by ignoring it. In fact, most of us seem to assume that death is someone else's problem. "Although everyone at least intellectually acknowledges the reality and the certainty of death," theologian Millard Erickson observes, "there nonetheless is often an unwillingness to face the inevitability of one's own death. . . . Persons do not die—they expire or pass away. We no longer have graveyards, but cemeteries and memorial parks."[2]

"Hell disappeared," Martin Marty says. "No one noticed."[3] Marty overstates, but according to the Pew Forum on Religion & Public Life, a 2008 study found that just 59 percent of Americans say they believe in a hell "where people who have led bad lives, and die without being sorry, are eternally punished." This compares with 71 percent who said so in a 2001 survey. (Incidentally, 74 percent in the 2008 survey say they believe in heaven.)[4]

Such a trend would have been unthinkable in centuries past. "The majority of men and women throughout the centuries of Western civilization," writes Al Mohler, "have awakened in the morning and gone to sleep at night with the fear of hell never far from consciousness—until now."[5] Today, the doctrine of hell is little more than a relic, an uncomfortable curiosity, in the modern mind. We have forgotten the biblical warning that "man is destined to die once, and after that to face judgment."[6]

Hell and the Church

But what exactly *is* hell? Mohler gives voice to the traditional understanding:

> The traditional doctrine of hell was developed in the earliest centuries of Christian history. Based in the New Testament texts concerning hell, judgment, and the afterlife, the earliest Christian preachers and theologians understood hell to be the just judgment of God on sinners without faith in Christ. Hell was understood to be spatial and eternal, characterized by the most awful biblical metaphors of fire and torment.[7]

Mohler cites such luminaries as Augustine of Hippo to buttress his claim. For Augustine, looking at Jesus's account in Matthew 25 of the sheep and the goats, the reality of conscious, everlasting punishment for the damned was no more strange than the promise of conscious, everlasting life for the saved: "For Christ . . . included both punishment and life in one and the same sentence when he said, 'So those people will go into eternal punishment, while the righteous will go into eternal life.'"[8] Dante imagined that above an archway to hell are inscribed the words, "Abandon all hope, you who enter here."[9]

Mohler also cites the great Puritan preacher and theologian Jonathan Edwards, who warned his parishioners, "Consider that if once you get into hell, you'll never get out. . . . Consider how dreadful it will be to suffer such an extremity forever. It is dreadful beyond expression to suffer it half an hour."[10] Many heeded his call to repentance before it was too late, leading to the first Great Awakening.

Today, the idea of hell is not a great motivator to repentance and faith— even among professing Christians. For many, it's simply a turn-off. "Attacks on the historic doctrine of hell," say authors Christopher W. Morgan and Robert A. Peterson, "that used to come from without the church are now coming from within."[11] Few conservative churches that claim to believe in this doctrine actually preach it. Researcher Kimon Howland noted that in "seeker-sensitive" churches, "today's cultural pluralism fosters an under-emphasis on the 'hard-sell' of Hell while contributing to an overemphasis on the 'soft-sell' of personal satisfaction through Jesus Christ."[12]

Some deny the doctrine of eternal punishment in order to protect God's reputation. While theologically liberal Christians claim that there is no hell because all people will be saved (universalism), increasing numbers of conservative Christians say they believe in a finally empty hell, as those without God are made to disappear from existence (conditionalism or annihilationism). "Scripture nowhere suggests that God is an eternal torturer," says conservative lawyer and theologian Edward William Fudge. "It never says the damned will writhe in ceaseless torment or that the glories of heaven will forever be blighted by the screams from hell. The idea of conscious everlasting torment was a grievous mistake, a horrible error, a gross slander against the heavenly Father, whose character we truly see in the life of Jesus of Nazareth."[13]

Jesus and Hell

Someone, however, forgot to tell all this reassuring pablum to Jesus. Notwithstanding slanderous ideas about God being an "eternal torturer," Jesus solemnly warned about the awful reality awaiting the unsaved. "I will show you whom you should fear," Jesus warned his disciples: "Fear him who, after killing the body, has power to throw you into hell. Yes, I tell you, fear him."[14]

Many have noted that Jesus spoke about hell more than anyone else in the Bible. Certainly God's judgment—both in this world and in the next—is a persistent subject of his questions, and it's sometimes hard to tell where earthly judgment ends and unearthly judgment begins. As we have seen, Israel was comfortable with the idea of divine judgment, at least when it was visited on the nation's enemies.[15]

But N. T. Wright notes that Jesus made sure that the Jews knew that they were not beyond the reach of divine wrath: "Israel was being redefined," Wright says; "and those who failed to heed Jesus' warnings would discover themselves in the position that they had thought was reserved for the pagans."[16] Judgment on the nation was coming, at the hands of the Roman Empire. And an even more terrible recompense awaited those who murdered Jesus.

The stakes were ultimate, and the Lord had a way of shaking people out of their spiritual complacency—and still does. While today he is universally admired as the Prince of Peace (at least for Christmastime), during his earthly sojourn he was just as likely to spark an argument or a mob scene as to bring peace and joy.

Jesus didn't originate the trouble, of course. He didn't have to. Trouble followed him wherever he went. Like a thermometer, his presence unerringly revealed the spiritual sickness raging unseen in the souls all around him.

> I came to cast fire on the earth, and would that it were already kindled! I have a baptism to be baptized with, and how great is my distress until it is accomplished! *Do you think that I have come to give peace on earth?* No, I tell you, but rather division. For from now on in one house there will be five divided, three against two and two against three. They will be divided, father against son and son against father, mother against daughter and daughter against mother, mother-in-law against her daughter-in-law and daughter-in-law against mother-in-law.[17]

The Once and Future Hell

Jesus came to bring peace, but earthly division comes first. It is a division that sometimes pits his followers against their own families, tribes, and nations. This parting of the ways points to an even greater judgment at the end of the world, between the saved and the lost, the sheep and the goats.

And while the last judgment will come suddenly, it will not come without warning. In fact, unmistakable harbingers of it are occurring all around us, every day. Those who persecute God's people, for example, are exhibiting their high-handed rebellion against the heavenly king. Noting Paul's statement, "The wrath of God is being revealed from heaven against all the godlessness and wickedness of men who suppress the truth by their wickedness,"[18] theologian Douglas J. Moo says the final judgment has already, in a sense, begun: "The judgment of hell is not, for Paul, the imposition of a new state of affairs but the continuation and intensification of a situation that already exists."[19]

Rebellion against God comes not just in the future, but now, in the decisions big and small that a person makes every day. The decision to go one's own way and not God's is not a healthy sign of independence; it is the darkest kind of rebellion against the benevolent heavenly King. But judgment will come, sooner or later.

Many who receive Christ as Savior can testify to the opposition that comes from family members who hold to their old allegiances and gods. In large swathes of the Muslim world, a profession that Jesus is Lord brings ostracism, the loss of employment, and, in some cases, martyrdom. Rightist Hindus in India regularly seek to forcibly "reconvert" destitute and despised people who for the first time in their lives have found dignity in Jesus. Secular parents comfortable in their religious veneer take offense when their children report encountering the living Lord. North Korean citizens who hear about Jesus over their radios are sometimes turned in by their brainwashed children.

This division is not merely regrettable; it is a call for God's judgment. And judgment may come immediately, in the form of consequences for our ungodly choices, such as arrest or a sexually transmitted disease. Or, as in most cases, in God's mercy, the judgment may wait. "He is patient with you," Peter said, "not wanting anyone to perish, but everyone to come to repentance."[20]

But those who reject God will sooner or later get what they desire—separation from him and his blessings. While in a sense the door of hell is locked on the inside, in another sense God sends all moral rebels into the outer darkness, with the chilling words, "I never knew you."[21]

Certainly this seems harsh, but would we really want to worship a God who winked at the atrocities of Adolf Hitler, Osama bin Laden, and Ted Bundy? Or at the parents who leave their defenseless children living in filth and squalor? No one would be safe if he did. No, in our sanest moments we admit that judgment is a necessary part of living in a moral universe. It is no wonder that the martyrs in heaven cry out, "How long, Sovereign Lord, holy and true, until you judge the inhabitants of the earth and avenge our blood?"[22]

All under Judgment

And yet we cannot assume that earthly suffering indicates God's special displeasure with any particular person or group. We *all* are accountable to the Judge. One day Jesus made that truth all too clear, referencing some well-known disasters—both political and natural—that had befallen contemporary Jews.

> There were some present at that very time who told him about the Galileans whose blood Pilate had mingled with their sacrifices. And he answered them,

"Do you think that these Galileans were worse sinners than all the other Gali-
leans, because they suffered in this way? No, I tell you; but unless you repent,
you will all likewise perish. *Or those eighteen on whom the tower in Siloam*
fell and killed them: do you think that they were worse offenders than all the
others who lived in Jerusalem? No, I tell you; but unless you repent, you will
all likewise perish."[23]

Here Jesus doesn't ask, like Rabbi Harold S. Kushner, why bad things happen to good people.[24] Instead, he simply asks us to consider why they happen
to bad people. There is no weeping that they didn't deserve it or theological
speculations, like those of Bart Ehrman, about "God's problem."[25] No, the
compassionate Jesus says that they got what they deserved. This is definitely
not the Jesus taught in most Sunday schools today.

Does this mean that we can chalk up all such disasters to God's immediate judgment on sin? Not at all. Jesus has already said the victims in Galilee
and Jerusalem were no more evil than anyone else. In fact, *they were just like*
us. That's the problem. God's default mode toward unrepentant, rebellious
sinners is not mercy, but judgment. Thus, we should not wonder at his judgment, but at his mercy.

Twice Jesus drives home the unsparing application for his listeners: "Unless
you repent, you will all likewise perish." It is a fearsome statement. We are in
a precarious posture toward the heavenly sovereign. As Edwards said, we are
sinners in the hands of an angry God. Yes, Jesus offers us mercy beyond all
our imagination or deserving, but first judgment must be satisfied.

Light and Judgment

Then, using a well-known biblical metaphor his Jewish audience would have
grasped immediately, Jesus warns that judgment on the entire nation is coming—which occurred in AD 70 with the fall of Jerusalem.

And he told this parable: "A man had a fig tree planted in his vineyard, and he
came seeking fruit on it and found none. And he said to the vinedresser, 'Look,
for three years now I have come seeking fruit on this fig tree, and I find none.
Cut it down. Why should it use up the ground?' And he answered him, 'Sir, let
it alone this year also, until I dig around it and put on manure. Then if it should
bear fruit next year, well and good; but if not, you can cut it down.'"[26]

Given the nation's history with Assyria, Babylon, and Persia, and the continuing
oppression of Rome, judgment was not the foreign concept for first-century
Jews that it is for many comfortable, twenty-first-century Americans. The real
scandal, then as now, involves understanding that a mere profession of faith
without a heart to match is no protection against temporal or eternal judg-

ment. In fact, merely possessing God's law and temple, as the Jewish people did, made the coming judgment that much more terrible. Unbelieving Jews faced an even more terrifying fate than the surrounding pagans, because they should have recognized their Messiah.

The Bible reminds us repeatedly that more light brings more responsibility. "This is the verdict," Jesus told Nicodemus in their nighttime meeting: "Light has come into the world, but men loved darkness instead of light because their deeds were evil."[27] All who rejected the light of Jesus and his kingdom were under judgment.

Sometimes people ask, "Will God judge those who have never heard the gospel?" The implication is that God ought not punish those who have no chance to receive Jesus as Lord. This question subtly shifts the discussion from our sin to our ignorance. And that is the serpent's territory. *Did God really say that if you eat from the tree you will die? You will not die! For God knows that your eyes will be opened.*[28]

Certainly ignorance can be a huge spiritual problem, which is one reason why we send missionaries around the globe—but it is not the only problem, or even the main one.

C. S. Lewis points out that the key issue is not ignorance, but disobedience to the light we have through conscience and the moral law, which he calls the Law of Nature. "First, . . . human beings, all over the earth, have this curious idea that they ought to behave in a certain way, and cannot really get rid of it," he says. "Secondly, . . . they do not in fact behave that way. They know the Law of Nature; they break it. These two facts are the foundation of all clear thinking about ourselves and the universe we live in."[29]

This disobedience to the moral law is true whether a person knows much or little. And the ignorance of a hypothetical person on the other side of the planet in no way absolves *us* from our disobedience to the light *we* have. We can leave *their* fate in the hands of God. We can trust, along with Abraham, that the Judge of the entire earth will do the right thing.[30]

Perhaps the question we *ought* to focus on is, "What about those who *have* heard?" We may not know for sure what God in his justice and mercy has in store for infants who die or the unevangelized (because he hasn't exhaustively spelled it out), but we do know what happens to those who willfully reject God. We are responsible for what we know, as Jesus made clear. The Jews who handled Jesus, heard his teaching, and saw his miracles had no excuse.[31] We, who have his Word and the sacred witness of his Spirit, are no less responsible.[32]

Facing Our Wretchedness

Sometimes we witness the sins of others, insulated from their crimes by time or distance, and believe we are not implicated. And we are dead wrong.

Rabbi Yehiel Poupko, to whom I referred to at the beginning of this section, reminds me that modern Christians are heirs of those so-called Christians who persecuted Jews down through the centuries. He has told me he knows *I* would never harm a hair on his head, and of course he is right. And yet I have an uncomfortable connection, a responsibility, for my anti-Semitic forebears. Would I do any better than they? I pray that I would. But do I *know* in my heart of hearts that if I lived during the first Crusade, I would not have murdered defenseless Jews who were "killed like oxen and dragged through the market places and streets like sheep to the slaughter"?[33] No, I do not. Do I know beyond a shadow of a doubt that I would have opposed public lynchings of blacks who "didn't know their place" during the detestable era of Jim Crow? Do I?

On the outside, the scribes and Pharisees appeared to be the cream of the crop, the best Israel had to offer. They were pious, zealous for the law, and eminently respectable. Jesus was never fooled by such religious appearances, however.

> Woe to you, scribes and Pharisees, hypocrites! For you build the tombs of the prophets and decorate the monuments of the righteous, saying, "If we had lived in the days of our fathers, we would not have taken part with them in shedding the blood of the prophets." Thus you witness against yourselves that you are sons of those who murdered the prophets. Fill up, then, the measure of your fathers. *You serpents, you brood of vipers, how are you to escape being sentenced to hell?*[34]

Aren't *we* vipers, too? We sometimes hold up Hitler as a cruel, inhuman monster as a way to distance ourselves from his unspeakable acts. Yes, Hitler was cruel. But he was *very* human. The man's sinfulness, shockingly, tragically, maddeningly, was on display for all to see. Hitler, as leader of the Third Reich, had the opportunity to give free rein to his hatreds, petty jealousies, and insecurities, and six million Jews and countless others perished. Yet there are others—teachers, spouses, office workers—who may not have the same opportunity to lash out but who nonetheless harbor a bitter spirit that would murder if it could.

Well did Jesus note the unseen connection between anger and murder—and hell.[35] Paul spoke for all of us when he cried out, "Wretched man that I am! Who will deliver me from this body of death?"[36] We are all, to borrow a phrase, sons of Adam and daughters of Eve. We are *all* guilty.

Matching Deeds and Words

When Jesus sends his disciples to the surrounding towns, he is under no illusion that they will be welcomed with open arms.

> Then he began to denounce the cities where most of his mighty works had been done, because they did not repent. "Woe to you, Chorazin! Woe to you, Bethsaida! For if the mighty works done in you had been done in Tyre and Sidon, they would have repented long ago in sackcloth and ashes. But I tell you, it will be more bearable on the day of judgment for Tyre and Sidon than for you."[37]

These towns were on Jesus's home turf. Chorazin, according to the later church father Jerome, was in Galilee, and ruins of a synagogue indicate it was quite important and known for its wheat.[38] Bethsaida, a city northeast of the Sea of Galilee, was the hometown of disciples Andrew, Philip, and Peter. In addition, Jesus fed over five thousand people and healed a blind man there.[39] Because Chorazin and Bethsaida had the advantage of seeing the Messiah up close, their rejection of him would make the historical judgment of the pagan Philistine cities of Tyre and Sidon look like a walk in the park. Then Jesus takes aim on Capernaum.

> *And you, Capernaum, will you be exalted to heaven?* You will be brought down to Hades. For if the mighty works done in you had been done in Sodom, it would have remained until this day. But I tell you that it will be more tolerable on the day of judgment for the land of Sodom than for you.[40]

Capernaum, of course, is known as "the headquarters of much of Jesus's ministry," which the Lord adopted as his own after he was rejected at Nazareth. In Capernaum, the City of Nahum, he healed a centurion's servant and Peter's mother-in-law, and exorcised an unclean spirit. Mark tells us Jesus performed many miracles in Capernaum.[41]

And yet Jesus reserves his searchlight question for Capernaum, which he knew so well. The inhabitants, many of whom counted Jesus as a local boy, might have expected to sidestep the fate of their neighbors in Chorazin and Bethsaida. After all, they had a *connection*. Jesus was one of them. But no. In effect, Jesus says, "I never knew you." With a question that verbalizes their arrogant presumption, Jesus dashes their ill-founded expectation of special treatment. The wicked pagan city of Sodom, destroyed in a conflagration of fire and sulfur, would get off easier than respectable Capernaum.[42] Why? Because Capernaum had sinned against more light.

Do we in the West have any less light? That would be hard to argue. According to David Barrett and Todd Johnson, we are awash in a vast sea of gospel opportunities. In 2009, globally there were 6.6 million books published about Christianity, 83 million Bibles distributed (on top of 1.67 billion already in circulation), 200 billion hours of evangelism offered, and 209 opportunities to become a Christian disciple per person.[43] Much of this embarrassment of riches is found in the West. While vast areas of the world still have too little gospel witness,[44] the fact is that we in the West have little of which to complain.

It gets more uncomfortable still. Even those of us who name Christ as Lord and Savior must not presume that our profession of faith will save us. As the Bible reminds us, we will be judged on the basis of our works, not our words, and we are to work out our salvation with "fear and trembling."[45] Yes, salvation is by faith, but it is a faith that expresses itself in works. Faith without works is not just a poor witness; it is "dead."[46]

Knowing Our Fate Now

Speaking of the destruction of Jerusalem in AD 70 and the undated but even greater eschatological judgment to come, Jesus says we can know *right now* whether we are saved or damned.

> But concerning that day and hour no one knows, not even the angels of heaven, nor the Son, but the Father only. . . . *Who then is the faithful and wise servant, whom his master has set over his household, to give them their food at the proper time?* Blessed is that servant whom his master will find so doing when he comes. Truly, I say to you, he will set him over all his possessions. But if that wicked servant says to himself, "My master is delayed," and begins to beat his fellow servants and eats and drinks with drunkards, the master of that servant will come on a day when he does not expect him and at an hour he does not know and will cut him in pieces and put him with the hypocrites. In that place there will be weeping and gnashing of teeth.[47]

For those who deny Jesus, the weeping and gnashing of teeth have, in a sense, already begun. The nightmares that torment us, the anxiety, loneliness, and pain that we experience on this earth, as terrible as they are, are only precursors to the eternal rejection we face because of our rejection of God. If we live like hell, we shouldn't expect heaven. Hell awaits those who by word or deed display their heart's contempt for the only Savior who can keep us out of the dreadful place where all hope is lost.

We easily recall Jesus's precious promise that "whoever believes in him shall not perish but have eternal life." But we forget his equally clear warning that "whoever does not believe stands condemned already."[48] Faithless and foolish servants face God's wrath—even those who call themselves Christians. If we do not seek his mercy, we will not escape his judgment.

Suggested Reading

Fudge, Edward William, and Robert A. Peterson. *Two Views of Hell: A Biblical and Theological Dialogue*. Downers Grove, IL: InterVarsity, 2000.

Hamilton, James. "The Glory of God in Salvation Through Judgment: The Centre of Biblical Theology?" *Tyndale Bulletin* 57.1 (2006): 57–84.

Lewis, C. S. *The Problem of Pain*. San Francisco: HarperSanFrancisco, 2002.

Morgan, Christopher W., and Robert A. Peterson. *Hell Under Fire: Modern Scholarship Reinvents Eternal Punishment*. Grand Rapids: Zondervan, 2004.

Discussion Questions

1. Why is it difficult to talk about hell?
2. Can God be loving if hell exists?
3. What do you think of the alternatives offered to the doctrine of eternal punishment? What parts of the Bible do they emphasize, and what parts do they miss?
4. Why do we need hell?
5. Do all people receive the same reward or punishment? Why or why not?
6. Do you really see yourself as a sinner deserving of hell?
7. If we are saved by grace through faith, why are we judged by our works?
8. If your works are not in line with your profession of faith, what ought you to do?

23

Fighting His Adversary

"What is your name?"

In the home of the Reverend Samuel Parris, two young girls began to act strangely. An investigation by a doctor, ministers, and local jurists began. They discovered to their horror that the two girls had attended secret meetings at which spells had been cast and the future had been foretold. The time was March 1692, and the place was Salem Village, Massachusetts.

During the height of the ensuing panic, twenty people were executed as witches (including one man who was crushed between stones), twenty-seven were convicted, fifty more confessed, one hundred were in prison awaiting trial, and another two hundred were accused.

A sermon by the great pastor Cotton Mather, however, turned the tide against the hysteria, and soon all the accused were freed. Several leading people of the day confessed their guilt in spreading the panic, and in 1711 heirs of the alleged witches were awarded reparations.[1] And ever since, the Salem witch trials have served as a warning against religious fanaticism for the wider culture.

Belief and Disbelief

While no one wants to see a return to the days of religious hysteria, I'm not sure the change from belief to today's skepticism regarding the devil has been altogether healthy. As C. S. Lewis noted, Satan can use either disbelief or an "excessive and unhealthy interest" in him to his advantage.[2]

Disbelief, however, is a relatively new phenomenon when it comes to Satan, and especially among those who counted themselves as followers of Yahweh. The heavens were not empty for the Jews, monotheists though they were. There was a whole panoply of intermediate beings, if not to be appeased, yet to be accounted for. On God's side were angels, who were often entrusted with special messages from Yahweh for his servants. On the other were the pagan deities who ruled the lives of Israel's enemies—pitiless gods such as Molech, Dagon, and Baal.

The Hebrew Scriptures recount the spiritual struggle of the Jews against these pagan deities, who were sometimes dismissed as mere demons—or angels who had rebelled with the devil against God's rule.[3] From the talking serpent in the Garden of Eden to the presence of Satan in the book of Job, the Hebrews knew evil as something personal and alive, something beyond their own sinful falleness, constantly opposed to the rule of Yahweh.

This worldview spread naturally from the Jews to those who accepted their Scriptures and their Jesus as the Jewish Messiah. Common folk down through the ages have accepted the presence of personified evil without question. According to authors David M. Kiely and Christina M. McKenna, "Few Christians living in the seventeenth century doubted the existence of hell and its rulers. . . . It was generally agreed that the Devil himself was a horned creature with a forked tail, who might sometimes appear as a serpent."[4] Some of the greatest minds in all history have believed in the devil without embarrassment: Augustine, Thomas, Luther, and Calvin among them.

The Once and Future Worldview

We sometimes think that this worldview was relegated to the ash heap of history by the inevitable march of science and reason. Mental and physical illness were said to be (at least in theory) completely explainable in naturalistic terms. A person who was formerly thought to be possessed by evil spirits might instead have a chemical imbalance in his brain, or be depressed by certain life experiences. And if the cause was not spiritual in origin, then the cure would not be, either. Medicine and psychology have grown in influence during the same span in which the heavens supposedly have become emptied of spiritual entities.

And yet a curious thing happened on the way to our enlightenment. Secularism has become known in our day not as a philosophy leading to the limitless skies of human freedom and dignity, but as an arid, mechanistic approach to life that drains our existence of its mystery and purpose. Secularism, lived out both by atheistic empires and social welfare states alike, has also been exposed as unlivable, because it does not fill the God-shaped vacuum in every human heart. However, when God does not fill that space, other forces happily rush in. While still nominally on the throne, secularism (known in other contexts as "scientific socialism") has been displaced by postmodernism, the New Age movement, conspiracy theories, and fascination with the occult. We are not nearly as rational as our press clippings might indicate.

Author Philip Jenkins notes,

> on closer examination, perhaps Euro-American proclamations of scientific objectivity are not quite as genuine as they appear. . . .
>
> Viewed at the most rationalistic level, the human mind is hard-wired to interpret happenings in supernatural ways, to seek causality and agency in the natural world. We plead and argue with cars and computers. . . . After September 11, it was dismaying to watch the upsurge of myths concerning the numerical significance of the event. According to a growing body of urban legend, transmitted verbally and electronically, the whole disaster was surrounded by omens and auguries, by arcane numerological patterns. . . . Individuals educated and articulate enough to construct sophisticated websites used them to promulgate ludicrous conspiracy theories blaming the disaster on any number of sinister dark forces, beside which demons seem almost plausible.[5]

So dissing the Bible or Christians for the "superstition" of believing in a personal devil—especially when you consider the monstrous evils committed by the human race quite apart from religious belief—seems ill founded indeed. As has been well documented, the supposedly enlightened twentieth century was the bloodiest (so far) in history, and the twenty-first has started off just as wickedly. From Hitler to Stalin to Saddam, from innumerable pedophiles and serial killers to the Unabomber and Islamic terrorists, our propensity to murder and torment one another for any reason (or for no reason at all) certainly opens up the possibility that evil is real, it is personal, and it is among us—even if in some quarters it is not widely acknowledged. As a demon says to a junior devil in *The Screwtape Letters* of C. S. Lewis:

> I wonder you should ask me whether it is essential to keep the patient in ignorance of your own existence. That question, at least for the present phase of the struggle, has been answered for us by the High Command. Our policy, for the moment, is to conceal ourselves.[6]

Three Foes

But Christians through the ages (at least before this one) have had no problem believing in a personal devil, along with other deleterious influences. This is in keeping with a balanced, biblical faith. A careful reading of Scripture describes the evils facing human beings, and clearly not all wickedness can be traced to a personal devil. In fact, Christians acknowledge three main opponents to their spiritual growth: the world, the flesh, and the devil.[7] Let's take these three foes of mankind in turn.

The world: The apostle John warns, "Do not love the world or the things in the world. If anyone loves the world, the love of the Father is not in him."[8] This is not the earth or simply human beings in aggregate, but "the evil system opposed to God and consisting of worldly things."[9] Theologian Millard Erickson defines the world as "a virtual spiritual force, the antithesis . . . of the kingdom of God." He continues,

> The world represents an organized force, a power or order which is the counterpoise to the kingdom of God. Paul in Ephesians 2 describes the structure that controls the unbeliever. The Ephesians had been dead through their trespasses and sins in which they "once walked, following the course of this world, following the prince of the power of the air, the spirit that is now at work in the sons of disobedience." . . . There is a permeating order of the world, a structure which affects and governs mankind.[10]

This order plays out on many levels. The devil uses it to control systems of thought and philosophy to bolster his work of blinding the minds of people so that they will not see God.[11] Indeed, he uses "cunning and crafty . . . plots, which seek to overthrow the reestablishment of God's rule upon the earth."[12]

The flesh: By this we mean not our skin or our physical bodies, but our natural sinful human nature, which produces all manner of disobedience to God in our lives: sloth, selfishness, lust, greed, indifference to the suffering of others, and any other nasty attitude or act you can think of. And we are helpless to rid ourselves of this sinfulness by our own striving.[13]

The apostle Paul struggled mightily against his flesh, his "members," which drove him closer to God's grace:

> when I want to do right, evil lies close at hand. . . . I see in my members another law waging war against the law of my mind and making me captive to the law of sin that dwells in my members. Wretched man that I am! Who will deliver me from this body of death?[14]

The devil: Also called Satan, Belial, and Lucifer, this dark spirit is known by his roles: the accuser, the slanderer, the prince of demons, the prince of this world, the adversary, the author of evil, the evil one, a murderer, and the father of lies.[15] Many Christians believe he was a good angel who rebelled against God's rule, taking some of the heavenly host with him.[16]

The apostle Paul, who had experience casting out demons in the name of Jesus Christ,[17] highlighted the continuing conflict between the kingdoms: "For we do not wrestle against flesh and blood, but against the rulers, against the authorities, against the cosmic powers over this present darkness, against the spiritual forces of evil in the heavenly places."[18]

For Jesus and the disciples, skirmishes with the devil and his minions were manifestations of a much wider war. According to Jenkins: "they signaled something far deeper that was going on, namely, the real battle of the ministry, which was not a round of fierce debates with the keepers of orthodoxy, but head-on war with the satan."[19]

As we saw in chapter 3, Jesus assumed the existence of a personal devil. While there we looked at several of Jesus's questions pertaining to his authority over the satanic kingdom, I will examine one more here that will shed light on how we ought to think about spiritual darkness, and about the ultimate victory of Christ. The event that sparked it occurred without warning one day in Galilee.

Jesus and the "Legion"

This day Jesus and the twelve stepped out of their boat and were suddenly faced with a fearsome man under the violent control of the demonic.[20] The man went around naked, not out of any lascivious intent, but as a sign of his alienation and degradation. People of the nearby city had chained and guarded the man—probably for his protection as much as for their own—but with superhuman strength he had shattered his bonds many times and fled into the desert. Seeming more dead than alive, he lived not in a home but "among the tombs."

Seeing Jesus, he runs toward the Master but suddenly falls in terror at his feet, as if hitting an invisible wall. After Jesus commands the spirit afflicting the man to leave, the man cries out, "What have you to do with me, Jesus, Son of the Most High God? I beg you, do not torment me." Jesus, while concerned that people understand who he was, refuses to trumpet his identity in this terrible moment. But perhaps surprised that the demon had not instantly vacated its human premises, Jesus replies with his own query: "*What is your name?*" He wasn't making a social introduction. In biblical times, when you knew a person's name, you knew something significant and revealing about his or her character. You knew his weakness.[21]

"Legion," came the evasive reply from the mouth of the demon-afflicted man, "for we are many." A Roman legion at the time consisted of six thousand soldiers and one hundred and twenty cavalry. While we don't know if the demons afflicting the man were telling the literal truth (and can probably assume that they weren't), it is safe to assume that the demonic host was massive.[22] Whatever their numbers, the demons, now exposed, were in no mood to fight: "they begged [Jesus] not to command them to depart into the abyss." Instead, they offered to enter a large herd of pigs nearby.

After Jesus approves their plan (and I cannot fathom why he did), the herd stampedes down a steep bank and drowns in the Sea of Galilee. End of problem; another captive freed; the ultimate destruction of the satanic kingdom prefigured. C. S. Lewis says much of the Christian life is like this—a conflict with Satan now, complete with struggles and advances, with God's ultimate victory yet to come:

> Why is God landing in this enemy-occupied world in disguise and starting a sort of secret society to undermine the devil? Why is He not landing in force, invading it? Is it that He is not strong enough? Well, Christians think He is going to land in force; we do not know when.[23]

And while some may try to explain away the incident by the sea using psychological or societal theories, it's hard to see how psychology drove a herd of swine into the Sea of Galilee. The man, soon "sitting at the feet of Jesus, clothed and in his right mind," was ready to tell the people who had feared him about the authority and grace of Jesus.

The swineherd narrative is full of curious details: Jesus slow to remove the demons, apparently not knowing the extent of their infestation, and seemingly little concerned about the destruction of a herd of pigs. So while this incident is full of strange twists and turns, the early church had no problem believing this supernatural power encounter—attested in all three Synoptics—literally happened.

Christian Credence

Certainly believers have had ample scriptural warrant, as we have seen. Genesis, the book of beginnings, speaks of God's judgment against an intelligent and volitional serpent—the one who tempted Adam and Eve into sin. The serpent is "cursed . . . above all livestock and above all beasts of the field." God tells the serpent, "I will put enmity between you and the woman, and between your offspring [or "seed"] and her offspring; he shall bruise your head, and you shall bruise his heel."[24] It is a declaration of ultimate defeat for this shadowy figure of evil, a declaration the rest of the Bible amplifies in many ways.

Psalm 91, for example, states that the one who follows the Lord "will not fear the terror of night, nor the arrow that flies by day, nor the pestilence that stalks in darkness, nor the destruction that wastes at noonday. . . . No evil shall be allowed to befall you, no plague come near your tent. . . . You will tread on the lion and the adder; the young lion and the serpent you will trample underfoot."[25] An amplification of God's promise of deliverance from the serpent in Genesis 3:15, the psalm is interpreted in spiritual terms throughout much of the global South, where it is a favorite text.[26]

Jesus's substitutionary death on the cross, resurrection, and ascension have been viewed down through church history as Satan's death knell.[27] The apostles Peter and Paul were both well known for confronting the power of Satan via their relationship with Jesus.[28] Early church fathers Origen and Justin Martyr maintained that the faith was proved "every time an ordinary Christian cast out demons, not through great occult learning, but through prayer and simply invoking the name of Jesus."[29] The great third-century theologian Gregory Thaumaturgus was "a singularly gifted exorcist and healer, who repeatedly overcame demons and pagan deities. . . . That record of accomplishments in spiritual combat added vastly to the credibility of his Trinitarian doctrines."[30]

We, however, live in a more skeptical age. As Jenkins notes, paraphrasing a typical response, "Even if the early Christian tradition accepted notions of the demonic—as it clearly did—surely, we have outgrown these ideas. Should we really fear darkness? Can any sane person in the modern world seriously believe in witchcraft or ancestral curses?"[31]

Taking the Devil Seriously

The three-pronged witness of Scripture, history, and current events clearly suggests we should take this little understood aspect of reality seriously, though Christians themselves need have no fear. Nevertheless, we also should recognize that we may face dangers, both natural and supernatural, if we decide to take the devil seriously.

These dangers are well known: demonic oppression (or demonization, such as the man afflicted by the "legion"), temptation, dissention among friends, lies, and other stratagems of the devil. We can unwittingly invite his presence into our lives through sin, too. As Paul stated, we are to "give no opportunity to the devil."[32] The apostle Peter, an eyewitness to Jesus's many exorcisms, nevertheless warns, "Be sober-minded; be watchful. Your adversary the devil prowls around like a roaring lion, seeking someone to devour."[33] The devil is not to be trifled with. We must be prepared.

If Satan is a deceiver, we need to make sure he does not deceive us. Sometimes, that deception comes in the form of respecting him too much, which Lewis termed "an excessive and unhealthy interest." Our focus on the devil can indeed go awry quickly. The Salem witch trials are but one example. The film *The Exorcism of Emily Rose* tells the true story of a child who died during a botched exorcism, and such ugly incidents are reported in the media all too frequently—giving a self-inflicted black eye to the church, besides all the damage they do to those involved. But fanaticism is not the inevitable byproduct of belief in the devil.

In the book *Defeating Dark Angels*, missiologist Charles Kraft lists twelve myths Christians must face before they should even think of doing ministry among those troubled by the devil. The book you are reading is not the place to delve deeply into the how-to of spiritual warfare, but Kraft's list will give you at least a general idea of what to expect. For more details, check out his book, as well as Clinton Arnold's *3 Crucial Questions about Spiritual Warfare*. Though you will likely not agree with everything inside the covers of these volumes (I don't), they will get you thinking. Remember to test everything by the unchanging standard of God's Word written, the Bible.

Here is Kraft's list of myths. See which ones you are holding:

1. Christians cannot be demonized;
2. people are "possessed" by demons;
3. deliverance is a one-shot deal;
4. demonization is simply psychological illness;
5. all emotional problems are caused by demons;
6. such problems are either demonic or emotional;
7. demonization is uncommon in the United States;
8. those with demons are guilty of spiritual rebellion;
9. only those with "special gifting" can cast out demons;
10. inner voices and personality switching are sure evidences of demonization;
11. deliverance always entails a big fight; and
12. the demonized speak in a different voice.[34]

It is worth noting that in none of his recorded exorcisms did Jesus resort to physical force to drive out demons, and neither should we. His authority as God the Son was enough, and still is. As Martin Luther wrote of Satan in his hymn "A Mighty Fortress Is Our God," "One little word shall fell him."

Ultimate Victory

As we contemplate Jesus's questions about Satan, we need to remember that the Bible teaches not a dualism between good and evil or an equal balancing of some mysterious Force's light and dark sides. No, Jesus knows the devil's name, and in that knowledge there is authority and ultimate victory for his people. On the flip side, deep down, for all their bluster, demons know that torment awaits them. As James said when warning of a mere intellectualized, non-transforming faith, "You believe that God is one; you do well. Even the demons believe—and shudder!"[35]

As Kraft notes, a power encounter needn't look like a gory scene from a horror movie. "We have learned that today, just as in Jesus's day, getting rid of demons is a normal part of the Christian life for those who would be his disciples. We have also learned that demonization is very common and that deliverance can be done in a loving, often even unobtrusive, way."[36]

In Scripture, our victory in Christ is assured. As the apostle John says,

> Now war arose in heaven, Michael and his angels fighting against the dragon. And the dragon and his angels fought back, but he was defeated and there was no longer any place for them in heaven. And the great dragon was thrown down, that ancient serpent, who is called the devil and Satan, the deceiver of the whole world—he was thrown down to the earth, and his angels were thrown down with him. And I heard a loud voice in heaven, saying . . . "But woe to you, O earth and sea, for the devil has come down to you in great wrath, because he knows that his time is short!"[37]

The good news is that Satan's time is indeed short as he awaits final judgment. The bad news is that he seeks to inflict as much harm as he can between now and then. The devil is working overtime to snare and spread misery among human beings, in many guises, using multiple strategies. But while he has many names, as far as the believer is concerned, only one ultimately matters: *defeated*.

Suggested Reading

Arnold, Clinton E. *3 Crucial Questions about Spiritual Warfare*. Grand Rapids: Baker, 1997.

Kraft, Charles H. *Defeating Dark Angels: Breaking Demonic Oppression in the Believer's Life*. Ann Arbor, MI: Servant Publications, 1992.

Lewis, C. S. *The Complete C. S. Lewis Signature Classics*. San Francisco: HarperSanFrancisco, 2002. Includes the theological works *Mere Christianity* and *The Screwtape Letters*, along with five more.

Discussion Questions

1. Do you tend more toward disbelief or an "excessive and unhealthy interest" when it comes to Satan? Why?
2. What are some of the reasons supporting belief in Satan in our technological age?
3. What are some of the dangers?
4. How might Satan be at work in the world today?
5. What are some of the other major barriers besides the devil when it comes to Christian growth?
6. How do we keep from going off the deep end when investigating this subject?
7. What's the good news about Satan when it comes to Scripture and church history?

24

Announcing His Kingdom

"What is the kingdom of God like?"

The kingdom of God is near," Jesus proclaimed when he began his public ministry. "Repent and believe the good news!"[1] Here we learn several things: (1) the kingdom of God was *near*; (2) that kingdom, as Jesus and John the Baptist preached, called for a response of *repentance* and *belief*; and (3) the kingdom was assuredly *good news*. So what was—and is—the kingdom? Jesus's questions will provide answers that can change your life, and your world.

A This-worldly Kingdom?

We have seen glimpses of the kingdom in our study of the questions Jesus asked. In chapter 5 we met Brian McLaren, who sees the kingdom Jesus preached in largely this-worldly terms. The kingdom, according to McLaren, has everything to do with what Jesus calls us to do and be in the here and now and says the church has gone seriously off track by emphasizing heaven-after-we-die.

While McLaren doesn't deny the afterlife, his passions lie elsewhere. "I've been convinced that [Jesus's message] has everything to do with public matters in general and politics in particular—including economics and aid, personal empowerment and choice, foreign policy and war." The kingdom message Jesus preached, McLaren suggests, went something like this:

> The radical revolutionary empire of God is here, advancing by reconciliation and peace, expanding by faith, hope, and love—beginning with the poorest, the weakest, the meekest, and the least. It's time to change your thinking. Everything is about to change. It's time for a new way of life. Believe me. Follow me. Believe this good news so you can learn to live by it and be part of the revolution.[2]

Revolution. Reconciliation. Peace. Love. Faith. Hope. Changed thinking. Here. Now.

It's a bracing vision, embraced by many young Christians today who put to shame old stereotypes about "apathetic youth." And McLaren isn't the only prophet calling for a new understanding of the kingdom. Rob Bell is another. Founding pastor of Mars Hill Bible Church in Grand Rapids, Bell says we must ditch our "evacuation theology" for one that seeks "the renewal of all things," shalom, starting right here.

"The story is about God's intentions to bring about a new heaven and a new earth," Bell says, "and the story begins with shalom—shalom between each other and with our Maker and with the earth. The story line is that God intends to bring about a new creation, this place, this new heaven and earth here. And that Jesus' resurrection is the beginning, essentially, of the future; this great Resurrection has rushed into the present."[3]

Pie in the Sky?

I must confess that my own understanding of the kingdom of God has been much more otherworldly. Yes, I understood that Jesus, when he walked on this earth, told his contemporaries that the kingdom of God was near, or even among them.[4] But, I reasoned, when Jesus left, the kingdom—which was essentially a spiritual reality—left, too. Didn't Jesus tell Pilate, after all, that his kingdom is *not* of this world?[5]

When the resurrected Christ was about to ascend to the Father, his disciples impatiently asked, "Lord, are you at this time going to restore the kingdom to Israel?" His answer indicated, against their hopes, that it was not yet time.[6] I believed that the kingdom was for another time, another place. I supposed that the kingdom would remain hidden with Jesus, the uncrowned and rejected King, until the church fulfilled the Great Commission and "The kingdom of the world has become the kingdom of our Lord and of his Christ."[7]

And anyway, wasn't it true that the church down through the centuries had fallen into pernicious errors such as the Crusades and the Inquisition when it mistook itself for the very kingdom of God? Charles Colson, the founder of Prison Fellowship, told me that this "is a strain of utopian thinking which has popped up time and again in the history of Christianity. It always leads to terrible dysfunction in the relationship between church and state, religion and politics."[8] While many of the Religious Right have been criticized for doing just this over the last three decades, can the Religious Left, and people like Brian McLaren, be far behind?[9]

Better to keep the kingdom as an impossible ideal, safely out of reach, until such time as God sees fit to inaugurate it on earth. When I prayed "thy kingdom come" from the Lord's Prayer, I was calling on God to do the heavy lifting. My job was to pray, be faithful, evangelize, and do works of righteousness. Bringing in the kingdom was *his* job. And that was okay with me.

A Persistent Promise

My approach, oddly enough, in some ways mirrored the apocalyptic worldview of Jesus's contemporaries, who bifurcated the Old Testament's persistent promise of God's earthly rule over his people into a kind of pie-in-the sky hope. But regardless of their understanding of the concept, the kingdom of God was no strange doctrine in the ears of Jesus's contemporaries, according to scholar John Bright:

> For the concept of the Kingdom of God involves, in a real sense, the total message of the Bible. Not only does it loom large in the teachings of Jesus; it is to be found, in one form or another, through the length and breadth of the Bible— at least if we may view it through the eyes of the New Testament faith—from Abraham, who set out to seek "the city . . . whose builder and maker is God" . . . , until the New Testament closes with "the holy city, New Jerusalem, coming down out of heaven from God."[10]

And indeed Jesus's contemporaries were steeped in the concept of the kingdom. God, the rightful ruler of the universe,[11] led his people out of Egypt as their covenant King and dwelt with them via the tabernacle, delivering them again and again from their difficulties. He later granted their rash request to end his direct rule and give them an earthly ruler, eventually epitomized in David, who was promised an endless kingdom in a redeemed creation.[12]

In light of that future, the Jews were expected to live like kingdom people now. The prophets, biblical scholar George Eldon Ladd notes, presented an eschatology that informed the people's ethics and indeed could transform all of life.

"A distinctive element in prophetic eschatology is the tension between history and eschatology," Ladd says. "By this is meant that as the prophets looked into the future, they saw an immediate historical judgment and a more remote eschatological visitation. For Amos, the Day of the Lord is both the immediate judgment of Israel and a final eschatological salvation."[13]

The dissolution and eventual destruction of the theocracy by Assyria and then Babylon fulfilled the warnings of immediate judgment. Yet there were persistent promises that one day God would return to set up his kingdom once more, this time perfectly. Bright calls the concept of the kingdom ubiquitous in both testaments.

"It involves the whole notion of the rule of God over his people," Bright says, "and particularly the vindication of that rule and people at the end of history. That was the Kingdom which the Jews awaited."[14]

A First-century Hangover

But according to Ladd, first-century Judaism suffered from a spiritual hangover because in the centuries since their return from exile, God had still allowed them to live as captives. The expected national salvation hadn't come. The Jews' exile as disobedient followers of Yahweh had been understandable; this new reality of continuing slavery when they were trying their best to obey was not. So they wrote a series of noncanonical religious documents called apocalypses (similar to the Book of Revelation) to try to understand why.

"Israel was obedient to the Law as never before," Ladd says. "The Jews abhorred idolatry and faithfully worshiped God. Still the kingdom did not come. . . . Where was God? Why did he not deliver his faithful people? Why did the kingdom not come?"[15]

The answer to the "why" question in Jesus's day involved a shift in the common understanding of God. While the prophets of old saw a link between God's judgments in history and at the end of time, thereby urging people to reform their lives now in expectation of God's coming, the first-century Jewish hope had withered to pie in the sky. Rather than being the personal Old Testament Lord who blesses and judges people and nations in history, the intertastamental God, in the imagination of many, became aloof from human affairs, almost like the deist conception of God. The deists, extant around the time of the American Revolution, rejected biblical notions of an active, personal God in favor of a deity who set up the world and allowed it to run by almost mechanical processes. God, the deists held, no longer needed to act in human affairs.

The Jews of Jesus's era didn't take it so far as this, of course. They still believed that Yahweh would vindicate himself at the end of history, with the sudden arrival of a messianic kingdom that would drive out the Romans; but they largely gave up the hope that he would act in the here and now. To paraphrase Rabbi Harold Kushner, they believed bad things happened to good people because God, for inscrutable reasons, had ceased to act in history.[16] Moving into this power vacuum were Satan and his minions.

"The present age is under the power of evil angelic and demonic forces and is irretrievably evil," Ladd says, summarizing the national mood. "God has abandoned this age to evil; salvation can be expected only in the age to come."[17] Such a vision of the present inspired not faith, at least not in the God who saves. Instead, it produced fatalism, legalism, and (in some, such as the Zealots) a man-centered desire to take matters into one's own hands—to rebel against the Romans and set up the kingdom by force.

Evangelicals have been caricatured in the mainstream press as being so enthralled by prophecies of the imminent destruction of the planet that we are supposedly unconcerned about this present world. This largely unfair stereotype has been belied by our designation by columnists such as Nicholas D. Kristof of *The New York Times* as "the new internationalists" because of our undeniable opposition to sex trafficking and the spread of AIDS in Africa.

And yet there is at least a grain of truth in this stereotype—or at least there was in my case. Perhaps it was the way I came to faith—hearing the gospel through books such as *The Late Great Planet Earth* and *There's a New World Coming*, by Hal Lindsey. These books, strong on the lostness of man, emphasized that the world was soon to be destroyed in judgment. Such a theology certainly captured my formerly secular attention. But it probably did not help me develop deep care for the world God made. That is to my shame, not Lindsey's. I reasoned that since everything was going to be burned up anyway, what mattered was escaping the coming conflagration.

"Is This All There Is?"

No wonder John the Baptist's message of repentance reverberated like a five-hundred-pound bomb in the first century.[18] The fire of judgment was coming, suddenly, and with overwhelming force. The age was coming to an abrupt end. One could do nothing but repent and wait. It was time to run for the hills.

Certainly this scenario must have been on the mind of John, who to his shock saw Jesus's ministry as only partly fulfilling his expectations. His later question from prison, based on the fact that Jesus had not come as the conquering figure everyone had expected, was simple yet profound: "Are you the one who is to come, or shall we look for another?"[19] His question echoed the Ascension Day confusion of the disciples: "Lord, what about the *kingdom*? Is this all there is?"

While Jesus never explicitly defined the kingdom for his listeners, he talked about it incessantly. In his hometown of Nazareth, Jesus quoted a messianic prophecy from Isaiah that spoke of preaching good news to the poor, proclaiming release to prisoners and sight to the blind, freeing the oppressed, and proclaiming the year of the Lord's blessing, adding, "Today this Scripture has been fulfilled in your hearing."[20] According to Ladd, "Jesus proclaimed that the messianic promise was actually being fulfilled in his person. This is no apocalyptic kingdom but a present salvation. . . . He boldly announced that the kingdom of God had come. The presence of the kingdom was a happening, an event, the gracious action of God."[21]

It was a *radical* message, in the true sense of the word. Jesus was calling the people to return to their Old Testament roots, to live ethically now in light of eternity, knowing that in a very real sense God's kingdom had already begun. In Jesus, Amos 4:12 had come true: "prepare to meet your God, O Israel!"[22] His questions about the kingdom encourage his followers, then and now, to work on behalf of the kingdom that is both already and not yet.

The Mustard Seed

Mark records Jesus as asking the following question:

> *With what can we compare the kingdom of God, or what parable shall we use for it?* It is like a grain of mustard seed, which, when sown on the ground, is the smallest of all the seeds on earth, yet when it is sown it grows up and becomes larger than all the garden plants and puts out large branches, so that the birds of the air can make nests in its shade.[23]

The kingdom ruled by God, whom the Psalmist says "reigns over the nations" and "sits on his holy throne,"[24] is such an awesome concept that Jesus must shrink it down to the level of his listeners. So he looks for an analogy that will pique their interest. He condenses the reign of God down to the size of a mustard seed—a mere grain two millimeters in diameter, in itself next to nothing, easily overlooked.

And yet we know, or should know, that size is no indicator of significance. This is obvious when we study human life. A microscopic human embryo grows into a composer, a scientist, a mother, a father. As Dr. Seuss's character Horton emphatically insisted, "A person's a person, no matter how small."[25] The human genome, hereditary information that guides the development of nascent life, is tinier still. William P. Cheshire, associate professor of neurology at the Mayo Clinic College of Medicine, describes the enormous purpose of this tiny material.

> The genome is simply the sum of hereditary information for the species. Written in the molecular language of DNA and organized into genes, the genome encodes all the instructions the organism needs to synthesize cellular building blocks and develop from an embryo into a unique, mature individual with a beating heart, sensitive fingers, and a brain that even in toddlers vastly outclasses the most advanced computers. Although microscopic in size, the human genome is enormous in its information content. Its 3.1 billion nucleotide base pairs are arranged along a double helical strand of DNA that, if removed from a single cell and stretched out, would measure more than five feet long, but only 50 trillionths of an inch in thickness. If written out as a book, the human genome would take up the equivalent of 200 volumes the size of a Manhattan telephone book at 1,000 pages each.

It would take 19 years to read aloud without stopping, at 5 bases per second, the entire sequence of the genome within the nucleus of the human embryo.[26]

Measuring the importance of anything by its size is a colossal mistake. Sometimes we sit perched on this lonely outpost of air, rock, and water, feeling small and insignificant as the "billions and billions" of majestic galaxies whirl over our heads at unfathomable distances. What is man, we ask, in all this emptiness? "Man at last knows that he is alone in the unfeeling immensity of the universe," philosopher Jacques Monod said, "out of which he has emerged only by chance."[27]

But we need to consider that at the beginning of creation, the universe was packed into an incredibly hot (100 trillion degrees Centigrade), infinitely dense state smaller than an atom.[28] Did this size make the universe less valuable? In that infinitesimal space were encoded all the potentialities for the structures of galaxies, the laws of physics, the stars, the planets, the trees, the flowers, the fish, the whales, the birds, and the people. Size is only one indicator of importance, and far from the most important one.

Small Is Beautiful

In making the case that "small is beautiful," Jesus presents the mustard seed as exhibit A. This seed, Jesus hyperbolically says, is exceedingly tiny. Yet it is pregnant with possibility, with nearly unlimited potential. From this unremarkable, minuscule sphere comes a gargantuan plant that is sometimes mistaken for a tree. A seed that is nearly too small to cast a shadow produces sturdy, leafy branches that provide a cool, shady haven from the noonday sun for an endless parade of avian visitors.

The easily overlooked mustard seed seems almost completely unlike the lush plant that will, in time, emerge from the dry Palestinian ground. And yet the two are connected; the farmer cannot have the plant without the seed. In fact, the seed produces the plant. They are the same substance. They share the same genetic structure, the same essence. They are both *mustard*. One is potential; the other, actual.

Luke presents the comparison more briefly:

[Jesus] said therefore, "*What is the kingdom of God like? And to what shall I compare it?* It is like a grain of mustard seed that a man took and sowed in his garden, and it grew and became a tree, and the birds of the air made nests in its branches."[29]

The kingdom, Jesus says, must come first as the mustard seed, then as the tree. It is both seed and tree. The kingdom is already here, but the kingdom in all its fullness is not yet. The kingdom of God is among you, in secret. Now.

Open your eyes. What you see now, however humble, is inextricably linked with what is to come.

It is like the first rays of dawn over the horizon before you see the sun in all its glory. And what is to come will be immeasurably, unmistakably greater, and yet the same. Now we see the kingdom in seed form, perhaps lying patiently in the ground, waiting for the right time to emerge. Then we will see it fully grown. The *eschaton* has, in a sense, already begun. The work begins now in anticipation of an even greater harvest.

"*Do you not say,*" Jesus says to his disciples, "'*There are yet four months, and then comes the harvest?*' Look, I tell you, lift up your eyes, and see that the fields are white for harvest."[30] We have but to lift up our eyes to see it.

God loves the small and insignificant. He pares down Gideon's army to less than one percent of its strength and with it routs the Midianites. He takes a boy's lunch and with it feeds thousands. He leaves ninety-nine sheep on a hill to pursue the one that is lost. The insignificant is never insignificant to God.

When Christ's followers pray, *Thy kingdom come*, we are praying for the tree, yes.[31] But we are also praying for the seed, knowing that the two are mystically united. You cannot have the tree without the seed. We ache for the shade of the tree, but first we must brave the day's heat and ultraviolet rays to plant the seed. If we desire to experience the kingdom banquet, we must do the kingdom work. *Thy will be done on earth as it is in heaven.*

Yet, like the prophets of old, we sow in hope, seeing the connection between our work today and our reward tomorrow. Unlike the prophets, however, we have seen the King with a clarity they can but envy. More than that, we live in his royal presence.

The King is gone and yet still here, in his kingdom people.

- "I am with you always, to the end of the age."[32]
- "Where two or three are gathered in my name, there am I among them."[33]
- "But thanks be to God, who in Christ always leads us in triumphal procession, and through us spreads the fragrance of the knowledge of him everywhere."[34]

The kingdom spreads through us because the King goes with us, as one unseen, like a mustard seed.

Word and Deed

And the results, though delayed, will be undeniable. But they begin now, like a mustard seed. Not only does giving a cup of cold water in Jesus's name spread the kingdom;[35] it exhibits the kingdom, in seed form. We don't know what the glorious tree will look like that grows from this simple seed of compassion, but we do know that it will be of the same kind as the seed, only more so. A few gulps of water no doubt will be transformed into a waterfall of blessing for both the giver and the receiver. This is the kingdom displayed.

But the kingdom is not merely a collection of good deeds. The presence of the kingdom calls for repentance and belief. This involves evangelism, the kingdom spoken. But it is more than talk. Not only does a conversation about Jesus encourage a fellow traveler to enter the kingdom; it advances the kingdom in a new realm. We don't know what the results will be from our verbal witness, but we can rest assured that the consummated kingdom will be full of people who responded to the humble words of the King's ambassadors.

In Nazareth, Jesus's signs of the kingdom, after all, had as much to do with verbal witness as with physical ministry, maybe more. As Jesus set free the oppressed, he did a lot of preaching. He *proclaimed* (1) good news to the poor, (2) freedom to the captives, (3) recovery of sight to the blind, and (4) the year of the Lord's favor to all.[36] With the kingdom, inevitably, comes the call to *repent and believe the good news*. There is no kingdom if there is no *news*.

Much of contemporary conversation about the kingdom, unfortunately, misses the verbal nature of the mustard seed. There seems to be a hole in our holism—not enough evangelism.[37] This should be no surprise. It's always easier to give a cup of cold water than to talk about the One in whose name we give it, but we are called to do both. The kingdom comes when we act compassionately, yes—and also when we speak compassionately for our King.

Our kingdom words and deeds may be small, and yet they are anything but weak or insignificant. They plant a flag in the hard ground of this dark world, making the audacious claim that the rightful King is coming with the armies of light, trumpets blowing, banners waving, to take possession. And one day he will. Every deed that we accomplish for the King today, every word we speak, however small, asserts his rule over the earth and hastens his coming to claim what belongs to him. And it *all* belongs to him. *For thine is the kingdom, and the power, and the glory*. Today and forever, *amen*.

Leaven's Worth

Jesus asked another question about the kingdom, and made another everyday comparison.

And again he said, *"To what shall I compare the kingdom of God? It is like leaven that a woman took and hid in three measures of flour, until it was all leavened."*[38]

The kingdom of God, again, is likened to something humble—at least at the beginning. This time it's leaven, or yeast, the living ingredient that makes bread rise. It's a common thing, but without it, the loaf is ruined. Like the mustard seed, the action of yeast is far-reaching but takes time. It must be patiently kneaded into the dough. But once present, it spreads. It does so surreptitiously, its presence recognized only in hindsight.

Yeast, like dripping water on stone, eventually leaves its mark. Dough with too much yeast in it has been known to blow the doors off ovens. Leaven is an invading force. But for some impatient people, it is too slow. We want the kingdom *now*, launching grandiose plans to "reclaim America for Christ" (through the reinstitution of prayer in the schools) or "bring justice to the poor" (defining "justice" by the amount of government spending on social programs). These approaches may or may not be good (depending upon your political convictions), but they are not the *kingdom*.

The kingdom is quiet, powerful, and *Christian*. There is no kingdom if the King is not proclaimed and recognized. Contra McLaren, it is assuredly not a political program, though the kingdom will transform everything it touches, including politics. And it touches everything, leaving nothing unchanged. The kingdom starts small, but spreads inexorably, like leaven.

And it works from the inside. At first, it seems humble. Later, its benevolent presence is everywhere, transforming ordinary dough into a life-sustaining meal. Theologian John Frame points out that Abraham Kuyper, the theologian-prime minister of the Netherlands, once said that "there is no square inch of territory in the whole universe over which Christ does not say, 'This is mine.'"[39] The kingdom spreads into all fields of human endeavor, to the glory of Christ.

Jesus's earthly ministry inaugurating the kingdom was like leaven. He started small, choosing twelve undistinguished men as his disciples. He spent three years teaching them about the kingdom through word and deed. He healed the sick, gave sight to the blind, opened the ears of the deaf, fed the hungry, and gave dignity and hope to the downtrodden. The Sermon on the Mount spoke of the righteousness of the kingdom, the parables the mystery of the kingdom as present in Jesus, the Lord's Supper the future consummation of the kingdom.[40] But with Jesus ascending to the Father, how is the kingdom to grow like a mustard seed, to spread like leaven in our day?

People of the Kingdom

When the disciples ask their resurrected Lord whether the kingdom is about to begin, Jesus hands the leaven to them. The gospel must first be preached and lived in Jerusalem, Samaria, and the uttermost parts of the world. While judgment is to fall on the Jewish nation, the kingdom will continue to spread. But its emissaries now are the people of the true kingdom, both Jew and Gentile. And the kingdom people constitute the church.[41] While the church is not the kingdom, the kingdom does not spread without the church.

New Testament scholar Scot McKnight appreciates McLaren's emphasis on the kingdom but asks for more specificity about the church. According to the New Testament, the kingdom vision of Jesus is, it seems, only implemented through the church. Only in the community of Jesus does one hear about the problem of Adam and Eve's rebellion . . . and the need for resolution through the life, death, and resurrection of Jesus Christ and the gift of the Holy Spirit. I believe the solution to the global crises that McLaren helpfully highlights will come as the followers of Jesus Christ live out the gospel, as they expand the presence of God's redemptive good news through evangelism, compassion, and justice. But the solution will only come through the Spirit-prompted kingdom gospel the church is called to embody and proclaim.[42]

Colson talks about the coming of Christ as "the invasion of planet earth" and the announcement of the kingdom. Colson notes Christians today are to avoid the extremes of thinking they can either establish that kingdom on this earth or simply resign themselves to awaiting the future kingdom. Instead, he calls for the church "to engage this world and bring God's truth and righteousness to bear against the unrighteousness of a fallen world."[43]

That engagement starts as a humble mustard seed and spreads, quietly and inexorably, like leaven, until the kingdom comes in inescapable power and glory, forever. Now *that's* a revolutionary vision.

Suggested Reading

Bright, John. *The Kingdom of God: The Biblical Concept and Its Meaning for the Church*. Nashville: Abingdon, 1981.

Colson, Charles, with Ellen Santilli Vaughn. *God and Government: An Insider's View on the Boundaries Between Faith and Politics*. Grand Rapids: Zondervan, 2007.

Frame, John M. *The Doctrine of the Christian Life: A Theology of Lordship*. Phillipsburg, NJ: P&R, 2008.

Ladd, George E. "Kingdom of God (Heaven)." In Walter A. Elwell, ed. *Baker Encyclopedia of the Bible*. 2 vols. Grand Rapids: Baker, 1988.

Olson, Ted. "Are Christians Overemphasizing Cultural Renewal?" *Christianity Today*, May 6, 2009. http://blog.christianitytoday.com/ctliveblog/archives/2009/05/are_christians.html.

Discussion Questions

1. What are the implications of holding a this-worldly view of the kingdom of God? Of a pie-in-the-sky view? Which do you find more compelling, and why?

2. How did Jesus's understanding of the kingdom agree with, and diverge from, the contemporary view?
3. Explain what you think the mustard seed analogy means.
4. How does a two-layered emphasis on the kingdom help us carry out God's work?
5. How is the leaven analogy different from the mustard seed analogy?
6. Do you agree that kingdom work involves both verbal and nonverbal witness?
7. In what areas of human life is the kingdom to spread?
8. How do Christians avoid the extremes of kingdom theology?

25

Anticipating His Gift of Resurrection

*"If it were not so, would I have told you
that I go to prepare a place for you?"*

To my elementary-school-aged eyes, my mother's father had always looked old. Certainly he appeared older than people his age do today. Living through the Great Depression and growing up in rural, mid-century Alabama will do that to you. He had no hair, or very little of it, and what he had was silver-gray. His face was lined with wrinkles, his eyes deep-set. Even his name sounded old: Hade.

Yet I remember him as lanky and strong. Years of blue-collar work in field and factory had given him a groundedness and authority that even I, a coddled child of a different era, could appreciate. Mom told me stories of how tough he was. There was never a lot in his house, but there was always enough, thanks to the hard work of Hade and Inez, his wife.

They kept the family together and on track after a fire burned down the house they were renting. They were regular churchgoers, and he was the ultimate disciplinarian. When Mom's brother and sisters would misbehave, "Daddy" would send them outside to select their switch and bring it back to him. Hade would administer the punishment, and that was the end of that.

I, however, saw only Hade's soft, grandfatherly side. Granddaddy played the harmonica and liked to sing a nonsensical ditty: "Sugar in the morning,

283

sugar in the evening, sugar at suppertime." Every summer our family made the
two-day drive from Delaware in our dark-green Pontiac Catalina to see him and
the rest of our Alabama kin. We enjoyed the chickens running around outside
Hade and Inez's small, white wood farm home, the sound of the rooster in
early morning (yes, they had a rooster), the gravel driveway, the butterscotch
always available in the candy dish, the homemade biscuits, and just the sense
of belonging. I remember those days as quiet, peaceful, and happy. I felt a
connection there, a rootedness that is almost impossible to recreate in today's
highly mobile, disconnected society.

It was a sunny day, the day I found out my grandfather had died. My parents
were on the phone, speaking in hushed tones behind closed doors. I was self-
absorbed, as many kids are, and basically oblivious. In the afternoon, Mom
and Dad asked us to come into their bedroom to hear the news: Granddaddy
had died, suddenly. The funeral would be next week, and we would go there
on an airplane. My older sister and younger brother quickly jumped up from
my parents' bed and ran off, crying. I sat there, physically and emotionally
unmoved. It didn't seem real. How could Granddaddy be dead? What is death,
anyway?

When we got off the plane, I craned my neck, half-expecting to see Granddaddy among my other somber-faced relatives. Still, the tears did not come.
I don't remember the funeral at all, only its aftermath in the kitchen of Hade
and Inez. Finally, somehow, the truth sank in. Death meant my grandfather
was gone, never coming back. The harmonica would be silent forever. Then
the tears poured out, and my voice got that hoarse, out-of-control tone that
would be utterly embarrassing to a kid if you weren't among relatives who
knew you had just lost your grandfather.

But I rebelled against the finality of it all. "We'll see him again," I wailed,
defiantly. I don't know why I did. Though I had heard of heaven, I didn't
know how to get there.

Already and Not Yet

In the last chapter we looked at the already-and-not-yet dimensions of the
kingdom of God (which Matthew the Jewish tax collector judiciously called
the *kingdom of heaven* out of his ingrained respect for God's name). We
saw that God's kingdom has both a present and a future aspect, and that the
future state should affect how we live in the present. Yes, the kingdom has an
inescapable ethical component. We live as kingdom people *now*, spreading
the seed today as we await the tree tomorrow.

Brian McLaren and others in the emerging movement are right to emphasize
the *alreadyness* of the kingdom. Unfortunately, in their zeal to remind us of
our ethical obligations today, they sometimes swing the theological pendulum

too far in the other direction and fail to give the heavenly *not yetness* of the kingdom its proper weight.

Karl Marx smeared religion, calling it the "opium of the people," giving oppressors the opportunity to exploit the pacified, heavenly minded masses. Others, taking a similar tack, say we have gone too far in emphasizing heaven over earth. Tom Wright, in his excellent book *Surprised by Hope*, says this is a false choice. Wright examines the old comment that "we are so heavenly minded that we are no earthly use" and finds that too often we dichotomize what ought to be left together.

But in the Bible heaven and earth are made for each other. They are the twin interlocking spheres of God's single created reality. You really understand earth only when you are equally familiar with heaven.[1]

Indeed, when Jesus talks about heaven he is usually talking about earth, too. The two realities are linked—or, to use Wright's word, interlocked. Rather than promoting a benign neglect of this world, Jesus used heaven as a spur to greater godliness, trust, and Christian activism. Just to take some examples from the Sermon on the Mount:

- The persecuted are to rejoice, anticipating their great reward in heaven.
- Followers of Christ are to do good works so that their heavenly Father receives praise.
- Christians are to love and pray for their enemies so that they may be sons of their Father in heaven.
- Disciples are to be perfect as their heavenly Father is perfect.
- Christ-followers are not to worry as they trust their Father in heaven to feed them.
- They are to seek first the kingdom, trusting that their heavenly Father has their needs in mind.
- Christians are to pray expectantly, counting on their heavenly Father to provide them with blessings.[2]

Heaven is the place of their reward. More important, it is the abode of their ultimate, loving Father, whom they are to emulate and glorify. Such heavenly mindedness frees us to be like our Father in heaven even as we do much earthly good.

Doubting Heaven

And yet evangelicals often don't exhibit this kind of lifestyle. We demonize our enemies (personal and political) rather than pray for them. The command to perfection seems an impossible ideal as our marriages collapse from within and our personal and professional indiscretions become common knowledge. Seeking our own kingdoms, we fear for the future, like pagans, wondering how we will ever save enough to retire on. We pray little, not really expecting God to do very much on our behalf.

A recent study finds that religious people who are sick are even more likely than their secular counterparts to choose invasive medical treatments such as breathing machines, even if such measures fail to improve their long-term chances.[3] Mark Galli openly wonders what this study reveals about our *real* belief—not what we *say* we believe—about heaven. He calls it an "addiction to longevity": "in other words, it was the most religious who seemed to want to hang on to life the hardest, no matter the prospects."[4] Journalist Rob Moll, who has researched the ways Christians die, says the fearlessness about death that one would expect from Christians because of their belief in the afterlife "is not at all apparent in the decision making of many, many Christians."[5]

Could all this be because we are so earthly minded that we're no heavenly good? Are we in fact afraid to die?

A Healthy Respect for Death

When I was a pimply-faced teen, I didn't think about my good health, but just assumed it would continue unabated. When I became a Christian in high school, I was interested in living forever, of course, and so Jesus's promise of eternal life definitely got my attention. But looking back, I would have to say that the bigger motive was simply knowing God and having purpose in life. Fear of death was not a daily part of my existence.

But as I've aged, if I don't exactly fear death, I certainly have developed a healthy respect for it. People tell me that I look young for my age, but there's no denying that Father Time is beginning to catch up with me. Wrinkles, the occasional white (or is it gray?) hair, and unexplained aches and pains tell me I'm not the kid I used to be. Nearly every day, I think about the brevity of my remaining time on this earth. As the writer of Ecclesiastes cryptically says, God "has put eternity into man's heart, yet so that he cannot find out what God has done from the beginning to the end."[6]

Perhaps reflecting a desire to avoid the Grim Reaper before my time, I've forsaken my sedentary lifestyle (an occupational hazard for writers), cut out most of the junk food that I love, and become a faithful swimmer. Because there is a history of cancer in my family, I have been more insistent with my doctor about certain issues, and I have begun to take some dietary supplements that might improve my chances.

There is no guarantee, of course, for any of us. I have seen increasing numbers of friends and colleagues struggle with cancer (sometimes repeatedly).

One battled a rare, life-threatening blood disorder—and survived. But three people I respected died unexpectedly after surgery. I've heard heart-breaking stories of neighbors whose children drowned in a bathtub or dropped dead in school. Every day, crime takes the lives of people who deserve to live every bit as much as I do.

The numbers can be downright alarming. According to the National Center for Health Statistics, some 2.4 million people died in the United States during 2004, or 816.5 for every 100,000 in population. (That's uncomfortably close to one in 100.) For my age range, the news is a little better. The death rate for us is 427 per 100,000; in eight years, however, it will be 910 per 100,000. Then the slope toward death gets awfully slippery. When I turn 75, it will be 2,164.6 per 100,000; when I turn 85, it becomes 13,823.5 per 100,000.[7] Those are hardly encouraging trends.

We know much more about death than the ancients did. And yet such knowledge, if anything, has only heightened our fear. We know—or think we know—of the lethal potential of food, sun, alcohol, long airplane flights, and practically every other activity. But as we seek control over death, fear of our own mortality controls us. As Galli says, "now every time I sit down to a polish sausage or hamburger, I will not be able to count it as joy. The New York steak sitting gloriously before me will not signal a gift of God but a temptation of the Health Devil and the Grim Reaper."[8] Well does the author of Hebrews speak of "all those who through fear of death were subject to lifelong slavery."[9] We are slaves to our fears.

If this is so, how do we develop a biblical heavenly mindedness, one that allows us to live unafraid, joyfully serving God amid the already while eagerly awaiting the not yet? Jesus's questions are a good place to start.

Premodern Skeptics

Perhaps our problem is we are like the Sadducees, whose unbelief in the resurrection rendered them unfit for the kingdom.[10] In chapter 20 we observed Jesus asking them, *"Is this not the reason you are wrong, because you know neither the Scriptures nor the power of God?"*[11] The focus then was on Scripture. Now let's examine the encounter through another lens, one focusing specifically on the afterlife.

The Sadducees, you will recall, had offered up a kind of "stump the pastor" question aimed at Jesus and his credibility. They were not actually interested in the truth. In this they were like the New Atheists, always asking hard questions but never open to the answers. Once in a public discussion I asked Christopher Hitchens, author of *God Is not Great: How Religion Poisons Everything*, whether there was any kind of evidence that would cause him to believe in God. Hitchens replied that I was probably going to think him closed-minded, but the answer was no.[12] Like the Sadducees, he was more interested in arguing than in listening, in teaching than in learning.

On this day the Sadducees were attempting to show what they considered to be the utter illogic of the doctrine of resurrection. As we saw in the last chapter, while much of the culture believed in a great disjunction between the current world and the one to come, most people at least believed in the one to come.

The Jews, unlike the Greeks, for example, believed that at the end of time people would not live in some shadowy, incorporeal state (which admittedly seemed to be the temporary destination of people immediately upon death[13]). They would not simply rise like ghosts from the graveyard, but be resurrected, their bodies reconstituted, changed but still somehow physical. The Hebrew Scriptures had always had a robust view of creation, which God had pronounced as "very good."[14] It only made sense to most Jews that the bodies of mankind, the crown of God's creation, would ultimately share in its re-creation. Though there are intriguing hints of this coming reality (Job, for example, declares, "And after my skin has been thus destroyed, yet in my flesh I shall see God"[15]), we must admit that in the main the focus of the Old Testament is decidedly on this world, on life in God's community now.

The Sadducees interpreted the Bible's relative silence on the intermediate state and the future resurrection as proof that these proto-doctrines were examples of wishful thinking in the face of death. Perhaps these in-the-know elite would have finally agreed with Marx that religion is the "opium of the people."

It helped their skeptical case that they held only the first five books of Moses as authoritative. Genesis, Exodus, Leviticus, Numbers, and Deuteronomy address many things: among them creation, God's covenant with Abraham and his descendants, the deliverance from Egypt, and God's law for his people. But they seemingly had nothing to say about the afterlife.

So the Sadducees tell Jesus a yarn about a woman who married a man who later died, and then married his six brothers in turn, each of whom later died—making her a widow of seven men. Were the story true, we would be justified in suspecting the woman of being a serial killer, and the dead husbands of being unbelievably naïve. Yet it is the Sadducees who are seeking to prove the naïveté of Jesus. "In the resurrection, therefore," the Sadducees ask Jesus smugly, "whose wife will she be? For they all had her."[16] It is an absurd question, and they know it. Their implication is that the resurrection itself is absurd.

The question reminds me of ridiculous theological questions we have all heard, such as, "If God is all-powerful, could he make a rock that's too heavy for him to lift?" These questions are not evidence of a searching heart, but of a closed one. Like the New Atheists, the Sadducees are not looking for information. They want to score points.

Jesus usually doesn't accommodate such people. That's why his gracious answer amazes me.[17] Evidently the resurrection doctrine is so important that he is willing to put up with verbal chicanery to counter their skepticism. Perhaps, too, he seeks to answer their speciousness publicly so that it will not spread among the common folk. Certainly this is a prime motive of Christian apologists such as William Lane Craig and Dinesh D'Souza in debating closed-minded atheists. The hope is not really to convert them, but to seed a listening world with truth.

Striking Out

Like a major league pitcher, Jesus throws a couple of fastballs right by them. Their intellectual bat remains on their shoulder, useless. First Jesus reminds the Sadducees of their scriptural ignorance: "you are wrong, because you know neither the Scriptures nor the power of God." They are speechless. Strike one.

Then he quickly moves on to their inaccurate premise, that marriage must continue in the next world if there is a resurrection. But Jesus points out that matrimony is a temporary institution, for this world only. "For in the resurrection they neither marry nor are given in marriage, but are like angels in heaven." Strike two.

The Mormons, of course, believe in a continuation of marriage, as do some other religions. Hope for matrimony to continue into the next life is natural— ask any happily married couple. But the two primary goals of matrimony— intimacy and children—will no longer be needed in the resurrection. The command to be fruitful and to multiply, to fill the earth and subdue it,[18] will finally be transformed.

The mutual vulnerability, acceptance, and self-giving that characterize the blessed intimacy of a good marriage in this life, of course, will never be retired but instead will be writ large in the next. We will experience a closeness not just with our former spouse(s), but also with God's people and with our Creator that will render earth's most rapturous intimacy superfluous, or, to borrow a phrase from C. S. Lewis, mere "milk and water." We will not miss any aspects of our earthly lives in heaven. They will not be removed but fulfilled.

Strange as it may seem to people who this side of death are built for heterosexual companionship, on that side we will be so full of God that we will not hunger for the things that on this side never quite satisfied us anyway. The best marriages, after all, are mere preparations for what awaits us on the other side. As Lewis says, "God will look to every soul like its first love because He is its first love. Your place in heaven will seem to be made for you and you alone, because you were made for it—made for it stitch by stitch as a glove is made for a hand."[19] No, we will be like the angels, loving and serving one another but loving and serving God supremely.

Having set up the Sadducees with two fastballs, now Jesus strikes them out on a curveball, basing his question on how God identified himself to Moses:

> *"And as for the resurrection of the dead, have you not read what was said to you by God: 'I am the God of Abraham, and the God of Isaac, and the God of Jacob'?* He is not God of the dead, but of the living." And when the crowd heard it, they were astonished at his teaching.[20]

And so were the Sadducees. Jesus here bases his argument for the resurrection on a verb tense (indicating that he believes in the verbal inspiration of Scripture). God, revealed as the great "I Aᴍ" in the Pentateuch, doesn't say, "I *was* the God of the patriarchs."[21] He remains their God, not just through historical identification ("there goes the God who worked with our long-dead fathers in the ancient past"), but because they share in his inexhaustible life. Abraham, Isaac, and Jacob, though temporarily hidden from our eyes through death, remain alive unto God.

All life, whether the smallest amoeba or the mightiest blue whale, the president of the United States or an unborn child with Down syndrome in her mother's womb, comes from God, for "he himself gives to all mankind life and breath and everything."[22] And those who in God's mercy go on to receive the gift of resurrection also have the King of life to thank. And what kind of King would he be, after all, if all his subjects were dead? "He is not God of the dead, but of the living." Strike three.

This is not an academic argument. My grandfather (if he knew Jesus, and I have strong reason for suspecting that he did) is not just a hazy memory from a long-lost childhood, a fading picture in a photo album, a brief line in a family genealogy. He is alive, not in theory, but in fact, with real thoughts and joys—perhaps praying, remembering, resting, waiting for me and for the resurrection body Jesus has promised, like the one the Lord has. My friend Jeff, who succumbed to brain tumors while a young man, leaving behind a beautiful family, is alive now, awaiting an even better future. "He is not God of the dead, but of the living."

A Place for Us

Of course, we have an even clearer hope of resurrection than the ancients did: not just a serendipitous verb tense, but the physical, space-time resurrection of Jesus. Answering believers who wondered whether there really will be a resurrection (believers who came out of a Greek mindset), Paul assured them that their future resurrection (and that of their deceased loved ones) is tied to Christ's historical resurrection:

But Christ has indeed been raised from the dead, the firstfruits of those who have fallen asleep. For since death came through a man, the resurrection of the dead comes also through a man. For as in Adam all die, so in Christ all will be made alive. But each in his own turn: Christ, the firstfruits; then, when he comes, those who belong to him. Then the end will come, when he hands over the kingdom to God the Father after he has destroyed all dominion, authority and power. For he must reign until he has put all his enemies under his feet. The last enemy to be destroyed is death.[23]

Normal Doubt

The New Atheists are at least right about the fact that doubt is a normal part of every life. Even religious people doubt amid their faith. When it comes to religious matters, we all live in the "show me" state. We are materialists like the apostle Thomas, who demanded physical evidence that Jesus had indeed risen.[24] The atheists' grievous mistake is not doubting, but prizing doubt over faith, when they should do the opposite.

The ground of all healthy life is faith, not doubt. We have faith, we trust, that God loves us, that there is a purpose for our lives and ultimate solace for our suffering. Such faith is a normal part of life, which is impossible without it. We trust, on good evidence, that the airplane that flies us cross-country will safely bear us across farm and field, depositing us to our destination, and return us home again. Those who take doubt as the ultimate ground of their being, by contrast, are never sure of anything and can become paralyzed with fear—if, that is, they can live consistently with their life-sapping philosophy of negation. Most cannot. They love others without knowing why; they trust their reason for no good reason; they assume they will not suffer a stroke while walking down the driveway to get their mail.

But doubt, if not sustainable as a comprehensive life philosophy, will nevertheless, until the *eschaton*, be with us always. Charles Taylor points out that "we cannot help looking over our shoulder from time to time, living our faith also in a condition of doubt and uncertainty."[25] In this life we will never get to a completely sunny spot where no shadows of doubt lurk. If the greats such as Mother Teresa, Martin Luther, and others experienced doubt, so will we. We struggle to believe what we do not see.[26] Even Jesus's disciples doubted, both before and after the resurrection. It's no surprise, then, that they should doubt the resurrection itself.

The Answer for Doubt

On the night he was betrayed, Jesus told his band of disciples that he was going away but would return for them.

Let not your hearts be troubled. Believe in God; believe also in me. In my Father's house are many rooms. *If it were not so, would I have told you that I go to prepare a place for you?* And if I go and prepare a place for you, I will come again and will take you to myself, that where I am you may be also. And you know the way to where I am going.[27]

Jesus tells the disciples not to be afraid in the face of all that is about to happen because of his personal credibility and equality with God. Jesus is as trustworthy and as powerful as God the Father. (1) Jesus's *trustworthiness* reminds us that his intentions, while he himself may be invisible to us, are always good; (2) Jesus's *power* assures us that whatever he plans will come to pass; he is able to do all that he wills. And he wills to be with us one day.

Further, Jesus equates believing in God with believing in himself: believing in him is the same qualitative act as believing in God. And this is the kind of belief that involves primarily the heart. It is a trusting belief amid doubt. Jesus is not calling for an abstract, intellectual assent, like acceptance of the periodic table of the elements. He is not the answer to a chemistry problem; he is someone to be trusted, a friend. His is the kind of friendship that Enoch, Abraham, David, and John experienced, a personal faith with a personal God. Echoing Job, the old hymn says:

> He lives, my kind, wise, constant Friend;
> He lives and loves me to the end.[28]

Such a friendship will be untouched by the cold hand of death. We will be going to his Father's house. Actually, we aren't required to go anywhere, as if we had to find the way, but simply to follow him. The text says that Jesus himself will take us to his Father's house. While Jesus mentions the many rooms (or dwelling places)[29] in God's house, his question is all about his trustworthiness: "*If it were not so, would I have told you . . . ?*" The word of Jesus, who never lies, can be counted upon, especially in death. And of what does he assure us? That he is going to *prepare* a *place* for us.

Let's tweak Lewis's trilemma here.[30] If Jesus's claim to be the Son of God can have only three explanations—liar, lunatic, or Lord—then his promise to prepare a place for us also has only three possibilities: lie, lunacy, or love. Jesus's appeal to us for trusting belief in our hour of death is grounded not in his logic but in his love.

I find his use of the word *prepare* (Greek: *hetoimazo*) fascinating. We encountered this word at the beginning of this book when John the Baptist told the masses to "prepare the way for the Lord."[31] Such preparations in the Baptist's day were substantial and deeply personal. Jesus chose the same word when he told the disciples to prepare the upper room for the

Last Supper at Passover, the very room in which he is now speaking.[32] Such preparation was considerable. It involved sacrificing the lamb at the temple, roasting the lamb, getting the room ready for the meal, and cooking the side dishes.[33]

Jesus says here, "Trust me; while I am gone, I will be making elaborate preparations for you, and then I will take you to the feast." Indeed, Jesus tells his disciples at this sad upper-room meal, "I tell you I will not drink again of this fruit of the vine until that day when I drink it new with you in my Father's kingdom."[34] But the kingdom feast will come.

He also says he will prepare a *place*. His use of the Greek word for *place*, *topos*, from which we get our word *topography*, is equally intriguing. It basically means a definite, specific area: "a solitary place," "a place called Golgotha," "the place where he lay," and so on.[35] The *topos* where we will feast with Jesus in his Father's house is real and definite, prepared with ultimate care by the master carpenter. And remember that he has been preparing this special place for us over the last two millennia. No detail will be missed.

Some Christians worry that if heaven involves simply sitting on clouds and strumming harps for eternity then they'll be eternally bored.[36] But the afterlife will be much more than this—perfectly fitted to us, satisfying our deepest desires, forever. As Lewis notes,

> All the things that have deeply possessed your soul have been hints of it—tantalising glimpses, promises never quite fulfulled, echoes that died away just as they caught your ear. But if it should really become manifest—if there ever came an echo that did not die away but swelled into the sound itself—you would know it. Beyond all possibility of doubt you would say 'Here at last is the thing I was made for.' We cannot tell each other about it. It is the secret signature of each soul, the incommunicable and unappeasable want, the thing we desired before we met our wives or made our friends or chose our work, and which we shall still desire on our deathbeds, when the mind no longer knows wife or friend or work.[37]

If it were not so, would Jesus have told us otherwise?

Suggested Reading

Alcorn, Randy. *Heaven*. Wheaton: Tyndale, 2004.

Keller, Timothy. *The Reason for God: Belief in an Age of Skepticism*. New York and Toronto: Dutton, 2008.

Wright, N. T. *Surprised by Hope: Rethinking Heaven, the Resurrection, and the Mission of the Church*. San Francisco: HarperOne, 2008.

Discussion Questions

1. How are heaven and the kingdom of God related?
2. Why is heaven called an intermediate state?
3. What difference should the doctrine of resurrection make in the life of the believer?
4. What do the Sadducees and the New Atheists have in common?
5. Why is it important that God is the God of the living?
6. How does the knowledge that Jesus is preparing a place for you change your view of death?
7. What is the significance of Jesus's statement that he will come for us?

26

Rejoicing in His Love

"What man of you, having a hundred
sheep, if he has lost one of them,
does not leave the ninety-nine in
the open country, and go after the
one that is lost, until he finds it?"

Hundreds of Christians and atheists were pouring into the ballroom in Dallas, all eager to hear well-known "anti-theist" pundit Christopher Hitchens debate four prominent Christian apologists on the theme, "Does the God of Christianity Exist, and What Difference Does It Make?" I was there to serve as moderator. The predebate buzz in the atheist blogging world was intense. In contrast to the rest of the convention, which was sparsely attended, the atmosphere here was electric. The organizers made sure there were two police officers and a couple of security guards on hand—just in case passions got out of control.

Hitchens, an accomplished editor and columnist, wrote *God Is Not Great* and other rants against religion. With a sonorous British accent, an engaging personality, and an attacking, take-no-prisoners style, the formidable Mr. Hitchens is an agent provocateur, and on this bright, early spring afternoon, he would not disappoint.

The night before I had briefly met Hitchens at a book signing (his) and told him sincerely that I was looking forward to the discussion. The way he looked at me suggested that I—or perhaps my disability—had caught him off guard. Sometimes the disabled have a sixth sense, some might call it an oversensitivity, for the way "normal" people see us. Regardless, the encounter got my mental wheels turning.

If the panel were going to examine whether Christianity has done any good in the world, it made sense to me to at least ask Hitchens whether his atheism could withstand similar scrutiny. I wanted to move the discussion beyond just an academic exercise into something more personal and practical—and to give him something to think about that perhaps he had not considered. And I think I succeeded.

So after the audience was seated and the guests had made their opening statements, I turned to Hitchens and said:

> Before I came on this business trip, I got a call that the car was sitting outside. I hurriedly went to grab my bag, threw myself off balance in that moment, and ended up on the floor. Quickly I got up, hoping that no one saw me—I don't think they did—but it's happened before, and it will happen again.
>
> But I'm wondering, Christopher, it seems to me that your anti-theism is a philosophy for the strong; it's a philosophy for the intelligent; it's a philosophy for the well-connected. And my experience is that Christianity has something to say for people who are not strong, for people who are not intelligent, for people who fall down. Christianity gives people a reason for dignity, *human* dignity: we're all created in God's image, and Jesus took on our suffering and our frailties and our sin.
>
> It also gives us a reason for hope, because he conquered death; he conquered the things that hold us down, and I know that as a believer, in the future I will receive a resurrection body, and these limitations that I've had to deal with, for whatever reason God has, will one day be taken away from me.
>
> And I guess my question for you, Christopher, is, regardless of the truth or falsity of my beliefs, I would like to know what your anti-theism has to offer in the way of dignity or hope for those who are not as intelligent as you, who are not as strong as you, who are not as well-connected. What hope do you and your philosophy give to people like me and, frankly, people who are much worse off than I am?[1]

My question, at its root, was an attempt to contrast the love of God—as evidenced by the compassion of Christ and countless of his followers down through the millennia for the outcast and forgotten—with the evident randomness and purposelessness of atheism. Christians can point to countless hospitals, clinics, orphanages and the like built for the glory of Christ. What can atheists point to? Without a loving God, what hope do people really have? It was an appeal not to the head, but to the heart. And the answer Hitchens gave revealed a stunning contrast in perspective.

"First, I don't believe it's true that Christianity is a religion of the weak, the downtrodden, the lost, the abject—those, perhaps, who have been dealt a bad hand by life in the first place," Hitchens replied, attacking my premise. Then he responded to my question with one of his own.

What does it mean to believe that there is a divinely supervising Father—not just that there is a Creator—in other words, not a deist belief that there must be a first cause—but a theist belief that there's someone who knows and watches and cares? What does it mean to believe that?

Countless Christians down through the ages would say that the knowledge of a personal God whose image we share and who cares for us is incredibly freeing. But for Hitchens, the effect is the precise opposite, creating fear of a celestial tyranny, akin to Kim Jong-Il's North Korea:

> We are subject all the time to a permanent, unending, round-the-clock surveillance that begins at least when we're born—some would say before—and doesn't even quit when we die. There's no privacy, there's no freedom, there's nothing you do that isn't watched over, and you can be convicted of thought crime. . . . Is this for the weak? No, it postulates "hideous strength," to borrow a C. S. Lewis term—a horrible, unchallengeable despotism that could never be voted out or overthrown or transcended, and a parody, a horrible parody of the idea of fatherhood. . . . It's the utter arrogance of absolute power.

When the bluster was over, I pressed Hitchens to actually answer my question: what dignity and hope does atheism offer? His answer, stated indirectly, finally was that we must accept "conclusions that may be unwelcome," and that choosing to reject something—atheism—simply because we don't like its implications would be "babyish." In other words, atheism provides *no* basis for hope or dignity for the weak, and wishing otherwise won't make it so.

Actually, I suspect that most of the New Atheists, Hitchens included, find atheism's conclusion, that there is no God who sees and cares, as *most* welcome, and that they reject Christianity, which Hitchens labels as "a horrible, unchallengeable despotism," precisely because they don't like its implication, that they and their freedom are accountable to the God who made them. So much for intellectual honesty.

Of course, the biggest problem for the New Atheists isn't in their heads; it's in their hearts. God's love, which should cause them to experience warmth and joy, produces in them only a cold dread. God calls them into a loving relationship as Father and, unforgiven, all they see is their Judge. The love he offers is twisted into a smothering dictatorship, because they will not submit to his loving rule.

God's Motive

This is, if I may say so, a particularly demonic twisting of God's love. As Screwtape said when attempting to fathom the incredible depths of God's love, "All His talk about Love must be a disguise for something else—He must have some *real* motive for creating them and taking so much trouble about them."[2] To the unconverted mind, God's desire for us and our good is incomprehensible. Catholic philosopher Michael Novak says that the New Atheists, in their zeal for human autonomy, forget the divine purpose for their freedom, which, after all, is God-given:

> If it has ever occurred to you to ask, even if you are an atheist, why did God create this vast, silent, virtually infinite cosmos, you might find your best answer in the single word "friendship." According to the Scriptures, intelligently read, the Creator made man a little less than the angels, a little more complex than the other animals. He made human beings conscious enough, and reflective enough, that they might marvel at what He had wrought, and give Him thanks. Even more than that, he made human beings in order to offer to them, in their freedom, His friendship and companionship.[3]

Certainly we can see this friendly, loving God throughout the Bible. As we saw in chapter 7, on relationships, he walked with Adam and Eve in the Garden. God was also a friend who confided in Abraham and spoke with Moses face to face. In Christ he was a companion to tax collectors and sinners and laid down his life for his friends. God desires not just to lead us, but also to walk beside us. God offers his hand and promises to pull us out of slavery, but, like Screwtape and the New Atheists, in our sin all we see is the fire and the cloud, all we touch are the stony tablets. All we hear are the "Thou shalt nots" and the trumpet blasts. We are offered an intimate friendship beyond anything available on this earth and call it dictatorship. Woe is us. As Jesus asked his accusers, "*I have shown you many good works from the Father; for which of them are you going to stone me?*"[4]

In fact, while this book has covered many topics, they all could be subsumed under one: God's love. Every question Jesus asked (and asks still) presupposes that he desires an answer. Yes, God is divine Lawgiver and Judge, but he is no dictator. Dictators do not ask questions and listen to answers. They give orders, pure and simple. God is not a celestial despot, and we are not mindless slaves. He has lips not just to order, but to question, and ears to listen. And God expects us to answer, and with the quickening of his Spirit, we can not only answer, but lay down our weapons and join him as his dear children. Our capacity to respond to God as creatures made in his image, as detailed in the Bible and confirmed throughout human history, sets biblical faith apart.

"No other world religions except Christianity and Judaism have put liberty and conscience so close to the center of religious life," Novak says. "For instance, Islam tends to think of God in terms of divine will, quite apart from nature or logic. Independently of reason, whatever Allah *wills*, does occur. Judaism and Christianity tend to think of God as *Logos* (reason), light, the source of all law and the intelligibility of all things. This difference in the fundamental conception of God alters, as well, the fundamental disposition of the human being proper to each religion: inquiry, versus submission."[5]

God's first question to humanity, "Where are you?"[6] and every subsequent question have the ultimate aim of drawing us into a relationship with himself. Jesus drove this point home not just with his life, but also with his questions.

Valuable to God

In chapter 15 we heard Jesus ask us not to worry because God will take care of us. This promised provision for our needs is rooted in our heavenly Father's loving relationship with us, which he freely entered out of his own goodness. It is sometimes said that you can choose your friends but not your family, but God has done both. Why? Because he loves and values us.

God's love and our value go together. We cannot really love what we do not see as precious. We can only truly love what we truly value, and God demonstrates our value to him by his death on the cross for our sins.[7] God's love is not a passive feeling of good will; it is active, and his continuous provision for helpless sinners—as our Creator, Sustainer, and Redeemer—proves how important we are to him.

A lady attending our church had heard about the good news of Christ's sin-bearing death and resurrection and understood it intellectually, but she hesitated to make a commitment. She just couldn't understand why a perfect, holy God would care about sinners. It just didn't make sense. On one level, of course, she was right. Why should a perfect, and perfectly happy, God bother about us? He certainly didn't have to. We add nothing to his perfections. He has no need of us.

My pastor struggled to find an answer, not wishing to leave her with the mistaken impression that God needs human beings. He doesn't. God's love, he finally admitted, is a mystery. In one sense, that is true. God chooses to save sinners out of sheer grace; there is nothing in us that compels his good will. As our Creator, God owes us nothing. He would have been completely justified in letting us all go to hell, with no diminishing of his goodness. As Jonathan Edwards said, "The sword of divine justice is every moment brandished over their heads, and it is nothing but the hand of arbitrary mercy, and God's mere will, that holds it back."[8]

Yes, God's mercy is free. I know not why he chooses some to be his children. And yet, is this the whole story? I think not. Rushing in where angels fear to tread, I told this lady that perhaps God chooses to save some of us because, as image-bearers of the divine, we are intrinsically worth something to him, and that rescuing and remaking us of his own free will, making us into reborn creations of incredible beauty—not because he has to, but because he wants to—brings him both glory and joy. God doesn't need us, but his acts on behalf of unworthy sinners express his essential love.

As an example: don't human parents derive great joy when a son or daughter who is on the wrong path comes home? Of course, and we all know such people. If this is true, doesn't it make sense that God, who made our personalities, would also rejoice when a sinner repents? Would we really expect the triune God who created us with emotions and wills be *less* relational, *less* able to rejoice than we are?

Edwards, notwithstanding the earlier quote, had a fundamental grasp of God's love, which expresses itself in relationships. Edwards biographer George M. Marsden notes that the eighteenth-century theologian had this key insight: "if there is a creator God, then the most essential relationships in the universe are personal. Edwards started every inquiry with reference to God. If we want to understand the universe, then we must understand why God would have created it. As he argued . . . the perfectly loving God of the Trinity must create in order to share that love with other morally responsible beings."[9]

The next time I saw this dear woman, with a peaceful smile she told me she had surrendered her life to the God who had sacrificed his only Son—not just for the world, but also for her. She finally grasped that we are valuable to God, and that knowledge allowed her to give her love to the one who loved her first.

Sparrows and Human Hairs

"*Are not two sparrows sold for a penny?*" Jesus asks. "And not one of them will fall to the ground apart from your Father. But even the hairs of your head are all numbered. Fear not, therefore; you are of more value than many sparrows."[10]

By one estimate, sparrows can live an amazing twenty-three years—although most live a far briefer lifespan.[11] Yet however long or short a sparrow's life, almost all fall to the ground in obscurity. No one notices when a sparrow dies and becomes food or fertilizer for the rest of creation, because this quiet tragedy happens every day. No one notices—except the God who made the sparrow. Novak named the book I earlier quoted from *No One Sees God*. That may or may not be true, but it is obvious that God sees everything, and everyone.

Small things, as we have noted, are not small to God.[12] By another estimate, on average the human head has approximately one hundred thousand hairs.[13] Each is nearly invisible, powerless. Yet our Creator knows intimately about all of them, to the extent of numbering each one: "There goes number 14,783! Here comes number 101,622!" If he cares about such seemingly insignificant details, we can trust him to watch over the rest of our lives.

Such care, meant to spark in us a sense of security and reciprocal love,[14] produces in atheists only dread and loathing. They fear a celestial dictator, and, tragically, instead of a heavenly Father, that is what they will receive. The problem, however, is not God, for God loves the world and indeed *is* love.[15] The problem is them, because they hate the light of Christ.[16] So God gives them what they ask for—a Christless eternity. As Lewis said, the "the doors of hell are locked on the inside."[17]

In contrast, Christ-followers receive what we ask for: God. We know we are God's because we love him. His love is displayed (imperfectly now) in our hearts by his Spirit.[18] One day, however, we will experience that love in full. My guess is the doors to heaven are not locked, on the inside or the outside. But it doesn't really matter, because no one will ever want to leave.

How Much More?

Jesus sometimes employs comparison to drive home his questions, often using the *how much more* technique. To assure us of our heavenly Father's love, he compares us to lesser things, such as sparrows. The point (sometimes implied) was: if God loves the lowly sparrows, *how much more* will he love you, a human being created in his image? Jesus also compares us to greater things, such as God himself. The point was similar: if you—sinful as you are—know how to love others, *how much more* can God be counted upon to love you? Jesus makes this second point in the Sermon on the Mount as he encourages his followers to look to God for their needs.

> Ask, and it will be given to you; seek, and you will find; knock, and it will be opened to you. For everyone who asks receives, and the one who seeks finds, and to the one who knocks it will be opened.[19]

We have already seen how prayer changes us, even if we don't always get precisely what we want.[20] But here Jesus assures us that those who ask really will get an answer; those who seek really will find; and those who knock really will see God's door open. We have looked at this extravagant—some might say dangerous—promise of Jesus before.[21] But how can we know God will actually do these wonderful things and this is not just spiritual hyperbole? Now we can see the *how much more* argument embedded in his questions.

> *Or which one of you, if his son asks him for bread, will give him a stone? Or if he asks for a fish, will give him a serpent?* If you then, who are evil, know how to give good gifts to your children, how much more will your Father who is in heaven give good things to those who ask him![22]

We can trust this promise because God is our *Father*. If *we* try to do right by our children, how much more will *he* be good to us? God is not a smooth-talking salesman who is gone after the warranty expires; he is not a flimsy internet come-on. He cares for us; he understands us; he is attuned to our needs. He is our Father, willing to take care of us. And because he is our Father in *heaven*, he is able.

As our Father, he knows how to give us gifts—*good* ones. Among the simple joys of parenthood are the birthdays of our children. The boys and girl in our house anticipate their birthdays weeks, even months, in advance. They are little mercenaries, angling for specific gifts. They scheme, they plan, they hope, they request. They write it down for us, just to make sure.

And while as a father I wish that they were not so materialistic about birthdays, our children needn't worry about our generosity. Christine and I delight in choosing just the right gifts (within reason). We carefully seek things that will delight them, develop their talents, express our love, and expand their world. Why do we go to all this trouble? In giving to them we share in their joy. It truly is more blessed to give than to receive.[23] If that is how *we* approach giving to *our* children, *how much more* will our heavenly *Father* give to *his* children?

Searching and Celebrating

When I was on the radio with Rabbi Poupko,[24] he asked me why Christians are so intent on converting the Jews, who probably constitute just 1 percent of the world's population. Why didn't we just leave his people alone and focus on the other 99 percent? I reminded him of the story that Jesus told the Pharisees and scribes, who were complaining that he was hanging out with sinners.

> What man of you, having a hundred sheep, if he has lost one of them, does not leave the ninety-nine in the open country, and go after the one that is lost, until he finds it?[25]

With this question Jesus tells the religious elite that God cares about sinners, like a man determinedly seeking his helpless, lost sheep. He is willing—no, eager—to leave the ninety-nine to find the one. God's math is not like ours. We might chalk up the loss of the one as the cost of doing business, much as the proponents of embryonic stem cell research are willing to trade off *a little unborn* human life now in the expectation (realistic or not) of saving *more born* human life later. God cares about the ninety-nine, of course, but not at the expense of the one. God is willing to go out of his way to rescue the one, to trouble about it, to inconvenience himself, to search for it. This is not the search of a dictator seeking to keep his slaves in line, but the quest of a lover.

As from the beginning, God's favorite question to the lost sheep—to *us*—continues to be: "Where are you?"[26] While many people in the world today doubt whether their lives possess any purpose or significance, the fact that the Shepherd is looking for them proves otherwise. God bothers about us because we matter to him. God so *loves* the lost sheep.

Although many Jews in Jesus's day were waiting anxiously for a revolution against the Roman oppressors, understanding that there exists a loving, searching God is more liberating than any armed rebellion. This is the love that, once it finds us, resonates in our hearts, little by little producing the same kind of love, which in turn touches the lost sheep around us. It is this love that builds hospitals, frees slaves, hides Jews, feeds the hungry, clothes the naked, visits the imprisoned, educates the ignorant, and provides dignity and hope for all—even for the forgotten of the world. This is the kingdom revolution that has changed our planet and will one day transform it, in a joyous, endless celebration of God's love, as Jesus reminds his self-righteous critics:

> And when he has found it, he lays it on his shoulders, rejoicing. And when he comes home, he calls together his friends and his neighbors, saying to them, "Rejoice with me, for I have found my sheep that was lost." Just so, I tell you, there will be more joy in heaven over one sinner who repents than over ninety-nine righteous persons who need no repentance.[27]

Heavenly Celebration

To make sure they get the point, Jesus asks another question:

> *Or what woman, having ten silver coins, if she loses one coin, does not light a lamp and sweep the house and seek diligently until she finds it?*[28]

One of my sons does some of his best work with Legos. The designs he comes up with—for forts, starships, and the like—using just plastic interlocking blocks, are breathtaking in their intricate ingenuity. The boy can spend contented hours on his "creations," and I believe in a small way he is reflecting the creativity and attention to detail of his heavenly Father, who forgets not the sparrow.

But should he misplace even one small piece, all bets are off. The satisfaction of the "nine" he still possesses is lost as he feverishly seeks out the "one." Telling him he still has the rest is no consolation. He *must* find the one, no matter how long it takes. And when he finally does find it, usually tucked away under a bookcase or in a corner, his relief is palpable. It is the same with the woman and the coin—only more so.

> And when she has found it, she calls together her friends and neighbors, saying, "Rejoice with me, for I have found the coin that I had lost." Just so, I tell you, there is joy before the angels of God over one sinner who repents.[29]

Can we say that God is similarly anxious over us in our lostness, or relieved when he finds us? Perhaps not, as these stories are parables making a main point or two, not allegories (in which every detail would correspond to some higher reality). But it is clear that Jesus is putting himself in the position of the searching shepherd and the seeking woman, and that in both cases the finding sets off a heavenly celebration. It is a celebration we are invited to join.

Years ago my wife and I were booked to travel to Ecuador to support a missionary and her ministry to the disabled, to meet and encourage the people, and (for me) to write and report. It was a significant challenge for both of us, and we asked friends in our Bible study group to pray for us. The final days before we were to leave, amid a miserably frigid November in Chicago, we came down with bad colds and were nearly immobilized in our wretchedness. Yet there was nothing to be done except to pray for the best—and get on the plane.

And indeed our heavenly Father watched over us on this visit. The illnesses quickly evaporated in the warm mountain air outside Quito, and we enjoyed the trip immensely and (we hope) were able to encourage the locals.

Thankful for all God had done, about a week later we boarded the plane for the return flight. After passing through U.S. Customs in Miami, we resumed our flight to O'Hare International Airport in Chicago, tired but happy. We were looking forward to sleeping in our own bed and getting back into our familiar routines.

When we stepped out of the tunnel at our gate, however, our plans were sweetly interrupted, and our contented weariness gladly gave way to an unexpected adrenaline surge of joy. Greeting us there were the smiling members of our study group, armed with a large sign welcoming us home by name. We were receiving the royal treatment in the world's busiest airport, and our friends who had prayed for us were eagerly awaiting our report. The final leg of our journey—to our townhome—would be delayed a bit longer, and our rest would have to wait. But it was a "sacrifice" I was only too glad to make. I can honestly say that, amid my surprise, I had never felt more loved, special, or important.

The joyous airport celebration at the end of our journey was worth far more than any inconveniences. And the reunion was a mere foretaste of the party awaiting those valued and loved by our heavenly Father. I have told various Christian friends and loved ones that when I die, they should throw a party. God knows I will already be celebrating, reveling in the One who is the Answer to all *my* questions.

Suggested Reading

Colson, Charles W. *Born Again*. Grand Rapids: Chosen, 2008.

Keller, Timothy. *The Prodigal God: Recovering the Heart of the Christian Faith*. New York and Toronto: Dutton, 2008.

Lewis, C. S. *Surprised by Joy: The Shape of My Early Life*. Rev. ed. New York: Houghton Mifflin Harcourt, 1995.

Discussion Questions

1. Why do Christians and atheists look at the same data and come up with radically different conceptions of God?
2. How does God's love provide a solid basis for human dignity and hope?
3. What are the dangers in saying that God values human beings?
4. If we love our children, how much more will our heavenly Father love us?
5. What details of your life—good and bad—do you wonder whether God notices?
6. What does it mean to say that an omniscient, omnipotent God searches for us?
7. In what ways does God's love spark a similar love in our own hearts, and how can we show this love in the way we live?
8. Why does God celebrate over us, and how might we return the favor?

Postscript

Answering the Questions

And now we come to the end of this book. We have navigated through all the questions Jesus asked as recorded in the New Testament. They are but one kind of signpost along the Way, and there are others. But they are divinely ordained means to help us come face to face with the God-Man— and with our own sinful hearts. I pray they have done so for you. Ever fresh and penetrating, twenty centuries ago and today, the questions point to the inestimable value and responsibility we have in the sight of our Creator and Savior.

The Lord has asked, and he awaits our answer. Are we ready to give it?

Questions Index

To help you in your study of all that Jesus asks, here are all of his questions as recorded in the New Testament, divided by the themes covered in the chapters of this book. This index will direct you to the chapter and verse location of each question. By grouping them in this way, I hope your thinking concerning these important themes will be enhanced. I have listed the questions roughly in the order that they appear in the main text of the book. I have not mentioned all 295 questions in the main part of the book in cases where the Synoptics are clearly describing the same event, though I usually have noted them. Nor have I covered some of the questions in the mouths of the characters in Jesus's parables, unless they are clearly speaking for him.

Jesus undoubtedly asked more questions than those recorded in this index during the course of his time on earth, for the scriptural writers never aimed to give an exhaustive account of his life. Their incompleteness carried over to other descriptions of key aspects of his ministry. As John the Evangelist said, "Now Jesus did many other signs in the presence of the disciples, which are not written in this book" (John 20:30). But these questions are complete in the sense that, with the rest of the Bible, they can make us "wise for salvation through faith in Christ Jesus" (2 Tim. 3:15).

The questions listed below are how the English Standard Version of the Bible words them. There is some overlap as some of the questions appear more than once. I have dealt with some of them in more than one chapter because they fall under more than one of my categories.

Some questions have slight differences in wording, according to how the different authors recorded them (for example, "Who touched me?" vs. "Who was it that touched me?" vs. "Who touched my garments?"). This is not a problem for the doctrine of scriptural inerrancy. The human authors, seeking to show Jesus as the way to God, were not slaves to verbal exactitude but used the events and words in the Lord's life to drive home spiritual points. We can trust the questions to be reliable indicators of what Jesus said, but we should not attempt to apply pristine, twenty-first-century journalistic standards to first-century literature. Sometimes, of course, Jesus asked the same question more than once. In these cases, I have recorded both instances because they represent different events.

Introduction

- Why are you afraid, O you of little faith?
  Matthew 8:26 (also chapters 10 and 15)

- Why are you so afraid? Have you still no faith?
  Mark 4:40

Chapter 1: His Forerunner

- What did you go out into the wilderness to see? A reed shaken by the wind? What then did you go out to see? A man dressed in soft clothing? . . . What then did you go out to see? A prophet?
  Matthew 11:7–9

- The baptism of John, from where did it come? From heaven or from man?
  Matthew 21:25

- Was the baptism of John from heaven or from man?
  Mark 11:30; Luke 20:4

- But to what shall I compare this generation?
  Matthew 11:16 (also chapter 16)

- To what then shall I compare the people of this generation, and what are they like?
  Luke 7:31

Chapter 2: His Teaching in Context

- And why do you break the commandment of God for the sake of your tradition?
  Matthew 15:3

- Where are we to buy bread so that these people may eat?
  John 6:5

- Salt is good, but if the salt has lost its saltiness, how will you make it salty again?
  Mark 9:50

- Salt is good, but if salt has lost its taste, how shall its saltiness be restored?
  Luke 14:34

- What is the kingdom of God like? And to what shall I compare it?
  Luke 13:18

- Can a blind man lead a blind man? Will they not both fall into a pit?
  Luke 6:39

- Where is my guest room, where I may eat the Passover with my disciples?
  Mark 14:14

- You see all these, do you not?
  Matthew 24:2

- Do you see these great buildings?
  Mark 13:2

Chapter 3: His Authority

- How then will [Satan's] kingdom stand? And if I cast out demons by Beelzebul, by whom do your sons cast them out? . . . Or how can someone enter a strong man's house and plunder his goods, unless he first binds the strong man?
  Matthew 12:26–27, 29 (also chapter 13)

- Do you think that these Galileans were worse sinners than all the other Galileans, because they suffered in this way? . . . Or those eighteen on whom the tower in Siloam fell and killed them: do you think that they were worse offenders than all the others who lived in Jerusalem?
  Luke 13:2, 4

Chapter 4: His Humanity

- Why were you looking for me? Did you not know that I must be in my Father's house?
  Luke 2:49

- Are you the teacher of Israel and yet you do not understand these things? . . . If I have told you earthly things and you do not believe, how can I tell you heavenly things?
  John 3:10, 12

- How long has this been happening to him?
  Mark 9:21

- What do you want me to do for you?
  Mark 10:36

- What do you want me to do for you?
  Mark 10:51

- What are you arguing about with them?
  Mark 9:16

- Do you say this of your own accord, or did others say it to you about me?
  John 18:34

- Who touched my garments?
  Mark 5:30

- Who was it that touched me?
  Luke 8:45

- Where have you laid him?
  John 11:34

- How many loaves do you have?
  Mark 8:5; Matthew 15:34

- Do you see anything?
  Mark 8:23

- My God, my God, why have you forsaken me?
  Mark 15:34 (also chapter 20)

Chapter 5: His Mission

- Woman, what does this have to do with me?
  John 2:4

- Do you think that I have come to give peace on earth?
  Luke 12:51

- You know how to interpret the appearance of earth and sky, but why do you not know how to interpret the present time?
  Luke 12:56 (also chapter 13)

- Are there not twelve hours in the day?
  John 11:9

- And how is it written of the Son of Man that he should suffer many things and be treated with contempt?
  Mark 9:12

- And what shall I say? "Father, save me from this hour"?
  John 12:27

- Is this what you are asking yourselves, what I meant by saying, "A little while and you will not see me, and again a little while and you will see me"?
  John 16:19

- Do you think that I cannot appeal to my Father, and he will at once send me more than twelve legions of angels? But how then should the Scriptures be fulfilled, that it must be so?
  Matthew 26:53–54

- Put your sword into its sheath; shall I not drink the cup that the Father has given me?
  John 18:11

Chapter 6: His Identity

- Who do people say that the Son of Man is?
  Matthew 16:13

- Who do people say that I am?
  Mark 8:27

- Who do the crowds say that I am?
  Luke 9:18

- But who do you say that I am?
  Matthew 16:15; Mark 8:29; Luke 9:20

- Have you never read in the Scriptures:

  "The stone that the builders rejected has become the cornerstone;

  this was the Lord's doing,
  and it is marvelous in our eyes"?
  Matthew 21:42; see also Mark 12:10–11

- What then is this that is written:

  "The stone that the builders rejected has become the cornerstone"?
  Luke 20:17

- Can the wedding guests fast while the bridegroom is with them?
  Mark 2:19

- What do you think about the Christ? Whose son is he? . . . How is it then that David, in the Spirit, calls him Lord, saying,

  "The Lord said to my Lord,
  Sit at my right hand,
  until I put your enemies under your feet"?

  If then David calls him Lord, how is he his son?
  Matthew 22:41–45

- How can the scribes say that the Christ is the son of David? . . . So how is he his son?
  Mark 12:35, 37

- How can they say that the Christ is David's son? . . . David thus calls him Lord, so how is he his son?
  Luke 20:41, 44

- Have you never read what David did, when he was in need and was hungry, he and those who were with him: how he entered the house of God, in the time of Abiathar the high priest, and ate the bread of the Presence, which it is not lawful for any but the priests to eat, and also gave it to those who were with him?
  Mark 2:25–26

- Have you not read what David did when he was hungry, he and those who were with him: how he entered the house of God and took and ate the bread of the Presence, which is not lawful for any but the priests to eat, and also gave it to those with him?
  Luke 6:3–4

- Why are you discussing the fact that you have no bread? Do you not yet perceive or understand? Are your hearts hardened? Having eyes do you not see, and having ears do you not hear? And do you not remember? When I broke the five loaves for the five thousand, how many baskets full of broken pieces did you take up? . . . And the seven for the four thousand, how many baskets full of broken pieces did you take up? . . . Do you not yet understand?
  Mark 8:17–21

- Why do you question these things in your hearts? Which is easier, to say to the paralytic, "Your sins are forgiven," or to say, "Rise, take up your bed and walk"?
  Mark 2:8–9

- O you of little faith, why did you doubt?
  Matthew 14:31 (also chapter 8)

- Which one of you convicts me of sin? If I tell the truth, why do you not believe me?
  John 8:46

- Why do you call me good?
  Luke 18:19; Mark 10:18

- Why do you ask me about what is good?
  Matthew 19:17

- Why were you looking for me? Did you not know that I must be in my Father's house?
  Luke 2:49 (also chapter 4)

- Have I been with you so long, and you still do not know me, Philip? . . . How can you say, "Show us the Father"? Do you not believe that I am in the Father and the Father is in me?
  John 14:9–10

- Do you think that I cannot appeal to my Father, and he will at once send me more than twelve legions of angels?
  Matthew 26:53 (also chapter 5)

- Have you anything here to eat?
  Luke 24:41

- Saul, Saul, why are you persecuting me?
  Acts 9:4; see also 22:7; 26:14

Chapter 7: Relationship with Him

- Do you believe in the Son of Man?
  John 9:35 (also chapter 8)

- What do you want me to do for you?
  Luke 18:41; Mark 10:51 (also chapter 4)

- Who touched my garments?
  Mark 5:30 (also chapter 4)

- Who touched me?
  Mark 5:32

- Who was it that touched me?
  Luke 8:45 (also chapter 4)

- Who is my mother, and who are my brothers?
  Matthew 12:48

- Who are my mother and my brothers?
  Mark 3:33

- Do you want to be healed?
  John 5:6

- Woman, why are you weeping? Whom are you seeking?
  John 20:15

- What is this conversation that you are holding with each other as you walk?
  Luke 24:17

- What things?
  Luke 24:19

- Children, do you have any fish?
  John 21:5

- What were you discussing on the way?
  Mark 9:33

- Simon, son of John, do you love me more than these? . . . Simon, son of John, do you love me? . . . Simon, son of John, do you love me?
  John 21:15–17 (also chapters 9 and 12)

- Why do you trouble the woman?
  Matthew 26:10

- Why do you trouble her?
  Mark 14:6

Chapter 8: Faith in Him

- Do you believe in the Son of Man?
  John 9:35 (also chapter 7)

- Do you believe this?
  John 11:26

- Did I not tell you that if you believed you would see the glory of God?
  John 11:40

- Do you now believe?
  John 16:31

- O you of little faith, why did you doubt?
  Matthew 14:31 (also chapter 6)

- Why are you making a commotion and weeping?
  Mark 5:39

- Do you believe that I am able to do this?
  Matthew 9:28

- Which of you by being anxious can add a single hour to his span of life?
  Matthew 6:27; Luke 12:25

- Do you see anything?
  Mark 8:23

- Do you want to be healed?
  John 5:6

- What do you want?
  Matthew 20:21

- Why do you trouble her?
  Mark 14:6

- Because I said to you, "I saw you under the fig tree," do you believe?
  John 1:50

- How many loaves do you have?
  Matthew 15:34; Mark 6:38; 8:5

- Where are we to buy bread, so that these people may eat?
  John 6:5

- Why are you troubled, and why do doubts arise in your hearts?
  Luke 24:38

- Where is your faith?
  Luke 8:25

- O you of little faith, why are you discussing among yourselves the fact that you have no bread? Do you not yet perceive? Do you not remember the five loaves for the five thousand, and how many baskets you gathered? Or the seven loaves for the four thousand, and how many baskets you gathered? How is it that you fail to understand that I did not speak about bread?
  Matthew 16:8–11

- So, could you not watch with me one hour?
  Matthew 26:40

- Simon, are you asleep? Could you not watch one hour?
  Mark 14:37

- Are you still sleeping and taking your rest?
  Mark 14:41

- Why are you sleeping?
  Luke 22:46

Chapter 9: Discipleship Directed by Him

- Are you able to drink the cup that I am to drink?
  Matthew 20:22

- Are you able to drink the cup that I drink, or to be baptized with the baptism with which I am baptized?
  Mark 10:38

- For which of you, desiring to build a tower, does not first sit down and count the cost, whether he has enough to complete it? . . . Or what king, going out to encounter another king in war, will not sit down first and deliberate whether he is able with ten thousand to meet him who comes against him with twenty thousand?
  Luke 14:28, 31

- What are you seeking?
  John 1:38

- For who is the greater, one who reclines at table or one who serves? Is it not the one who reclines at table?
  Luke 22:27

- Do you understand what I have done to you?
  John 13:12

- If then you have not been faithful in the unrighteous wealth, who will entrust to you the true riches? And if you have not been faithful in that which is another's, who will give you that which is your own?
  Luke 16:11–12

- When I sent you out with no moneybag or knapsack or sandals, did you lack anything?
  Luke 22:35

- You are the salt of the earth, but if salt has lost its taste, how shall its saltiness be restored?
  Matthew 5:13

- So you are Simon the son of John?
  John 1:42

- Simon, son of John, do you love me more than these? . . . Simon, son of

into a person from outside cannot defile him, since it enters not his heart but his stomach, and is expelled?
Mark 7:18–19 (also chapter 13)

- And why do you not judge for yourselves what is right?
  Luke 12:57

- Why do you seek to kill me?
  John 7:19

- I have shown you many good works from the Father; for which of them are you going to stone me?
  John 10:32

- What do you want?
  Matthew 20:21

- Now which of them will love him more? . . . Do you see this woman?
  Luke 7:42, 44

Chapter 15: Overcoming Anxiety for Him

- Can you make wedding guests fast while the bridegroom is with them?
  Luke 5:34

- Are not five sparrows sold for two pennies?
  Luke 12:6

- Is not life more than food, and the body more than clothing?
  Matthew 6:25

- Are not two sparrows sold for a penny?
  Matthew 10:29 (also chapter 26)

- Are you not of more value than they?
  Matthew 6:26

- And which of you by being anxious can add a single hour to his span of life? If then you are not able to do as small a thing as that, why are you anxious about the rest? . . . But if God so clothes the grass, which is alive in the field today, and tomorrow is thrown into the oven, how much more will he clothe you, O you of little faith!
  Luke 12:25–26, 28

- Why are you afraid, O you of little faith?
  Matthew 8:26 (also Introduction and chapter 10)

Chapter 16: Unbelief Rejects Him

- How can you believe, when you receive glory from one another and do not seek the glory that comes from the only God?
  John 5:44

- But to what shall I compare this generation?
  Matthew 11:16 (also chapter 1)

- Why does this generation seek a sign?
  Mark 8:12 (also chapter 14)

- O faithless and twisted generation, how long am I to be with you and bear with you?
  Luke 9:41

- O faithless generation, how long am I to be with you? How long am I to bear with you?
  Matthew 17:17; Mark 9:19

- How can you speak good, when you are evil?
  Matthew 12:34

- And should not you have had mercy on your fellow servant as I had mercy on you?
  Matthew 18:33

Chapter 20: Understanding His Word

- And why do you break the commandment of God for the sake of your tradition?
  Matthew 15:3

- Woman, where are they? Has no one condemned you?
  John 8:10

- Are you also still without understanding? Do you not see that whatever goes into the mouth passes into the stomach and is expelled?
  Matthew 15:16–17 (also chapters 13 and 14)

- Is this not the reason you are wrong, because you know neither the Scriptures nor the power of God?
  Mark 12:24 (also chapter 25)

- Have you not read this Scripture?
  Mark 12:10

- Have you not read what David did when he was hungry, he and those with him: how he entered the house of God and took and ate the bread of the Presence, which is not lawful for any but the priests to eat, and also gave it to those with him?
  Luke 6:3–4

- Or have you not read in the Law how on the Sabbath the priests in the temple profane the Sabbath and are guiltless?
  Matthew 12:5

- What did Moses command you?
  Mark 10:3 (also chapter 21)

- Is it not written, "My house shall be called a house of prayer for all the nations"?
  Mark 11:17

- My God, my God, why have you forsaken me?
  Mark 15:34 (also chapter 4)

- But if you do not believe his writings, how will you believe my words?
  John 5:47

- Has not Moses given you the law?
  John 7:19

- Was it not necessary that the Christ should suffer these things and enter into his glory?
  Luke 24:26

- Do you think I cannot appeal to my Father, and he will at once send more than twelve legions of angels? But how then should the Scriptures be fulfilled, that it must be so?
  Matthew 26:53–54

Chapter 21: Following His Design for Marriage

- What did Moses command you?
  Mark 10:3 (also chapter 20)

- Have you not read that he who created them from the beginning made them male and female, and said, "Therefore a man shall leave his father and his mother and hold fast to his wife, and they shall become one flesh"?
  Matthew 19:4–5

Chapter 26: Rejoicing in His Love

- I have shown you many good works from the Father; for which of them are you going to stone me?
  John 10:32

- Are not two sparrows sold for a penny?
  Matthew 10:29 (also chapter 15)

- Or which one of you, if his son asks him for bread, will give him a stone? Or if he asks for a fish, will give him a serpent?
  Matthew 7:9–10

- What father among you, if his son asks for a fish, will instead of a fish give him a serpent; or if he asks for an egg, will give him a scorpion?
  Luke 11:11–12 (also chapter 11)

- What man of you, having a hundred sheep, if he has lost one of them, does not leave the ninety-nine in the open country, and go after the one that is lost, until he finds it?
  Luke 15:4

- Or what woman, having ten silver coins, if she loses one coin, does not light a lamp and sweep the house and seek diligently until she finds it?
  Luke 15:8

Notes

Introduction

1. Gene Weingarten, "Pearls Before Breakfast," *Washington Post*, April 8, 2007. Thanks to my friend Chris Castaldo for this illustration.

2. Matthew 8:23–27; see also Mark 4:35–41. Throughout this book I will italicize the questions of Jesus so that readers can find them more easily.

3. Stephen Prothero, *Religious Literacy: What Every American Needs to Know—and Doesn't* (San Francisco: HarperSanFrancisco, 2007), 192.

4. Mark Galli, *Jesus Mean and Wild: The Unexpected Love of an Untamable God* (Grand Rapids: Baker, 2006), 19.

5. This does not mean he asked three hundred separate questions, since the Synoptic Gospels—Matthew, Mark, and Luke—often cover (from different angles) many of the same events of Christ's life—including his questions.

6. Marcus Borg, *Jesus: Uncovering the Life, Teachings, and Relevance of a Religious Revolutionary* (San Francisco: HarperSanFrancisco, 2006), 150–57.

7. Mary Schaller, personal interview with the author, May 13, 2009.

8. To a lesser extent, we will also quote some of his disciples, who, better than anyone, are in position to give context to and interpret his questions.

9. John Piper, *What Jesus Demands from the World* (Wheaton: Crossway, 2006), 33.

10. Michael Weisskopf, "Energized by Pulpit or Passion, the Public Is Calling," *Washington Post*, February 1, 1993.

Chapter 1

1. Matthew 3:5, emphases mine.
2. Matthew 3:1–4.
3. Mark 8:28.
4. Luke 1:41, 43–44.
5. Judges 13:7.
6. Luke 3:11–14.
7. Matthew 3:7–8.
8. John 1:19–23; my paraphrase.
9. Matthew 3:11–12.
10. Matthew 3:13–14.
11. John 3:30.
12. Matthew 3:15.
13. Matthew 11:2–3.
14. Matthew 11:4–6; see also Isaiah 35:5–6.
15. Matthew 11:7–9; see also Luke 7:24–26.
16. Matthew 11:9–10.
17. Luke 7:29–30.
18. Matthew Henry, *Matthew to John*, vol. 5 of *Commentary on the Whole Bible* (McLean, VA: MacDonald Publishing Company, 1985), 149–50.
19. Matthew 21:23–25; see also Mark 11:30.
20. Matthew 4:17.
21. This is not to insist on a wooden, mechanical gospel presentation in which we must

first convince people of their sinfulness before we can offer the solution—convincing people of their sin and need for Christ is the Holy Spirit's job (see John 16:8). In our evangelism we must be sensitive both to cultural trends and to individual hearts. We cannot just shove a bit of information down people's throats. Jesus, after all, invited people to follow him and then shared more information along the way. In our postmodern milieu, many people respond more readily to an invitation to our community, where they see the faith lived out. Knowledge of their evil will come later, and, with it, a thorough conversion. But the point is, we cannot skimp on the bad news while attempting to share the good news.

22. Christian Smith with Melinda Lundquist Denton, *Soul Searching: The Religious and Spiritual Lives of American Teenagers* (Oxford: Oxford University Press, 2005).

23. Mark D. Regnerus, *Forbidden Fruit: Sex and Religion in the Lives of American Teenagers* (Oxford: Oxford University Press, 2007), 205–6.

24. Stan Guthrie, "The Evangelical Scandal," *Christianity Today*, April 2005, http://www.ctlibrary.com/ct/2005/April/32.70.html.

25. Matthew 11:16–19; see also Luke 7:31–35.

26. Charles Colson, "What Would Wilberforce Do?" *Christianity Today*, March 2007, http://www.christianitytoday.com/ct/2007/march/11.28.html.

27. Stan Guthrie, *Missions in the Third Millennium: 21 Key Trends for the 21st Century*, 2nd ed. (Waynesboro, GA: Paternoster, 2005), 42.

28. Rob Moll, "The New Monasticism," *Christianity Today*, September 2005, http://www.ctlibrary.com/ct/2005/September/16.38.html.

29. Mother Teresa, *My Life for the Poor* (San Francisco: HarperSanFrancisco, 2005), 211–16.

30. Gezim Alpion, *Mother Teresa: Saint or Celebrity?* (London: Routledge, 2007), 182.

31. Mother Teresa, "National Prayer Breakfast Speech Against Abortion—1994," OrthodoxyToday.org, January 22, 2004.

32. Matthew 14:1–12.

33. Matthew 11:11.

Chapter 2

1. Matthew 2:1–8, 13–18.

2. N. T. Wright, *Jesus and the Victory of God* (Minneapolis: Fortress, 1996), 150–51.

3. See Jaroslav Pelikan, *The Illustrated Jesus through the Centuries* (New Haven, CT: Yale University Press, 1997), 9–23.

4. Norman Cousins, quoted in "Some Jewish Views of Jesus," Jews for Jesus, January 1, 2005, http://www.jewsforjesus.org/answers/jesus/jewssay.

5. Wright, *Jesus and the Victory of God*, 98.

6. Matthew 24:35.

7. Jim Croce, "Bad, Bad Leroy Brown," *Life and Times* (New York: ABC Records, 1973).

8. John 1:46, emphasis mine.

9. Luke 22:59.

10. Adrian Curtis, *Oxford Bible Atlas*, 4th ed. (Oxford and New York: Oxford University Press, 2007), 153.

11. Rabbi Arthur Blecher, *The New American Judaism: The Way Forward on Challenging Issues from Intermarriage to Jewish Identity* (New York and Houndmills: Palgrave Macmillan, 2007), 140.

12. Matthew 15:3–7.

13. Walter A. Elwell, ed., *Baker Encyclopedia of the Bible* (Grand Rapids: Baker, 1988), 2:1914.

14. Ibid., 1880–81.

15. Matthew 10:28.

16. I am grateful to J. I. Packer for this insight.

17. Matthew 5:20.

18. Luke 16:17.

19. Matthew 7:28–29.

20. Matthew 23:8.

21. Matthew 28:20.

22. A. B. Bruce, *The Training of the Twelve*, 4th ed. (New Canaan, CT: Keats, 1979), 14.

23. Ibid., 37.

24. Luke 5:10.

25. Mark 3:13–15.

26. Robert E. Coleman, *The Master Plan of Evangelism* (Old Tappan, NJ: Spire Books/Revell, 1964), 40.

27. Ibid., 33.

28. Ibid., 18.

29. Matthew 5–7.

30. Luke 15:11–32.

31. Matthew 20:16 NIV.

32. Borg, *Jesus*, 152–53.

33. Ibid., 151.

34. See, for example, Matthew 5:22.

35. Borg, *Jesus*, 150.

36. For an excellent discussion of context and other principles of sound interpretation, see J. Robertson McQuilkin, *Understanding and Applying the Bible: An Introduction to Hermeneutics* (Chicago: Moody, 1983).

37. John 6:6.

38. John 6.

39. Wright, *Jesus and the Victory of God*, 171–72.

40. John 20:30–31.

41. Henry Parry Liddon, *Liddon's Brompton Lectures 1866* (London: Rivingstons, 1869), quoted in Ravi Zacharias, *Jesus among Other Gods* (Nashville: W Publishing Group, 2000), 148.

42. Debra Nails, "Socrates," *Stanford Encyclopedia of Philosophy*, November 7, 2009, http://plato.stanford.edu/entries/socrates.

43. *The Paper Chase*, DVD (1973; Los Angeles: 20th Century Fox, 2003).

44. Luke 14:34; see also Mark 9:50.

45. Luke 14:35.

46. Luke 13:18–19.

47. Luke 6:39.

48. Mark 14:14.

49. Matthew 24:2; see also Mark 13:2.

Chapter 3

1. R. E. K. Mchami, "Demon Possession and Exorcism in Mark 1:21–28, *Africa Theological Journal* 24, no. 1 (2001), 31, quoted in Philip Jenkins, *The New Faces of Christianity: Believing the Bible in the Global South* (New York: Oxford University Press, 2006), 107.

2. Ibid., 105.

3. Ibid., 100.

4. Borg, *Jesus*, 150.

5. Clinton E. Arnold, *3 Crucial Questions about Spiritual Warfare* (Grand Rapids: Baker, 1997), 20.

6. Luke 4:18–19.

7. Matthew 4:23–24.

8. Borg, *Jesus*, 146.

9. Mark 1:27.

10. Acts 19:13–16.

11. Matthew 9:34.

12. Matthew 12:22–30.

13. Abraham Lincoln, "House Divided," delivered in Springfield, Illinois, June 16, 1858, quoted in full at "'House Divided' Speech," The History Place, http://www.historyplace.com/lincoln/divided.htm.

14. Matthew 12:27.

15. Walter A. Elwell, ed., *Evangelical Commentary on the Bible* (Grand Rapids: Baker, 1987), 821.

16. Luke 10:1–19.

17. Matthew 12:29.

18. Jenkins, *The New Faces of Christianity*, 5.

19. Genesis 3:18–19.

20. Luke 13:10–17.

21. Luke 13:2–5.

22. 2 Corinthians 12:7.

23. See Stan Guthrie, "Stumbling After Jesus," *Christianity Today*, July 2007, 52.

24. Tony Snow, "Cancer's Unexpected Blessings," *Christianity Today*, July 2007, 32.

25. John 9:1–3.

26. Revelation 21:4.

27. Jenkins, *The New Faces of Christianity*, 113.

28. Ibid., 114.

29. See Gregory Fung and Christopher Fung, "What Do Prayer Studies Prove?" *Christianity Today*, May 2009, http://www.christianitytoday.com/ct/2009/may/27.43.html.

30. Jenkins, *The New Faces of Christianity*, 99.

31. Borg, *Jesus*, 149.

32. Jenkins, *The New Faces of Christianity*, 118.

33. Ibid., 118–22.

34. Ibid., 123.

35. Martin Ssebuyira and Zurah Nakabugo, "Pastor Arrested with 'Miracle' Machine," *Daily Monitor*, October 3, 2007, http://www.monitor.co.ug/News/National/-/688334/791328/-/w19yvt/-/index.html.

36. Michael Cuneo, *American Exorcism: Expelling Demons in the Land of Plenty* (New York: Doubleday, 2001).

37. Borg, *Jesus*, 146.

38. See, for example, Fred Heeren, *Show Me God: What the Message from Space Is Telling Us About God* (Wheeling, IL: Searchlight Publications, 1995).

39. J. P. Moreland, *Kingdom Triangle: Recover the Christian Mind, Renovate the Soul, Restore the Spirit's Power* (Grand Rapids: Zondervan, 2007), 172.

40. Ibid., 177–78.

41. Matthew 28:18–20.

42. John 14:12.

43. 2 Corinthians 12:9.

44. Moreland, *Kingdom Triangle*, 182–86.

45. C. S. Lewis, *The Screwtape Letters*, in *The Complete C. S. Lewis Signature Classics* (San Francisco: HarperSanFrancisco, 2002), 125.

Chapter 4

1. Mark 15:16–22.

2. Mark 15:18.

3. Stephen J. Nichols, *For Us and for Our Salvation: The Doctrine of Christ in the Early Church* (Wheaton: Crossway, 2007), 23.

4. Gary M. Burge, "Assessing the Apocryphal Gospels," *Christianity Today*, June 2006, 28.

5. For a good overview of the various scholarly "quests," see Wright, *Jesus and the Victory of God*, 3–144.

6. Anne Rice, *Christ the Lord: Out of Egypt—A Novel* (New York and Toronto: Alfred A. Knopf, 2005), 5.

7. Nichols, *For Us and for Our Salvation*, 26.

8. C. S. Lewis, *Mere Christianity*, in *The Complete C. S. Lewis Signature Classics*, 39.

9. For the prophecy, see Isaiah 53:3–4; for the fulfillment, see Matthew 27:46; Luke 19:41–42, 22:44; John 7:1–9, 11:35; Hebrews 2:18, 5:8.

10. Nichols, *For Us and for Our Salvation*, 26.

11. See, for example, Matthew 9:4; Mark 2:8; Luke 5:22; and John 6:64, 70–71.

12. Luke 2:41–52.

13. John 3:10, 12.

14. Mark 9:21.

15. Mark 10:36.

16. Mark 9:16.

17. John 18:34.

18. Philippians 2:7.

19. Luke 4:3–4.

20. Philippians 2:6.

21. John 5:19, 36; 7:16; 8:26.

22. Luke 6:12–16.

23. See, for example, Matthew 17:22–23.

24. For a good discussion of how the Spirit led Jesus, see Graham A. Cole, *He Who Gives Life: The Doctrine of the Holy Spirit* (Wheaton: Crossway, 2007), 59–91.

25. Matthew 4:1.

26. Mark 1:12.

27. Luke 4:1–2.

28. Mark 5:30–31; see also Luke 8:42–48.

29. Mark 8:1–10; 6:30–44.

30. Mark 8:5.

31. Mark 8:23.

32. Romans 8.

33. Mark 15:34.

34. Brian Kolodiejchuk, *Mother Teresa: Come Be My Light—The Private Writings of the "Saint of Calcutta"* (New York: Doubleday, 2007), 210.

35. Hebrews 4:15.

Chapter 5

1. Brian D. McLaren, *The Secret Message of Jesus: Uncovering the Truth That Could Change Everything* (Nashville: Thomas Nelson, 2006), 90–91.

2. Ibid., 14.

3. Ibid., 33.

4. Why refer to the teachings of Jesus's disciples and apostles in a book about his questions? Because if Jesus is the unparalleled teacher we all say he is—and even more—then we should be able to trust his students to faithfully convey what he taught. If not, then we must conclude that the man from Galilee was a pedagogical failure. For good reasons on why this conclusion is highly unlikely, see chapter 2.

5. Elwell, *Evangelical Commentary on the Bible*, 849.

6. John 2:1–11.

7. Exodus 4:10.

8. Exodus 4:11–12.

9. Walter A. Elwell, ed., *Evangelical Dictionary of Theology*, 2nd ed. (Grand Rapids: Baker, 2001), 1201.

10. Henry, *Matthew to John*, 872.

11. Isaiah 25:6; Joel 3:18.

12. Luke 12:49–56.

13. Isaiah 9:6.

14. Matthew 5:9.

15. Elwell, *Evangelical Dictionary of Theology*, 1201.

16. John 20:30–31.

17. Matthew 9:13; Mark 2:17; Matthew 5:17; Matthew 10:34; John 9:39 (but see also John 3:17); Luke 19:10; John 18:37.

18. John 10:31 and 11:8.

19. Henry, *Matthew to John*, 521.

20. Matthew 20:28; see also Mark 10:45.

21. John 11:8–10.

22. John 8:12.

23. Mark 9:12.

24. John 12:27–36.

25. John 16:16–22.

26. Matthew 26:52–54; see also John 18:11.

27. Two of the many passages from the Old Testament that point to the death of Christ centuries before it ever happened are Psalm 22 and Isaiah 53. For a thorough examination of Bible prophecies about Jesus, see McDowell, *Evidence That Demands a Verdict* (San Bernardino, CA: Here's Life, 1979), 141–78.

28. John 1:29.

29. John Stott, *Basic Christianity* (Downers Grove, IL: InterVarsity, 2006), 103.

30. Acts 9:1–30.

31. 1 Corinthians 15:1–8, emphasis mine.

32. 1 Peter 3:18.

33. 1 Corinthians 1:18–25.

34. John 8:24.

Chapter 6

1. David Hilborn, "The Da Vinci Code—Teabing"; see http://www.eauk.org/theology/filmreviews/the-da-vinci-code-teabing.cfm.

2. Robert M. Bowman and J. Ed Komoszewski, *Putting Jesus in His Place: The Case for the Divinity of Christ* (Grand Rapids: Kregel, 2007), 18.

3. Refutations from a Christian perspective are numerous. See, for example, Darrell L. Bock and Daniel B. Wallace, *Dethroning Jesus: Exposing Popular Culture's Quest to Unseat the Biblical Christ* (Nashville: Thomas Nelson, 2007).

4. Larry W. Hurtado, *Lord Jesus Christ: Devotion to Jesus in Earliest Christianity* (Grand Rapids: Eerdmans, 2003), 135, quoted in Bowman and Komoszewski, *Putting Jesus in His Place*, 30.

5. Bowman and Komoszewski, *Putting Jesus in His Place*, 18.

6. Josephus, *Jewish Antiquities* 18, quoted in Borg, *Jesus,* 30.

7. See Matthew 16:13–15; Mark 8:27–29; Luke 9:18–20; emphasis mine.

8. John 3:30.

9. John 8:24.

10. Borg, *Jesus*, 9. See previous discussion of Docetism in chapter 4.

11. Millard J. Erickson, *Christian Theology* (Grand Rapids: Baker, 1985), 683.

12. Matthew 21:42; see also Mark 12:10–11 and Luke 20:17.

13. Mark 2:19.

14. Psalms 2:6–8.

15. Psalms 2:12.

16. Matthew 22:41–45; see also Mark 12:35–37 and Luke 20:41–44.

17. Mark 2:25–28; see also Luke 6:3–5.

18. Acts 14:11–18.

19. See, for example, John 10:37–38.

20. Mark 6:30–44 and 8:1–9.

21. Mark 8:17–21.

22. Mark 2:1–12.

23. Lewis, *Mere Christianity*, 36.

24. Matthew 14:22–33.

25. Bowman and Komoszewski, *Putting Jesus in His Place*, 23.

26. John 8:44–46.

27. 1 John 1:5.

28. 1 Peter 2:22.

29. Luke 18:18–30; Matthew 19:16–30; Mark 10:17–30.

30. Matthew 5:8.

31. Bowman and Komoszewski, *Putting Jesus in His Place*, 74.

32. Hosea 11:1. The ultimate fulfillment of this verse about God's son being called out of Egypt, is, of course, Jesus.

33. See Psalm 2:7, 12. The ultimate fulfillment of the king who is God's son, of course, is Jesus.

34. Luke 2:49.

35. John 10:22–39.

36. John 14:1–14.

37. Matthew 26:53.

38. See chapter 23 for a discussion of the "legion" of demons.

39. Luke 24:41.

40. Stephen Charnock, *The Existence and Attributes of God* (Grand Rapids: Baker, 1996), 1:563.

41. Acts 9:1–9.

42. Matthew 28:18, 20.

Chapter 7

1. Miller McPherson, Lynn Smith-Lovin, and Matthew E. Brashears, "Social Isolation in America," *American Sociological Review* 71 (2006): 353–75.

2. See also "Look at All the Lonely People," *Christianity Today*, November 2006, 31.

3. See, for example, the triune doxology in 2 Corinthians 13:14.

4. Genesis 2:18.

5. Romans 5:8.

6. James F. Lewis, "Hindu, Hinduism," in *Evangelical Dictionary of World Missions* (Grand Rapids: Baker, 2000), 434–37.

7. J. Isamu Yahamoto, "Buddhism and Christianity," in Sinclair B. Ferguson, David F. Wright, and J. I. Packer, eds., *New Dictionary of Theology* (Downers Grove, IL: InterVarsity, 1988), 112.

8. Terry C. Muck, "Buddhist, Buddhism," in *Evangelical Dictionary of World Missions*, 149–50.

9. Warren Larson, "Who Is God for Muslims and Christians?" unpublished paper, Columbia International University, Columbia, South Carolina, 2007.

10. John Stott, *Why I Am a Christian* (Downers Grove, IL: InterVarsity, 2003), 95.

11. Matthew 5:3.

12. See John 9.

13. Joni Eareckson Tada, "Fear Not the Disabled," *Christianity Today*, November 2005, 28.

14. "Siloam, Pool of," in Elwell, *Baker Encyclopedia of the Bible*, 2:1964.

15. John 9:35–38. "Son of Man" is a messianic title for Jesus Christ; see Daniel 7:13–14.

16. See the discussion of this title in chapter 6.

17. Luke 18:35–43.

18. Mark 5:30.

19. Mark 5:32–34.

20. Matthew 12:46–50; also Mark 3:31–35.

21. See John 5:1–17.

22. John 20:14–16.

23. Luke 24:17–19.

24. Once when the disciples were arguing over which was the greatest, Jesus launched his teaching response with a question: "What were you discussing on the way?" As the context in Mark 9:33–37 indicates, Jesus already knew the answer, but he was looking for a response, not for information.

25. John 21:5.

26. John 21:15–19.

Chapter 8

1. See Romans 3:20–26, for example.

2. Stan Guthrie, "Answering the Atheists," *Christianity Today*, November 2007, 74.

3. Hebrews 11:6.

4. Edward W. Goodrick and John R. Kohlenberger III, *The NIV Exhaustive Concordance* (Grand Rapids: Zondervan, 1990), 1776–77.

5. John 9:35; see chapter 7.

6. John 11:25–26; see chapter 4.

7. John 11:40.

8. Emphasis mine; see John 16:25–33.

9. James 2:19.

10. Stott, *Basic Christianity*, 160.

11. Matthew 14:31.

12. Matthew 14:33.

13. Mark 5:39.

14. Matthew 9:27–31.

15. Matthew 17:20.

16. Mark 9:14–29; see also Matthew 17:14–19.

17. Matthew 6:27 and Luke 12:25.

18. Mark 8:22–26.

19. But see John 9 for another progressive healing of a blind man.

20. John 5:6; see chapter 7.

21. Mark 2:1–12.

22. Romans 8:18–21.

23. 1 Corinthians 15:53.

24. James 4:2–3.

25. Matthew 20:20–23.

26. Matthew 7:8.

27. Isaiah 55:9.

28. Luke 7:9; emphasis mine.

29. Luke 7:50.

30. Mark 14:6–7; also Matthew 26:10.

31. John 1:47–50.

32. Luke 21:1–4.

33. See Matthew 15:32–39; Mark 6:40–44; and Mark 8:1–10. See also in John 6:1–14 his related question, "Where are we to buy bread, so that these people may eat?"

34. Luke 24:38.

35. Luke 8:25.

36. Matthew 16:5–12.

37. Matthew 13:33; see chapter 24.

38. Matthew 22:37.

39. 1 Corinthians 3:2.

40. Matthew 26:36–46, Mark 14:32–42, and Luke 22:39–46.

41. Hebrews 3:7–4:13.

42. Romans 13:11.

43. Bill Curry, interview on "Mike and Mike in the Morning," ESPN Radio, December 12, 2007.

Chapter 9

1. G. Leibholz, "Memoir," in Dietrich Bonhoeffer, *The Cost of Discipleship* (New York: Macmillan, 1963), 11–35.

2. Bonhoeffer, *The Cost of Discipleship*, 99.

3. Luke 6:40.

4. See Mark 10:35–45; also, Matthew 20:20–28.

5. See, for example, Matthew 16:24–26 and 2 Timothy 3:12.

6. Isaiah 53:3.

7. Luke 14:25–33.

8. Romans 3:28.

9. Mark 10:17–22.

10. Matthew 13:1–9, 18–23.

11. John 1:38.

12. Hebrews 12:1–2.

13. Acts 20:35.

14. Luke 22:25–27.

15. John 13:12–17.

16. Luke 16:1–13.

17. Goodrick and Kohlenberger, *The NIV Exhaustive Concordance*, 1674.

18. 1 Timothy 6:10.

19. See Elisabeth Elliot, *Through Gates of Splendor* (Wheaton: Tyndale, 2005), 172.

20. empty tomb, inc., "U.S. Per Capita Inflation Adjusted Income/Per Member Giving as Percentage of Income," http://www.empty tomb.org/fig1_07.html.

21. See Guthrie, *Missions in the Third Millennium*, 22–24.

22. Colossians 3:5.

23. This represents my slightly altered paraphrase of Romans 1:25, which I am using as a literary allusion.

24. Luke 22:35. But this accounting is no guarantee that the disciple's life will be trouble-free, only that it will be under the Lord's control, whether there is opposition or not (see verses 36–38).

25. See Bonhoeffer, *The Cost of Discipleship*, 201, for a good discussion of this passage.

26. Romans 12:1.

27. 1 John 4:19.

28. Matthew 5:13.

29. Bonhoeffer, *The Cost of Discipleship*, 51.

30. John 1:40–42.

31. John 21:15–19.

32. See a parallel discussion of this passage in chapter 7.

33. Acts 4:19–20.

34. Hebrews 12:1–2 and Ephesians 2:10.

35. John 21:22.

36. Revelation 2:17.

Chapter 10

1. John 13:23.

2. John 14:15, 24.

3. 1 John 2:4.

4. Piper, *What Jesus Demands from the World*, 23.

5. John M. Frame, *The Doctrine of God: A Theology of Lordship* (Phillipsburg, NJ: P&R, 2002), 24n10.

6. Ibid., 22.

7. See http://www.vincelombardi.com.

8. Luke 6:46.

9. See the discussion of Peter's character in chapter 9.

10. John 13:36–38.

11. Michelle Beardon, "Hillsborough Judge Resigns to Become Missionary," *The Tampa Tribune*, February 1, 2008, www2.tbo.com/content/2008/feb/01/hillsborough-judge-resigns-become-missionary/news-breaking/.

12. Tim Stafford, *Surprised by Jesus: His Agenda for Changing Everything in A.D. 30 and Today* (Downers Grove, IL: InterVarsity, 2006), 113.

13. See Luke 20:19–26; also Matthew 22:15–22 and Mark 12:13–17.

14. Genesis 1:27.

15. Matthew 12:1–8.

16. Henry, *Matthew to John*, 163; emphasis in original.

17. Elwell, *Evangelical Commentary on the Bible*, 744.

18. Luke 2:49.

19. See Matthew 21:12–16; Mark 11:15–18; Luke 19:45–47; and John 2:14–16.

20. Matthew 17:24–27.

21. See Matthew 12:46–50; also Mark 3:31–35; see also chapter 7.

22. Matthew 8:23–27.

23. See Daniel 3.

24. Stan Guthrie, "A Hole in Our Holism: Why Evangelicals Might Be Shy About Sharing Their Faith," *Christianity Today*, January 2008, 56.

25. Perhaps he was obliquely addressing the common prejudice that disability is the result of sin; see discussion in chapter 7.

26. See Matthew 9:1–9, also Luke 5:17–26; a parallel discussion of this incident is in chapter 6.

27. See, for example, Tim Stafford, "The Joy of Suffering in Sri Lanka," *Christianity Today*, October 2003, http://www.christianitytoday.com/ct/2003/october/5.54.html.

28. Luke 8:35.

29. Stafford, *Surprised by Jesus*, 97.

30. Luke 12:35–48.

31. Luke 12:42–46.

32. Ephesians 2:8.

33. Bonhoeffer, *The Cost of Discipleship*, 69.

34. Augustine, *Confessions*, trans. R. S. Pine-Coffin (New York: Penguin, 1961), 40.

35. Bonhoeffer, *The Cost of Discipleship*, 47.

36. Luke 17:7–10.

37. R. Kent Hughes, *Disciplines of a Godly Man* (Wheaton: Crossway, 1991), 17.

Chapter 11

1. See Karen Breslau, "Overplanned Parenthood: Ceauşescu's Cruel Law," *Newsweek*, January 22, 1990, 35, reprinted at www.Ceauşescu.org, http://www.Ceauşescu.org/Ceauşescu_texts/overplanned_parenthood.htm.

2. Patrick Johnstone and Jason Mandryk, *Operation World: 21st Century Edition* (Carlisle and Waynesboro, GA: Paternoster, 2001), 536.

3. "On This Day: 25 December 1989: Romania's 'First Couple' Executed," BBC News, http://news.bbc.co.uk/onthisday/hi/dates/stories/December/25/newsid_2542000/2542623.stm.

4. Psalm 2:4–5.

5. See The Open Doors World Watch List 2010, compiled by Open Doors USA, Santa Ana, California. See also the Open Doors February 11, 2008 press release, "North Korea Tops List of Persecutors."

6. Psalm 44:22–24.

7. Luke 18:1–8.

8. Elwell, *Evangelical Commentary on the Bible*, 830.

9. See Sandi Dolbee, "Discrepancies in Bible Turn Scholar into Agnostic," *San Diego Union-Tribune*, February 16, 2008.

10. Henry, *Matthew to John*, 774.

11. Tim Stafford, "How Tim Keller Found Manhattan," *Christianity Today*, June 2009, 25.

12. J. I. Packer, *Knowing God* (Downers Grove, IL: InterVarsity, 1973), 125.

13. Romans 8:21–23.

14. Steven J. Keillor, *God's Judgments: Interpreting History and the Christian Faith* (Downers Grove, IL: InterVarsity, 2007), 71.

15. Luke 3:7.

16. Keillor, *God's Judgments*, 79.

17. Luke 18:7.

18. Matthew 24:34.

19. Romans 2:4.

20. More on that in chapter 22.

21. 2 Thessalonians 1:6–8.

22. Henry, *Matthew to John*, 692.

23. Luke 11:1–13.

24. For the longer version, presented in the Sermon on the Mount, see Matthew 6:9–13.

25. C. S. Lewis, *A Grief Observed*, in *The Complete C. S. Lewis Signature Classics*, 444.

26. Augustine, *The Confessions*, trans. Sister Maria Boulding (Hyde Park, NY: New City Press, 1997), 307.

27. D. G. Bloesch, "Prayer," in Elwell, ed., *Evangelical Dictionary of Theology*, 847.

28. Luke 11:13.

29. Henry, *Matthew to John*, 695.

Chapter 12

1. Luke 12:13–21.

2. Interview with Chris Duhon, broadcast on WMVP AM 1000 in Chicago, March 10, 2008.

3. Genesis 1:27.

4. Psalm 139:14.

5. 1 Corinthians 3:9.

6. 1 Corinthians 6:3.

7. John 10:10.

8. See the discussion in chapter 9.

9. Matthew 16:13–28; Mark 8:29–9:1; Luke 9:18–27.

10. While harmonizing the Gospel accounts has an honored tradition, in general I believe it is best to read each of the Gospels on their own terms. Each writer had important reasons for including, emphasizing, or excluding certain incidents and sayings, and we can get at them best by reading these books independently. There are important differences in the ways the Synoptics treat the narrative under discussion, but we will treat these variances only lightly here while focusing on Jesus's questions.

11. Acts 5:35–39.

12. John 19:12.

13. See John 21:15–17; see also the related discussion in chapter 9.

14. Alan M. Dershowitz, "Worshippers of Death," *The Wall Street Journal*, March 3, 2008.

15. Galatians 3:13, citing Deuteronomy 21:23.

16. Tony Snow, "Cancer's Unexpected Blessings," *Christianity Today*, July 2007, http://www.christianitytoday.com/ct/2007/july/25.30.html?start=2.

17. H. D. McDonald, "Life," in Elwell, *Evangelical Dictionary of Theology*, 692.

18. See chapter 9.

19. McDonald, "Life," in Elwell, *Evangelical Dictionary of Theology*, 692.

20. Job 2:4.

21. Randy Alcorn, *The Treasure Principle: Discovering the Secret of Joyful Giving* (Sisters, OR: Multnomah, 2001), 17.

22. Luke 16:19–31.

23. Mark 8:37–38.

24. Tim Stafford, "The Joy of Suffering in Sri Lanka."

25. This story is from personal email correspondence on March 5, 2008, with Warren Larson from the Zwemer Institute for Muslim Studies, Columbia International University, Columbia, South Carolina.

26. Philippians 3:3–11.

27. Colossians 3:1–4.

Chapter 13

1. Mark A. Noll, *The Scandal of the Evangelical Mind* (Grand Rapids: Eerdmans, 1994), 3.

2. Matthew 22:37.

3. Rodney Stark, *The Victory of Reason: How Christianity Led to Freedom, Capitalism, and Western Success* (New York: Random House, 2005), xi.

4. Ibid., 7.

5. Ibid., xiii.

6. Ibid., 5.

7. Ibid.

8. Luke 10:27.

9. Luke 10:26.

10. Matthew 18:12–14.

11. Luke 11:11–13.

12. For more on God's judgment, see chapter 22.

13. Luke 23:28–31.

14. See Matthew 21:33–46 (quoted) and Mark 12:1–12.

15. The subject of chapters 22 and 23.

16. Job 1:7–12.

17. See chapters 3 and 24.

18. See Luke 11:14–23; Matthew 12:22–32; and Mark 3:22–27.

19. Luke 11:18.

20. Matthew 12:27; see also Luke 11:19.

21. Mark 3:23.

22. Matthew 12:29.

23. Psalm 18:28–33.

24. Psalm 1:1–2.

25. John 13:12–17.

26. Matthew 13:51.

27. N. L. Geisler, "Analogy," in Elwell, *Evangelical Dictionary of Theology*, 57.

28. Mark 4:21–23.

29. See the discussion of the Bible's concept of time in chapter 5.

30. Luke 12:54–56; see chapter 5.

31. William Lane Craig, "God Is Not Dead Yet," *Christianity Today*, July 2008, 22; see

also Alvin Plantinga, *God and Other Minds: A Study of the Rational Justification of Belief in God* (Ithaca, NY: Cornell University Press, 1967) and "Is God Dead?" *Time*, April 8, 1966.

32. See, for example, Dallas Willard, *Knowing Christ Today: Why We Can Trust Spiritual Knowledge* (San Francisco: HarperOne, 2009).

33. God's Spirit is vital in the process of our choosing God, and the faith choice is never a strictly rational, purely human decision. "And without faith it is impossible to please [God]" (Hebrews 11:6); "And this [faith] is not your own doing; it is the gift of God" (Ephesians 2:8); "Unless one is born again, he cannot see the kingdom of God" (John 3:3). We will look at this indispensable truth in chapter 16.

34. Craig Detweiler, "The Gospel and the Cinematic Imagination: A Journey into the Dark," Evangelism Roundtable V, "Imagination and the Gospel: Harnessing the Imagination to Engage Contemporary Culture and Communicate the Life-changing Gospel," Billy Graham Center, Wheaton College, Wheaton, Illinois, April 24, 2008.

35. John 7:17.

36. Matthew 7:15–17.

37. Matthew 21:28–31.

38. Luke 10:29–37.

39. John 3:1–21.

40. Luke 6:39–42.

41. Ibid.

42. Mark 4:13.

43. Mark 7:14–23.

44. Mark 2:19; see also Luke 5:34.

45. Craig, "God Is Not Dead Yet," 27.

46. Luke 14:25–33.

Chapter 14

1. David Kinnaman and Gabe Lyons, *unChristian: What a New Generation Really Thinks about Christianity . . . and Why It Matters* (Grand Rapids: Baker, 2007), 29.

2. Ron Sider, *The Scandal of the Evangelical Conscience: Why Are Christians Living Like the Rest of the World?* (Grand Rapids: Baker, 2005).

3. Collin Hansen and Tony Jones, "Emergent's New Christians and the Young, Restless Reformed—Day 4," *Christianity Today*, May 7, 2008, http://www.christianitytoday.com/ct/2008/mayweb-only/119-32.0.html.

4. C. J. Mahaney, *Humility: True Greatness* (Sisters, OR: Multnomah, 2005), 22. I am indebted to Collin Hansen for bringing this quote to my attention.

5. Luke 11:40.

6. Hebrews 4:12.

7. Mark 12:15; Matthew 22:18 quotes the question simply as, "Why put me to the test, you hypocrites?"

8. Matthew 11:28.

9. George Orwell, "In Front of Your Nose," *Tribune*, March 22, 1946.

10. Mark 8:11–12.

11. Luke 22:48.

12. John 18:4, 7.

13. Luke 22:52; see also Mark 14:48.

14. Frank Morrison, *Who Moved the Stone? A Journalist's Classic Investigation into the Truthfulness of Christ's Resurrection* (Grand Rapids: Zondervan, 1971), 16.

15. See John 18:19–23; see also the Synoptic accounts: Matthew 26:59–68; Mark 14:55–65; and Luke 22:66–71.

16. Morrison, *Who Moved the Stone?*, 16.

17. Ibid., 17–25.

18. John 18:20–21.

19. John 18:22–23.

20. Acts 9:4.

21. John 19:11.

22. Matthew 7:3–5.

23. See Matthew 5:21–48.

24. John 7:23–24.

25. Matthew 23:23.

26. Luke 5:12–13.

27. Luke 7:1–10.

28. Luke 7:11–17.

29. Isaiah 1:11–17.

30. Elwell, *Evangelical Commentary on the Bible*, 751.

31. Matthew 23:19.

32. Elwell, *Evangelical Commentary on the Bible*, 751.

33. Mark 7:14–16.

34. Larry Crabb, *Inside Out* (Colorado Springs: NavPress, 1988), 33.

35. Mark 7:17–23.

36. 1 Corinthians 12:7.

37. 1 Corinthians 15:10.

38. Crabb, *Inside Out*, 15–16.

39. Luke 12:56.

40. See Luke 12:57–59; also Elwell, *Evangelical Commentary on the Bible*, 824.

41. Luke 7:36–50.

42. John 1:10–11.

43. John 7:19.

44. John 10:25–33.

45. John 3:19.

46. Matthew 20:17–28.

47. See John Piper, *God Is the Gospel: Meditations on God's Love as the Gift of Himself* (Wheaton: Crossway, 2005).

48. 1 Timothy 6:5.

49. Acts 9:1–9; 22:1–11; 26:1–18.

50. Philippians 3:1–11.

51. John Calvin, *Institutes of the Christian Religion*, trans. Henry Beveridge (Grand Rapids: Eerdmans, 1990), 38.

Chapter 15

1. Bob Phillips, *Overcoming Anxiety and Depression: Practical Tools to Help You Deal with Negative Emotions* (Eugene, OR: Harvest House, 2007), 8.

2. "Anxiety," *The American Heritage Dictionary, Second College Edition* (Boston: Houghton Mifflin Company, 1985), 117.

3. "Generalized Anxiety Disorder (GAD)," National Institute of Mental Health, http://www.nimh.nih.gov/health/topics/generalized-anxiety-disorder-gad/index.shtml.

4. Author search on June 3, 2008.

5. Matthew 6:34.

6. Some mental states, of course, involve more than wrong or unproductive thinking, such as schizophrenia and bipolar disorders. They result from chemical imbalances in the brain and must be dealt with medically. The worst thing you can do in these cases is to deny the problem. Sometimes we need outside help, whether medical or psychological, or both. We cannot do it on our own. We are sinful, fractured beings. We are on the mend through Christ's grace, yes, but we are not whole yet. Our dependence—on others and on God—is a fact of the Christian life.

7. Mark Galli, "A Refugee's Quiet Dignity," *Christianity Today*, June 2008, http://www.christianitytoday.com/ct/2008/junewebonly/123-11.0.html.

8. 2 Timothy 3:12.

9. Luke 5:34–35 NIV.

10. Luke 12:4–7.

11. Hebrews 4:13 NIV.

12. Goodrick and Kohlenberger, *The NIV Exhaustive Concordance*, 1804.

13. Psalm 64:1.

14. Luke 12:31.

15. Attributed to John Keith, "How Firm a Foundation," in Tom Fettke, ed., *The Hymnal for Worship and Celebration* (Waco, TX: Word Music, 1986), hymn 275, verse 2.

16. In the parallel account of Matthew 10:29, Jesus says two sparrows are sold for a penny, so those who could afford to pay more—two pennies—received an extra sparrow for buying in bulk!

17. *ESV Classic Reference Bible* (Wheaton: Crossway, 2001), 1049n2.

18. Stephanie O. Hubach, *Same Lake, Different Boat: Coming Alongside People Touched by Disability* (Phillipsburg, NJ: P&R, 2006), 29.

19. Or, as Proverbs 30:8–9 says, "give me neither poverty nor riches . . . lest I be full and deny you . . . or lest I be poor and steal and profane the name of my God."

20. Matthew 6:26 NIV.

21. Luke 12:22–31.

22. J. I. Packer and Carolyn Nystrom, *Guard Us, Guide Us: Divine Leading in Life's Decisions* (Grand Rapids: Baker, 2008), 238.

23. 1 Kings 17:6.

24. Matthew 19:29.

25. Luke 12:25 NIV.

26. Luke 12:26 NIV.

27. Jeannine Aversa, "Stress Taking Toll on Health," *USA Today*, June 29, 2008.

28. Phillips, *Overcoming Anxiety and Depression*, 11.

29. Matthew 18:3 NIV.

30. See also Matthew 6:28–30.

31. Luke 12:28.

32. Psalm 8:3–5 NIV.

33. Romans 8:31 NIV.

34. Psalm 127:2.

35. Isaiah 35:4.

36. Jeremiah 17:8.

37. Matthew 6:25.

38. Matthew 10:19; see also Mark 13:11 and Luke 12:11.

39. Philippians 4:6.

40. Matthew 8:23–27.

Chapter 16

1. Stan Guthrie, "Answering the Atheists."
2. Read an eyewitness account in John 11:1–12:9.
3. G. K. Chesterton, *Orthodoxy* (New York: Doubleday, 1908), 158–59.
4. Luke 12:10.
5. John 1:5.
6. John 1:11, a classic understatement if ever there was one.
7. Matthew 28:11–15.
8. Acts 3–4:22. Quotes are from the NIV.
9. Goodrick and Kohlenberger, *The NIV Exhaustive Concordance*, 127–28, 1776–77.
10. John 20:31 NIV.
11. The incident and its aftermath are told in John 5. For another discussion of the encounter, see chapter 7.
12. Genesis 1:27 and 2:18.
13. Dietrich Bonhoeffer, *Life Together: The Classic Exploration of Faith in Community* (San Francisco: HarperSanFrancisco, 1978).
14. Matthew 11:16–17; see also Luke 7:31–32.
15. Mark 10:14.
16. Psalm 1:1.
17. Mark 8:11–12.
18. Luke 9:37–43; also Matthew 17:14–21 and Mark 9:14–29.
19. Mark 9:24 NIV.
20. Matthew 12:34.
21. John 8:39–47.
22. R. C. Sproul, *Willing to Believe: The Controversy Over Free Will* (Grand Rapids: Baker, 1997), 63.
23. John 6:60–65.
24. See, for example, Matthew 20:20–28.
25. 1 Peter 1:20–21.
26. Philippians 2:8–9 NIV.
27. Ephesians 2:8–9 NIV.
28. John 3:3 NIV.
29. John 6:66 NIV.
30. John 6:67.
31. John 6:70.
32. Psalm 139:7.
33. 2 Peter 3:16 NIV.
34. John 6:68 NIV.
35. 2 Corinthians 13:5 NIV.
36. John 8:31–32.
37. John 3:16 NIV.

Chapter 17

1. See chapter 25 for more about that.
2. "Compassion," *The American Heritage Dictionary, Second College Edition* (Boston: Houghton Mifflin, 1985), 300.
3. Luke 13:10–17.
4. Mark 5:25–34.
5. John 9.
6. James 1:2–4.
7. Although Job and 2 Corinthians 12:7 demonstrate that God sometimes uses Satan to accomplish his good purposes in us.
8. Luke 13:12–13.
9. Mark 1:41 NIV.
10. Acts 3:8.
11. Luke 13:14.
12. 2 Samuel 12:7.
13. Exodus 20:8–11 NIV.
14. Mark 2:27 NIV.
15. Luke 13:15–17.
16. James 1:27 and Amos 5.
17. Luke 11:42 NIV.
18. Elwell, *Evangelical Commentary on the Bible*, 824.
19. Ibid.
20. Ibid., 736.
21. See Matthew 12:9–14 (quoted); Mark 3:1–6; and Luke 6:6–11.
22. See Acts 20:7; 1 Corinthians 16:2; and Revelation 1:10. (The "Lord's Day" is Sunday, the first day of the week.)
23. See R. Kent Hughes, *Genesis: Beginning and Blessing* (Wheaton: Crossway, 2004), 41–47.
24. Luke 14:1–6.
25. Elwell, *Evangelical Commentary on the Bible*, 825.
26. This commandment is discussed in Leviticus 19:18; Matthew 19:19, 22:39; Mark 12:33; Luke 10:27; Romans 13:9; Galations 5:14; James 2:8.
27. 1 John 3:16–18 NIV.
28. Kay Warren, "Joining the Resistance," *Christianity Today*, August 2008, 48.

Chapter 18

1. Peter J. Gomes, quoted in Robert Emmons, *Thanks! How the New Science of Gratitude Can Make You Happier* (Boston and New York: Houghton Mifflin, 2007), 16.

2. Ibid.

3. Henry, *Matthew to John*, 766.

4. Elwell, *Baker Encyclopedia of the Bible*, 2:1886.

5. John 4:9.

6. John 8:48.

7. Luke 9:51–55 NIV.

8. Elwell, *Baker Encyclopedia of the Bible*, 2:1887.

9. John 4:20–22.

10. Luke 17:11–13; the rest of the passage about the ten lepers, through verse 19, is quoted and discussed throughout this chapter.

11. Elwell, *Baker Encyclopedia of the Bible*, 2:1323.

12. Ibid., 1324–25.

13. Henry, *Matthew to John*, 767.

14. Luke 17:14.

15. See Leviticus 13.

16. Luke 17:14.

17. 2 Kings 5.

18. Henry, *Matthew to John*, 767.

19. Mark 6:5–6 NIV.

20. Psalm 1:1–3 NIV.

21. James 2:24 NIV.

22. Luke 17:15–16.

23. Psalm 30:4 NIV.

24. Psalm 79:13 NIV.

25. Psalm 100:4 NIV.

26. Emmons, *Thanks!*, 95.

27. Ibid., 97.

28. Ibid., 98.

29. Luke 17:17–18.

30. Ibid., 6.

31. Chesterton, *Orthodoxy*, 46.

32. Emmons, *Thanks!*, 6.

33. C. S. Lewis, *Reflections on the Psalms* (New York: Harcourt, 1958), 93–95.

34. John Piper, *Desiring God: Meditations of a Christian Hedonist* (Portland, OR: Multnomah, 1986), 37.

35. Psalm 19:1 NIV.

36. Psalm 96:11, 12 NIV.

37. Luke 19:38–40 NIV.

38. Luke 17:19.

39. Emmons, *Thanks!*, 54.

40. Henry, *Matthew to John*, 767; emphasis in original.

41. Matthew 25:29 NIV.

42. Matthew 23:12.

Chapter 19

1. Paul Johnson, *Intellectuals* (New York: Harper & Row, 1988), 10–11.

2. 1 Corinthians 13:13.

3. Galatians 5:22–23 NIV.

4. Galatians 3:24 NIV.

5. Matthew 19:16–22 NIV.

6. The Ten Commandments are found in Exodus 20; the command to "love your neighbor as yourself" is found in Leviticus 19:18.

7. Or, as Paul said, "The entire law is summed up in a single command: 'Love your neighbor as yourself'" (Galatians 5:14).

8. Luke 10:25–37.

9. Matthew 22:34–40 (NIV quoted) and Mark 12:28–34.

10. The gospel is good *news*, after all (1 Corinthians 15:3–8), and those who put their trust in Christ can *know* they are saved (1 John 5:13).

11. This statement in no way denies the necessity and sufficiency of saving faith, but it describes what that faith looks like in the real world. Love has arms and legs, and a faith without them will get you nowhere—except to hell. "You believe that there is one God. Good!" James wrote. "Even the demons believe that—and shudder" (James 2:19 NIV).

12. See related discussion in chapter 13.

13. Luke 10:30–37.

14. Galatians 5:6.

15. 1 John 3:17–18 NIV.

16. Matthew 5:43. The rest of this section will discuss and quote from Matthew 5:44–48.

17. Henry, *Matthew to John*, 66.

18. Matthew 5:44–45.

19. See Stan Guthrie, "The Scandal of Forgiveness," *Christianity Today*, January 2007, http://www.christianitytoday.com/ct/2007/january/15.58.html.

20. Miroslav Volf, "To Embrace the Enemy," interview with Tony Carnes, *Christianity Today*, September 2001, http://www.christianitytoday.com/ct/2001/septemberweb-only/9-17-53.0.html.

21. Romans 12:21.

22. Mark Twain, "Mark Twain Quotes," Thinkexist.com, http://thinkexist.com/quotation/it_ain-t_those_parts_of_the_bible_that_i_can-t/262060.html.

23. "Turkey: Widow of Slain Christian: 'A Cross for Me Every Day,'" *Compass Direct News*, October 1, 2007, http://www.compass direct.org. Thanks to Tim Morgan for pointing out this example.

24. Exodus 34:6–7 NIV. The rest of this section describes God as a righteous judge, but that is the subject of chapter 22.

25. Matthew 18:33.

26. Matthew 5:46–48.

27. Matthew 6:19–21.

28. Alcorn, *The Treasure Principle*, 12.

29. Henry, *Matthew to John*, 67.

30. Luke 6:27–36; see Elwell, *Evangelical Commentary on the Bible*, 1813.

31. Luke 6:32–36.

32. Piper, *God Is the Gospel*, 11.

Chapter 20

1. For commentary and links about the controversy, go to the December 2008 archives of http://www.stanguthrie.com.

2. See, for example, Romans 1:26–27; 1 Corinthians 6:9; and 1 Timothy 1:10.

3. Frank Newport, "One-Third of Americans Believe the Bible Is Literally True," *Gallup News Service*, May 25, 2007, http://www.gallup.com/poll/27682/onethird-americans-believe-bible-literally-true.aspx.

4. For a helpful description of the implications of the phrase "the Bible is the Word of God," see Packer and Nystrom, *Guard Us, Guide Us*, 91–92.

5. See, for example, Psalm 119:18 and 2 Timothy 3:16.

6. Packer and Nystrom, *Guard Us, Guide Us*, 92.

7. Deuteronomy 8:3 NIV.

8. *The NIV Study Bible* (Grand Rapids: Zondervan, 1985), 1464, note on Matthew 15:2.

9. "Tradition," in Elwell, *Baker Encyclopedia of the Bible*, 2:2093.

10. For a brief explanation, see the *NLT Study Bible* (Wheaton, Tyndale, 2008), 1662, note on Mark 7:2–4.

11. Matthew 15:3–9.

12. McQuilkin, *Understanding and Applying the Bible*, 255.

13. See "Dietary Laws," in Elwell, *Baker Encyclopedia of the Bible*, 1:626–28.

14. Matthew 15:10–20.

15. Matthew 9:17.

16. J. I. Packer, *God Has Spoken: Revelation and the Bible* (Grand Rapids: Baker, 1988), 84; emphasis in original.

17. William Larkin, quoted in McQuilkin, *Understanding and Applying the Bible*, 50.

18. Psalm 85:10.

19. John 7:53–8:11; for a brief defense of this passage's authenticity, see Elwell, *Evangelical Commentary on the Bible*, 858.

20. John 1:14.

21. Hebrews 2:18.

22. Mark 12:18–27. For a discussion of this passage in relation to heaven, see chapter 25.

23. See, for example, Job 19:26 and Psalm 16:11.

24. 1 Corinthians 15:20.

25. Mark 12:24.

26. Psalm 19:1–6; Romans 1:19–20.

27. Psalm 19:7–11.

28. Many of the references cited in this book are excellent tools for Bible study.

29. Mark 12:10.

30. Luke 6:3.

31. Matthew 12:5.

32. Mark 11:17.

33. Mark 10:3. See chapter 21 for more on this topic.

34. Mark 15:34; his actual words in Aramaic: "*Eloi, Eloi, lama sabachthani?*"

35. John 5:37–39 NIV.

36. John 5:46.

37. John 7:19.

38. Mark 9:2–8.

39. Philippians 3:5.

40. Romans 9:2.

41. Rabbi Yehiel E. Poupko and Stan Guthrie, "Christian Evangelism and Judaism," *Christianity Today*, April 2008, http://www.christianitytoday.com/ct/2008/aprilwebonly/114-33.0.html.

42. Romans 11:28–29 NIV.

43. Luke 24:25–27.

44. Matthew 5:17.

45. Isaiah 53.

46. Micah 5:2.

47. Matthew 2:13–15.

48. John 8:29.

49. Psalm 22.

50. Isaiah 53:5–7, 12.

51. Deuteronomy 18:18, Hebrews 3:3; 4:14; John 18:36–37.

52. Matthew 26:53–54.

53. Packer, *God Has Spoken*, 50.

Chapter 21

1. Jennifer Lee, "A Rush Into Marriage on the Last Day of the Year," *The New York Times*, December 31, 2008, http://www.ny times.com/2009/01/01/nyregion/01marriage .html.

2. Yet sociologist Bradford W. Wilcox notes that Christians who are committed to regular church attendance fare much better than these dismal averages would seem to indicate. See his thoughts in Stan Guthrie, "What Married Women Want," *Christianity Today*, October 2006, http://www.christianitytoday.com/ ct/2006/october/53.122.html.

3. Stan Guthrie, "The Evangelical Scandal."

4. R. Albert Mohler Jr., *Desire and Deceit: The Real Cost of the New Sexual Tolerance* (Colorado Springs: Multnomah, 2008), 47.

5. Glenn T. Stanton and Bill Maier, *Marriage on Trial: The Case Against Same-Sex Marriage and Parenting* (Downers Grove, IL: InterVarsity, 2004), 22.

6. Hughes, *Genesis*, 62.

7. Ibid.

8. See Matthew 26:59–60.

9. Matthew 19:1–12 and Mark 10:1–12.

10. See, for example, David Instone-Brewer, "What God Has Joined," *Christianity Today*, October 2007, http://www.christianitytoday .com/ct/2007/october/20.26/html.

11. Deuteronomy 24:1.

12. Instone-Brewer, "What God Has Joined."

13. Genesis 1:27 and 2:24.

14. Hughes, *Genesis*, 57.

15. Ibid.

16. Steve Tracy, "Good Question," *Christianity Today*, January 2002, http://www .christianitytoday.com/ct/2002/january7/37.63/ html.

17. Genesis 2:20–25 NIV.

18. Genesis 3:12 NIV.

19. Donna Freitas, *Sex and the Soul: Juggling Sexuality, Spirituality, Romance, and Religion on America's College Campuses* (New York: Oxford University Press, 2007).

20. Tracy, "Good Question."

21. Lauren F. Winner, *Real Sex: The Naked Truth about Chastity* (Grand Rapids: Brazos, 2005), 33–34.

22. Hughes, *Genesis*, 63.

23. Matthew 5:28 NIV.

24. Paul seemingly gives another exception for divorce in 1 Corinthians 7:15: desertion by an unbelieving spouse.

25. Mohler, *Desire and Deceit*, 6.

26. Ibid.

27. Lewis, *Mere Christianity*, 63–64.

28. Genesis 3:1 NIV, emphasis mine.

29. Chesterton, *Orthodoxy*, 49.

30. Revelation 21:2–3 NIV; see also Revelation 19:6–8.

31. Ephesians 5:21–33 (NIV quoted).

Chapter 22

1. C. S. Lewis, *The Problem of Pain*, in *The Complete C. S. Lewis Signature Classics*, 420.

2. Erickson, *Christian Theology*, 1168.

3. R. Albert Mohler Jr., "Modern Theology: The Disappearance of Hell," in *Hell Under Fire: Modern Scholarship Reinvents Eternal Punishment*, ed. Christopher W. Morgan and Robert A. Peterson (Grand Rapids: Zondervan, 2004), 16.

4. Charles Honey, "Belief in Hell Dips, but Some Say They've Already Been There," *Religion News Service*, August 14, 2008, http://pew forum.org/news/display.php?NewsID=16260.

5. Mohler, "Modern Theology: The Disappearance of Hell," 40.

6. See Hebrews 9:27 NIV.

7. Mohler, "Modern Theology: The Disappearance of Hell," 17.

8. Ibid.

9. Dante Alighieri, *Inferno*, trans. Robert Hollander and Jean Hollander (New York: Doubleday, 2000), 43.

10. Mohler, "Modern Theology: The Disappearance of Hell," 18.

11. Morgan and Peterson, *Hell Under Fire*, 11.

12. Mohler, "Modern Theology: The Disappearance of Hell," 40.

13. See Edward William Fudge and Robert A. Peterson, *Two Views of Hell: A Biblical*

and *Theological Dialogue* (Downers Grove, IL: InterVarsity, 2000), 20.

14. Luke 12:5 NIV.

15. See chapter 2.

16. Wright, *Jesus and the Victory of God*, 329.

17. Luke 12:49–53.

18. Romans 1:18 NIV.

19. Douglas J. Moo, "Paul on Hell," in Morgan and Peterson, *Hell Under Fire*, 94.

20. 2 Peter 3:9 NIV.

21. Matthew 7:23.

22. Revelation 6:10 NIV.

23. Luke 13:1–5.

24. Harold S. Kushner, *When Bad Things Happen to Good People* (New York: Anchor, 2004).

25. Bart D. Ehrman, *God's Problem: How the Bible Fails to Answer Our Most Important Question—Why We Suffer* (San Francisco: HarperOne, 2008).

26. Luke 13:6–9.

27. John 3:19 NIV.

28. Genesis 3:1–5.

29. Lewis, *Mere Christianity*, 13.

30. Genesis 18:22–33.

31. Romans 2:1–3.

32. John 16:8 and 1 Corinthians 2:6–16.

33. Thomas Asbridge, *The First Crusade: A New History* (New York: Oxford University Press, 2004), 87.

34. Matthew 23:29–33.

35. Matthew 5:21–26.

36. Romans 7:24.

37. Matthew 11:20–22; see also Luke 10:13–16.

38. Elwell, *Baker Encyclopedia of the Bible*, 1:430–31.

39. Ibid.

40. Matthew 11:23–24.

41. Elwell, *Baker Encyclopedia of the Bible*, 1:415.

42. The story of the destruction of Sodom is told in Genesis 19:1–28.

43. See David Barrett and Todd M. Johnson, "Status of Global Mission, 2010, in the Context of 20th and 21st Centuries," Gordon-Conwell Theological Seminary, http://www .gcts.edu/sites/default/files/IBMR2010.pdf.

44. See, for example, Guthrie, *Missions in the Third Millennium*, 199–211.

45. See, for example, Matthew 25:31–46; Romans 2:6–11; 1 Corinthians 3:11–15; and Philippians 2:12.

46. See James 2:14–26 and related discussion in chapter 19.

47. Matthew 24:36, 45–51.

48. John 3:16–18 NIV.

Chapter 23

1. "Salem Witch Trials," *Grolier Encyclopedia of Knowledge* (Danbury, CT: Grolier, 1991), 16:255–56.

2. Lewis, *The Screwtape Letters*, 125. See discussion of and more of this quote at the end of chapter 3.

3. Leviticus 17:7; Deuteronomy 32:17; Psalm 106:37.

4. David M. Kiely and Christina McKenna, *The Dark Sacrament: True Stories of Modern-Day Demon Possession and Exorcism* (San Francisco: HarperOne, 2007), xvi.

5. Jenkins, *The New Faces of Christianity*, 125–26.

6. Lewis, *The Screwtape Letters*, 139.

7. 1 John 2:13–16.

8. 1 John 2:15.

9. Elwell, *Evangelical Commentary on the Bible*, 1181.

10. Erickson, *Christian Theology*, 644.

11. 2 Corinthians 4:4.

12. Elwell, *Evangelical Commentary on the Bible*, 1032.

13. Romans 3:20.

14. Romans 7:21–25.

15. For a list of biblical references of Satan and his attributes, see the Religious Tolerance website, http://www.religioustolerance.org/ chr_sat3.htm.

16. Isaiah 14:12–20; Ezekiel 28:13–17; Revelation 12:7.

17. Acts 16:16–18.

18. Ephesians 6:12.

19. Wright, *Jesus and the Victory of God*, 195.

20. Luke 8:26–39; see also Mark 5:1–20 and Matthew 8:28–34

21. See "Names, Significance of," in Elwell, ed., *Evangelical Commentary on the Bible*, 1522–24.

22. Elwell, *Evangelical Commentary on the Bible*, 1322–23.

23. Lewis, *Mere Christianity*, 42.

24. Genesis 3:14–15.

25. Psalm 91:5–6, 10, 13.

26. Jenkins, *The New Faces of Christianity*, 91–92, 107–9, 116.

27. Colossians 2:15.

28. Acts 8:9–24; 19:11–20.

29. Jenkins, *The New Faces of Christianity*, 103.

30. Ibid., 99.

31. Ibid., 122.

32. Ephesians 4:27.

33. 1 Peter 5:8.

34. Charles H. Kraft, *Defeating Dark Angels: Breaking Demonic Oppression in the Believer's Life* (Ann Arbor, MI: Servant Publications, 1992), 34–58.

35. James 2:19.

36. Kraft, *Defeating Dark Angels*, 9.

37. Revelation 12:7–12.

Chapter 24

1. Mark 1:15 NIV.

2. Quoted in Scot McKnight, "McLaren Emerging," *Christianity Today*, September 2008, http://www.christianitytoday.com/ct/2008/september/38.59.html.

3. Mark Galli, "The Giant Story," *Christianity Today*, April 2009, 36.

4. Luke 10:9; 17:21.

5. John 18:36.

6. Acts 1:6–7 NIV.

7. Revelation 11:15 NIV.

8. Personal email from Charles Colson, March 18, 2009.

9. See Stan Guthrie, "When Red Is Red," http://www.stanguthrie.com/2009/04/when-red-is-red.html.

10. John Bright, *The Kingdom of God: The Biblical Concept and Its Meaning for the Church* (Nashville: Abingdon, 1981), 7.

11. Psalm 29:10; 103:19.

12. 1 Samuel 8:7; 2 Samuel 7:13.

13. George E. Ladd, "Kingdom of God (Heaven)," in Elwell, *Baker Encyclopedia of the Bible*, 2:1271.

14. Bright, *The Kingdom of God*, 18.

15. Ladd, "Kingdom of God (Heaven)," 2:1272.

16. Kushner, *When Bad Things Happen to Good People*.

17. Ladd, "Kingdom of God (Heaven)," 2:1272.

18. See chapter 1.

19. Matthew 11:3.

20. Luke 4:16–21.

21. Ladd, "Kingdom of God (Heaven)," 2:1275.

22. Ibid., 1272.

23. Mark 4:30–32.

24. Psalm 47:8.

25. Theodor Seuss Geisel, *Horton Hears a Who* (New York: Random House, 1954), n.p.

26. William P. Cheshire Jr., "Human Embryo Research after the Genome," The Center for Bioethics and Human Dignity, November 14, 2002, http://www.cbhd.org/resources/genetics/cheshire_2002-11-14.htm.

27. Quoted in Dinesh D'Souza, *What's So Great About Christianity* (Wheaton: Tyndale, 2008), 143.

28. Ibid., 120.

29. Luke 13:18–19.

30. John 4:35.

31. To read the Lord's Prayer in its entirety, see Matthew 6:9–14.

32. Matthew 28:20.

33. Matthew 18:20.

34. 2 Corinthians 2:14.

35. Matthew 10:42 and Mark 9:41.

36. See Luke 4:18–19.

37. Stan Guthrie, "A Hole in Our Holism."

38. Luke 13:20–21.

39. Frame, *The Doctrine of God*, 950.

40. Ladd, "Kingdom of God (Heaven)," 2:1273–1277.

41. Ibid.

42. McKnight, "McLaren Emerging."

43. Colson, personal email.

Chapter 25

1. N. T. Wright, *Surprised by Hope: Rethinking Heaven, the Resurrection, and the Mission of the Church* (San Francisco: HarperOne, 2008), 250–51.

2. Matthew 5:11–12, 16, 44–45, 48; 6:26, 32–33; 7:11.

3. Mark Galli, "Man Up, Christians," *Christianity Today*, http://www.christianitytoday.com/ct/2009/marchweb-only/112-41.0.html.

4. Ibid.

5. Rob Moll, "More on Faith and End-of-Life Care," *Christianity Today*, March 2009, http://blog.christianitytoday.com/ctliveblog/archives/death_and_dying.

6. Ecclesiastes 3:11.

7. See "Mortality Data," Centers for Disease Control and Prevention, January 25, 2010, http://www.cdc.gov/nchs/deaths.htm.

8. Galli, "Man Up, Christians."

9. Hebrews 2:15.

10. See my discussion of the Sadducees in chapter 2.

11. Mark 12:24.

12. Stan Guthrie, "Does the God of Christianity Exist, and What Difference Does It Make?" *Christianity Today*, April 2009, http://blog.christianitytoday.com/ctliveblog/archives/2009/04/does_the_god_of.html.

13. See, for example, Numbers 16:30; 1 Samuel 2:6; and Job 7:9.

14. Genesis 1:31.

15. Job 19:26.

16. Matthew 22:23–28.

17. Matthew 22:29–33; see also Mark 12:18–27.

18. Genesis 1:28.

19. Lewis, *The Problem of Pain*, 428.

20. Matthew 22:31–33.

21. Exodus 3:6, 14.

22. Acts 17:25.

23. 1 Corinthians 15:20–26 NIV.

24. John 20:25.

25. Charles Taylor, *A Secular Age* (Cambridge, MA: Harvard University Press, 2007), 11. I am indebted to Dinesh D'Souza for this reference.

26. For more reflections on doubt, see chapter 8.

27. John 14:1–4.

28. Samuel Medley, "I Know That My Redeemer Lives," 1775, http://www.ccel.org/a/anonymous/luth_hymnal/tlh200.htm.

29. *ESV Study Bible* (Wheaton: Crossway, 2008), note on John 14:2–3, 2052.

30. See chapter 6.

31. See chapter 1.

32. Luke 22:8–9; see Goodrick and Kohlenberger, *The NIV Exhaustive Concordance*, 901–2, 1725.

33. *ESV Study Bible*, note on Luke 22:7–13, 2004–5.

34. Matthew 26:29.

35. Goodrick and Kohlenberger, *The NIV Exhaustive Concordance*, 885, 1798.

36. See the comment by author Sam Storms at http://blog.christianitytoday.com/ctliveblog/archives/2009/04/a_guided_tour_o.html.

37. Lewis, *The Problem of Pain*, 428.

Chapter 26

1. The podcast for this panel discussion can be found at http://blog.christianitytoday.com/podcasts/upload/Does%20the%20God%20of%20Christianity.mp3. The video is available at http://blog.christianitytoday.com/ctliveblog/archives/2009/04/does_the_god_of.html. My question to Hitchens begins at about the thirty-minute mark. For clarity and brevity I have condensed and edited the quoted statements for this chapter, but the differences between the spoken and written words are minor.

2. Lewis, *The Screwtape Letters*, 163.

3. Michael Novak, *No One Sees God: The Dark Night of Atheists and Believers* (New York: Doubleday, 2008), 47–48.

4. John 10:32.

5. Novak, *No One Sees God*, 47.

6. Genesis 3:9.

7. Romans 5:8.

8. Jonathan Edwards, "Sinners in the Hands of an Angry God," Enfield, Connecticut, July 8, 1741, Christian Classics Ethereal Library, http://www.ccel.org/ccel/edwards/sermons.sinners.html.

9. George M. Marsden, *A Short Life of Jonathan Edwards* (Grand Rapids: Eerdmans, 2008), 137.

10. Matthew 10:29–31.

11. "The Life Span of Animals," *Nature Bulletin* 486-A, March 24, 1973, Forest Preserve District of Cook County, http://www.newton.dep.anl.gov/natbltn/400-499/nb486.htm.

12. See chapter 24.

13. "Q: Approximately how many hairs are on a human head?" WikiAnswers.com, http://wiki.answers.com/Q/Approximately_how_many_hairs_are_on_a_human_head.

14. 1 John 4:19.

15. John 3:16; 1 John 4:16.

16. John 3:20.

17. See chapter 22.

18. Romans 5:5.

19. Matthew 7:7–8.
20. See chapter 11.
21. See chapter 11.
22. Matthew 7:9–11. See also Luke 11:11–12, discussed in chapters 11 and 13.
23. Acts 20:35.
24. See chapter 22.
25. Luke 15:4.
26. Genesis 3:9.
27. Luke 15:5–7.
28. Luke 15:8.
29. Luke 15:9–10.

Stan Guthrie is editor at large for *Christianity Today* and author of *Missions in the Third Millennium: 21 Key Trends for the 21st Century*. Stan has assisted Darrow Miller with the books *Discipling Nations* and *Nurturing the Nations* and Brian Kluth with *Experience God as Your Provider*. He is a columnist for BreakPoint.org, speaker, and regular guest on Moody Radio. Stan moderated a panel discussion with Christopher Hitchens, William Lane Craig, and Lee Strobel on the question "Does the God of Christianity Exist, and What Difference Does It Make?" A literary agent, Stan has a bachelor of science in journalism from the University of Florida and a master's in missions from Columbia International University. His website is found at http://StanGuthrie.com/. Stan and his wife, Christine, live with their three children near Chicago.